I0823594

BEAUTIFUL ISLANDS

Publisher
Balthazar Pagani

Graphic design
Davide Canesi / PEPE *nymi*

Editing and fact checking
Giulia Bilancetti

Iconographic research
Rachele Adda

Piazzale Luigi Cadorna, 6
20123 Milan, Italy
www.whitestar.it

Translator: Neil Davenport
Editing: Abby Young

ISBN 978-88-544-2177-6
1 2 3 4 5 6   30 39 28 27 26

Printed in China

~ NICOLA BALOSSI RESTELLI ~

BEAUTIFUL ISLANDS

Incredible stories of adventure, legends, mysteries
of breathtaking natural wonders

whitestar

. CONTENTS .

ISLAND MARVELS

Nature is our mirror. We perceive its beauty, its light, and at the same time its mystery, its dark side. In the face of certain landscapes, we are torn between wonder and fear, as if we were in flight: there is not only the desire to be carried away on the wings of enchantment but also the fear of falling, mistrust of that bewitching unknown, that slender ridge separating curiosity from the urge to curl up for protection. It is inevitable that every element becomes charged with meaning and intertwines with our imagination, amplifying its emotional impact.

The island lends itself perfectly to this back-and-forth between dream and nightmare. It is the escape and holiday destination par excellence, it is both a privilege and an evocative promise of discovery, while at the same time it is the metaphorical place in which we remain alone with ourselves, for better or for worse, between aspirations and ghosts. Tropics and coral seas, tranquil northern landscapes, but also treasures, wrecks, and mystical journeys.

Islands, protected by water and inaccessible, are unparalleled metaphors for the human condition. There are myriad examples, some uninhabited or even unexplored, outposts wrested from the oceans, fragile but stalwart: each has a face and a story to tell. Indelible places that mark you and capture your heart forever. We have chosen to describe some of them, through portraits in which photographic images intertwine with words to paint a picture—inadequate by definition—of these places, some of which sometimes seem too beautiful to really exist. The underlying question is always the same, both when we have the good fortune to spend time there and when we are content to observe them from afar, to study them, to understand them: how is it possible that these islands are always there, even when they are far from our eyes and the lens of our camera, and how is it possible that people spend their entire lives there? It seems unthinkable to us that such a state of wonder is the norm. Islands are stars in a miniature firmament. The enraptured bewilderment we experience as we lose ourselves among the oceans on the map is closely related to the sensation we feel when faced with a night sky, as we try to find our way among those countless tiny lights that trace myriad alternative scenarios, imaginary and metaphysical worlds that scramble our thoughts. Such are the islands, which in our increasingly globalized, connected, and uniform habitat remain true to themselves, unique, tenacious, and beautiful. It has not been easy to make a selection from this limitless vastity and we know we have overlooked more than we have managed to recount. However, as is well-known, infinity is to be found in the detail. And just as there are remote mysteries that cannot be grasped, so we content ourselves with skimming them, circumnavigating the globe armed with patience and imagination, among humpback whales and giant tortoises, rainforests and northern lights, classical memories and primitive origins, virgin routes and alternative trajectories, conflicts and paradoxes. Take, for example, two very odd but closely related islands: Great Diomede and Little Diomede. Both lie in the Bering Strait, 2.4 miles (3.8 kilometers) apart and climatically twins, while at the same time belonging to two opposing galaxies. Little Diomede is part of Alaska, inhabited by an ethnic group of Inuit stock, while the now deserted Big Diomede is Russian territory. That stretch of sea, once known as "the ice curtain," freezes over in winter and can be traversed on foot. Not only the geopolitical boundary passes here, but also the International Date Line: while in Russia it is one day, in the United States it is the one before. It is as if this place has been designed to stage the relativity of time. It is precisely from this line that we begin our journey, heading east, toward a future that is simultaneously also the past. Lost in complexity, we shall allow ourselves to be guided by a single powerful voice: that of beauty, in its multiplicity of nuances.

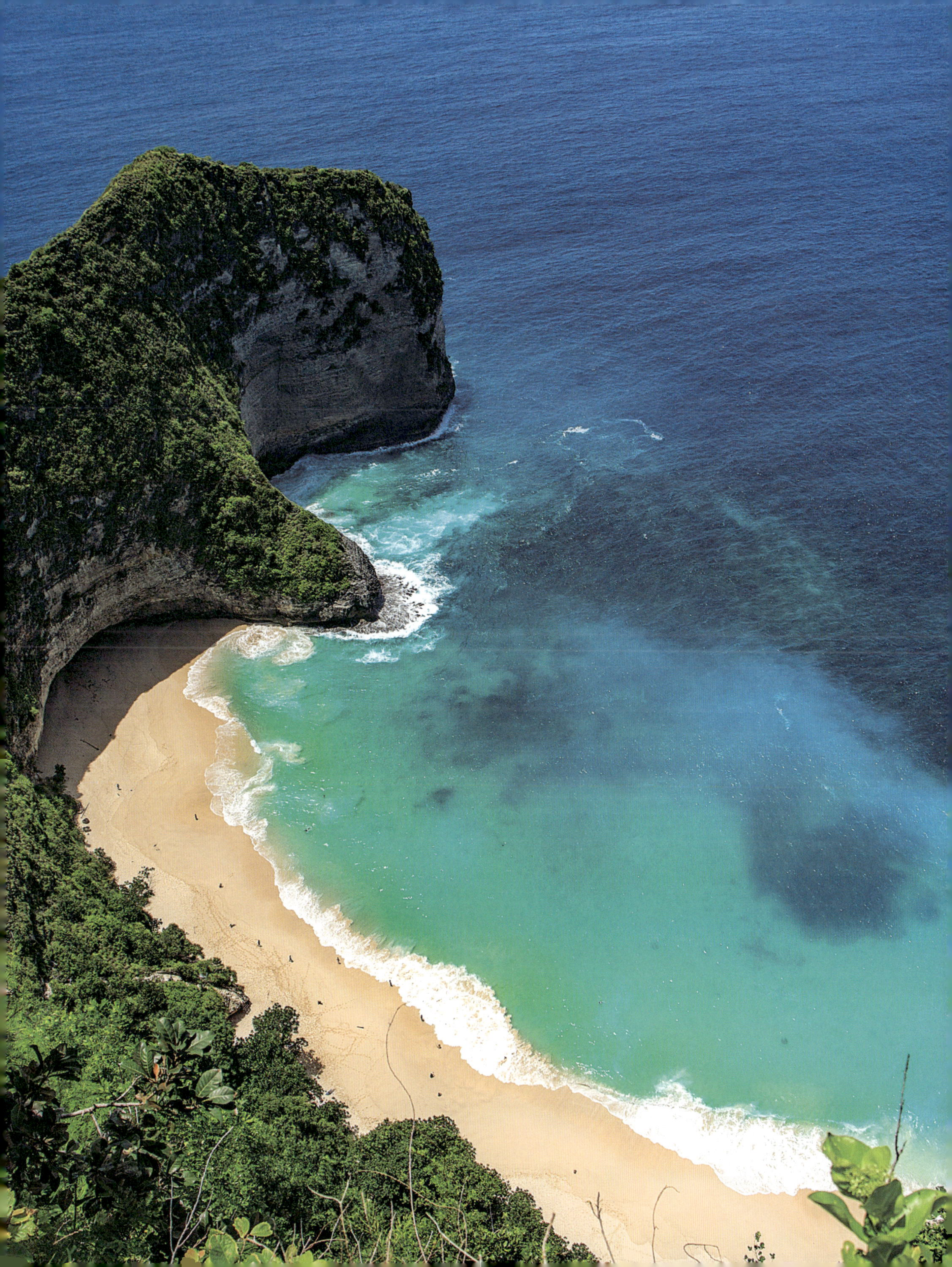

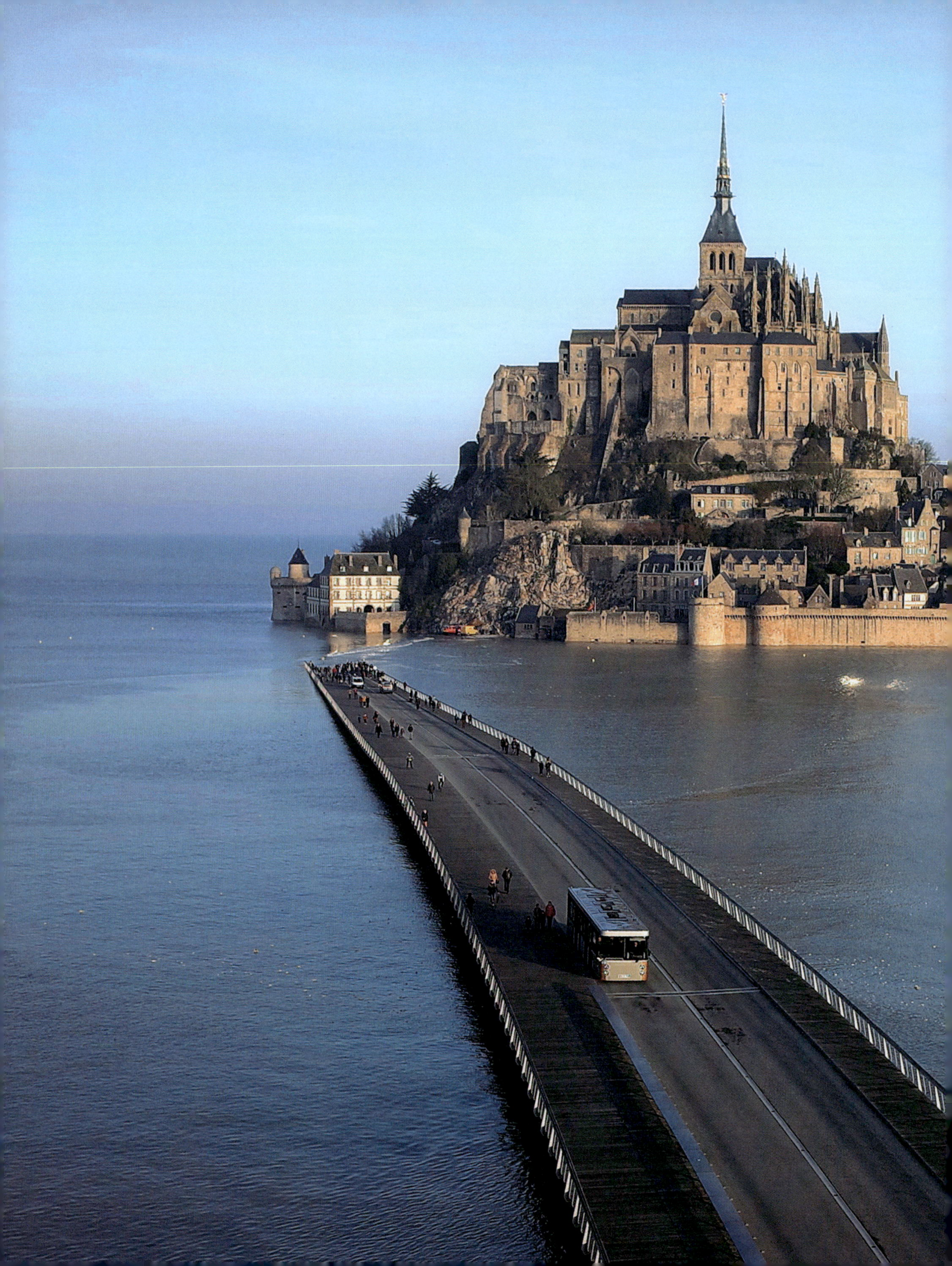

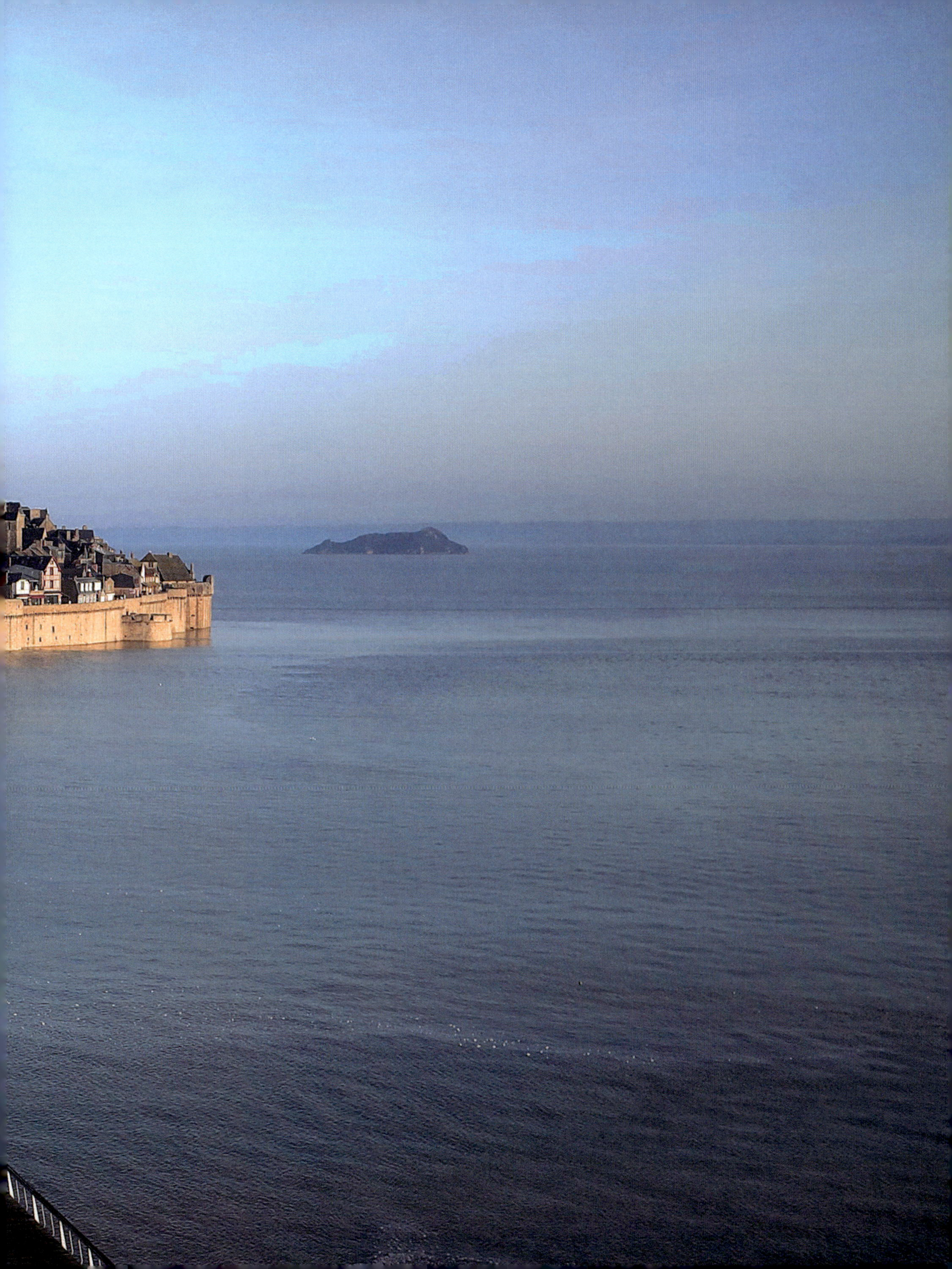

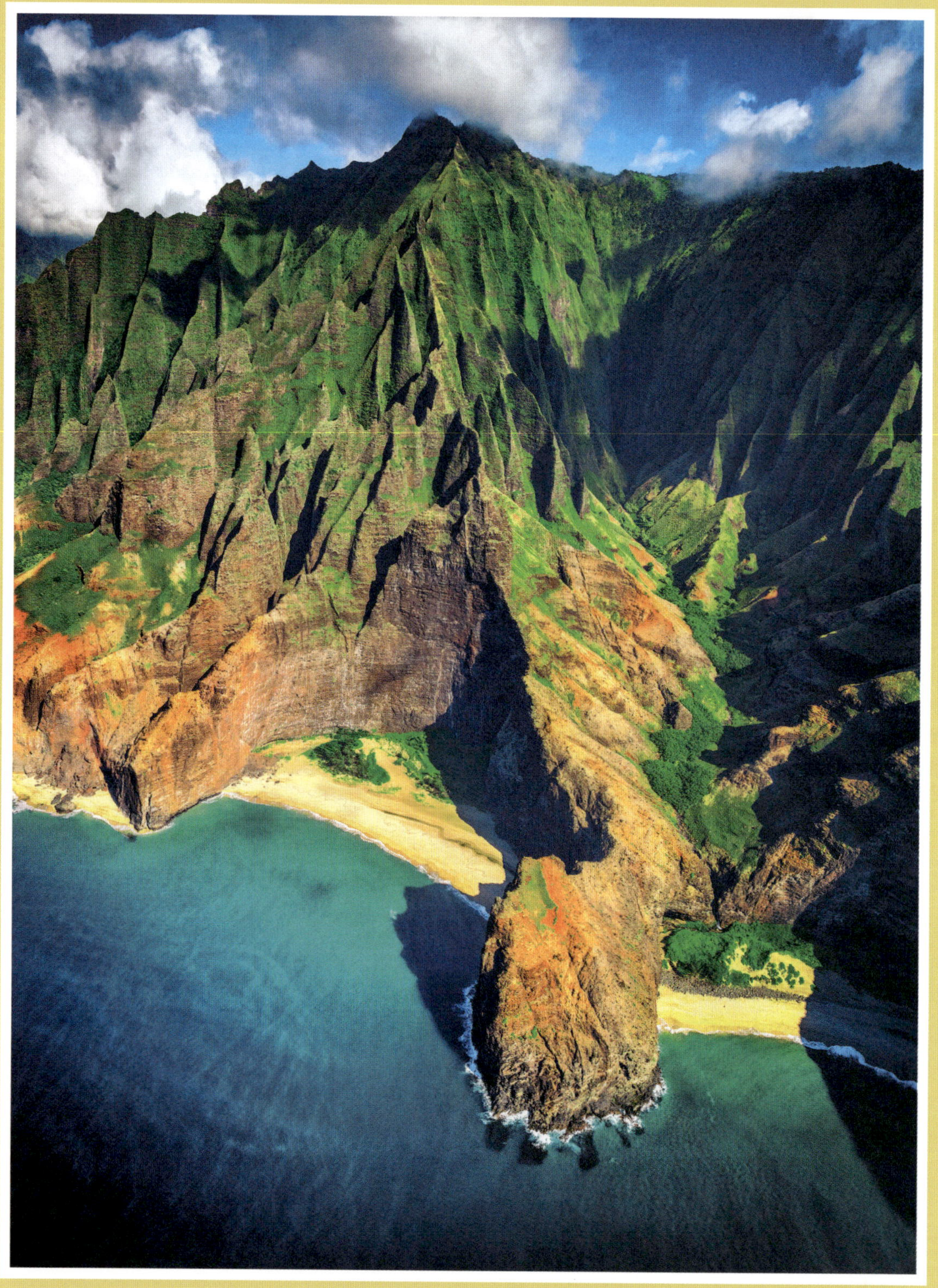

Hawaii, USA

KAUA'I

Geographical coordinates: 22°04'12" N; 159°29'51" W
Waters: Pacific Ocean
Population: 73,298 inhabitants
Surface area: 551 square miles (1,427 km²)
Principal settlement: Līhu'e

THE UNSPEAKABLE GARDEN

Kaua'i is the oldest of the Hawaiian Islands; if the others emerge from the ocean like restless adolescents, she rises with the grace of one who has already lived many lives, bearing the lines and creases of her history. She was born five million years ago from a hot spot in the heart of the Pacific, shaped by volcanic eruptions that slowly diminished and gave way to erosion, lush vegetation, and the silent work of time. This is the northernmost of the group, more than 60 miles (95 kilometers) from O'ahu, the island on which Honolulu and Pearl Harbor are located. Its center is the Waialeale volcano, one of the wettest places on the planet. Deep gorges, sheer waterfalls, and valleys covered in proud, impenetrable greenery descend its slopes. Nature here has carved, smoothed, and sculpted works of art such as the Waimea Canyon—the so-called "Grand Canyon of the Pacific"—with its conspicuous fissures like open wounds in the bare red rock. The island is almost perfectly circular, incised by radial valleys converging like the veins of a leaf. The coasts are changeable: rugged cliffs in the north; wide, golden beaches in the south; windswept headlands in the west. Kaua'i's morphology seems to be written in an archaic language composed of curves, paths, and sudden drops often concealed by the vegetation, which the downpours make confusing to read. It is a language that allows itself to be intuited but not translated literally, because it refers to deep and ineffable concepts as it speaks directly to the soul without concerning itself with a need to be.

THE FAVORITE SON

~

Human presence on Kaua'i has remote roots: the first Polynesians sailed here between 300 and 600 AD, guided by the starry sky and led perhaps by the legendary chieftain Hawai'iloa, who named the island after his favorite son. They built temples, villages, and terraces and cultivated taro and sugarcane. For centuries, Kaua'i was a closed society, with traditions and deities that families passed down from generation to generation. In 1778, James Cook landed in Waimea: for the West it was a discovery, for the islanders a catastrophe. Epidemics decimated the population, and the established equilibrium crumbled with the invasion of missionaries, landowners, and American traders. In the 19th century, Kaua'i became a pawn in the greater game of colonial power in the Pacific. The Hawaiian monarchy was overthrown, the United States annexed the archipelago, and the island was transformed into an extensive plantation and an agricultural and military laboratory. Today, the population is a mosaic composed of native Hawaiians, Japanese, Filipinos, Portuguese, and mainland Americans. The economy revolves mainly around tourism, but at the end of the day the island has resisted over-development: there are no skyscrapers, the buildings are low, and the roads have no traffic lights outside the main towns, Līhu'e and Kapa'a. There is a sense of harmony that is based on an innate respect for the environment, but which is being tested by inevitable and increasing pressure. With every new resort that rises, a small crack opens.

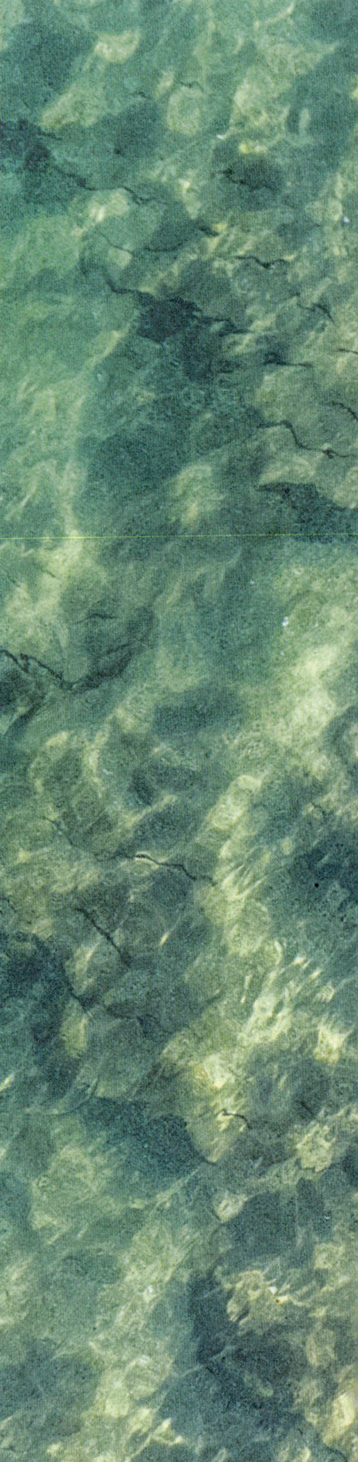

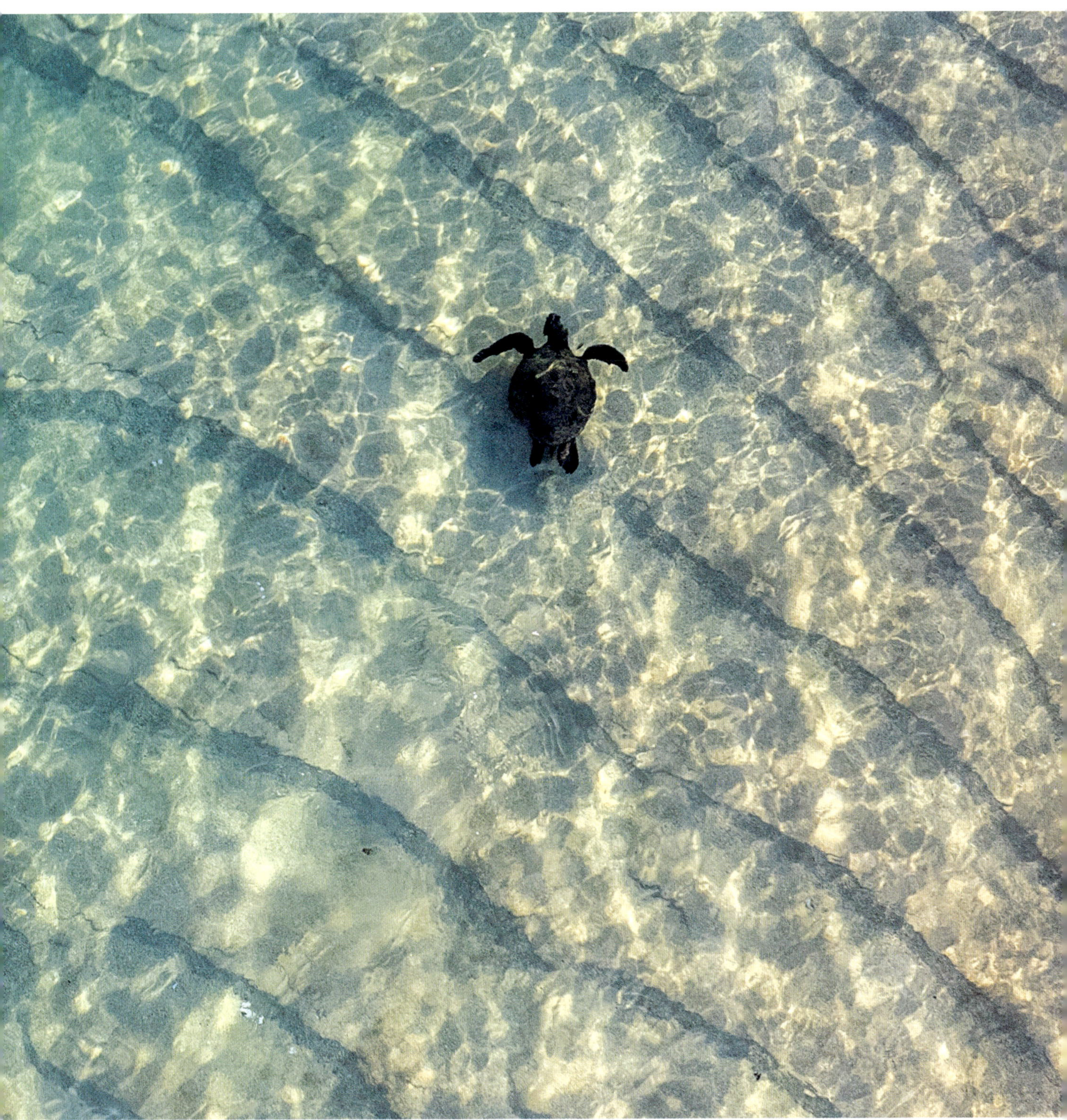

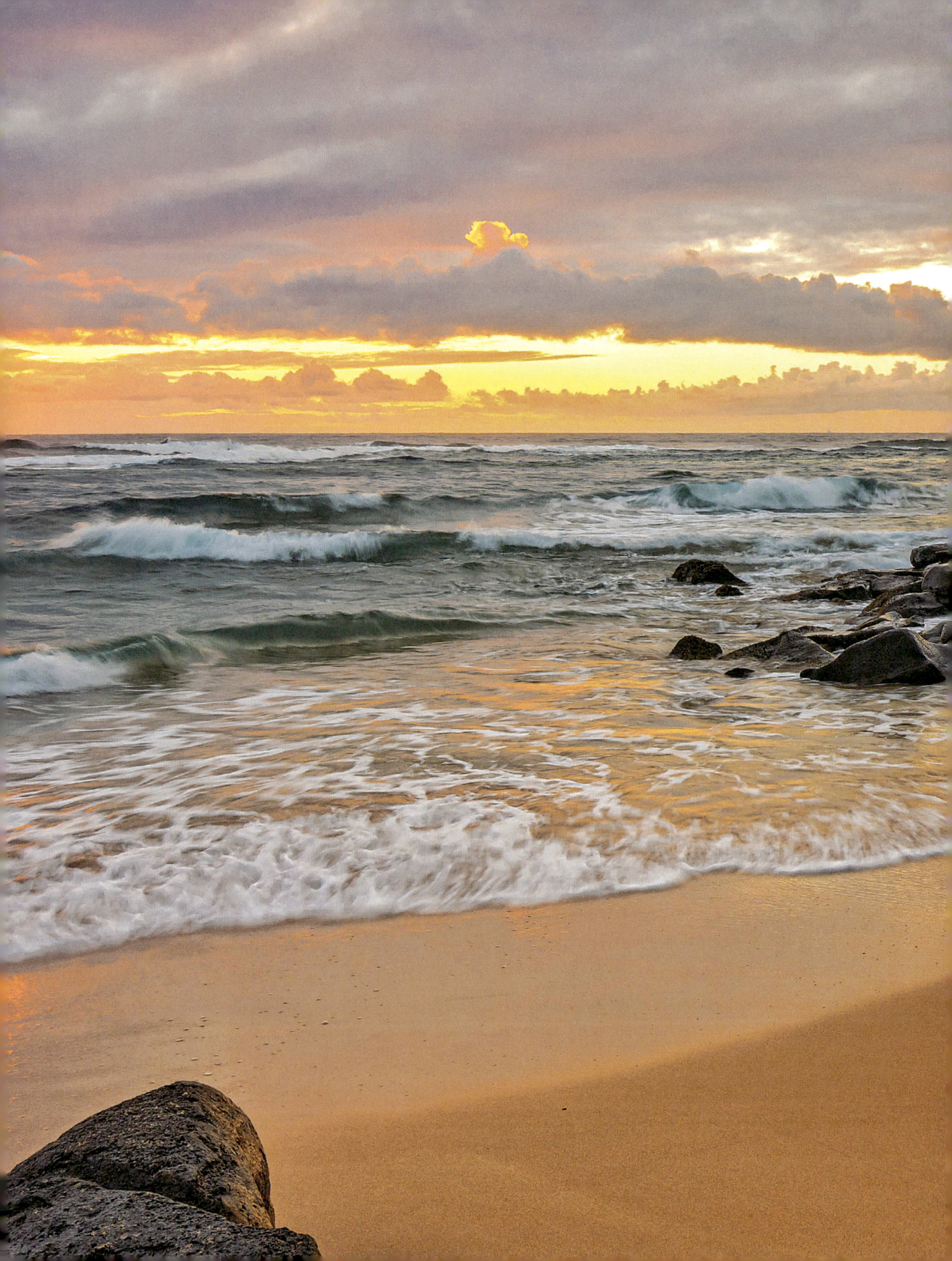

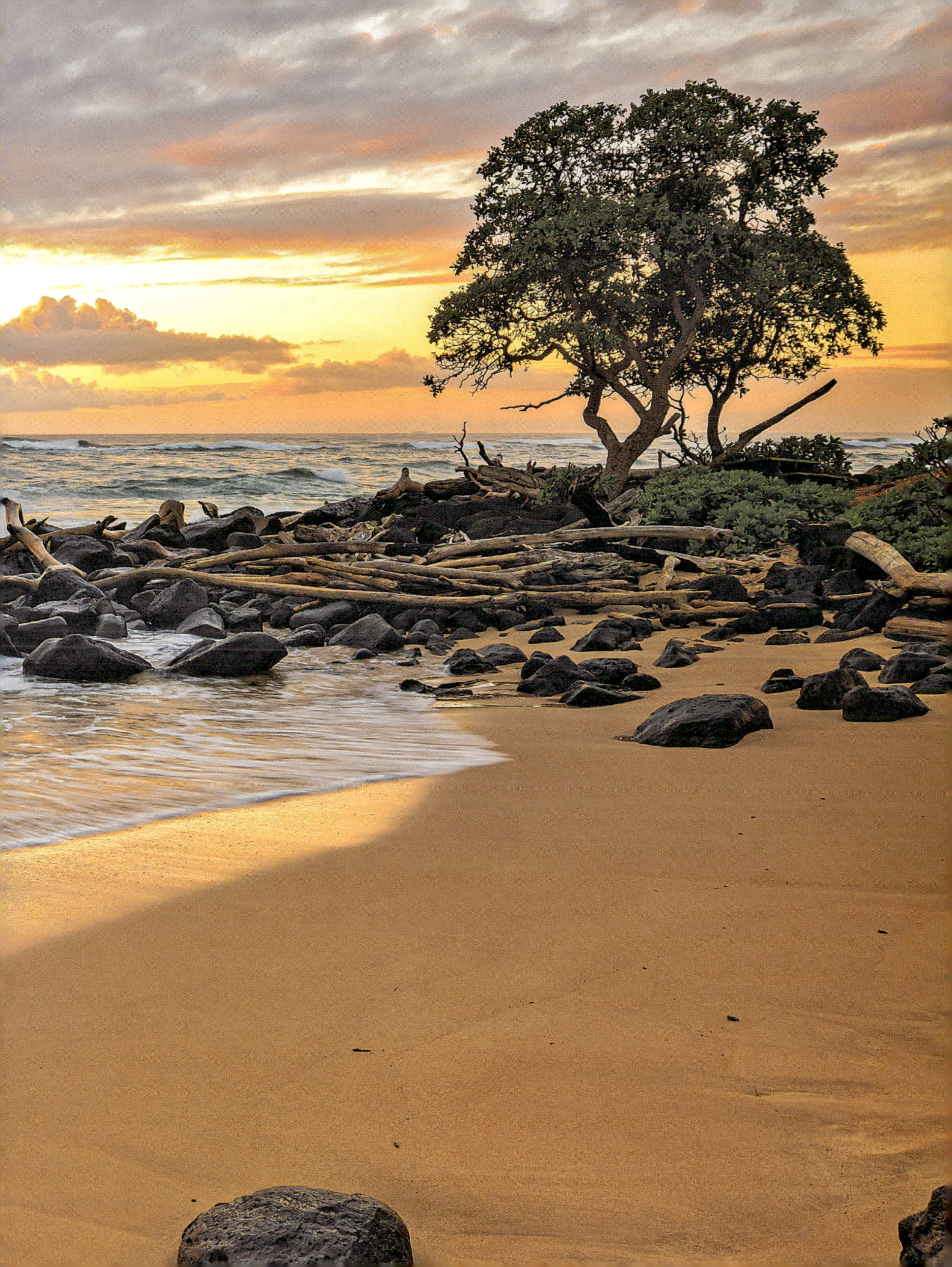

NEVERLAND

~

KAUA'I IS NATURE AT ITS MOST MYTHICAL. THE RAINFORESTS ARE ALIVE AND EVER-CHANGING, GROWING LUSH AS FAR AS THE EYE CAN SEE, RECLAIMING THE SPACE CONCEDED TO THE HUMANS, WHILE THE ROCKS THAT DASH STRAIGHT INTO THE WAVES ALSO SEEM ALIVE.

The Nā Pali coast cannot be reached by car, but only by sea in rubber dinghies or catamarans, on foot after a long hike, or from the sky by helicopter: it is a succession of sharp peaks, waterfalls, and secret bays. Its appearance from above is confirmation that the world existed before man, that it exists regardless of man, and that it will perhaps continue to exist in spite of man. Here, life in the wild is not an experience to brag about on social networks: it is a condition to be accepted and internalized. Your every step is to confront the unstable balance between beauty and danger: paths get lost in the mud, rivers disappear, the ocean changes mood in minutes, as does the sky. Those who stop to watch without pretending to understand receive something rare in return: the clear impression that even in its most inanimate components, Earth itself is living, changing, and surprising. It is no coincidence that many films have chosen Kaua'i as a backdrop conjuring up the origins of the world, as in *Jurassic Park* and *King Kong* and even a world that goes beyond fantasy, like Neverland in *Hook*. Not in search of exoticism, but of authenticity. No setting can hold a candle to the unpredictability of the vegetation engulfing the ruins of an ancient temple or the profile of Kalalau traced by the light. Yet, despite these displays of power, the island also has an intimate face: it lets you meet it on an empty beach, in a Saturday market, in the light rain that accompanies you for a stretch of road. It has no need to shout to be remembered. Kaua'i is what happens when nature remains mistress, and man, for once, does not try to steal her thunder.

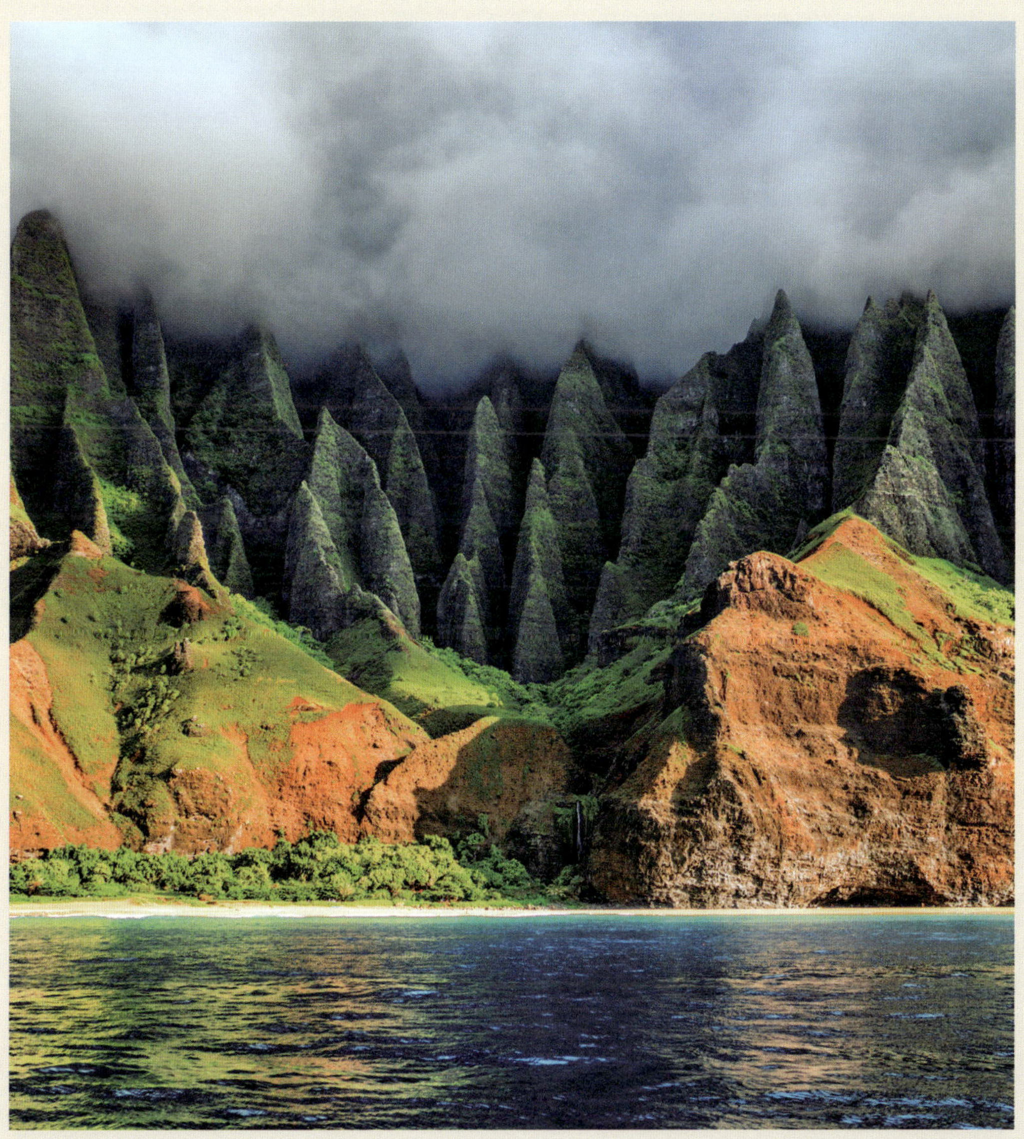

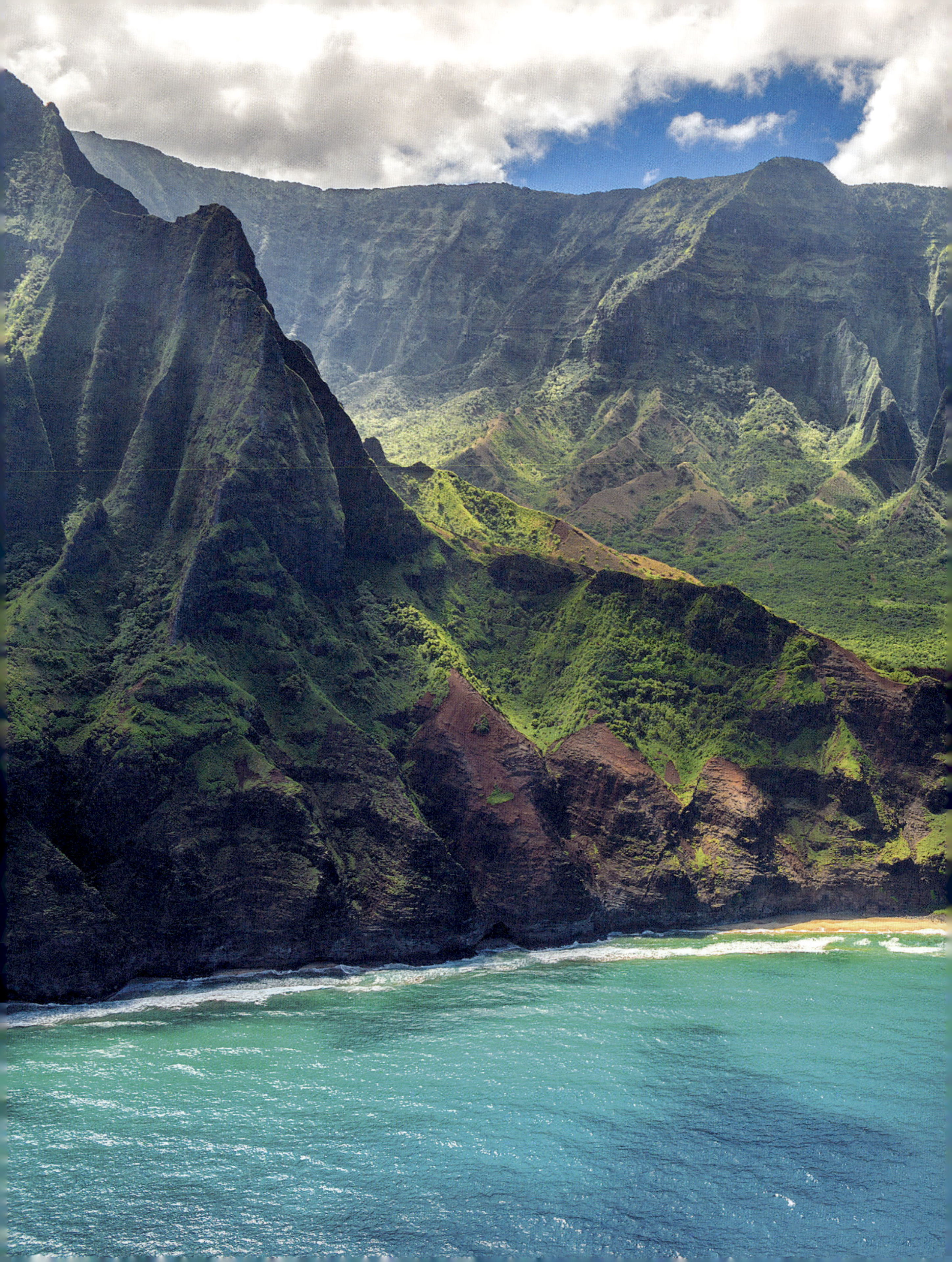

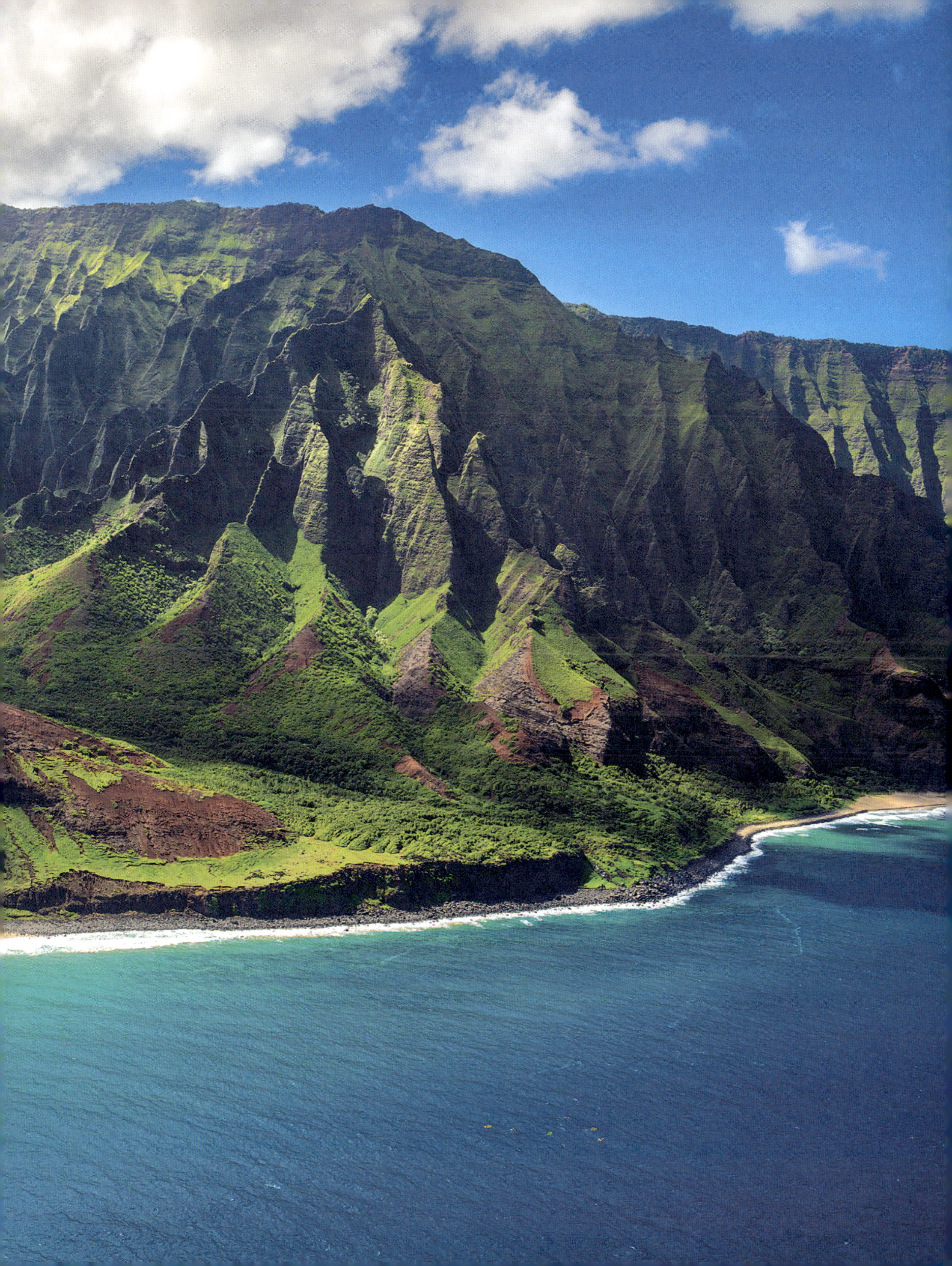

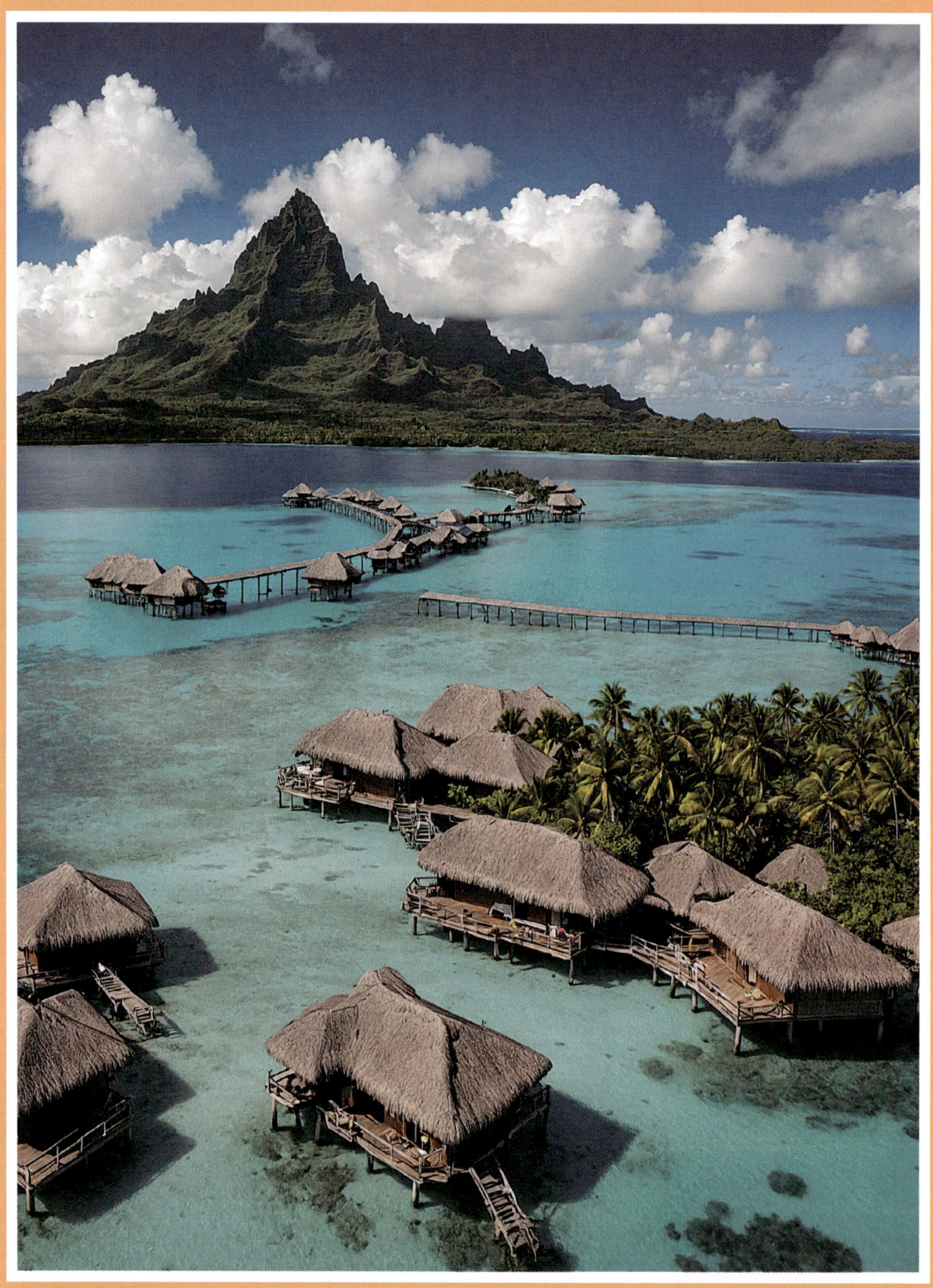

French Polynesia

BORA BORA

Geographical coordinates: 16°30'04" S; 151°44'29" W
Waters: Pacific Ocean
Population: 10,605 inhabitants
Surface area: 11.80 square miles (30.55 km²)
Principal settlement: Vaitape

THE PEARL OF THE PACIFIC

Every place bears the marks of its past, both recent and distant: this island was once a volcano that sank, creating a lagoon surrounding the last remaining peak. The term "lagoon" may evoke an image of murky, stagnant water, but here it is crystal clear, merging from blue to emerald green. It is almost entirely encircled by a coral reef and long islets fringed with white sand, called motu, two larger and several smaller ones. Mount Otemanu, what remains of the ancient volcano, is 2,385 feet (727 meters) of rock covered with dense green vegetation, like a soft garment draped over a sleeping creature. First reported to the Europeans by Jacob Roggeveen in 1722 and then in 1769 by James Cook, who landed there in 1777, the "Pearl of the Pacific" is now frequented by thousands of tourists, mainly honeymooners, attracted by the sea, the coral reef, and the unspoilt vegetation. The resorts are mainly located on the motus, facing the lagoon: wooden stilt houses with luxurious interiors. It is difficult to describe these places without resorting to words such as paradise, Eden, dreamlike, and all the other adjectives that spring to mind when we see fireworks or similar wonders: the fact is that our vocabulary is simply inadequate when it comes to describing nature's greatest gifts. Perhaps rather than struggling to find appropriate words, we should just abandon ourselves to contemplation and adopt the local philosophy *aita pea pea*, which roughly translates as "don't worry."

OPERATION BOBCAT

~

Pearl Harbor, dawn on December 7, 1941: the Japanese airborne forces unleash a massive surprise attack on the United States' Pacific Fleet. What Roosevelt was to define as the *day of infamy* resulted in the USA immediately joining the conflict. The Americans needed a supply base between Australia and the Panama Canal, and the island of Bora Bora was ideal. So it was that, within the ambit of an operation code-named Bobcat, this remote and peaceful corner of the world, with just over 1,000 inhabitants, was suddenly invaded by 5,000 men from Admiral Turner's fleet and their ships. In short order, a landing strip, bunkers, jetties, roads, and a power station were constructed. Naval guns that are still visible on the island's uplands were part of the fortifications installed to defend against a Japanese attack, something that fortunately never took place. Despite its brief life (it was decommissioned in June 1946), this base had a considerable impact both in terms of temporary disruptions to local customs—its subsidiary activities drew many inhabitants away from their usual subsistence activities of fishing and farming, which were not easy to revive—and long-term effects given that a large number of soldiers decided to remain in that magical place. However, despite the inevitable contaminations, the native culture still remained strong and deeply rooted: language, religion, songs, dances, and traditions have been jealously conserved by the descendants of the ancient Polynesians, who were probably already living here in the fourth century AD. The precolonial history of Bora Bora is marked by the rivalry between two clans through to the ascent of Puni, the great chieftain who in the 18th century united the entire island and neighbouring Ra'iatea, Taha'a, and Maupiti under his control. His successor, his grandson Tapoa II, was forced to give up Ra'iatea, retired to Bora Bora, and declared himself sovereign. The kingdom, bound by family ties to those of the other islands, was recognized by the colonial powers and lasted until France decided to annex it, obliging the last queen, Teriimaevarua III, to abdicate. This was in 1888.

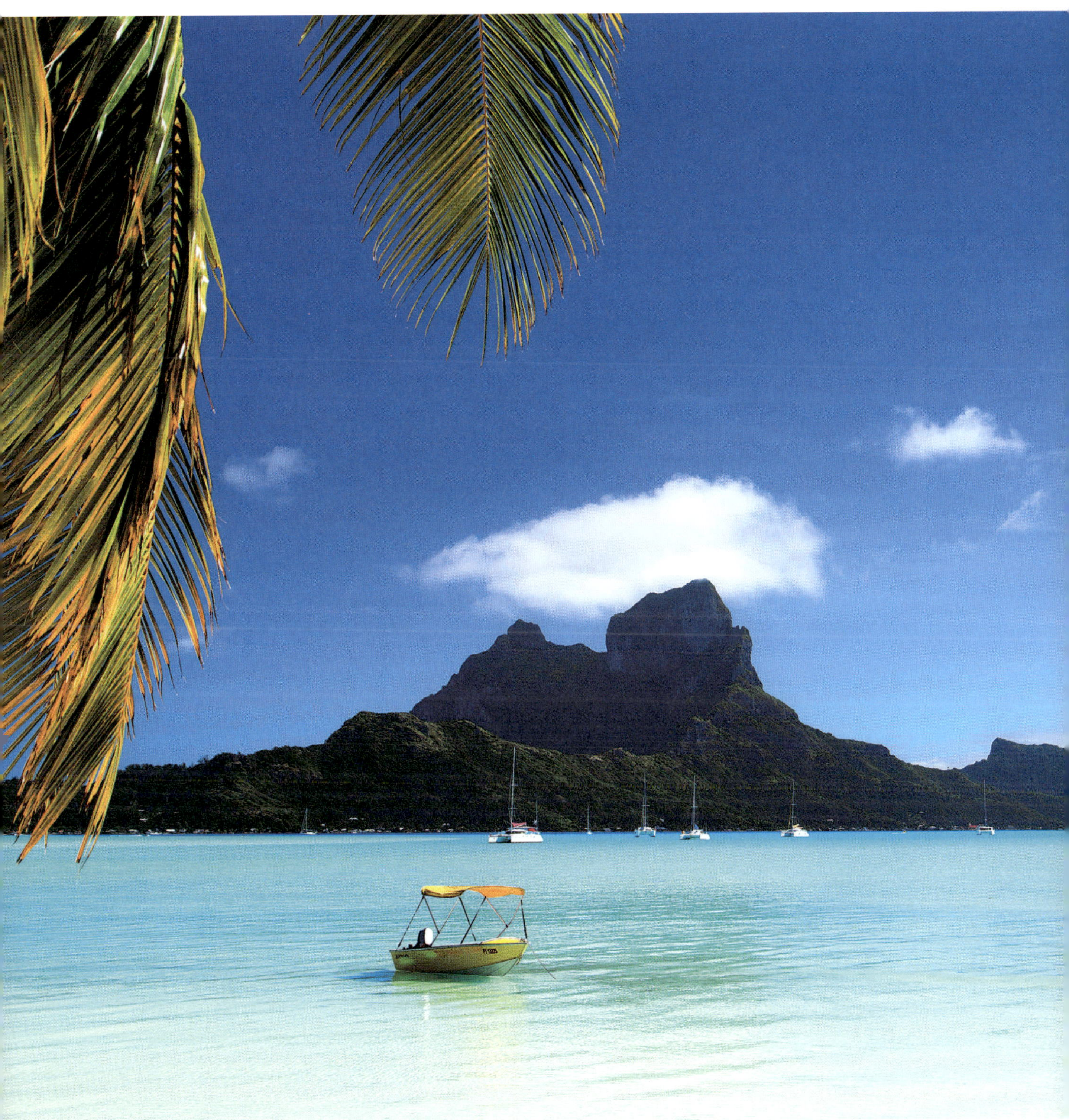

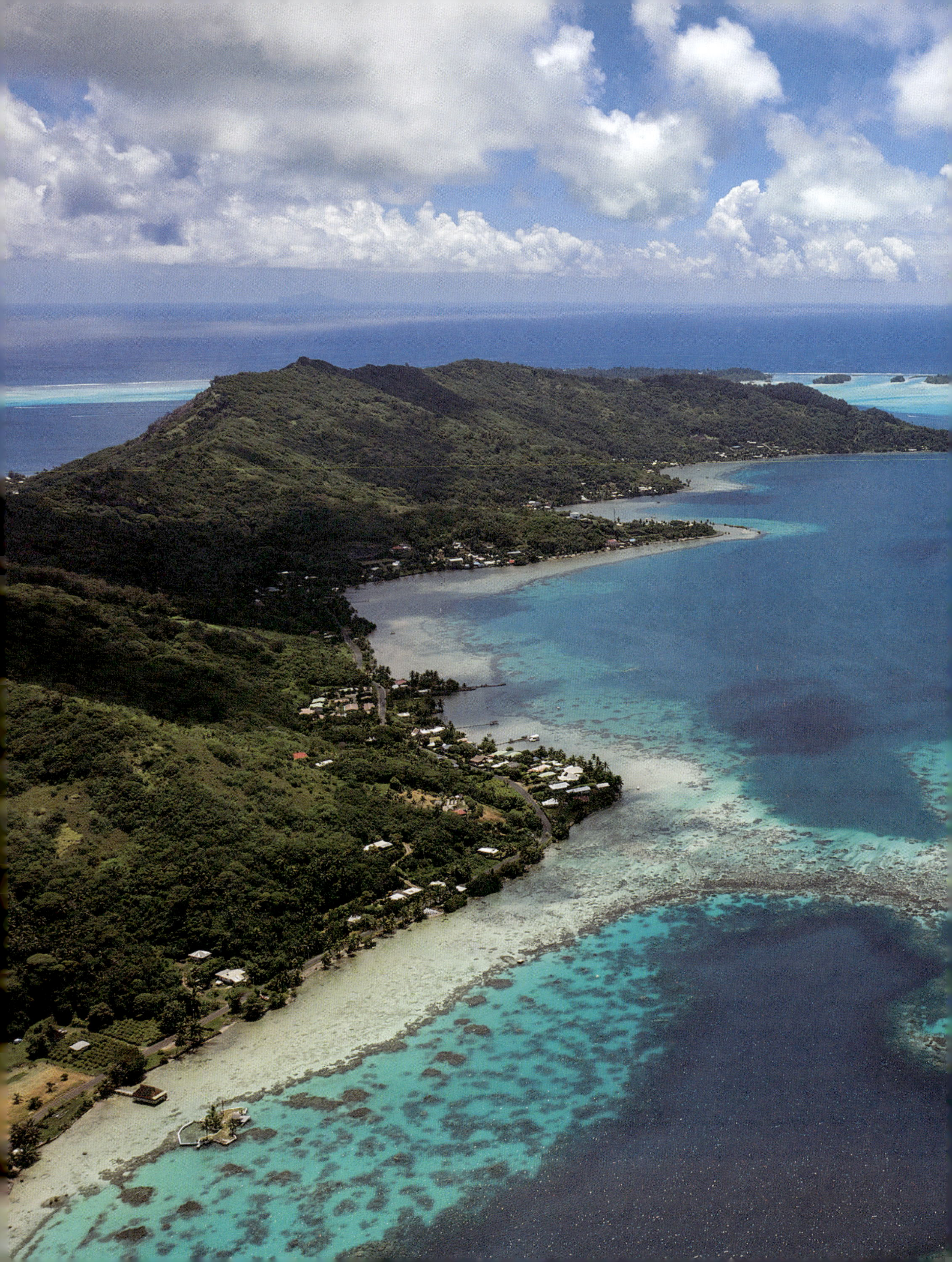

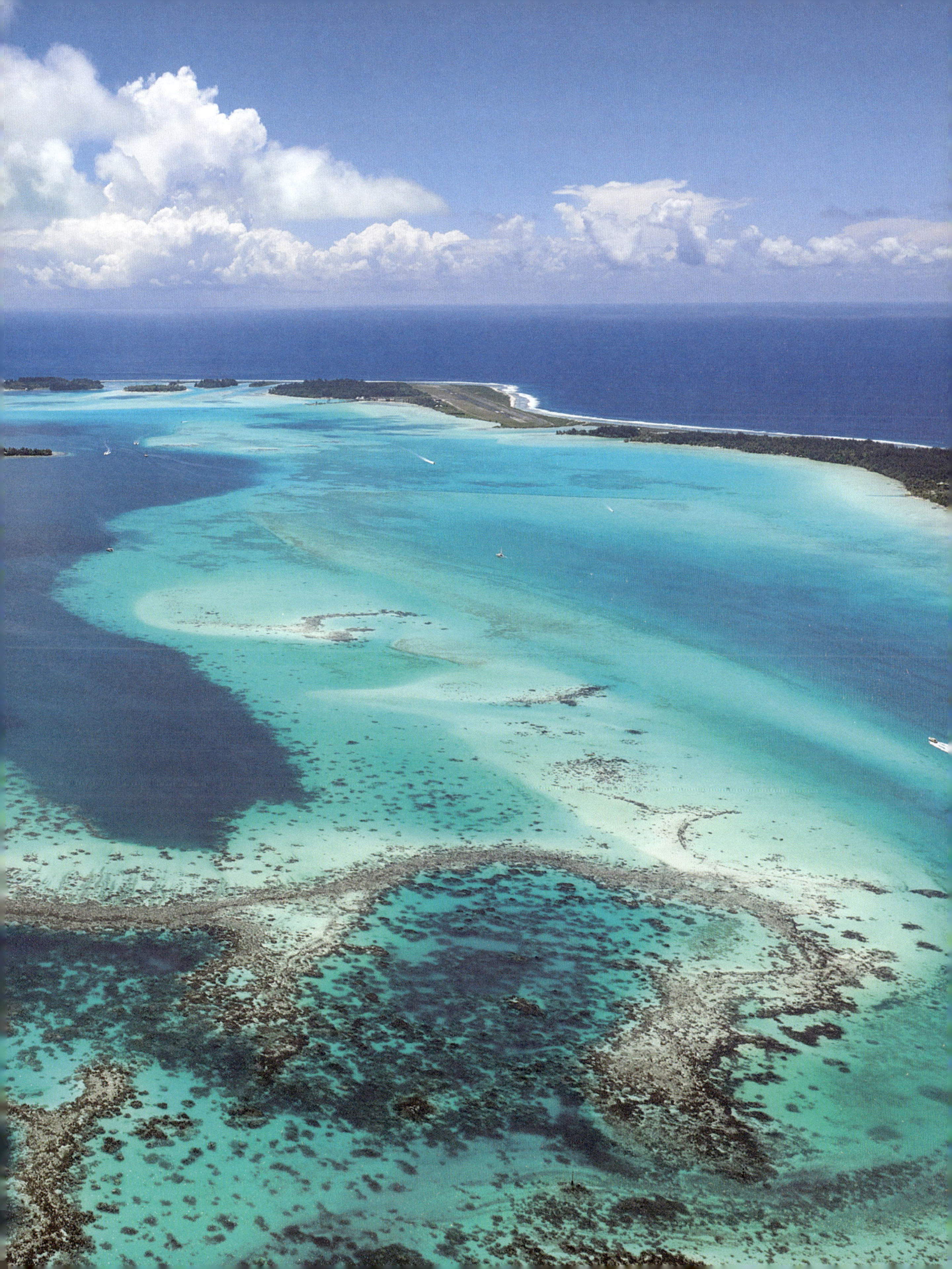

MARLON BRANDO AND THE OTHERS

MARLON BRANDO IS THE EPITOME OF APPEAL, CHARISMA, AND MYSTERY; PASSION WITHOUT COMPROMISE. HIS ENCOUNTER WITH THESE PLACES WAS AKIN TO THAT BETWEEN A FLAME AND GASOLINE.

Places that were then even more remote than they are today had already been evoked by the pens of Jack London, Herman Melville, Robert Louis Stevenson, and Mark Twain or captured on the canvases of Gauguin. When Brando first landed here in 1960 for the shooting of the cult film *Mutiny on the Bounty*, a remake of the 1935 movie with Clark Gable, his heart was captured and with it that of the rest of the world. While it is true that the line separating an actor and the character he plays is frequently slim and ambiguous, in this case the short-circuit took the most classic of forms: the love between Fletcher Christian and Maimiti, the daughter of the king of Tahiti, also overwhelmed the stars of the film, Marlon Brando and the beautiful Tarita Teriipia, daughter of a local fisherman. The two married on August 10, 1962 (for him it was the third time), and they remained together for 10 years and had two children. The actor also bought an atoll that he transformed into a love nest and a resort inspired by ecological criteria, a business that survived the couple's break-up and Brando's death, developing into *The Brando*, an example of the trend combing luxury with eco-friendly ethics. A simple phrase by Brando neatly summarizes the effect and spiritual value these place hold for humanity: "My mind is always soothed when I imagine myself sitting on my South Sea island at night."[1]

1 Rosemary McClure, "Marlon Brando's island paradise in Tetiaroa, French Polynesia," *Los Angeles Times*," 2/28/2015

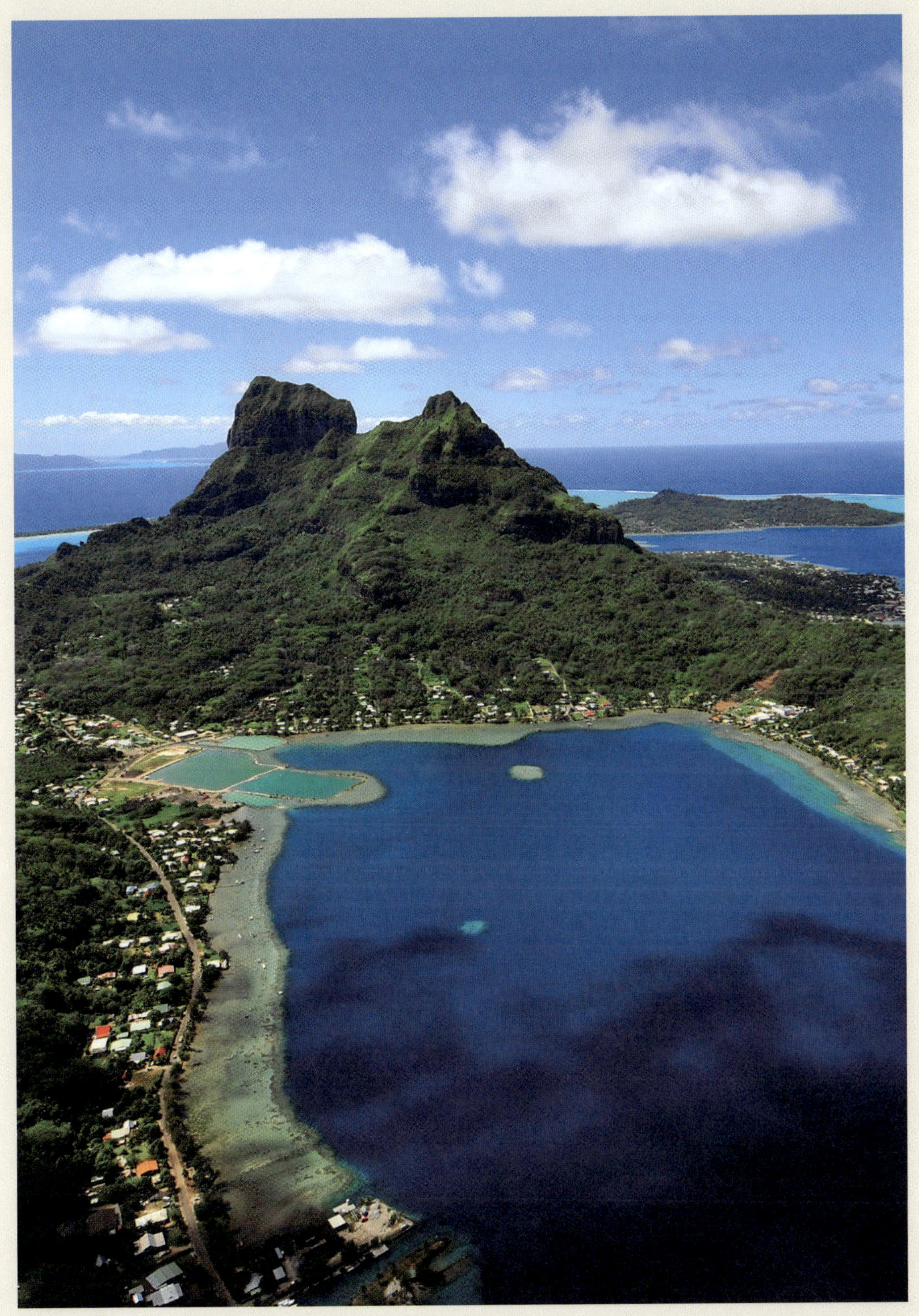

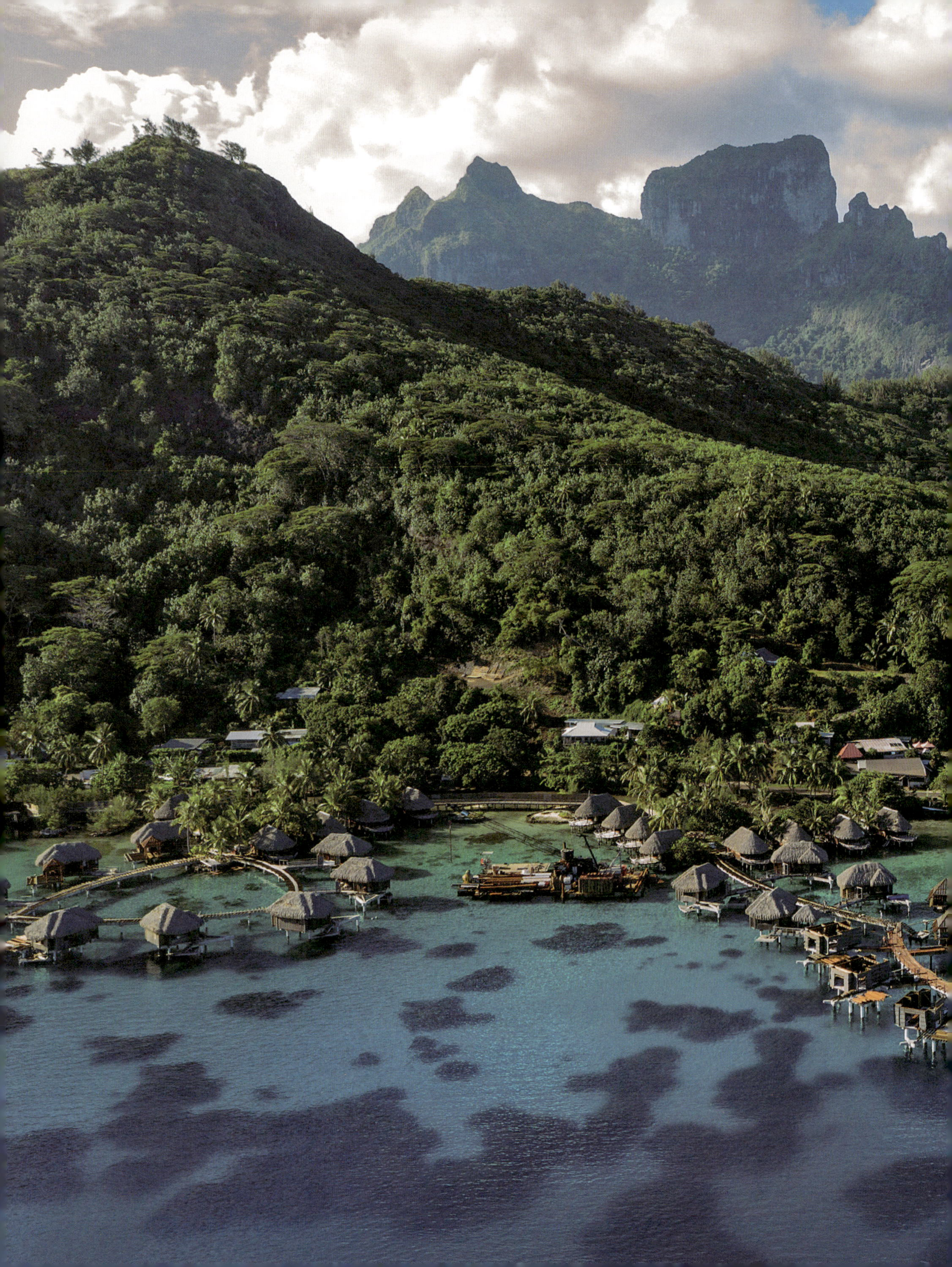

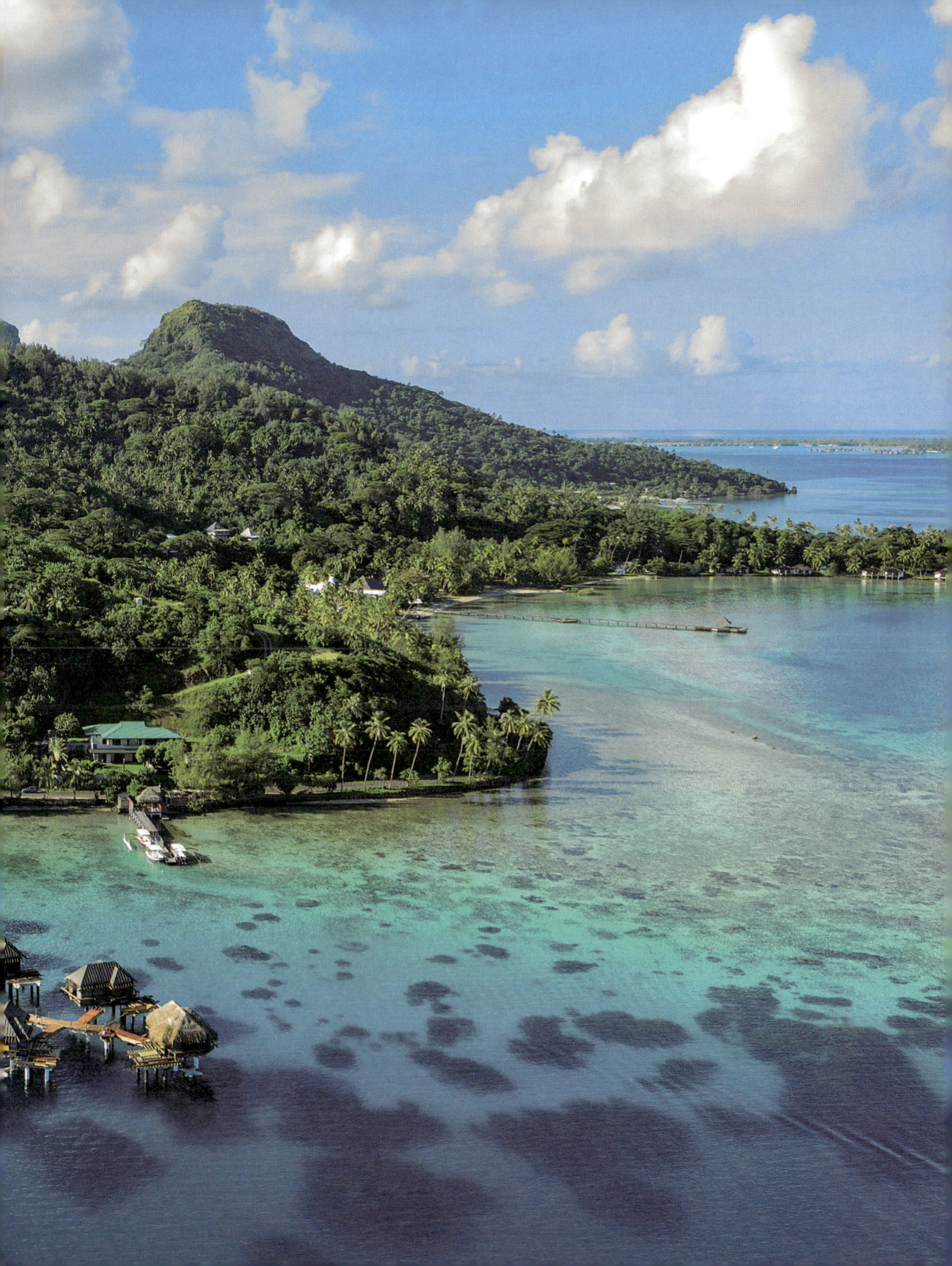

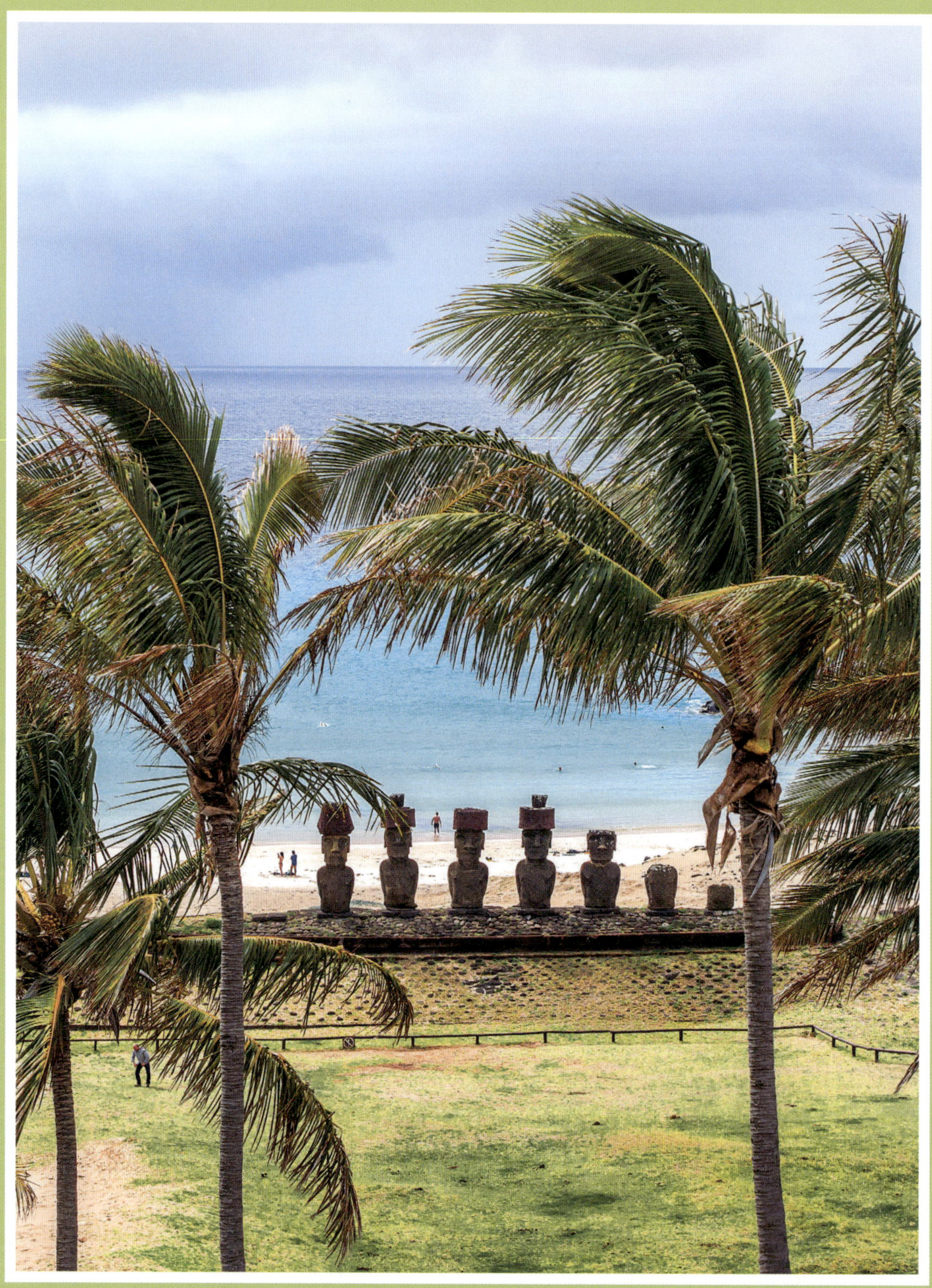

Chile

EASTER ISLAND

Geographical coordinates: 27°07'14" S; 109°21'05" W
Waters: Pacific Ocean
Population: 7,750 inhabitants
Surface area: 63.20 square miles (163.7 km²)
Principal settlement: Hanga Roa

CENTER OF THE WORLD

All it takes is to point to it on the globe to gain a sense of isolation: lying around 2,240 miles (3,600 kilometers) off the coast of Chile, lost in the Pacific Ocean, Easter Island hosts one of the most remote settlements on the planet. This patch of harsh rock, bordered by basalt cliffs, with few beaches, constantly battered by the trade winds, was born out of an eruptive process that began three million years ago on the oceanic ridge and forms a right-angled triangle, the corners of which are presided over by extinct volcanoes. These spectral craters are joined by a multitude of smaller cones and caves and tunnels, the remains of the volcanic activity of the past. All around, the seabed plunges rapidly to a depth of more than 6,500 feet (2,000 meters). It was on Easter Sunday 1722 that the Dutchman Jacob Roggeveen landed on the island, circumstances that were decisive in it being given a new name, destined to coexist for centuries with the original Rapa Nui (the "Great Rock") given by the local peoples. The island had in fact been inhabited for some time. This small but generous stretch of land favored the development of an evolved and flourishing society devoted to fishing and agriculture, a community of around 20,000 people, with their own written language, traditions, customs, and religion. It was the inhabitants of Rapa Nui who dedicated themselves to the construction of the Moai, anthropomorphic statues between 16 and 33 feet (5 and 10 meters) tall and weighing tens of tons. These enigmatic figures with their severe features were transported from the quarries to their final site via a complex system of trunks on which they were rolled for miles. They were almost all positioned around the coast, facing inland, and are so evocative that they have become the symbol of the island.

MOTU NUI

~

When the crisis was at its lowest depth, around 1500, the islanders ceased sculpting the Moai and abandoned them to the elements; some were actually destroyed, perhaps because the ancestors or divinities they were associated with failed to provide the protection and benevolence expected of them. This then led to the rise of the Bird Man Cult, as testified by figures carved into the rocks. This was a more nebulous period than the others and perhaps no study will ever shed light on the great number of questions and mysteries. What we do know is a series of intertwining threads from which more questions than answers emerge; the silence remains, filled by the stories narrated by the wind. Thus we can still hear the echo of the drums that rumbled during the competitions between the strongest warriors. Once a year, the champions from each tribe threw themselves into the water to swim to the rocky islet of Motu Nui. The first to collect a sooty tern egg and bring it back intact to the village of Orongo became the Tangata-manu (Bird Man) and claimed the position of chieftain through to the next challenge. Many of the participants were killed in the shark-infested waters, renewing the short circuit of light and shadow that alternates in these parts. This mechanism for legitimizing power brought an end to tribal struggles and favored a period of peace and equlibrium that lasted until the arrival of the white man.

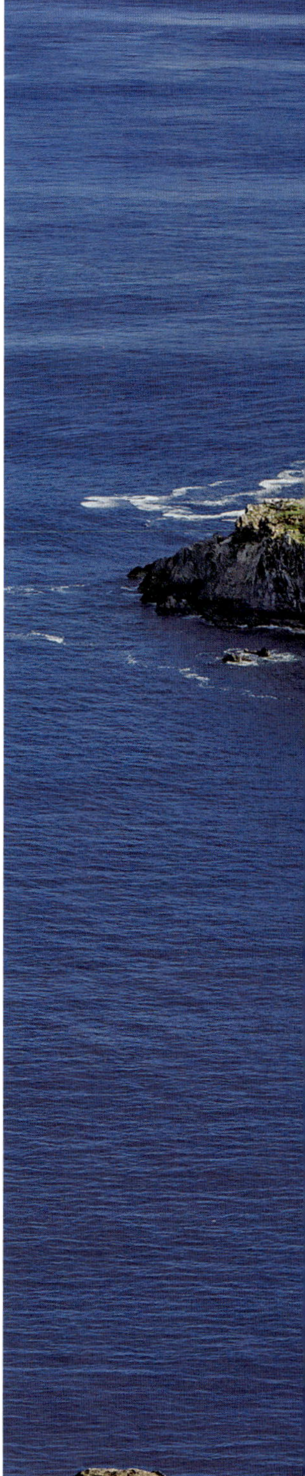

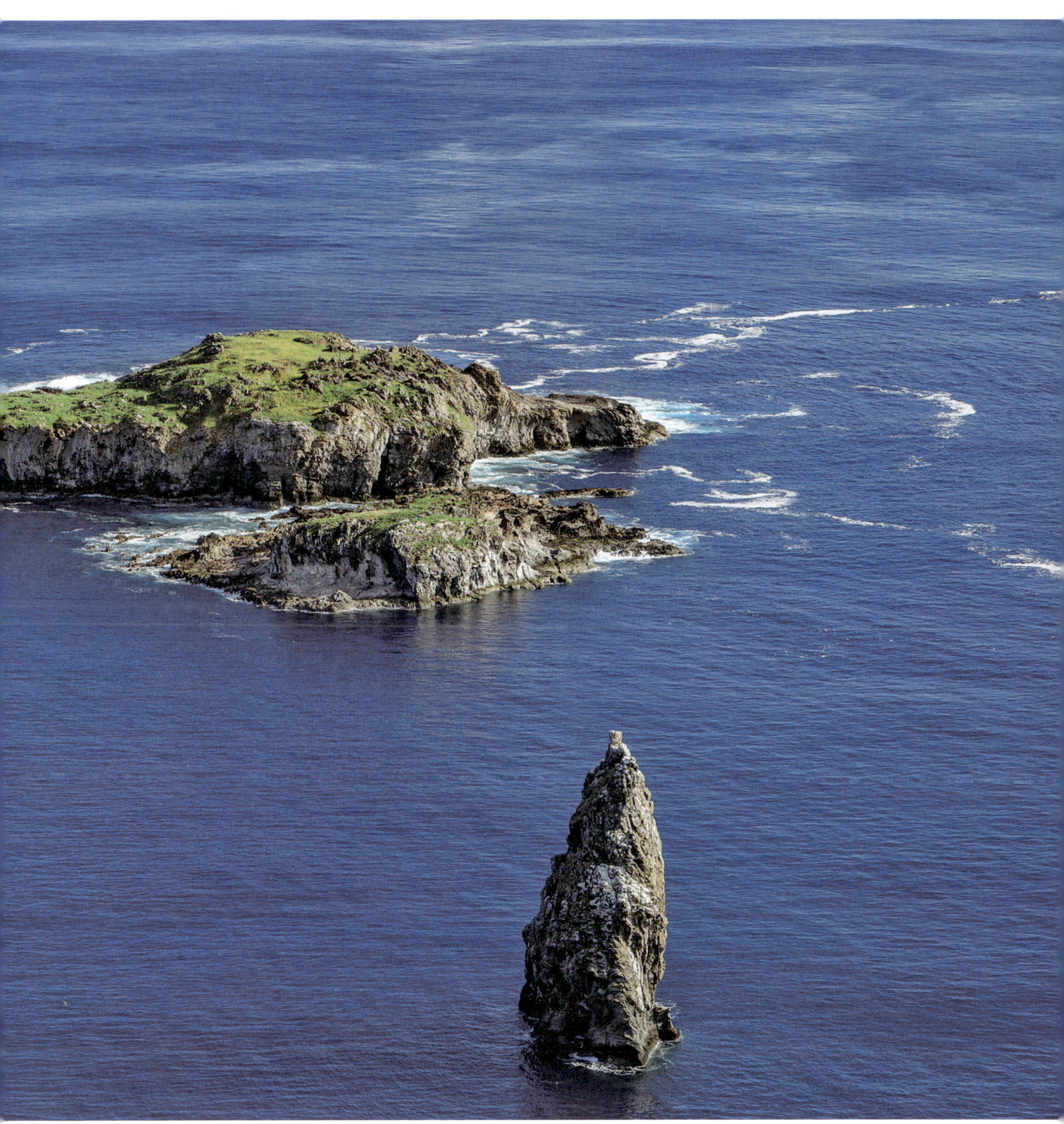

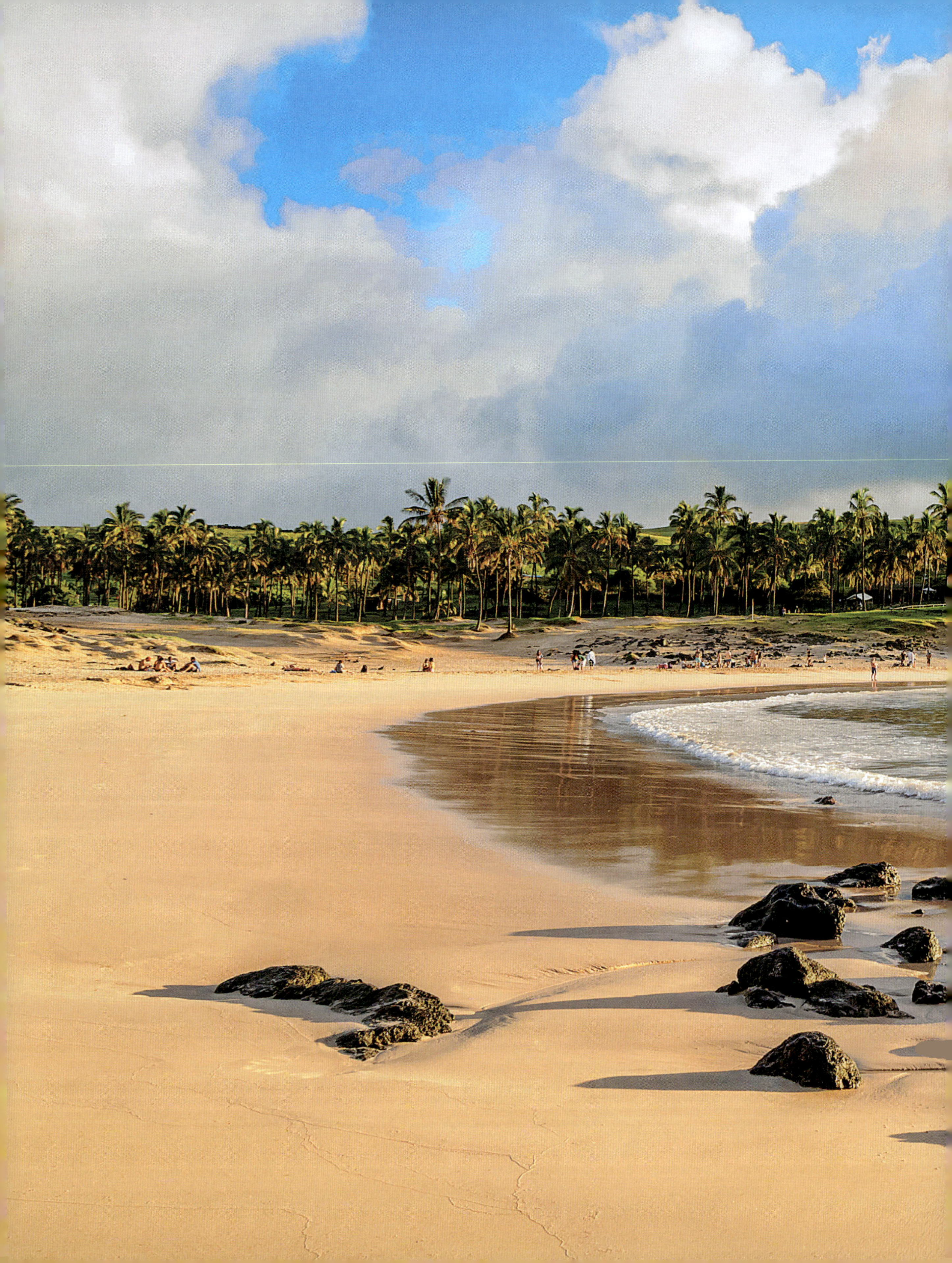

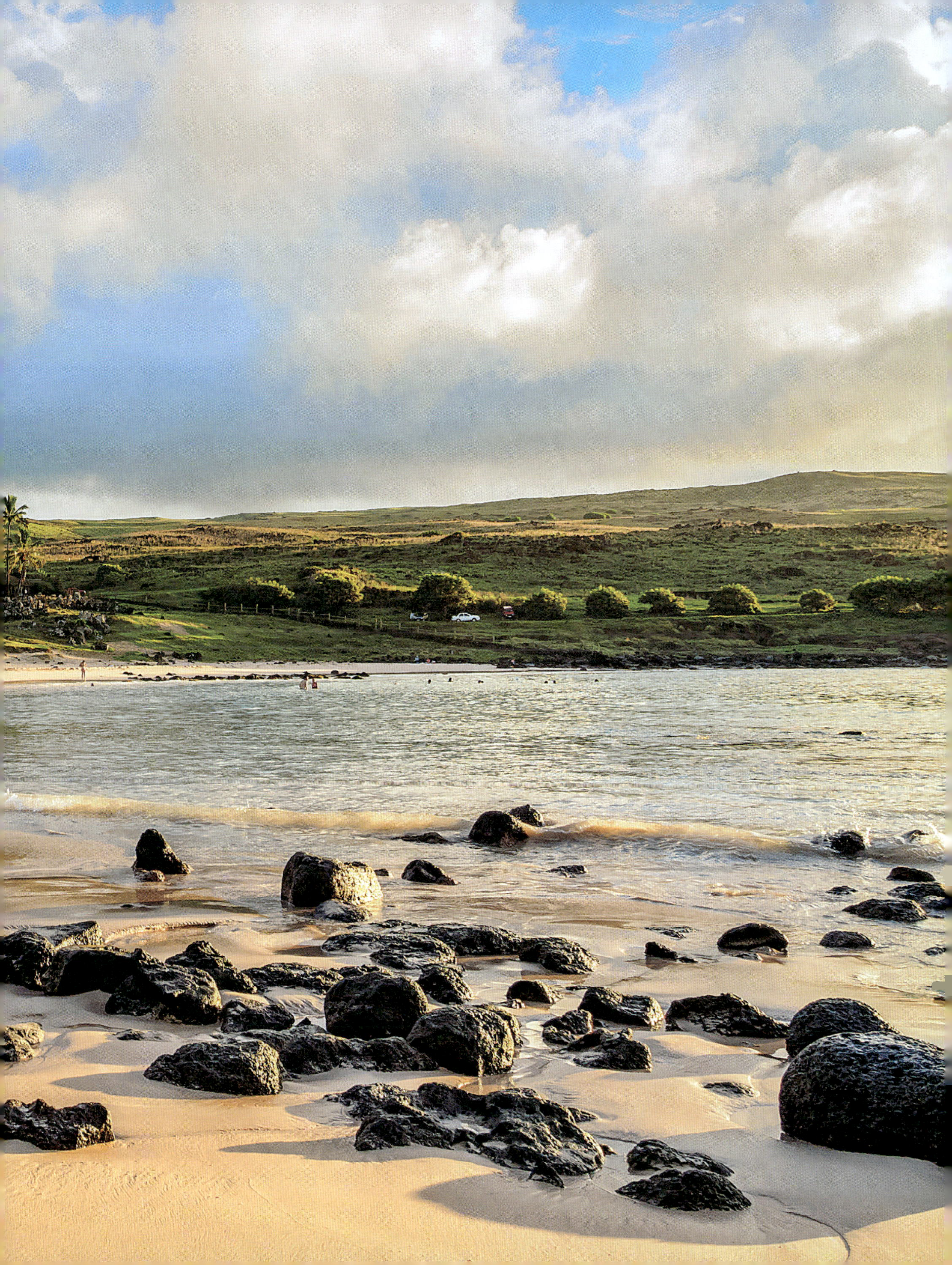

ASCENTS AND DECLINES

THE STORY OF RAPA NUI IS STILL SHROUDED IN MYSTERY. MANY ARCHAEOLOGISTS AND ANTHROPOLOGISTS HAVE TAKEN ON THIS FASCINATING CHALLENGE, ALONG WITH SEVERAL COLORFUL CHARACTERS, SUCH AS THE WRITER ERICH VON DÄNIKEN, WHO IN THE 1960S WROTE ABOUT A GROUP OF ALIENS STRANDED ON THE ISLAND DUE TO A SPACESHIP MALFUNCTION WHO PASSED THE TIME BY SCULPTING 1,000 GIANT-HEADED STATUES.

In light of etymological comparisons, research into artifacts, and genetic studies of skeletal remains, it seems that the first permanent inhabitants, who arrived around 1000 AD, were brave Polynesian explorers capable of tackling the ocean aboard rafts and canoes, sailing more than 1,800 miles (3,000 kilometers) under the guidance of their ruler and leader Hotu-Matua. When they arrived, the island was covered with giant palm trees and was home to numerous plant and animal species. So why, when Roggeveen landed there in 1722—and James Cook two years later—did the environment appear barren and inhospitable? It is a tragic parable about the balance between man and nature, which took place long before Westerners arrived to import disease, abuse, and various other disasters. The original population conducted savage deforestation, exploiting the wood from the trees to build boats and houses and above all as rollers to move their enormous Moai. Another hypothesis, not necessarily alternative, attributes decisive importance to the introduction of the Polynesian rat, which reproduced undisturbed in the absence of predators. In the process it almost completely

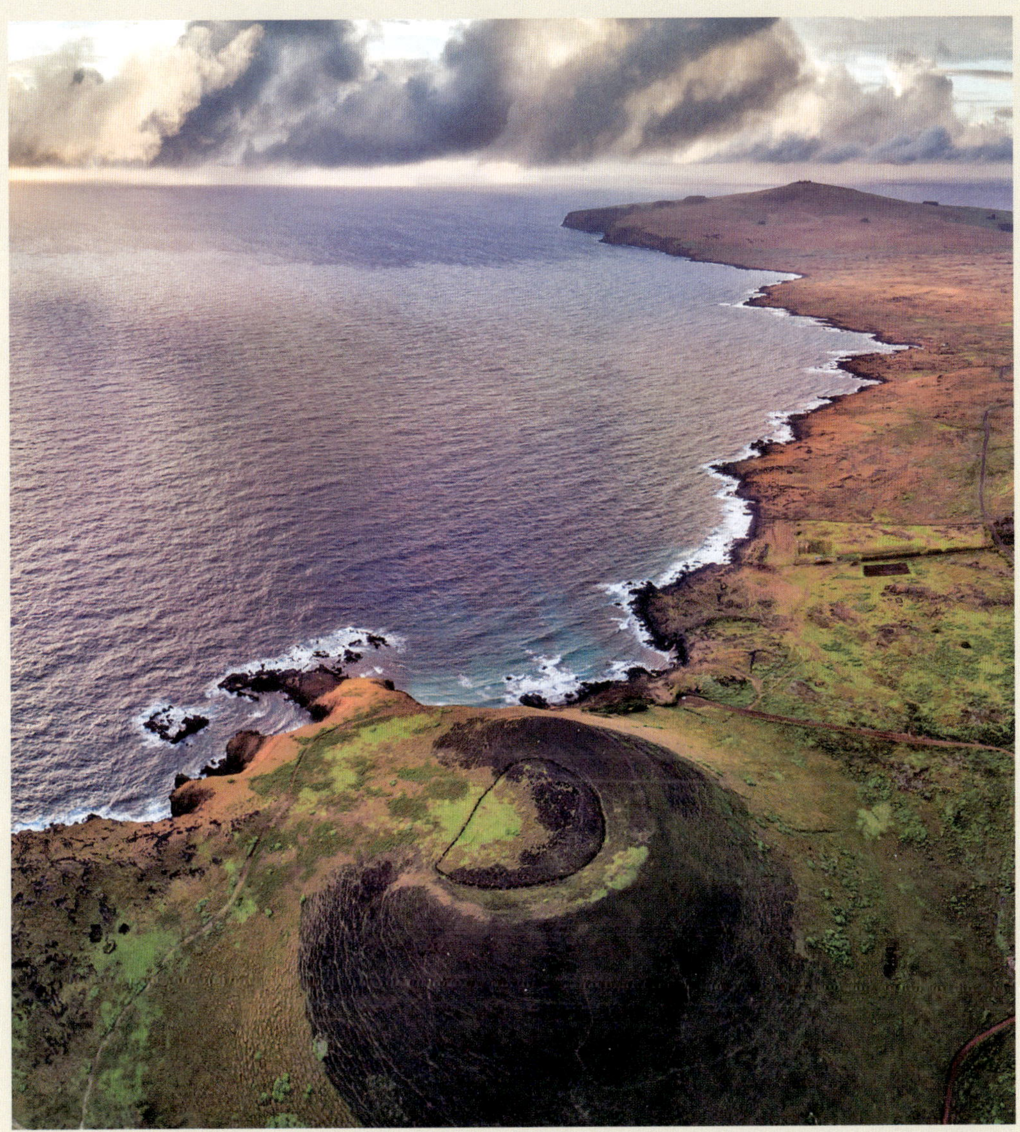

wiped-out other species and by including palm seeds in its diet, severely limited the regeneration and development of the typical vegetation. In short, within just a few centuries, human presence was responsible for the disappearance of about one million palm trees. This desertification triggered a process that peaked in the 16th century with famine, hunger, disease, violence, and cannibalism. The arrival of Westerners contributed to this dynamic. Even the early visits were not without clashes in which the indigenous people always came off worse. Syphilis, smallpox, multifaceted exploitation, various forms of abuse and harassment, and slave deportations did the rest, and by the end of the 19th century only 100 or so natives remained on the island.

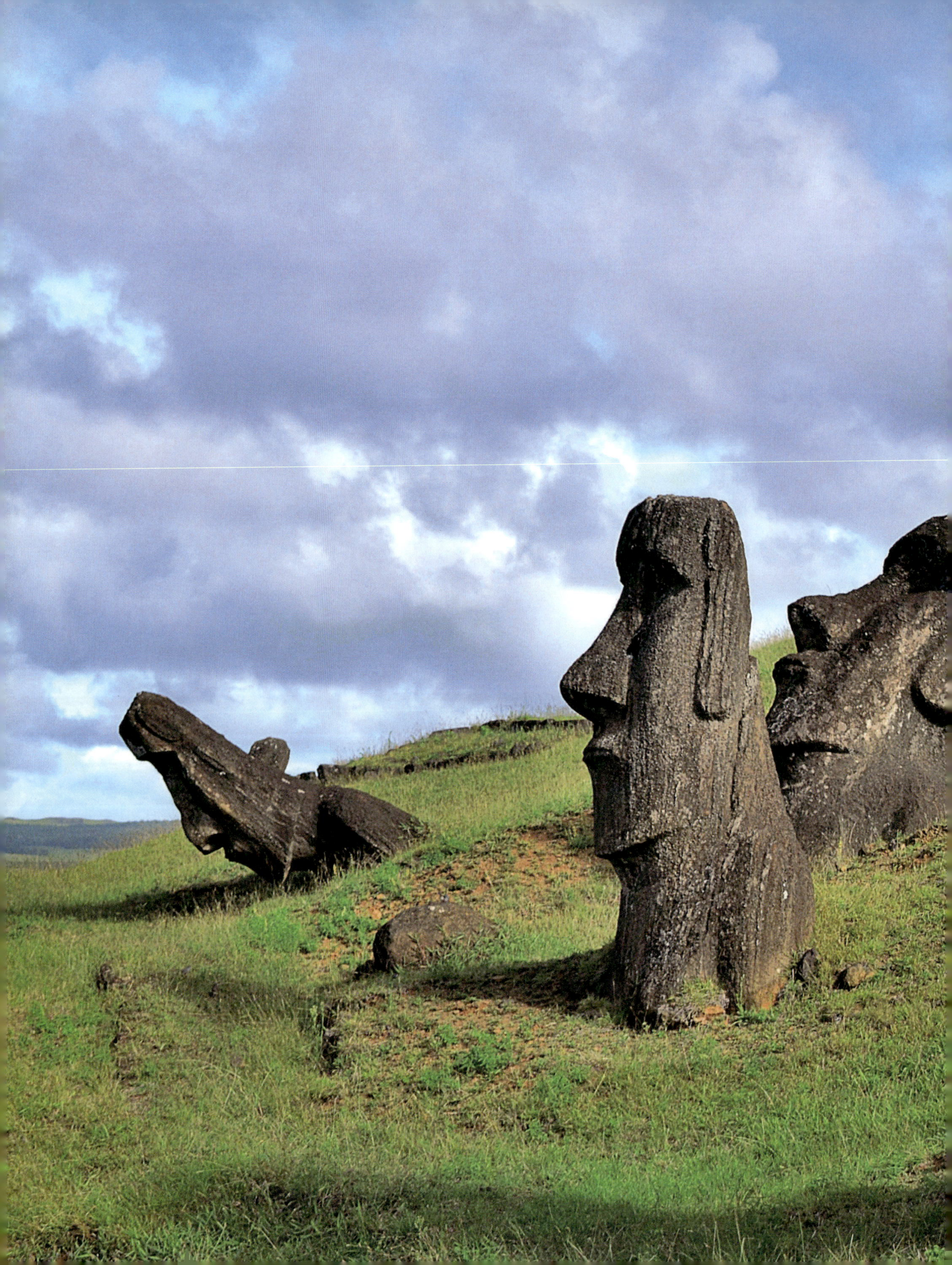

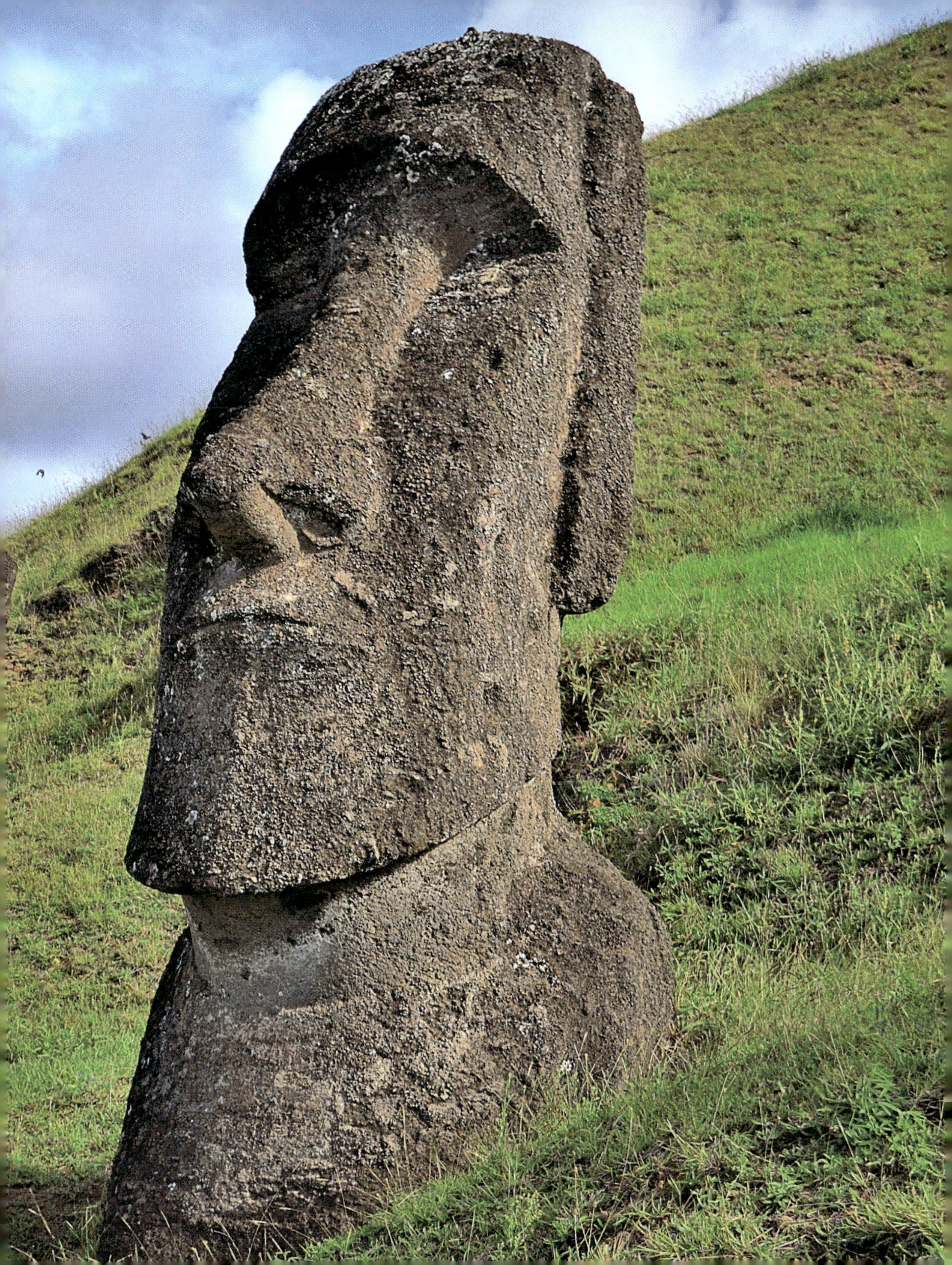

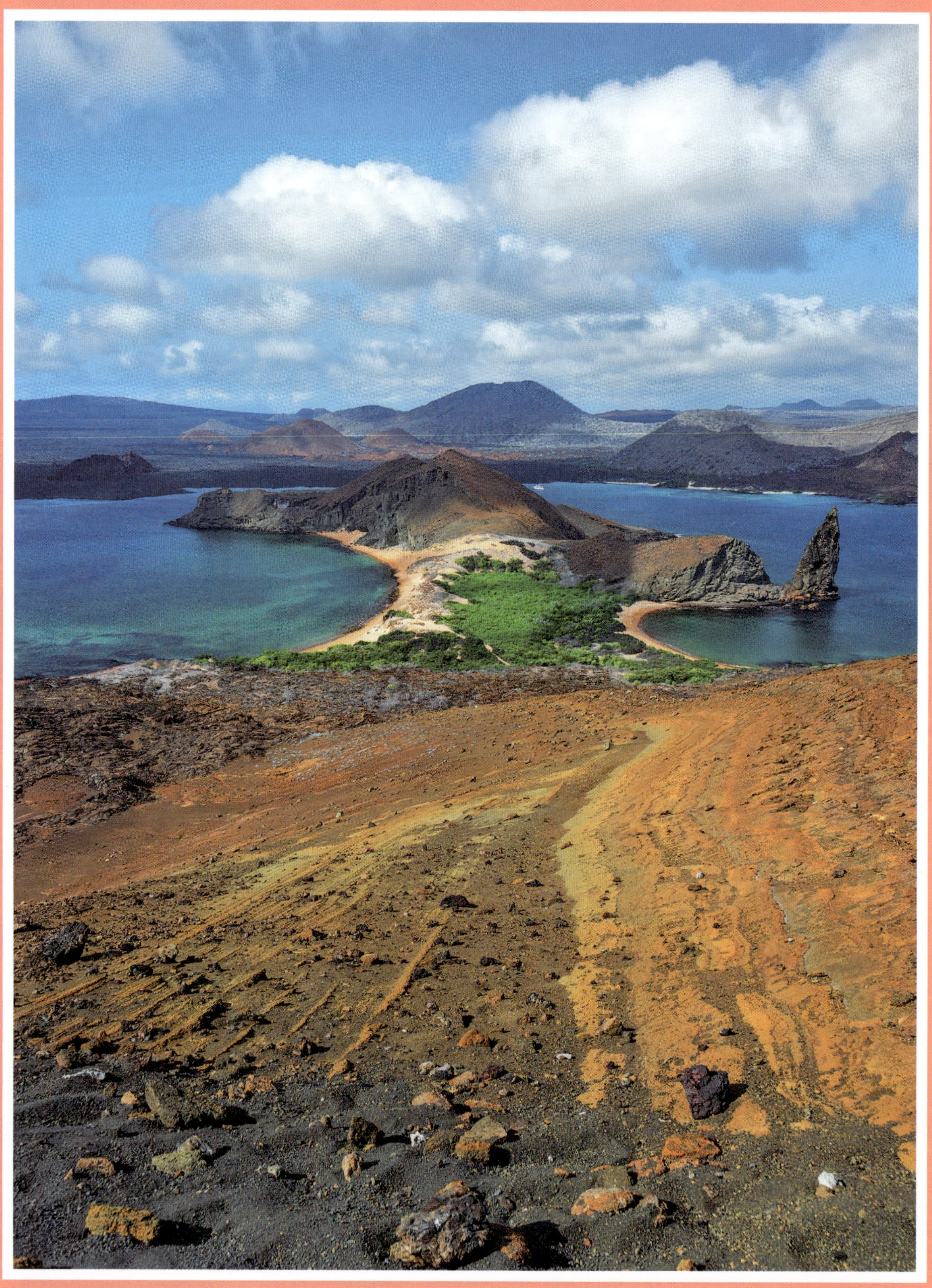

Ecuador

GALÁPAGOS

Geographical coordinates: 0°40'00" S; 90°33'00" W
Waters: Pacific Ocean
Population: 28,583 inhabitants
Surface area: 3,094.60 square miles (8,015 km²)
Principal settlement: Puerto Baquerizo Moreno

A WORLD APART

The Galápagos archipelago, situated at least 560 miles (900 kilometers) from the continent, is composed of 13 major islands and around 40 minor formations, all resting on a single submerged platform of volcanic origin: a system that is still active, with around 20 principal craters and thousands of derivations. The islands—colonized on multiple occasions and renamed by the Spanish and the British before being annexed by Ecuador in 1832—enjoy a mild climate and have a recent geological history given that they date from ten to two million years ago. Discovered by chance in March 1535 by the Bishop of Panama Tomás de Berlanga, who had drifted there while heading for Peru, the islands were perhaps already known to certain South American peoples, but remained untouched and uninhabited. The description provided by the bishop mentions his wonder at the giant tortoises that inspired the name and the naivety of the local fauna, in particular the birds that, by no means disturbed by the human presence, allowed themselves to be captured easily. Seals and tortoises were massacred and embarked as reserves of meat by the whalers who would frequently land on the islands and were also responsible for wildfires that destroyed what had hitherto been uncontaminated landscapes. Over the following centuries, these lands were the occasional refuge of pirates and buccaneers, until the first Ecuadorean governor decided to populate them with colonies of former prisoners, farmers, and craftsmen. Today the archipelago is divided between intensive tourism and the absolute need to preserve its globally unique biodiversity, gravely threatened by any contact with alien species.

THE ORIGIN OF SPECIES

~

The Galápagos Islands are inseparable from Charles Darwin. The Pacific archipelago occupied just a single chapter in the English naturalist's epic journey, yet it represents a milestone in the development of his evolutionary theory. It was in September 1835 when the brig-sloop *Beagle*, which had been sailing for almost four years of alternating fortunes, storms, disease, and exploration, reached the Galápagos, where it was to remain for five weeks. In this period, Darwin concentrated on the study of species that while similar presented different characteristics from one island to the next. The giant tortoises, for example, differed in the shape of their shells, while the finches presented a mutated morphology of their beaks. The wealth of endemic species and the total isolation triggered a revolutionary spark in Darwin. As he was to write years later, it was on that occasion his basic idea regarding evolution took shape: *I am fully convinced that species are not immutable.* He added that, in expressing these theories, he felt as though he was confessing to a crime. In effect, its conception was in stark contrast to the assumption of the immutability of divine creation. Curiously, following his return home, Robert FitzRoy, the captain of the *Beagle* and the man that had invited the naturalist to join the expedition, transformed into one of the most fervent opposers of the theories of evolution, protesting bible in hand and decrying heresy.

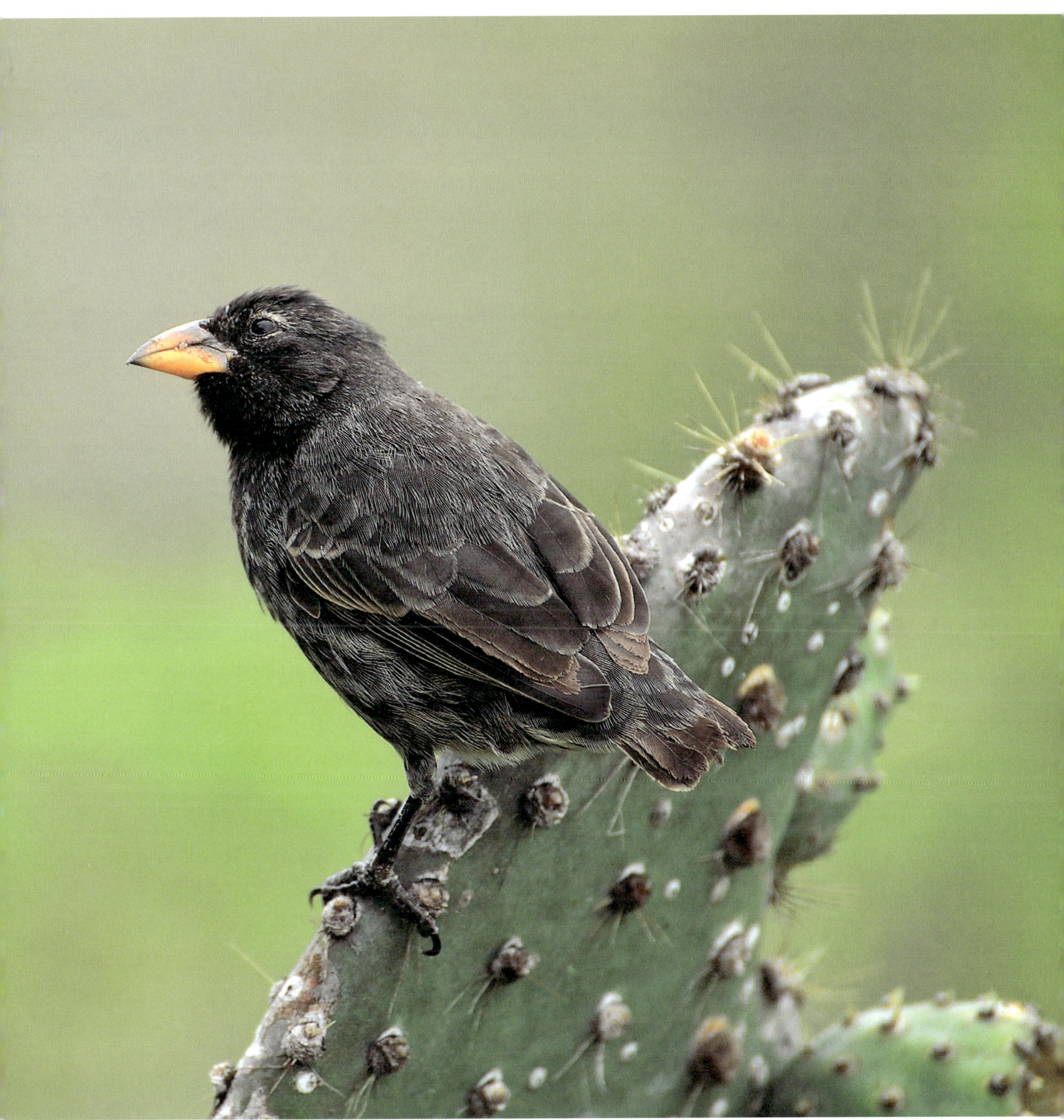

SATAN CAME TO EDEN

∾

THE STORY OF THE ISLAND OF FLOREANA IS ONE OF DREAMS AND UTOPIAS THAT SHATTER WITH NO EXPLANATION OTHER THAN PERHAPS MADNESS. THIS WAS 1929, NOT JUST ANY YEAR FOR THE WORLD AND FOR GERMANY IN PARTICULAR. DORA STRAUCH AND FRIEDRICH RITTER DECIDED TO LEAVE EVERYTHING BEHIND THEM—BERLIN, WORK, SPOUSES, AND RELATIVE BURDENS—AND TO REINVENT THEMSELVES IN A PLACE WITH NEITHER RULES NOR CONSTRAINTS. AFTER SAILING FOR A MONTH THEY REACHED THE GALÁPAGOS BEFORE DECIDING TO SETTLE ON THE UNINHABITED FLOREANA, A KIND OF TERRESTRIAL PARADISE.

The epic adventure of the would-be Adam and Eve attracted the attention of the media, and the visits of numerous journalists were the only occasions on which the couple had to wear clothes. Three years later, Heinz and Margret Wittmer, along with their son Harry and another child on the way, left Cologne to join the company. So far, so good: agriculture and a savage lifestyle, following in the footsteps of the first two inhabitants. Then Eden was rocked by the arrival of Eloise Wehrborn de Wagner Bosquet, the so-called Baroness, together with her two lovers, Alfred Lorenz and Robert Philippson. Driven by the dream of opening a hotel for billionaires on the island—and armed with a pistol—Eloise proclaimed herself the Empress of Floreana and began to tyrannize the other inhabitants as well as her protégés, especially the young Lorenz, the target of true torment. The situation was unsustainable and in fact soon came to a head: the empress and Philippson, her favorite, disappeared into thin air. The others claimed they had left, but they almost certainly were killed. Lorenz decided to return to Germany, but his ship also disappeared and his skeleton was found months later on a neighbouring island. This was not the end: Friedrich Ritter also died, perhaps poisoned by Dora, who then fled. The Wittmers remained and actually did open a tourist business, which is still run by their heirs. Local legend has it that this episode was secretly orchestrated by the giant tortoises, capable of unmasking and cursing those who approach the islands with evil intentions. The story inspired the novella by Simenon, *Ceux de la Soif,* the documentary by Geller and Goldfine *The Galapagos Affair: Satan Came to Eden*, and the very recent *Eden*, starring Jude Law and directed by Ron Howard.

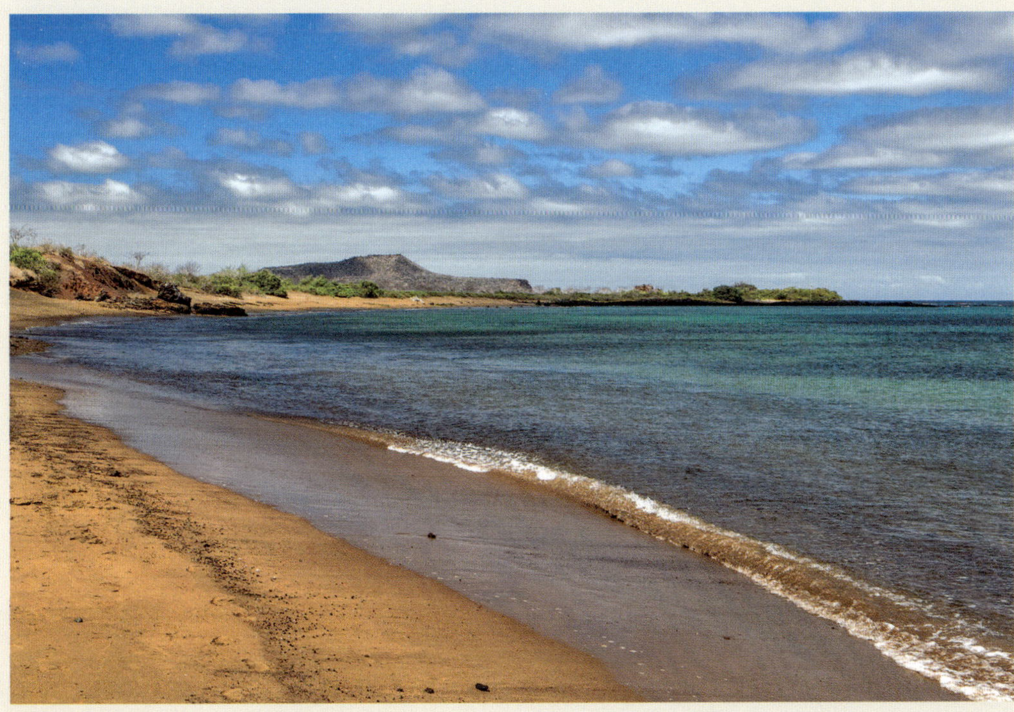

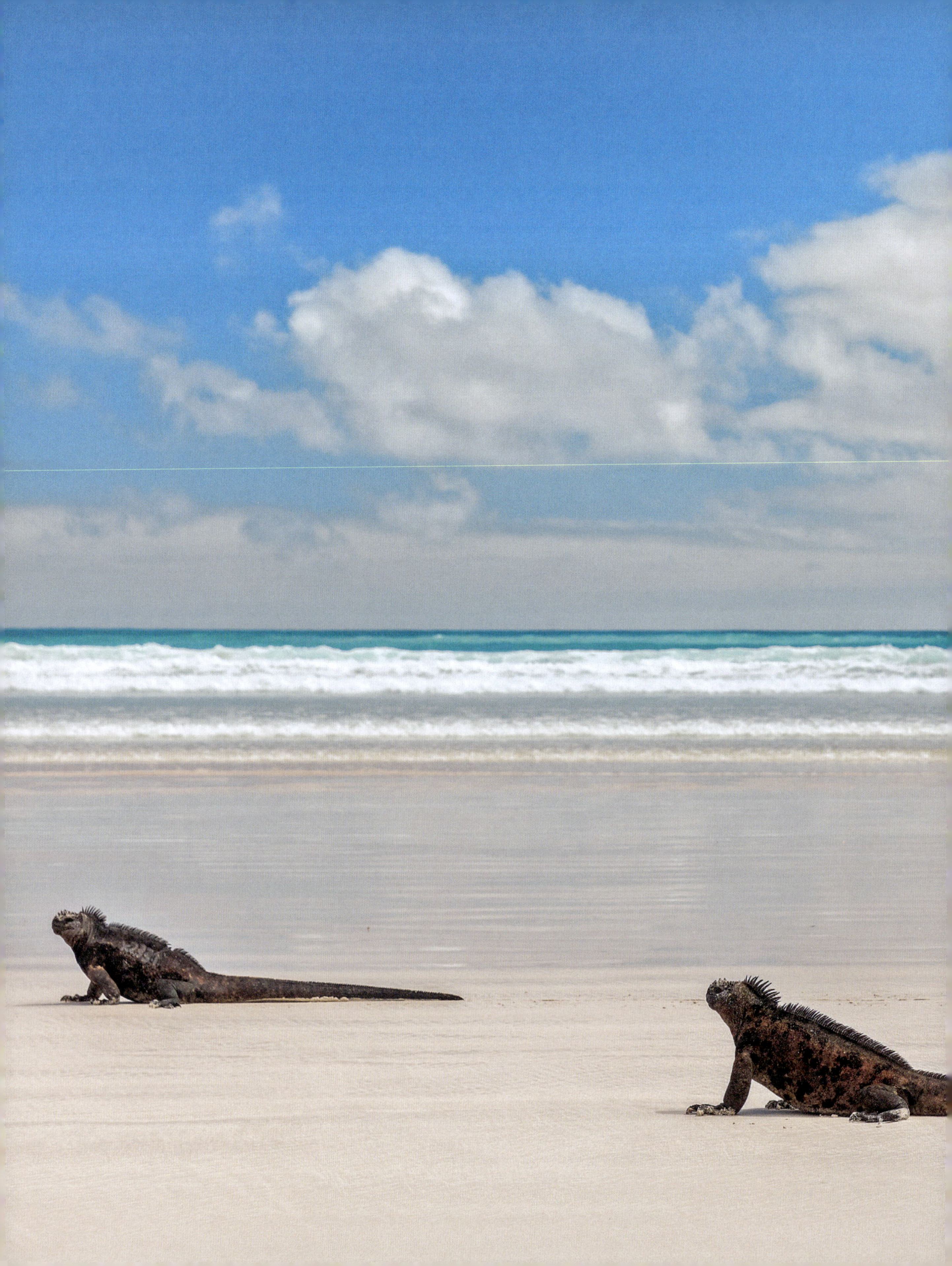

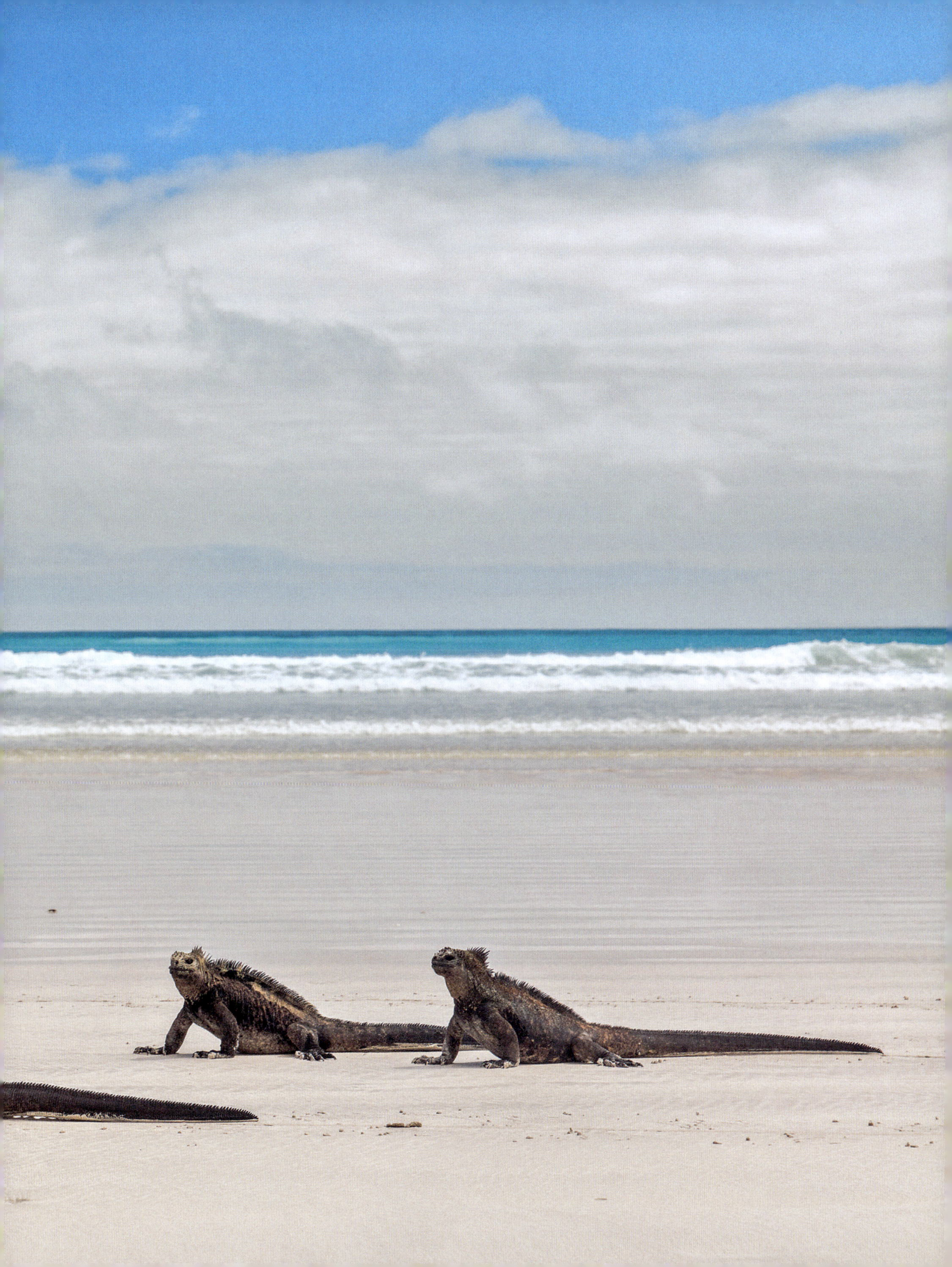

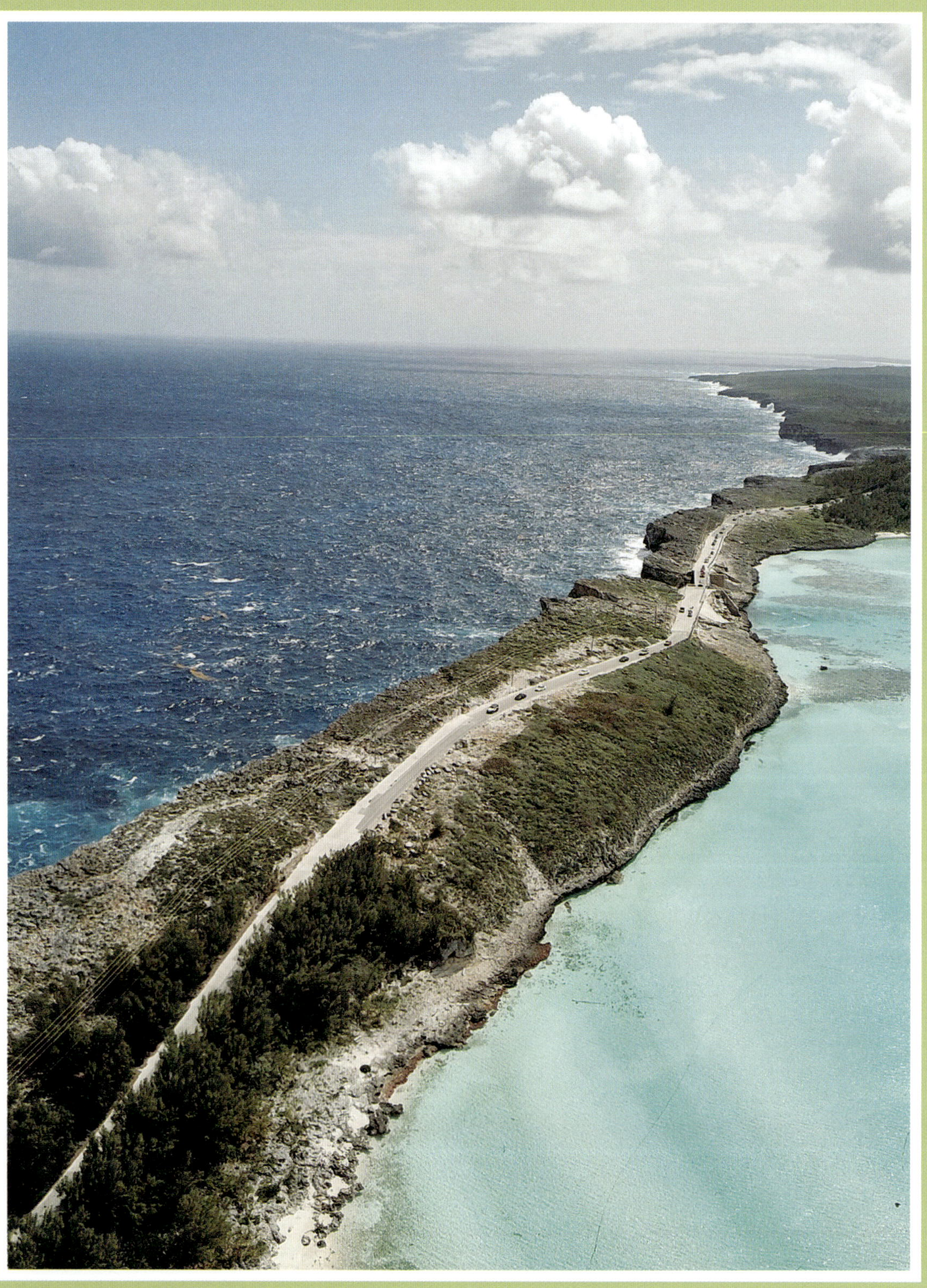

ELEUTHERA

Geographical coordinates: 25°8'05" N; 76°08'39" W
Waters: Atlantic Ocean, Caribbean Sea
Population: 12,716 inhabitants
Surface area: 176.60 square miles (457.4 km²)
Principal settlement: Governor's Harbour

THIN AS A PROMISE

Eleuthera has nothing of the shape of a typical island. It is a line traced on the sea, long and thin, a thread of land that has unwound itself into the Atlantic for over 110 miles (177) kilometers. This extension emphasizes its negligible breadth, which in some places barely exceeds one mile. It is as if it had been designed more to separate than to unite. It is almost an open wound in the blue, a strip poised between permanence and drift. To the north, it breaks away from the submerged platform of the Great Bahama Bank; to the south, it slides into the deep ocean. Its profile is atypical among the hundreds of islands and islets that make up the archipelago as a whole. Composed of coral and sand, Eleuthera has no mountains, only gentle undulations, fragmented coastlines, and low promontories. Beneath its surface, a karstic world of caves, sinkholes, and submerged cavities opens up. Water seeps everywhere, filling brackish lakes and combining with the soil, so porous and fragile yet capable of sustaining life. Lopsided palms, shrubs, breadfruit trees, and proud, elegant bougainvilleas grow with the pride of those struggling to survive without losing their beauty and dignity, as if every root were an act of resistance and every bloom a declaration of identity. Color is part of the geography: the pink of the fine sands, the turquoise of the shallow waters, and the blue of the ocean that changes shade with every passing hour. The Glass Window Bridge is one of the most emblematic sites, showing the sharp confine between the two seas: the placid Caribbean Sea on one side and the restless Atlantic on the other. A single glance reveals that everything here is a balance between sweetness and abyss.

VOLUNTARY CASTAWAYS, TRADERS, DISCONNECTED TRAVELERS

~

Eleuthera was one of the first islands in the Bahamas to be settled by Europeans. Its name, deriving from the Greek word for freedom, was chosen by a group of English Puritans fleeing religious persecution. They landed in the 17th century with a clear idea: to build a new society, a tropical utopia, an experiment in democracy in the middle of the ocean. Things turned out differently thanks to hunger, isolation, and complicated relations with the indigenous Lucayan people. The name remained, however, and with it a sort of vocation for escape. Over time, others arrived: freed slaves, settlers from neighboring islands, fishermen, and seekers of salvation and silence. Eleuthera experienced alternating cycles of splendor and abandonment. In the 19th century, it produced excellent pineapples, which were exported as far as Europe. Then came the agricultural crisis, emigration, and a slow slide into obscurity. Today, it is home to just over 12,000 people, scattered in villages like dots on a line. Governor's Harbour retains a discreet colonial charm, with wooden houses in pastel-colors and verandas overlooking the sunset. Harbour Island, just off the principal island, is livelier, with its golf carts instead of cars, hidden boutiques, and the famous Pink Sands Beach. Tourism has arrived on tiptoe, often through small sustainable resorts, private rentals, and forms of hospitality that still seek authentic contact. Eleuthera is not for those seeking run of the mill luxury: it is for those who want to lose that obsessive connectivity that hammers away at us every day and find a deeper connection by spending a few days in a bubble of slow time.

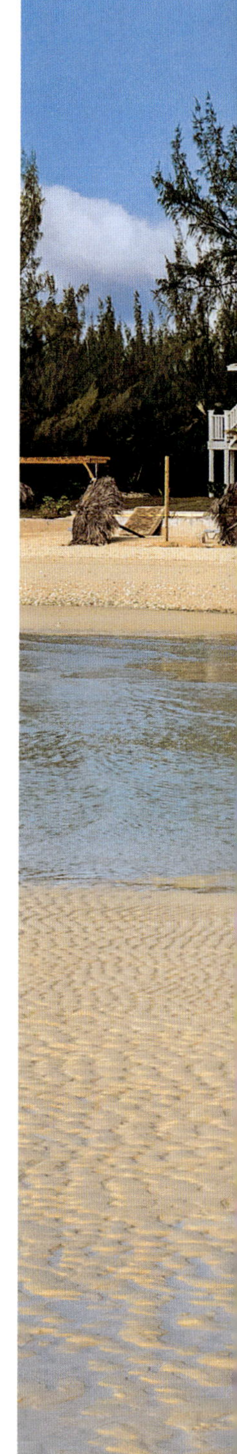

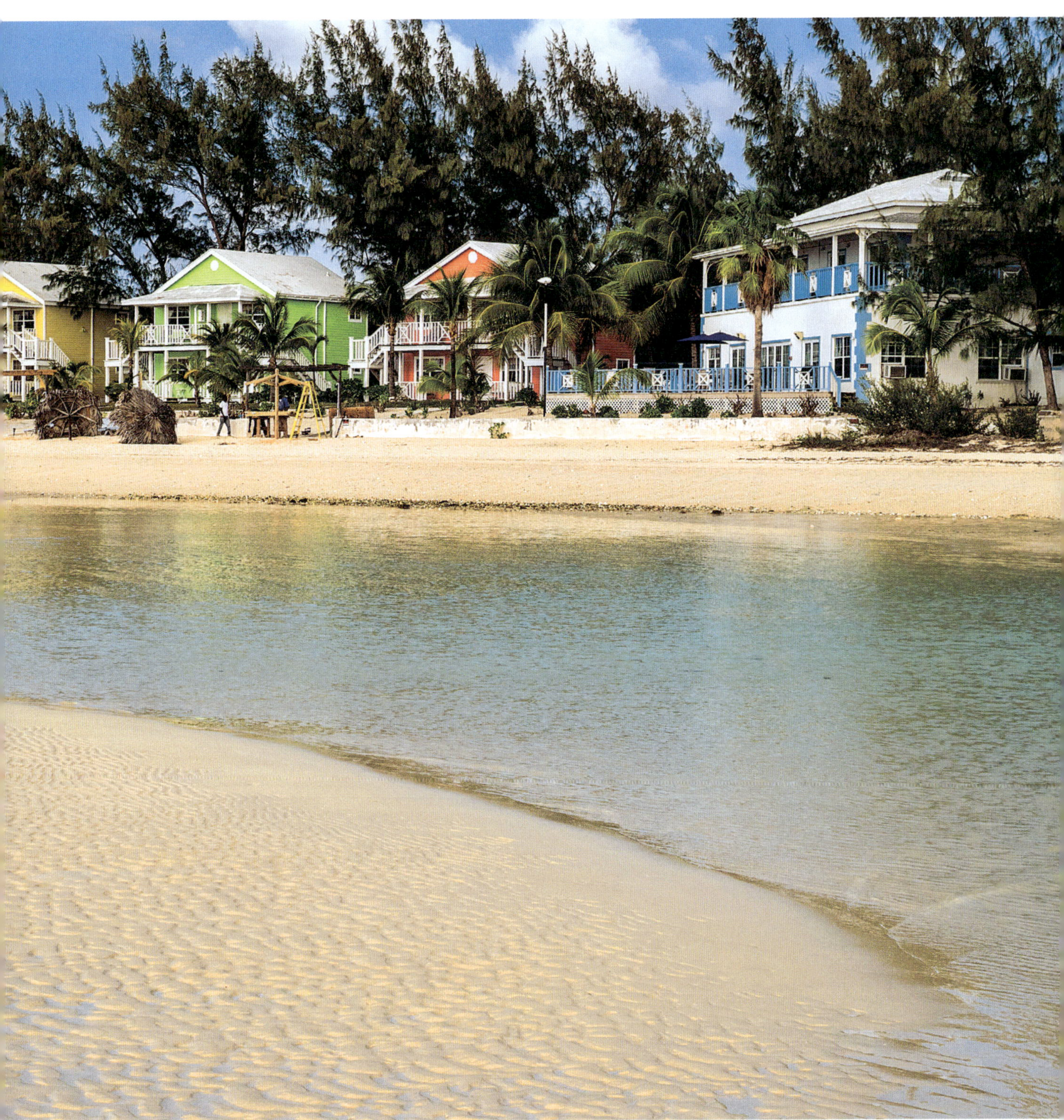

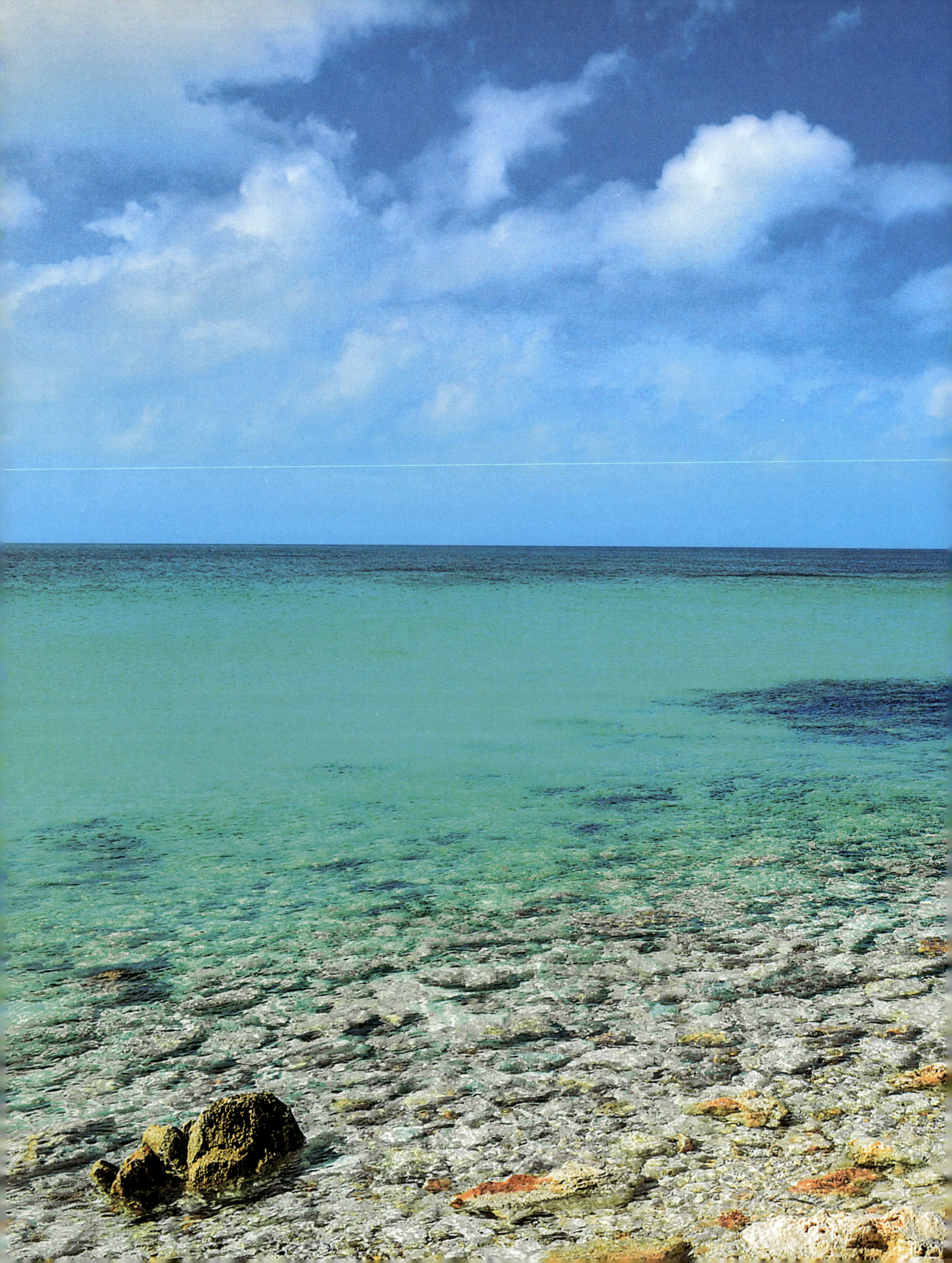

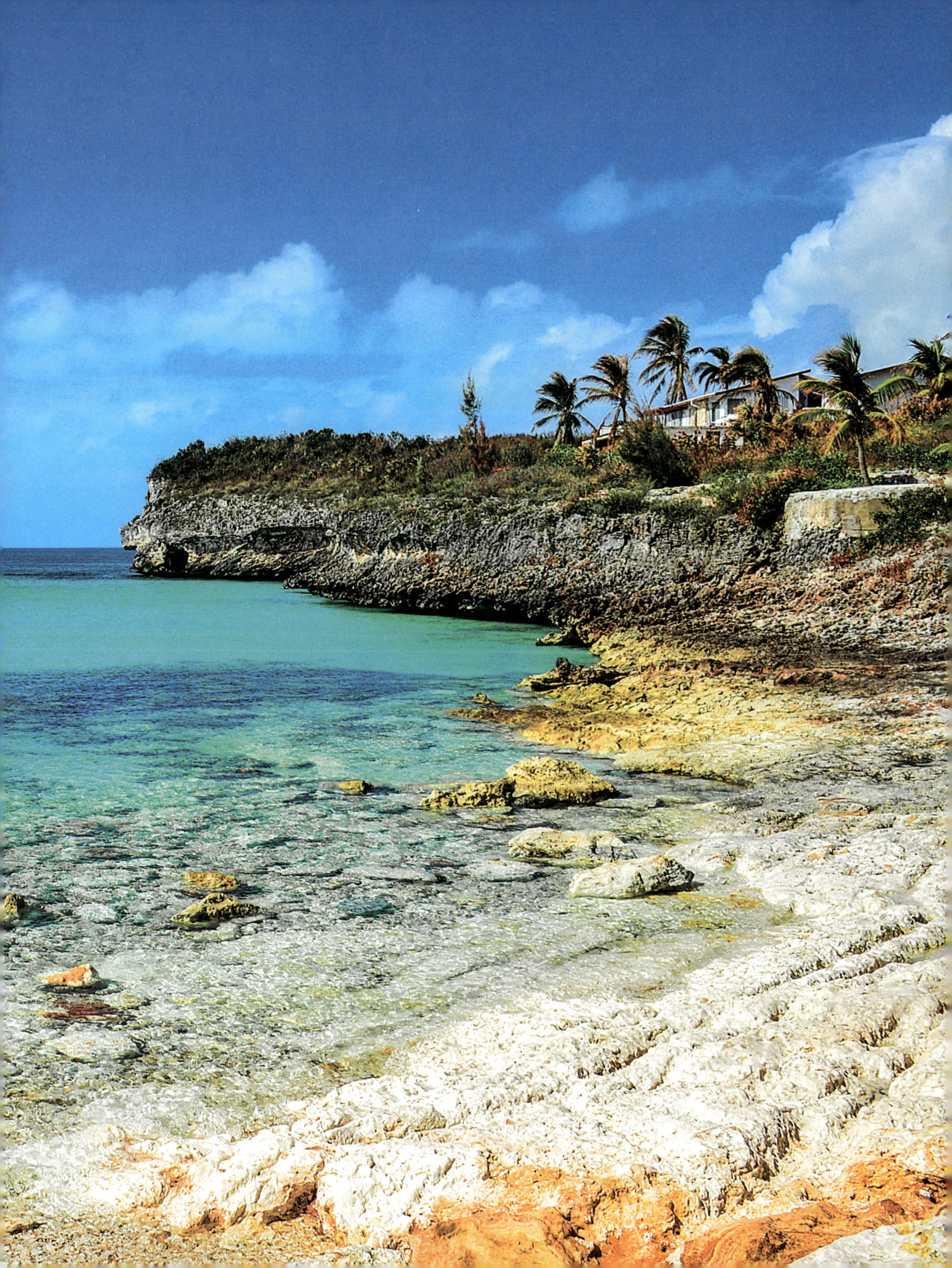

WHERE THE WORLD HAS YET TO FINISH BEING BORN

∾

NATURE ON ELEUTHERA IS NOT SPECTACULAR IN THE CONVENTIONAL SENSE: IT IS NOT MADE TO ASTOUND AT FIRST SIGHT. IT IS THERE TO BE TRAVERSED AND SAVORED; IT IS WILD YET DISCREET.

The beaches appear to be suspended in time: long, deserted, lacking points of reference, with a sand that changes color and consistency. The ocean presents itself with an ever-different voice; on certain days it whispers, on others it breaks across the coral reef with mighty and ferocious waves. The interior conceals sea caves, lagoons and secret estuaries where the saltwater encounters its fresh counterpart in a perpetual ritual. Hatchet Bay Cave, a subterranean labyrinth of stalactites, with centuries-old charcoal graffiti, is still a place that retains intact its aura of mystery. Then there is Surfer's Beach, which contradicts the sugar-coated image of the Bahamas with an ocean as rebellious and untameable as only the riders of the waves truly understand. Nature here is so strong that it has become the perfect setting for those wishing to describe archaic and symbolic worlds. Eleuthera has been used as a set for documentaries, films and advertisements, without ever losing its identity: it does not let itself be transformed. At certain points it seems as though the land is still emerging, that creation is still on-going, and perhaps it really is like that. Here the world has never been canceled by humankind. It is still possible to walk for hours without meeting anyone, to hear the wind speaking an ancient language, to swim in waters that have only just been invented. Eleuthera does not ask to be understood, but experienced. It never promises, it happens.

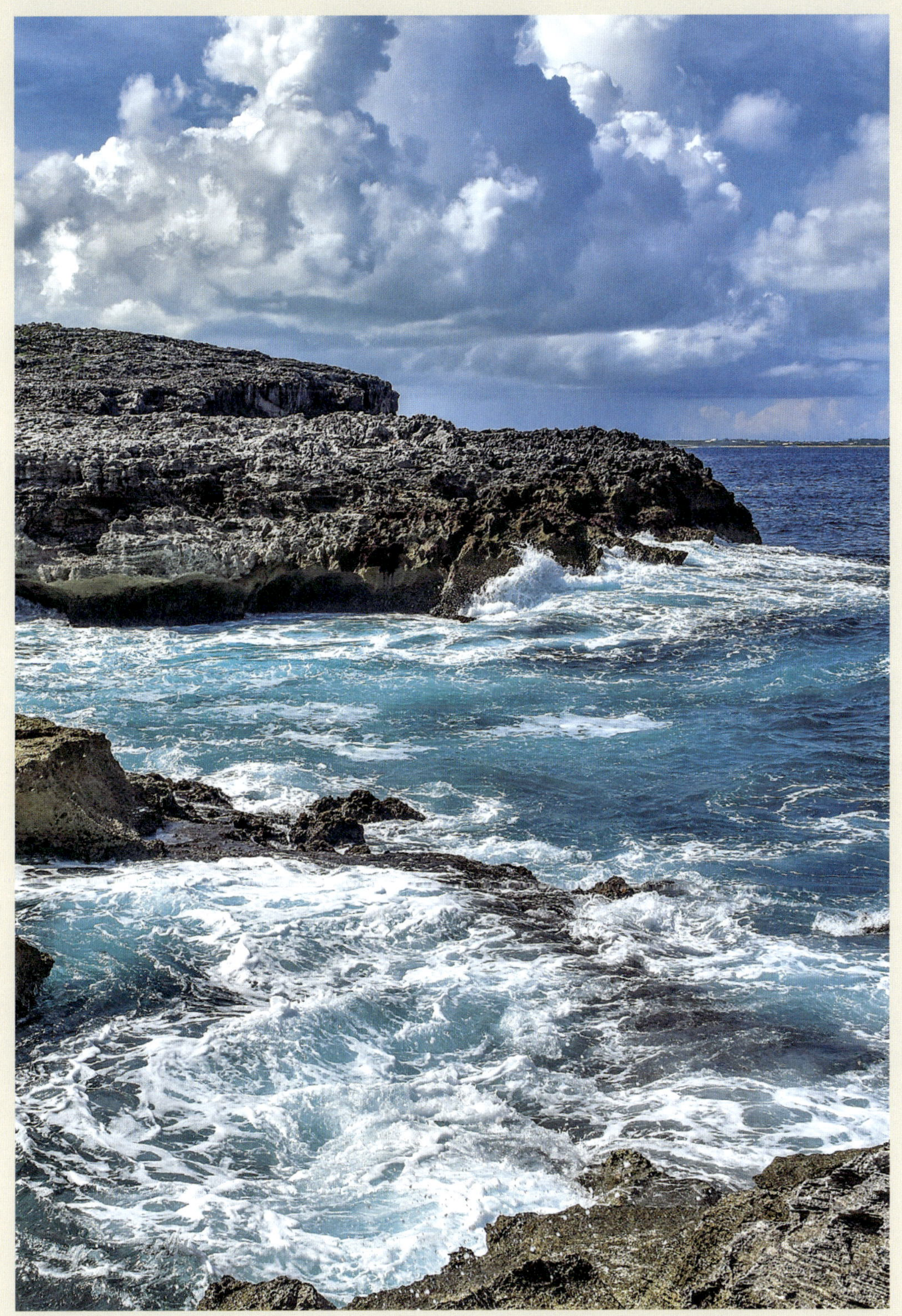

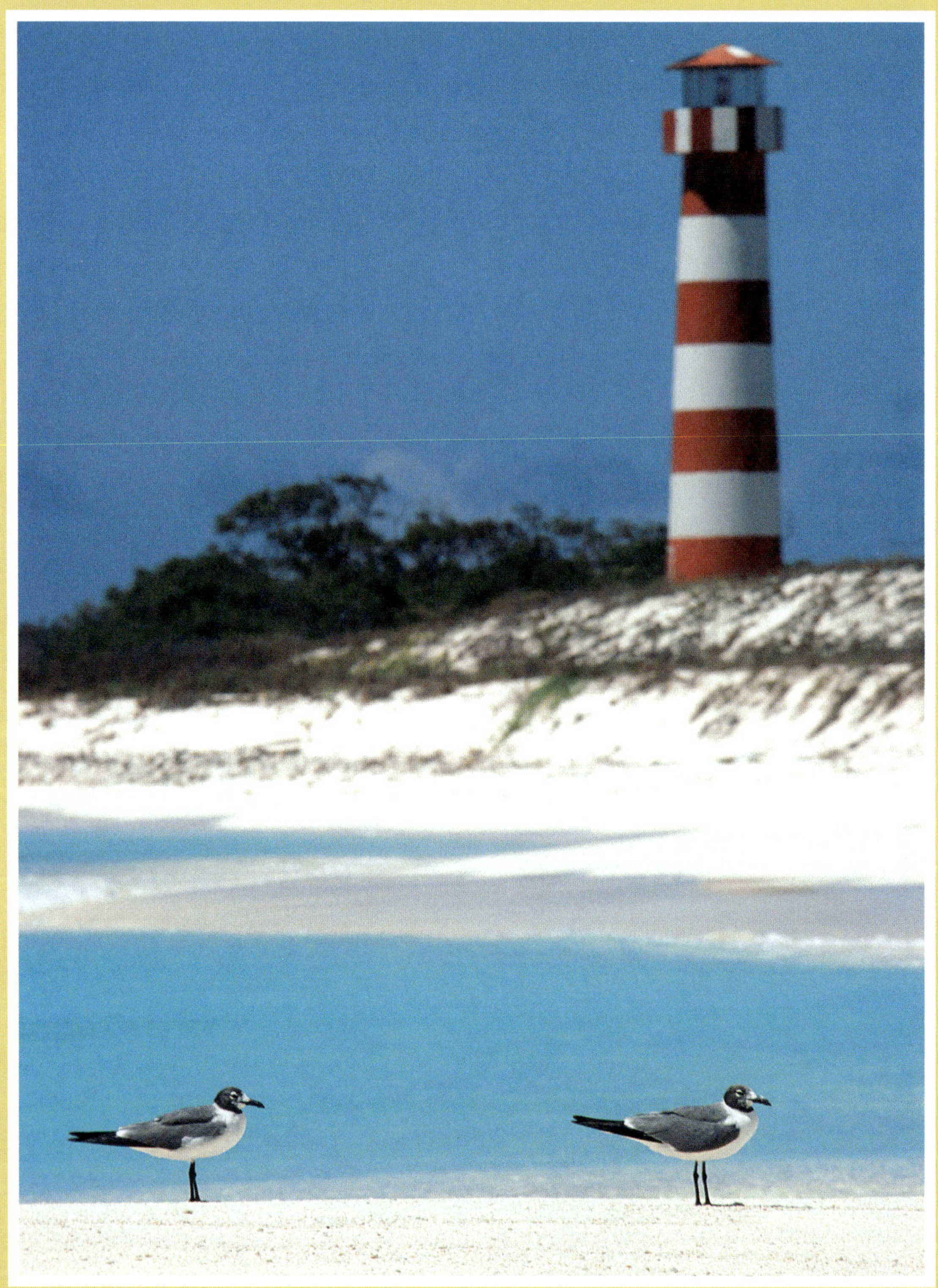

Venezuela

LOS ROQUES

Geographical coordinates: 11°52'27" N; 66°46'4" W
Waters: Caribbean Sea
Population: 3,100 inhabitants
Surface area: 15.67 square miles (40.61 km^2)
Principal settlement: Gran Roque

AN ARCHIPELAGO OUT OF THIS WORLD

It is easy, yet also difficult, to imagine the stillness of the afternoon sky rapidly fading into evening, to follow the syncopated, graceful flight of the pelicans, which up to a certain point retains a semblance of harmony before becoming a free fall toward the surface of the water, complete with a disheveled landing. Then a big mouthful of fish and off they go, their goiters bulging like Mary Poppins's handbag. The dinner of these strange creatures turns into a hypnotic dance: up and down, down and up. This all takes place at Los Roques, about 100 miles (160 kilometers) off Caracas, with its crystal-clear sea and white, beautiful and above all deserted beaches. Since 1972, these islands have been a national park and Gran Roque is the only site where it is possible to build, while the other 50 formations can be visited by day or by spending the night in very spartan accommodation. These are places with a recent geological history—born 10,000 to15,000 years ago—and not of volcanic origin, which is quite rare for an archipelago of this type. Here, the terrestrial fauna is sparce due to the scarcity of drinking water and the arid conditions—the only native mammal is the fisherman bat, which is accompanied by iguanas, lizards and spiders—but on the other hand, the sea is full of surprises, with 300 species of fish, 200 crustaceans, 140 molluscs, along with sponges, countless varieties of coral, sharks, dolphins, whales, manta rays and sea turtles. However it is the avifauna that leaves enthusiasts open-mouthed with over 90 species of birds, such as pelicans, gannets and flamingos, which migrate seasonally to these shores.

ANCIENT PRESENCES

~

Los Roques feels like a place that exists outside of time. There are human traces, but they are faint and precarious. Nonetheless, certain artifacts, such as statuettes and everyday utensils, testify to settlements dating back a thousand years, well before the arrival of the Europeans. However, these islands were again uninhabited when in around 1500 they began to be used as a staging post for explorers and pirates: the indigenous people had abandoned them, and in any case, according to some interpretations, the islands had never had permanent settlements, but were places visited seasonally for rituals and religious festivals. The archipelago became a Venezuelan province at the end of the 16th century, later gaining a certain prominence through the guano trade, before being abandoned once again. It was only at the beginning of the 20th century that fishermen from the neighbouring island of Margarita occupied Gran Roque and established the principal settlement there. Fishing, which still flourishes today, long remained the primary occupation for the few inhabitants, before tourism took over after the establishment of the natural park.

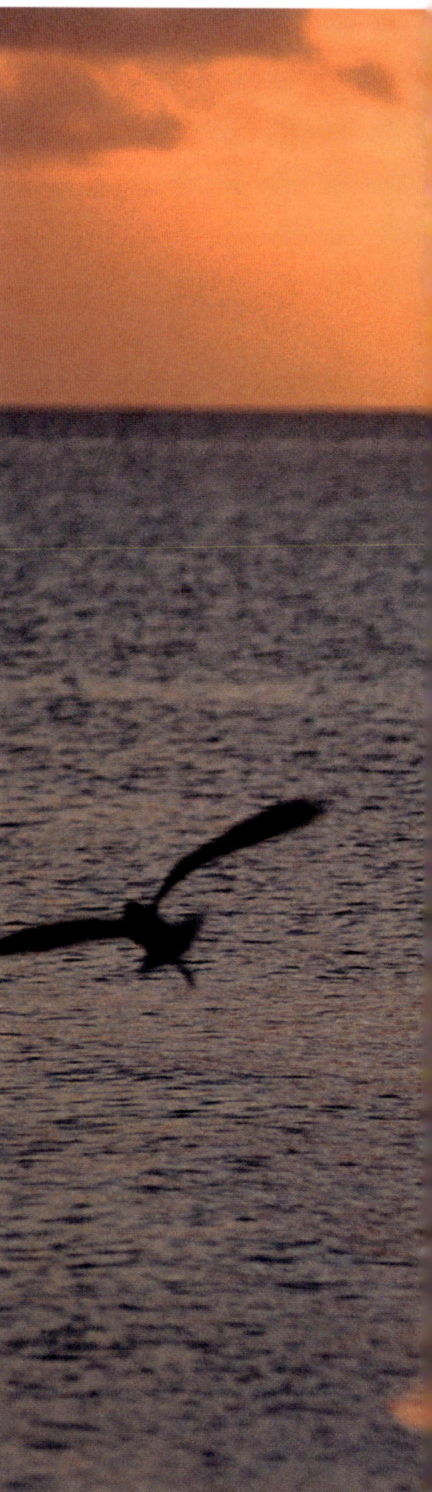

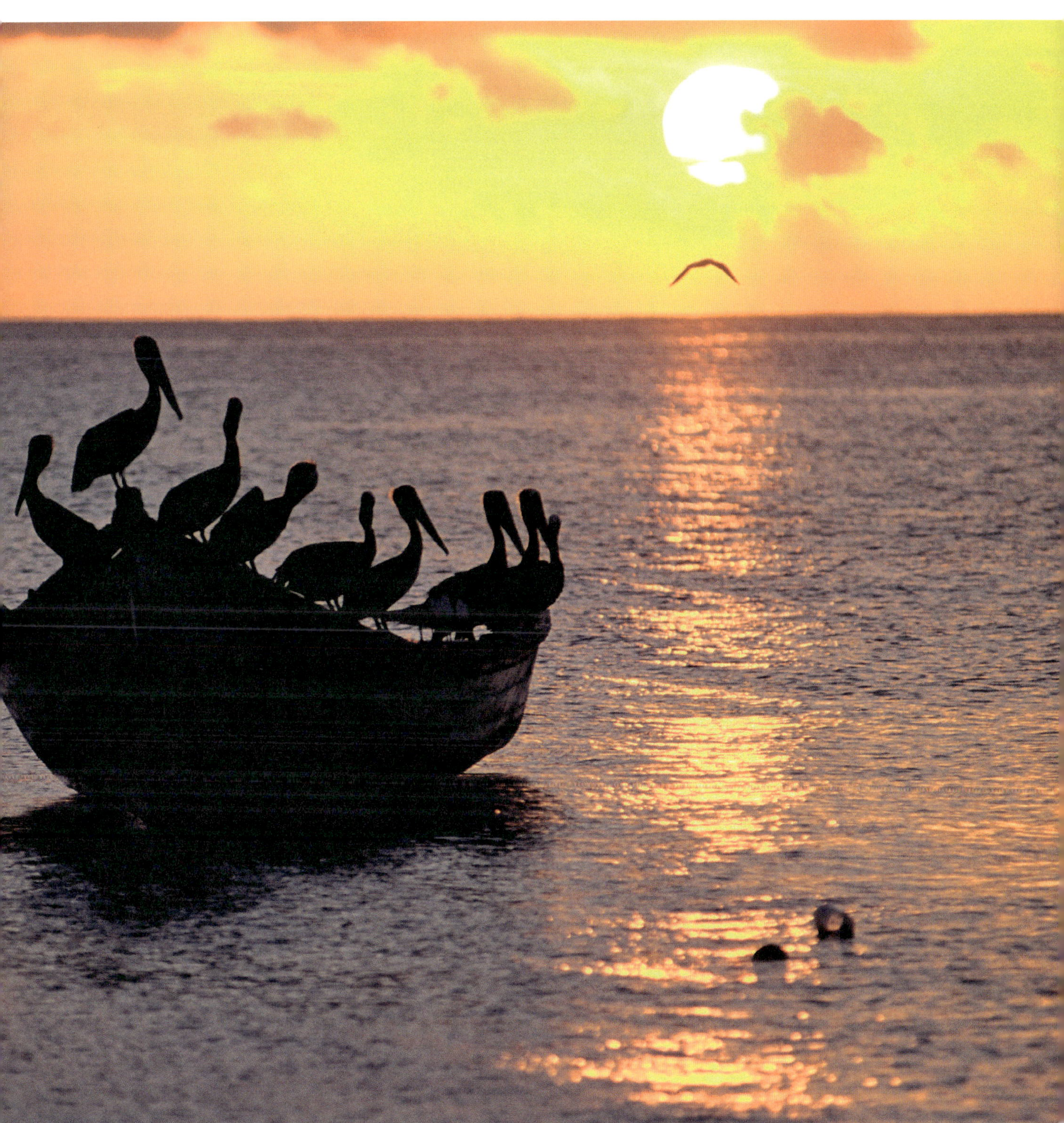

MYSTERIES AND MISDEEDS

~

VENEZUELA IS KNOWN FOR ITS BEAUTY, BUT CERTAINLY NOT FOR ITS SECURITY. IN CARACAS, ARMED GUARDS STAND OUTSIDE THE ENTRANCES TO BUILDINGS AND YOU ONLY HAVE TO SET FOOT IN THE WRONG NEIGHBORHOOD TO FIND YOURSELF IN ONE OF THOSE AREAS WHERE A LIFE CAN BE WORTH AS MUCH AS A PAIR OF SHOES. NOT AT LOS ROQUES THOUGH: IN THIS EDEN-LIKE LAND, NO ONE PULLS GUNS OR KNIVES, NO ONE STEALS WALLETS, NO ONE THREATENS.

This is why this story stands out like a purple elephant on a snowy expanse. It began in 2006 with the murder of a tourist, Elena, which caused quite a stir. Despite investigations complicated by underworld interference and an attempt to pass it off as a robbery gone wrong, it was probably a tragic case of mistaken identity: the manager of the *posada*, the real target of the ambush, had lent his own room to a honeymooning couple. A settling of scores or perhaps an affair with the wrong woman: the hypotheses overlapped without ever identifying a certain motive. Several suspects have been silenced forever, others have been arrested over the years, but the truth has faded along with the will to seek it. Elena's memory will never have

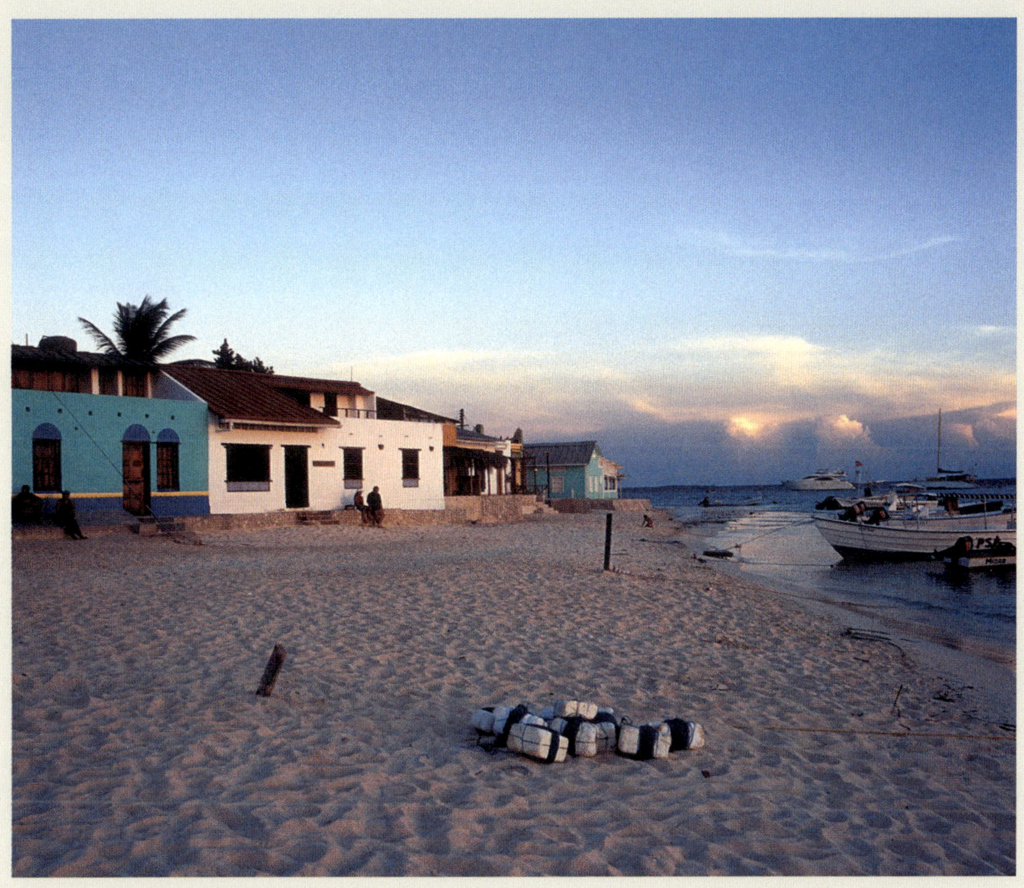

the peace of an explanation. Another mystery has attracted a lot of attention: the number of plane crashes on the route connecting the islands with the mainland. It was early January 2013 when a twin-engined plane that had taken off from Gran Roque bound for Caracas vanished into thin air. On board, among others, was Vittorio Missoni, son of the famous fashion designer Ottavio, with his wife and a couple of friends. This is not the first time something like this has happened: in 2008 a plane had disappeared on the same route. At that time, only the body of the co-pilot was fished out off the coast. According to some, he had died before impact, a detail that had fueled theories about a possible hijacking or kidnapping. The latest disappearance gave new impetus to the search, leading in a few months to the discovery of both wrecks, lying at a depth of 230 feet (70 meters) for the most recent and almost 3,280 feet (1,000 meters) for the earlier incident. On such short and uncontrolled routes, cases of hijackings linked to kidnappings or more straightforward drug trafficking is hardly rare, but in the case of Los Roques it was probably a matter of tragic fatalities that the collective imagination has made more enigmatic. Secrets remain guarded by the sky and the sea in this sublime place where tragedy has occasionally made an unwelcome appearance.

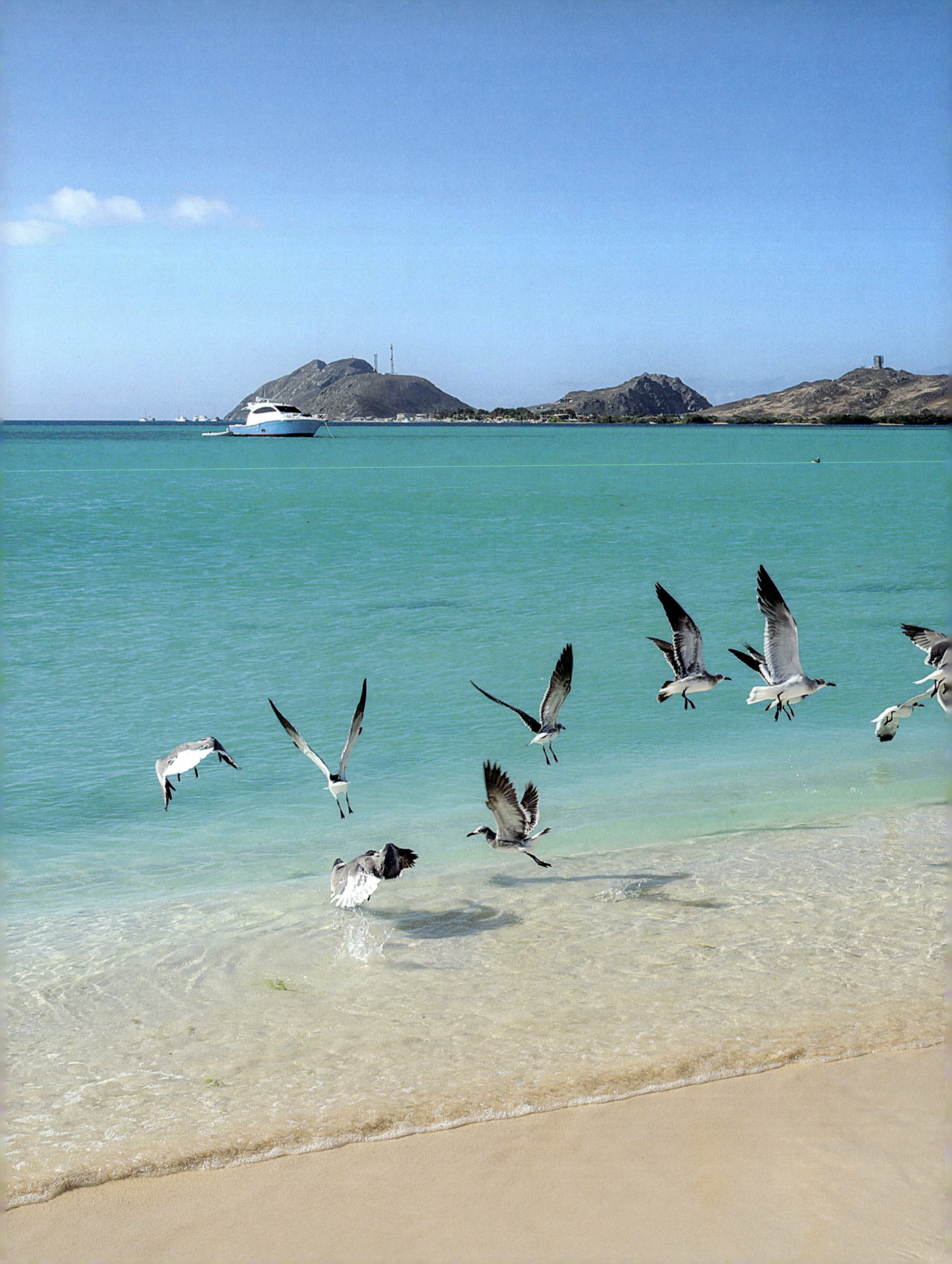

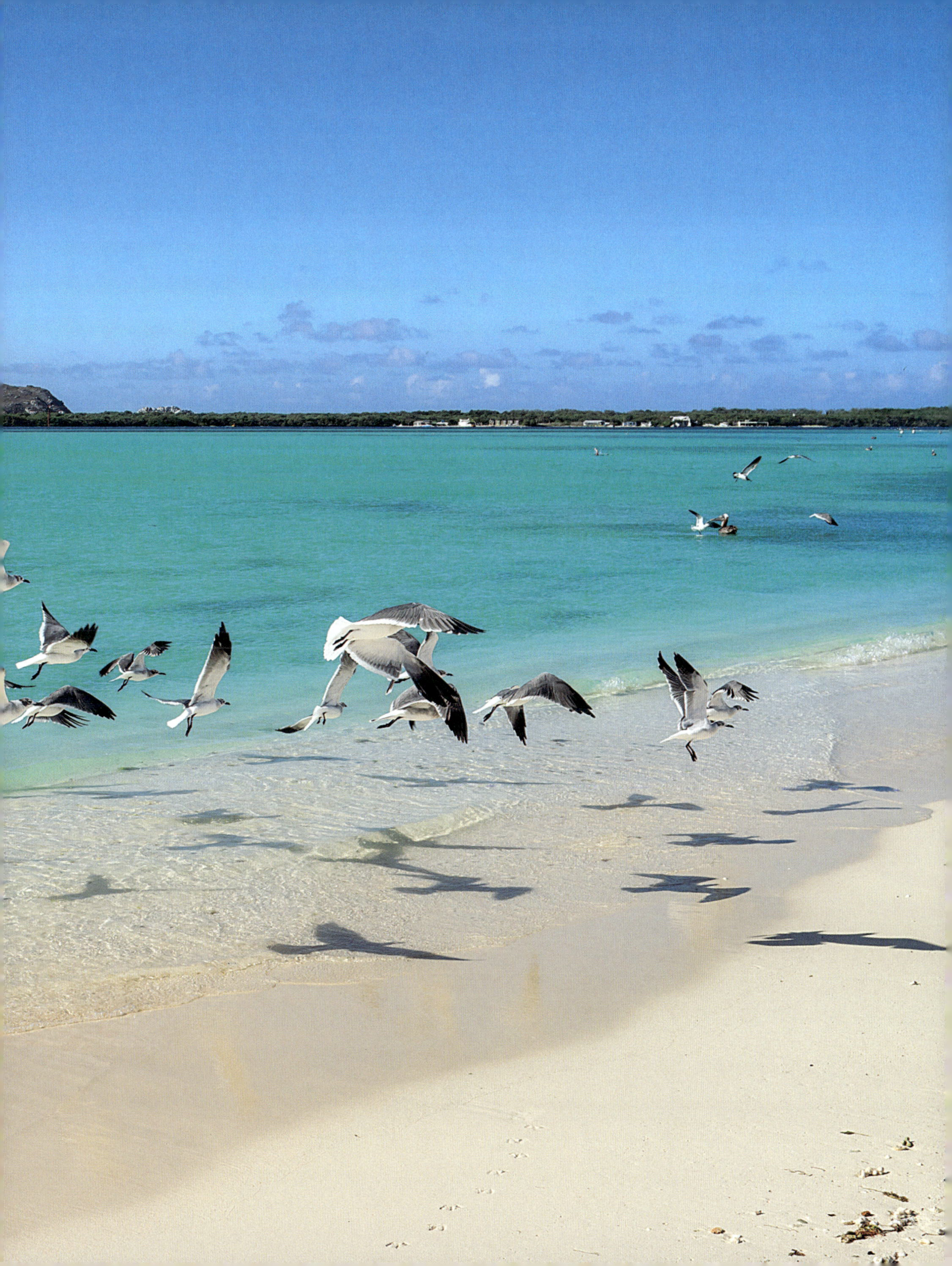

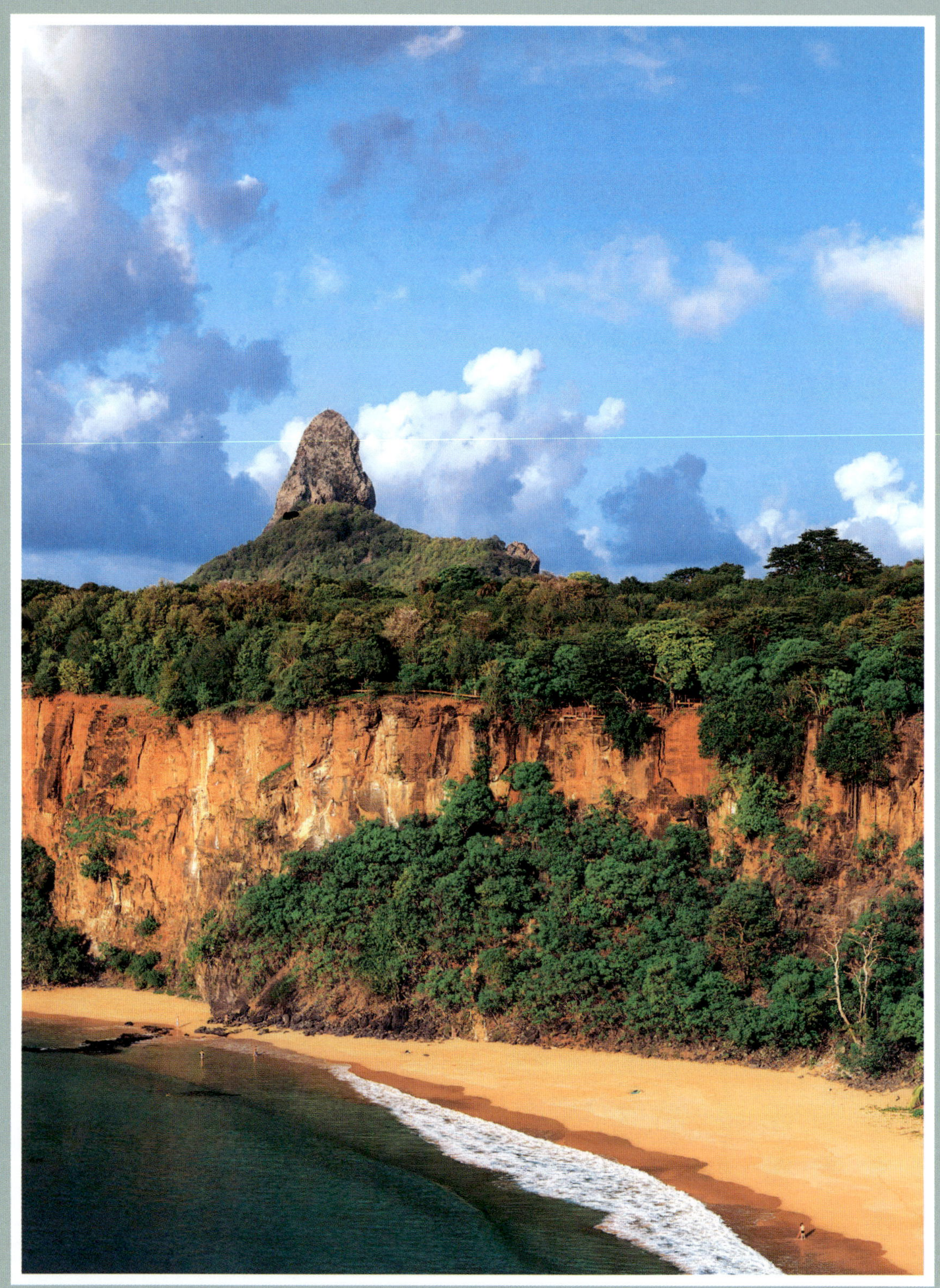

Brazil

FERNANDO DE NORONHA

Geographical coordinates: 3°50'47" S; 32°24'49" W
Waters: Atlantic Ocean
Population: 3,167 inhabitants
Surface area: 10 square miles (26 km²)
Principal settlement: Vila dos Remédios

STONES IN THE OCEAN

The archipelago of Fernando de Noronha is located in the state of Pernambuco, where Brazil stretches out into the ocean, 215 miles (346 kilometers) from its northeastern coast, yet it could be anywhere, suspended between reality and imagination. A magma surge from an ancient wound in Earth's crust has generated a handful of islands, barely visible from the sky, sculpted from the incandescent lava by the patience of the Atlantic Ocean. The principal formation is the island that lends its name to the entire archipelago, a labyrinth of curves, highlands, bays and cliffs plunging unhesitatingly into the abyss. The living volcanic rock is black, flayed by the wind, scarred like a face that has seen too many springs. The sparse but tenacious vegetation climbs the steep hillsides: cacti, shrubs, a few patches of green that seem to defy the scorching sun dominating from above. Then, standing among the waves is the symbol of this place: the Morro do Pico, a stone tooth piercing the sky, 1,000 feet (304 meters) of basaltic solitude. A natural lighthouse, a silent eye that scans the horizon without ever looking away. Around it, 20 other smaller islands, rocks, formations that look like unfinished sketches. Only the main island is inhabited, the others belong to the wind, the birds and time. This is Fernando de Noronha: a presence that emerges from the sea without asking permission, a place that has more to do with geology than with geography, the result of an ancient compromise between fire and sea, where every stone tells an ancient story and every wave guards a secret.

ISLAND VOICES

~

Walking here is like crossing an invisible threshold: time has different rules, it expands and contracts, it bends to the light. Every path is a promise, every beach an encounter. There is something primitive, something absolute, in the beauty of Fernando de Noronha. It is a beauty to be conquered by accepting its rules and respecting its silences. The beaches are among the most spectacular in the world, but to call them beaches is almost insulting. Baía do Sancho, for example, is reached by clambering down through the cracks in the rock as if through a secret passage leading to a golden crescent. Here the ocean changes color every hour: emerald, sapphire, turquoise. Living water that looks at you and whispers mysterious words. Then there are Baía dos Porcos, with its sharp rocks emerging like gaping jaws, and Baía do Sueste, where turtles move slowly as if deep in thought. The sea here is an underwater garden: you swim among rays, barracudas, curious sharks and dolphins animating the waves at dawn. Noronha is a natural cathedral, and like any cathedral it demands respect. The number of visitors is restricted, access regulated by an Environmental Preservation Fee. The island defends itself elegantly, without hostility but with firmness. Those who visit it lightly remain on the surface. Those who listen and look with clear eyes receive in return an experience they will never forget. Nature here is not a landscape, but a voice. Birds, the Noronha elaenia and the Noronha vireo (both endemic), then the frigate birds, terns and gannets, which hover above the cliffs like spirits, and crabs that dance on the rocks with mechanical, impassive movements. Even the wind has a precise sound: rather than whistle, it tells stories.

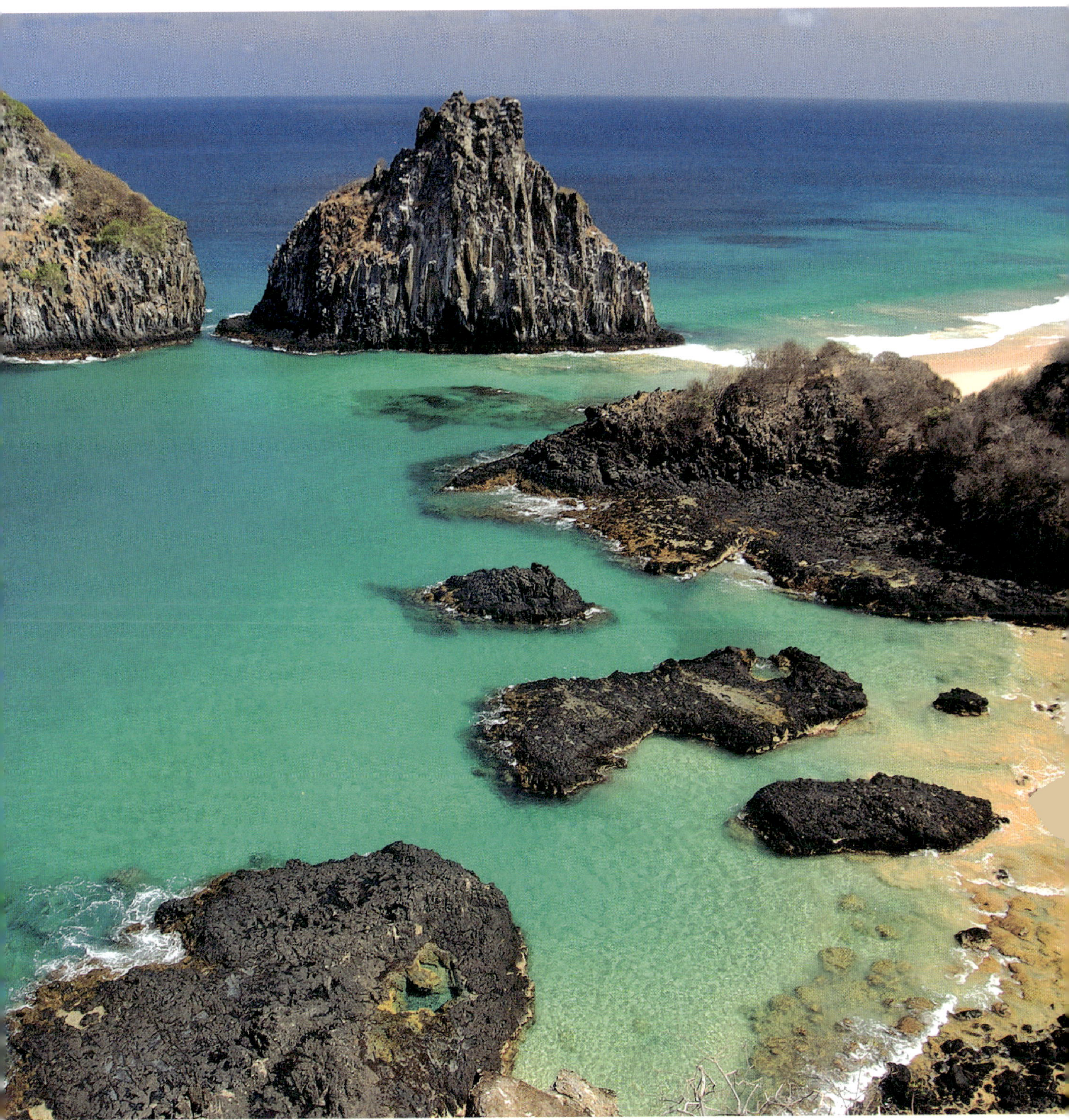

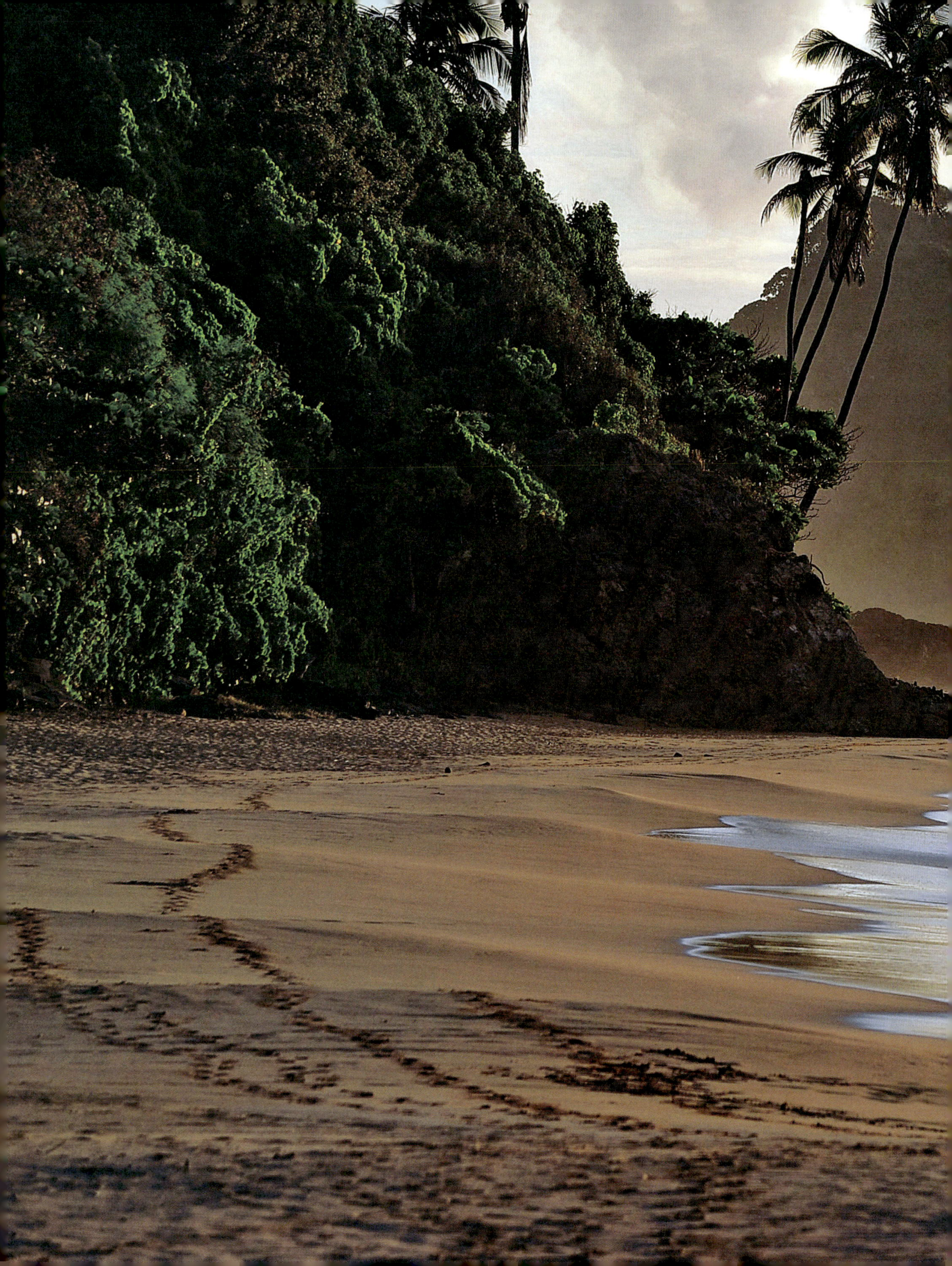

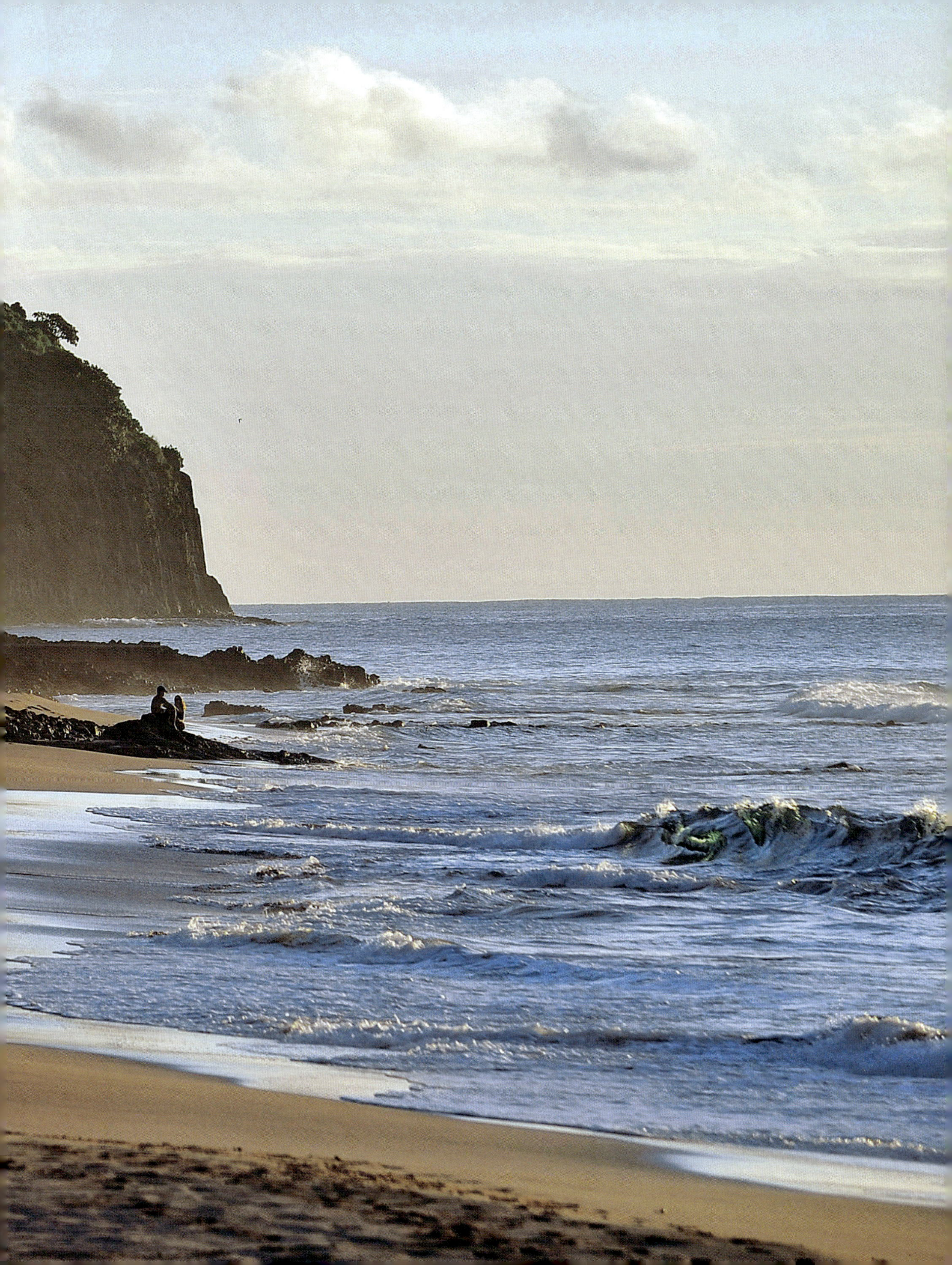

SHADOWS AND LEGENDS

THERE IS A DEEP, DARK MEMORY ALIVE AMONG THE ROCKS OF FERNANDO DE NORONHA. THE ARCHIPELAGO HAS HAD MANY FACES. IN THE 16TH CENTURY, IT WAS MAPPED BY PORTUGUESE EXPLORERS, BUT THE ORIGIN OF ITS NAME IS UNCERTAIN: IT PERHAPS DERIVES FROM A MERCHANT WHO HAD FINANCED ONE OF THE EXPEDITIONS, PERHAPS FROM NO ONE.

For centuries it was fought over and then forgotten before reappearing. The French, the Dutch, the Portuguese: they all tried to claim it, but this place never wholly succumbed. The main island has been a military base, a penal colony and a land of exile. It is in fact a perfect natural prison: no escape routes, just the sea. The most dangerous prisoners were sent here, the sick and the undesirables. Still today, along the internal paths, the ruins of the old walls emerge, the carcasses of buildings gutted by the vegetation. Vegetation that in the 19th century had been almost completely cleared to prevent the prisoners from hiding. An operation that takes a rightful place among the certified proofs of human stupidity. No less questionable was the deliberate introduction in the 1950s of a species of lizard—the *Tupinambis merianae*—to control the rat population. A pointless and damaging idea: rats are nocturnal animals and coexist happily with these reptiles, which instead put the avifauna at risk, feeding on the eggs of the sea birds. And then there are the stories. There are those who swear they have seen fires lit on the beaches at night, signs of ancient presences, lights that belong to no fisherman. There are those who speak of a ghost ship, swallowed up by the Baía dos Golfinhos, which reappears every ten years. The most silent legend is the one that shrouds the entire archipelago: it is said that Noronha is not entirely real, that it exists only for those who search for it with their eyes open, that it is actually a geological mirage, a collective vision generated by the sea to remind us that beauty is not a right, but a gift. Those who leave here carry with them a nostalgia that resembles no other, nostalgia for a place that does not belong to you but that recognizes you. A dream that is more real than everything else.

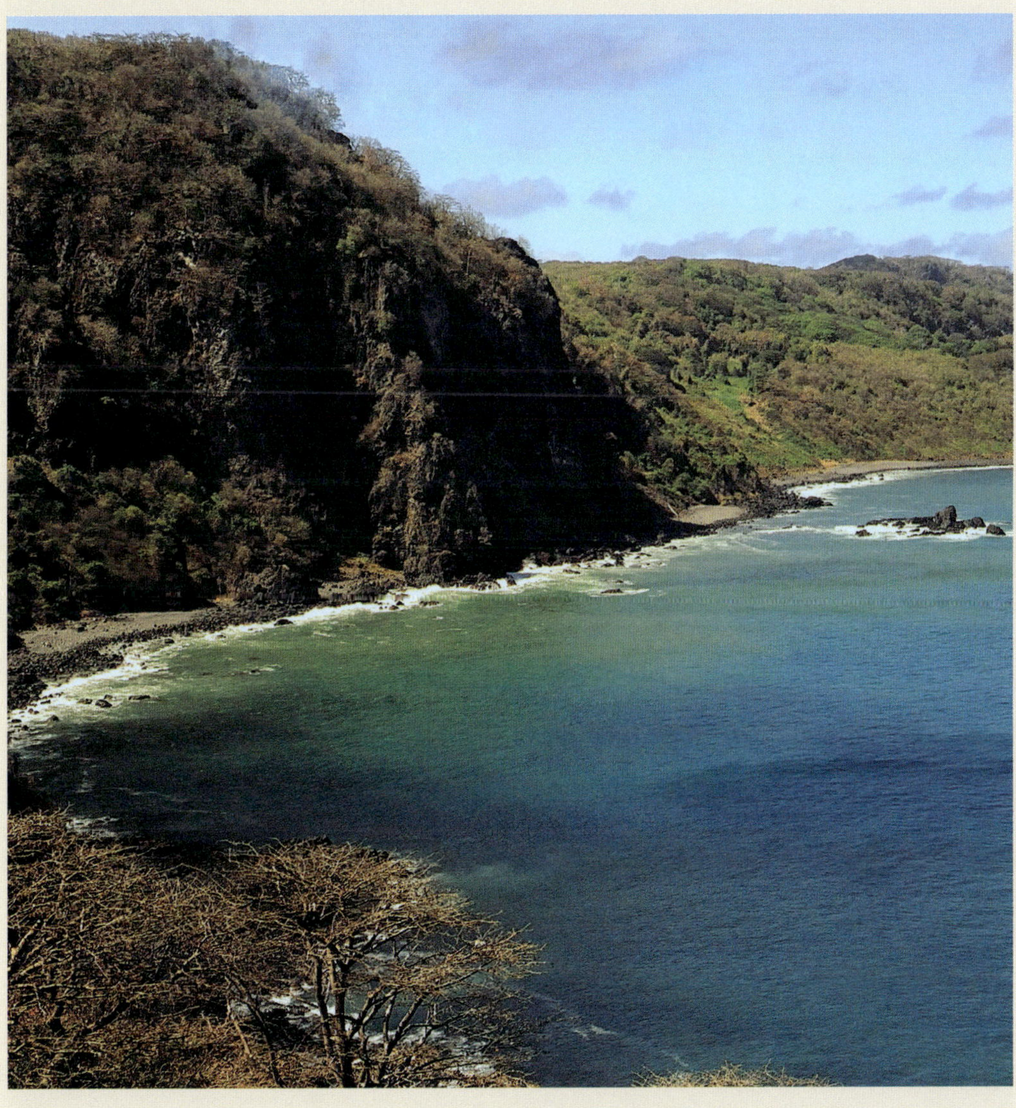

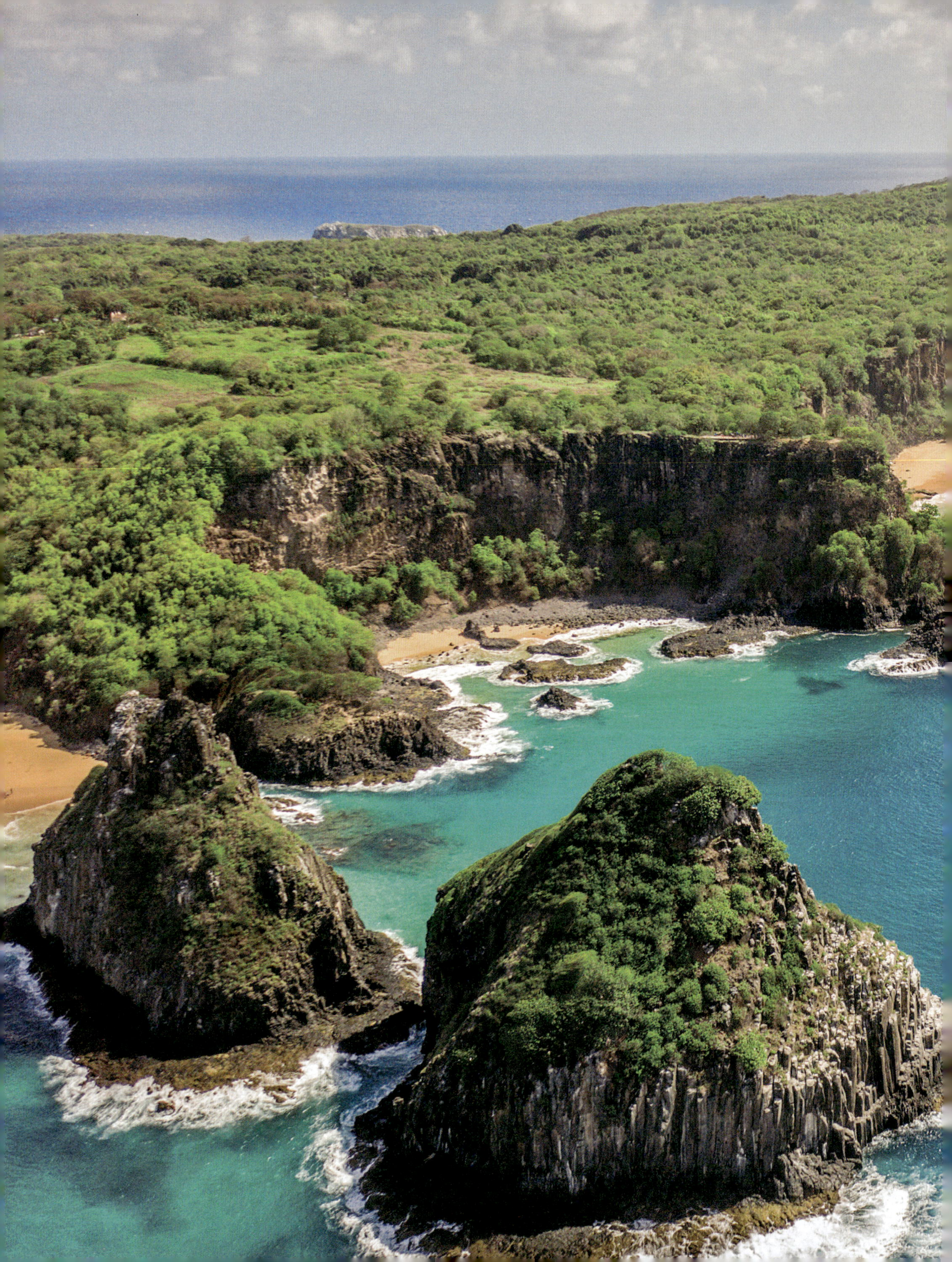

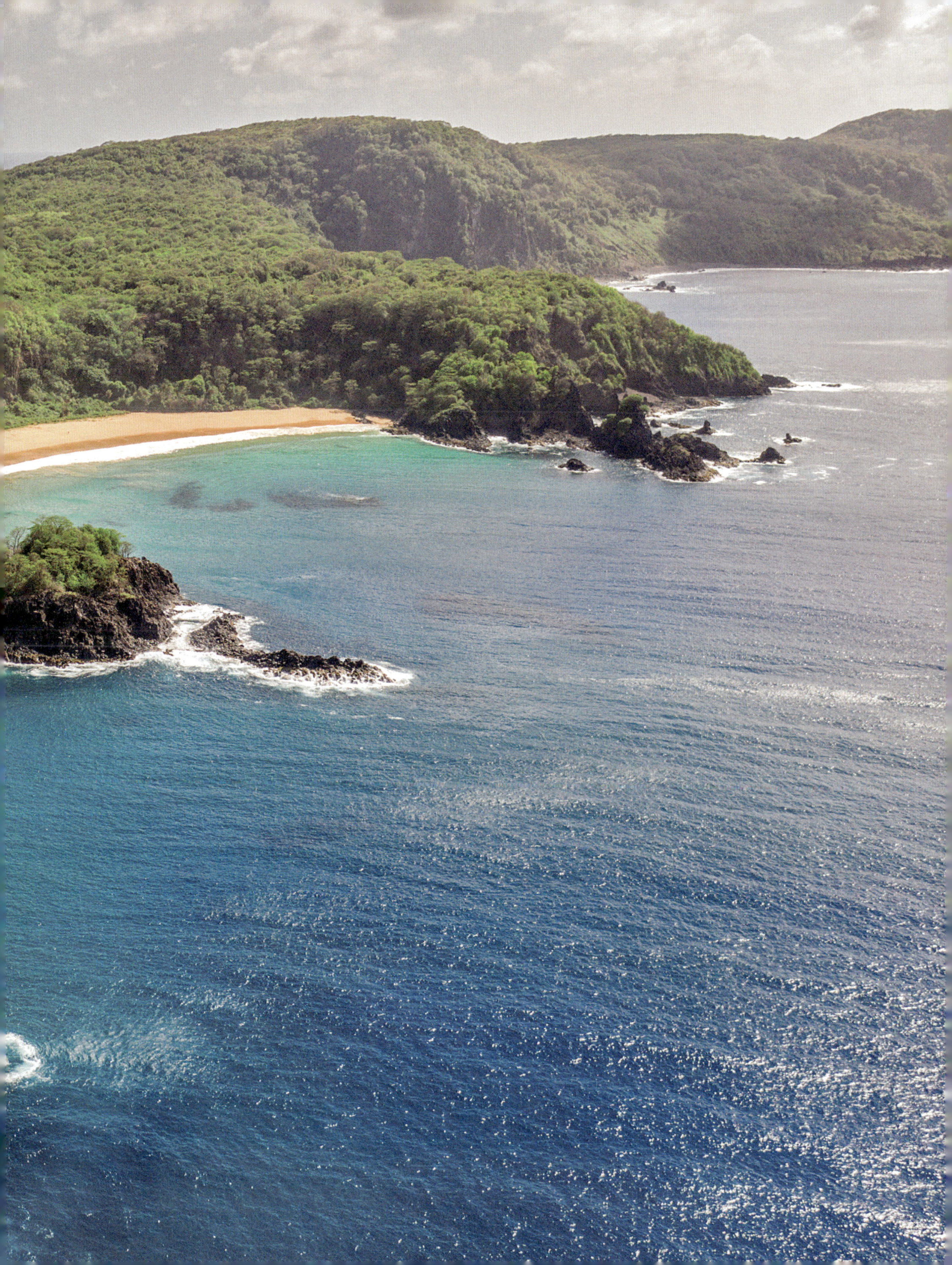

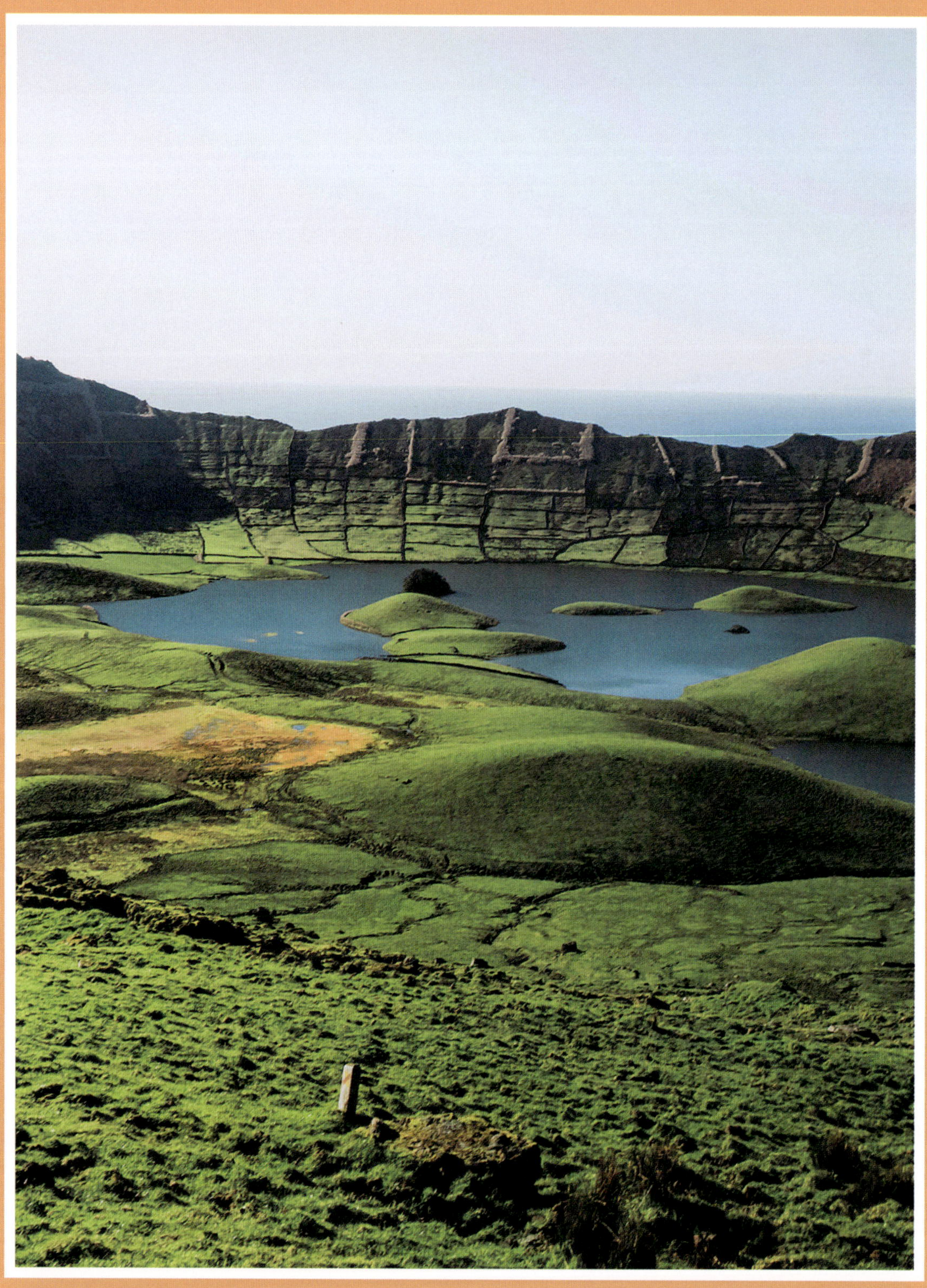

Azores, Portugal

CORVO ISLAND

Geographical coordinates: 39°41'51" N; 31°6'19" W
Waters: Atlantic Ocean
Population: 435 inhabitants
Surface area: 6.61 square miles (17.13 km²)

AZURE ISLANDS

Corvo is part of a very well known archipelago that takes its name from the color these lands take on when seen from afar, as if they were part of the sky into which their forms dotted with magnificent hydrangeas fade; others instead suggest that the Azores are so-named due to the presence of certain buzzards that the first explorers mistook for examples of the Eurasian goshawk, *açor* in Portuguese. It is the smallest of the nine sisters, 15 miles (24 kilometers) north of Flores. The entire island is an extinct volcanic edifice composed of the principal crater Caldeirão and around 20 minor cones inside it and on its slopes. Elliptical in shape, this is the main feature of Corvo's landscape: the crater houses a shallow lake dotted with small formations that recall the archipelago itself. Certain sources date the discovery of the two western islands of the Azores to 1452 and Diogo de Teive, but an isula Corvi marini had already appeared on maps dating from a century earlier, such as the Medici Atlas from 1351. In any case, the finding of several Carthaginian artifacts and coins suggest that landings had been made as early as the 4th century BC. The building of the first church in 1570 certified the birth of stable settlements. Corvo is a harsh, wild place, with low-growing vegetation and sheer cliffs, continuously subjected to the erosion of both wind and waves; the most impressive is on the western side, a drop of hundreds of feet overlooking the ocean. In terms of meteorology, the high pressure of this area, the well-known Azores High, is highly significant for its ability to influence the climate of the bands situated along the same parallel, including the Mediterranean area.

COURAGEOUS CORVINOS

~

The community established here devoted itself to arable farming and livestock, but its remote location was not sufficient to guarantee that the Corvinos could enjoy a peaceful existence. The merchant ships traversing these waters were in fact particularly attractive to pirates and corsairs as closer to the mainland they would be defended or escorted by vessels from their mother country. The frequent raiding encouraged the locals to attempt to befriend their enemies, offering food and shelter, care for the wounded and repairs for their ships. Not even these measures proved sufficient to avoid the repeated incursions. In 1632, a particularly ferocious attack was made by a fleet of pirates from the Barbary coast of North Africa. It is said that 200 inhabitants defended themselves with what little they had on hand, including rocks and everyday objects. Their courage was rewarded and supported by the Madonna of the Rosary, who intervened to protect the islanders from gunshots by deflecting them back to the attackers. Confused and frightened, the invaders fled under full sail. A couple of centuries later, the Corvinos were equally combative in claiming their rights: in 1832 a determined delegation headed to the island of Terceira to protest against the excessive taxes and tributes that were draining the population. In this case, too, their prayers were answered. During the following centuries, the assiduous frequentation of Corvo by Canadian and North American whalers created a privileged relationship with these countries. Over time, this translated into a major migratory phenomenon, with a sharp decline in the population from over 1,000 in the mid-19th century to the 370 counted in 1980. Since then the decline has halted; the conditions of extreme isolation has eased thanks to the construction of the airport—small and not always operational—and the regular maritime connections with the other islands, weather conditions and tides permitting of course.

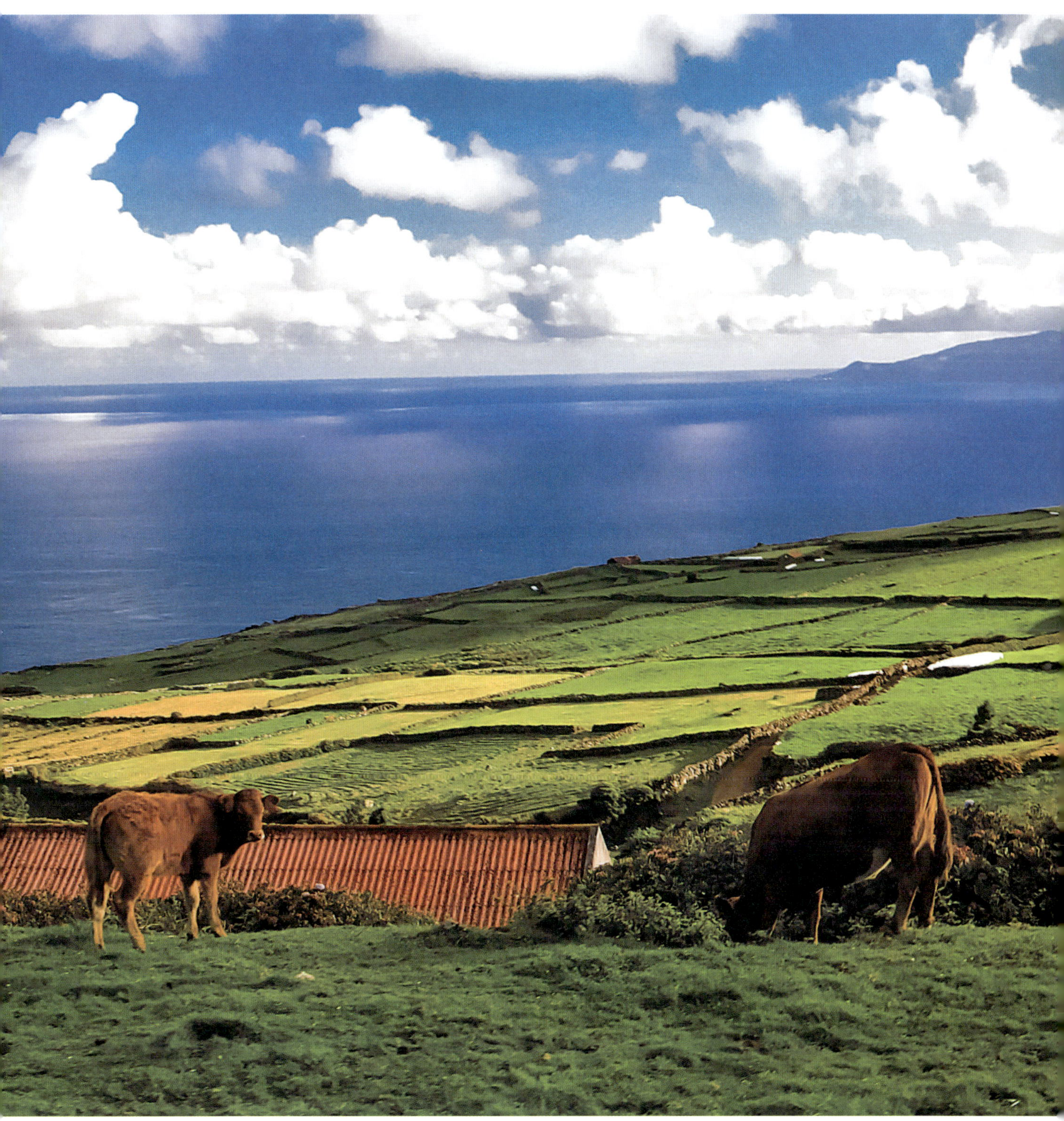

CORVINO LIFE

~

THE VILLAGE OF CORVO, THE SMALLEST OF THE AZORES AND THE MOST REMOTE OF THE WHOLE OF PORTUGAL IN TERMS OF DISTANCE FROM OTHER SETTLEMENTS, IS A GROUP OF NEIGHBORING HOUSES, SEPARATED BY THE *CANADAS*, NARROW, TWISTING STREETS CLIMBING THE STEEP SLOPES. THIS COMPACT FORMATION, SIMILAR TO THAT OF A MEDIEVAL HAMLET, IS DESIGNED TO OFFER GREATER PROTECTION FROM THE WINDS AND OTHER ATMOSPHERIC AGENTS. THE DARK PATHS CONTRAST WITH THE WHITE HOUSES, ALTERNATING WITH OTHER OLDER BUILDINGS IN BLACK BASALT.

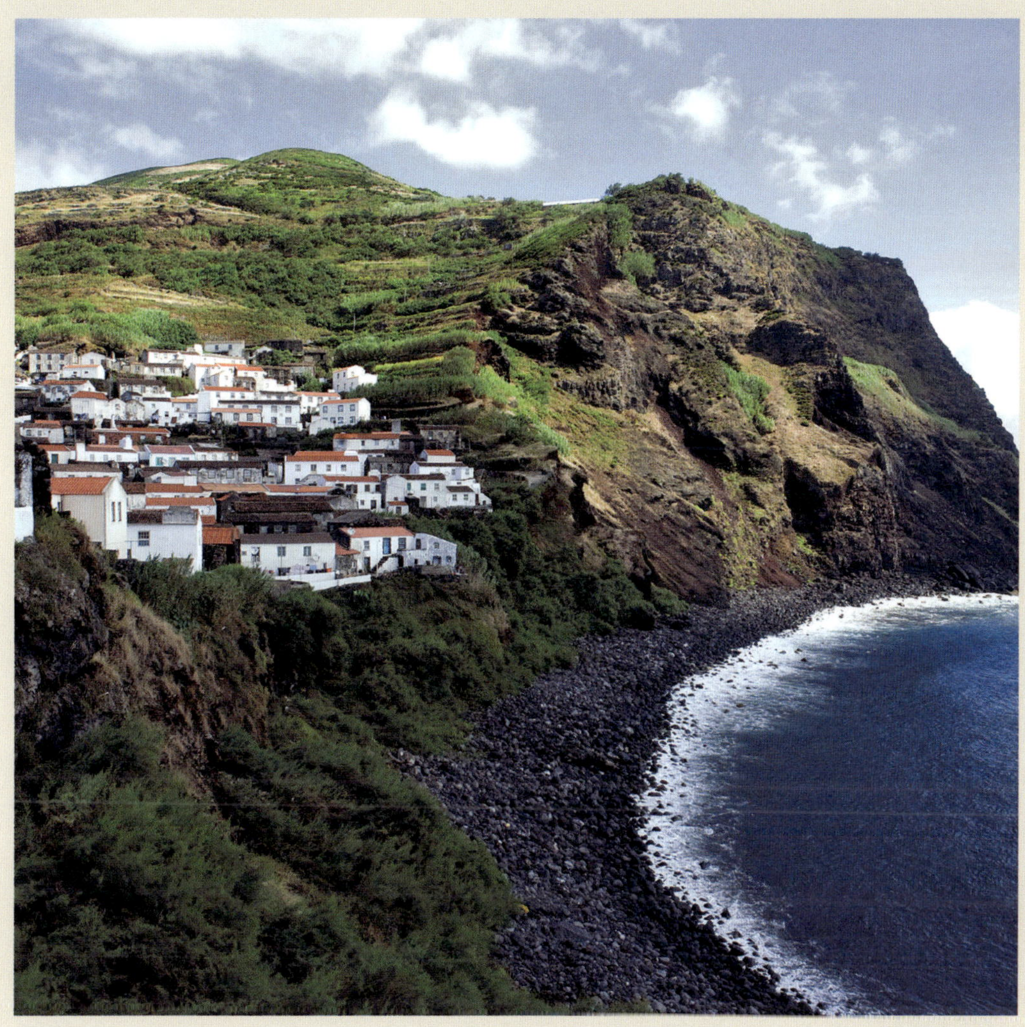

There is a simple society here, with close links to cattle husbandry and crafts, a community that gathers in the central square to share news and stories from the past. In this setting, the traditional summer festivals are an essential element. Here there are none of the theatrical excesses of the more popular islands, such as the running of the bulls on Terceira or the famous floral arches that adorn Flores for the Holy Spirit festival, but there is certainly no lack of enthusiastic participation. On the 15th of August, for example, coinciding with the religious celebrations of Our Lady of Miracles, the Festival dos Moinhos comes to life, bringing together the Corvo philharmonic orchestra and bands from other islands for two days of music. At the end of the summer, in September, there is a lively procession in honour of Nossa Senhora do Bom Caminho. These local folk traditions are complemented by growing tourist interest, with travelers attracted by this world apart at the edge of the world, with its fascinating marine and bird life and wild landscapes that speak directly to the spirit of those who find themselves in these parts.

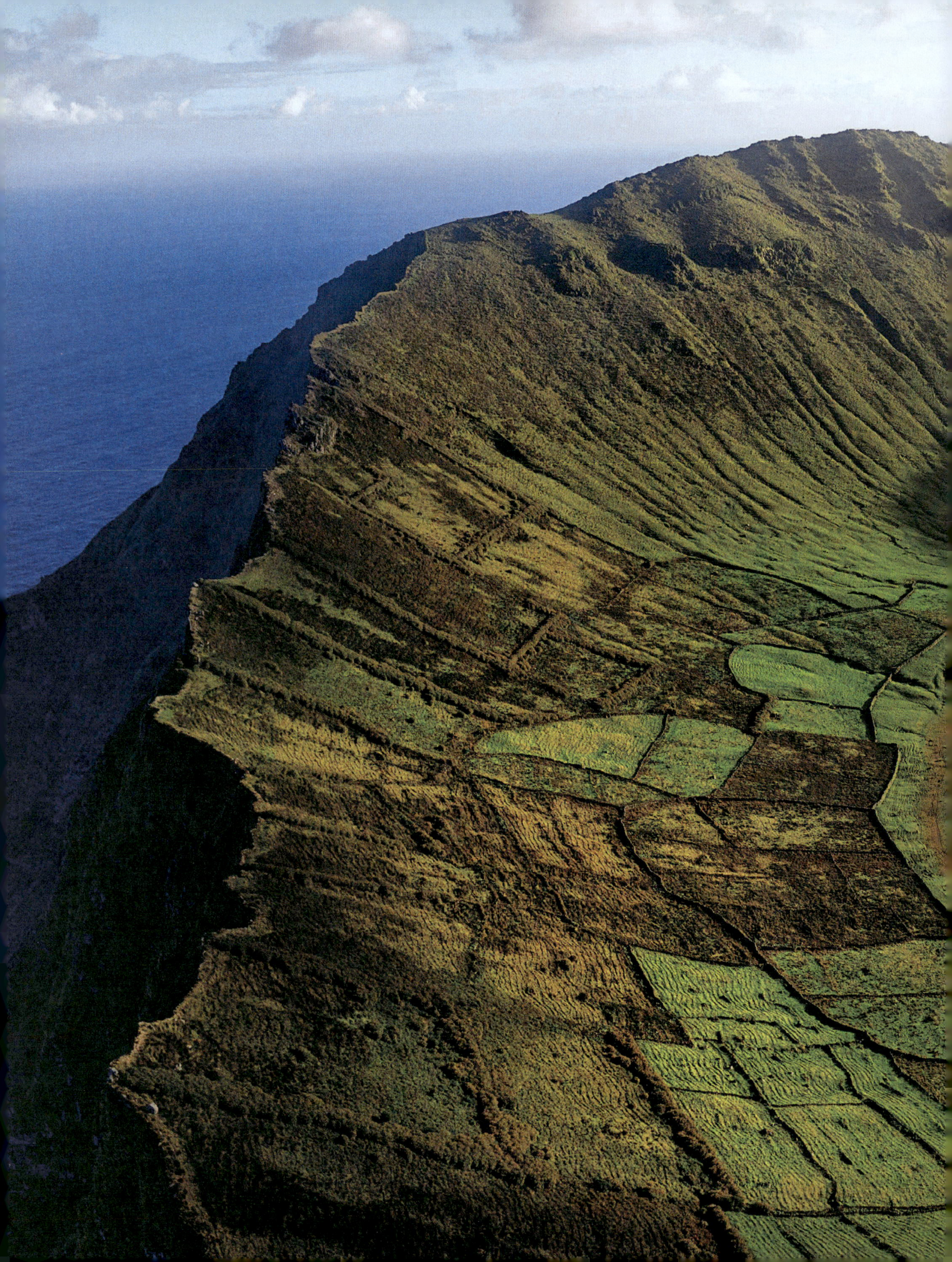

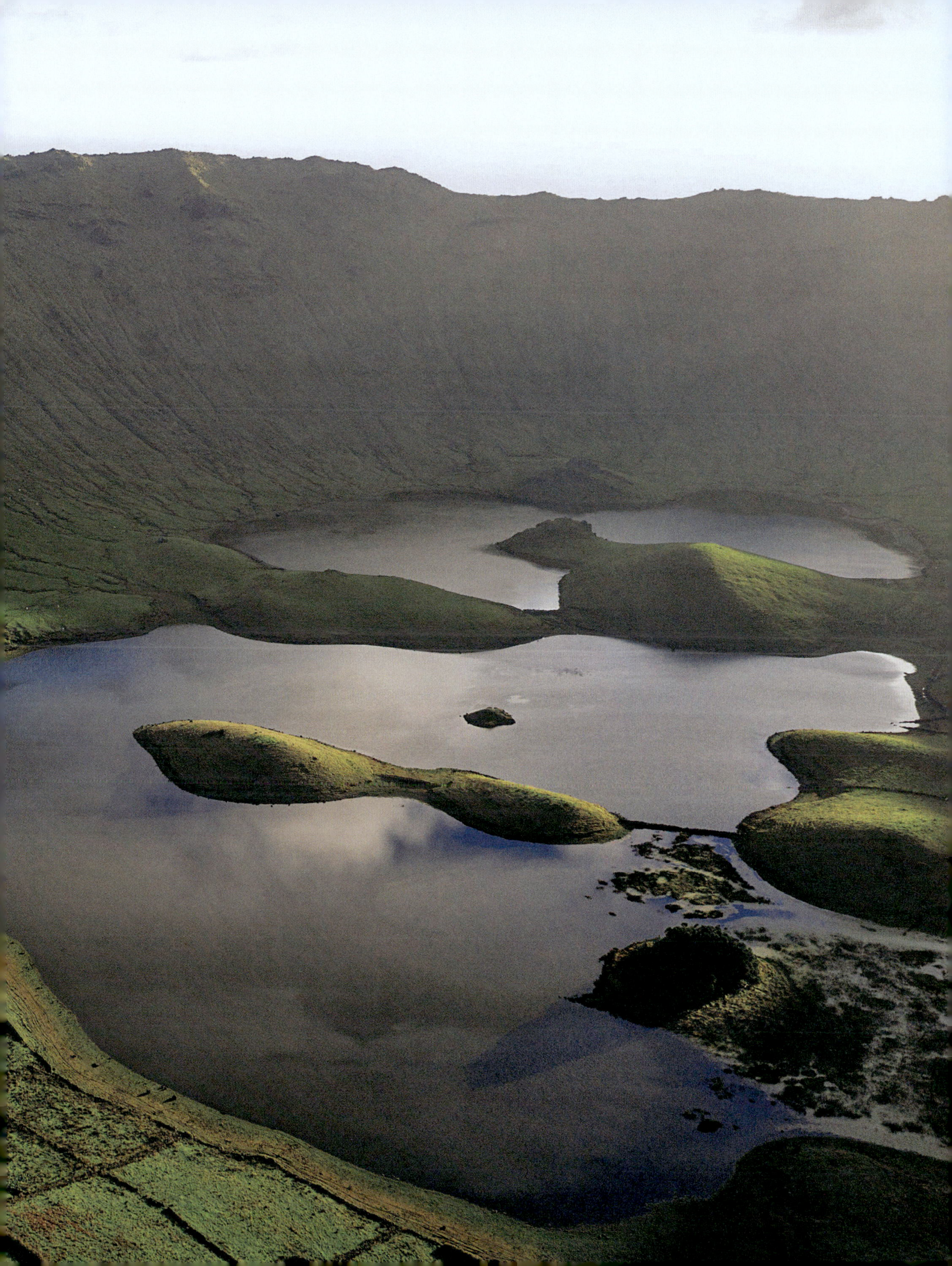

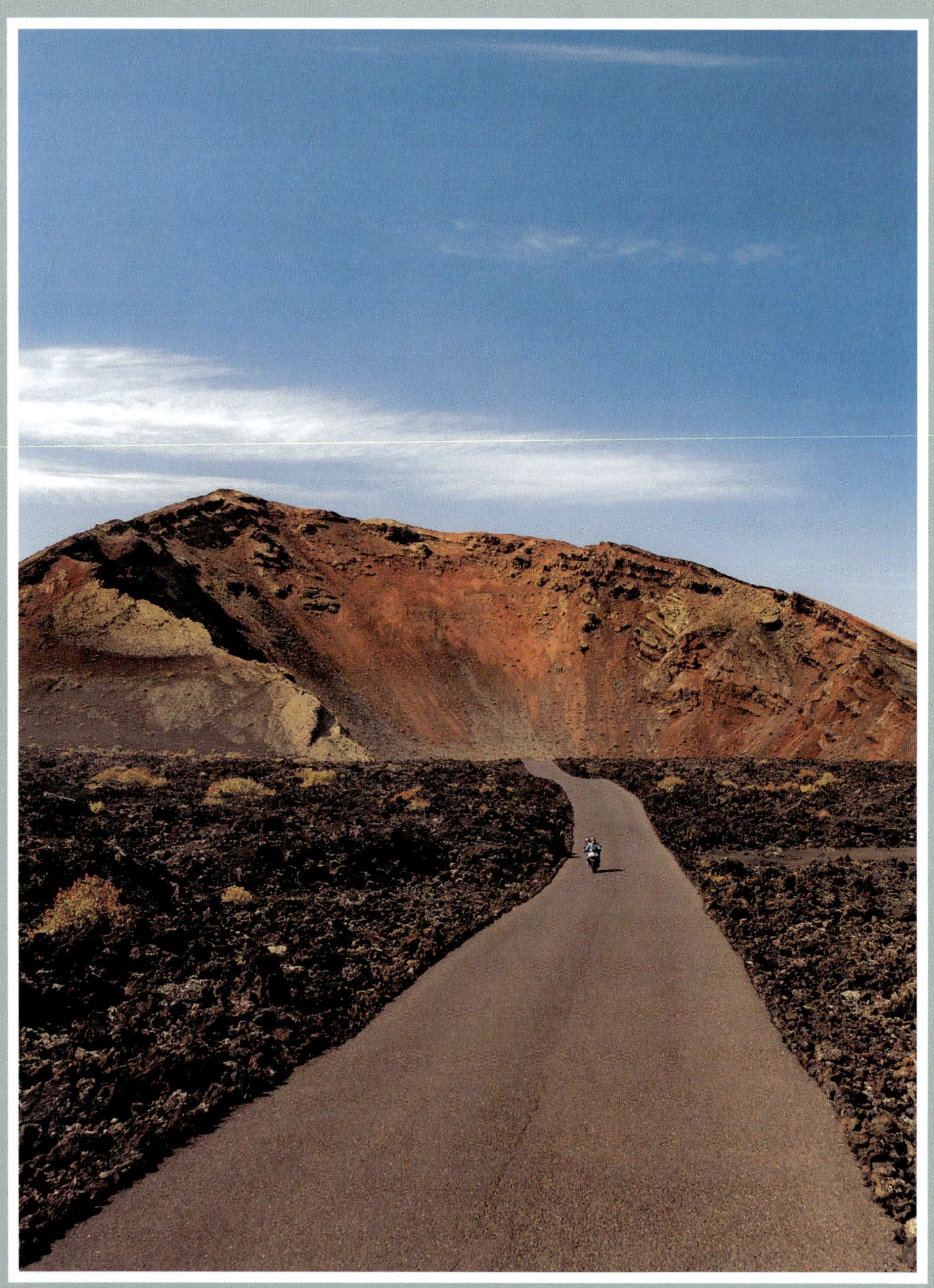

Canary Islands, Spain

LANZAROTE

Geographical coordinates: 29°02'06" N; 13°38'06" W
Waters: Atlantic Ocean
Population: 163,230 inhabitants
Surface area: 326.61 square miles (845.94 km^2)
Principal settlement: Arrecife

THE BONE OF THE WORLD

Porous rocks that resemble blackened lava sponges, hills like graphite rubbed on a sheet of paper, open craters like hungry mouths: here, nature hardly welcomes you with a friendly smile. When the wind blows, it carves rather than caresses. The sun sculpts rather than illuminates. And the sea? The sea restricts itself to surrounding the island as it would something it does not fully recognize, an unexpected guest in its vast blue expanse. There is a point in the Atlantic where the earth tires of being earth and allows itself to burn. Lanzarote is the flayed bone of a world that once was, a geological relic where the landscape seems to have transcended the very concept of landscape. There are no rivers, no woods, no meadows. Yet Lanzarote is alive. Palm trees sprout like survivors and prickly pears cling to the rocks with the silent stubbornness of life that needs no reasons or explanations, but simply resists. Then there are the lichens, equally stubborn, interrupting the volcanic black with their yellow and red patterns, and there is the ocean bringing salty news from afar. The air here has a rough, dark scent: it carries with it the memory of eruptions, the hot breath of craters, the dust scorched by the sun. As soon as you set foot here, a feeling of alienation is almost inevitable: you will almost certainly wonder if you have landed on Mars or the moon, and you will be forced to rethink your concept of beauty. Nothing is taken for granted, nothing is easy, but if you know how to look at it, the island can reveal a mineral poetry, a harsh and absolute harmony, as if the earth had abandoned all modesty and complacency to display a wild and frightening nakedness.

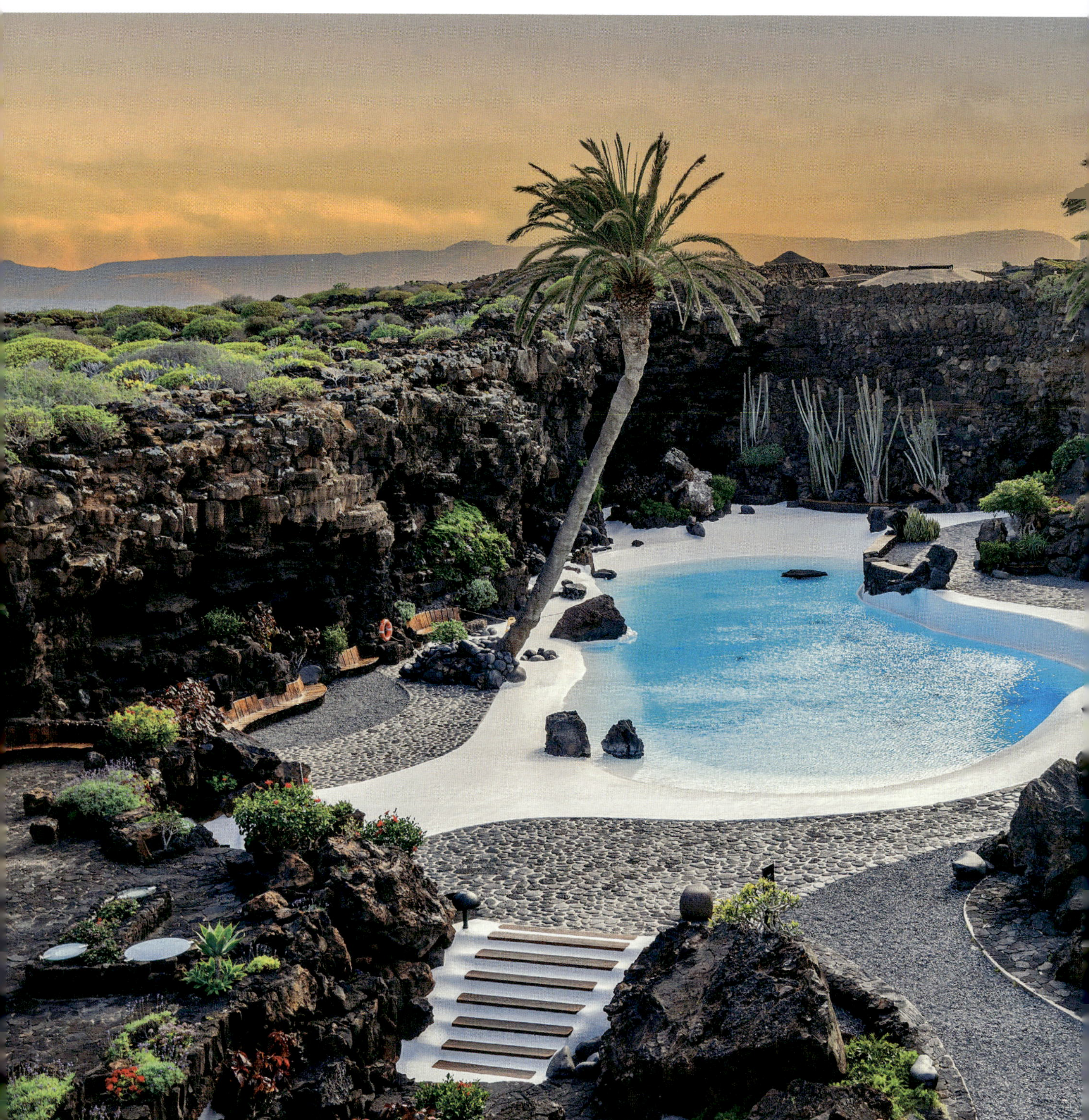

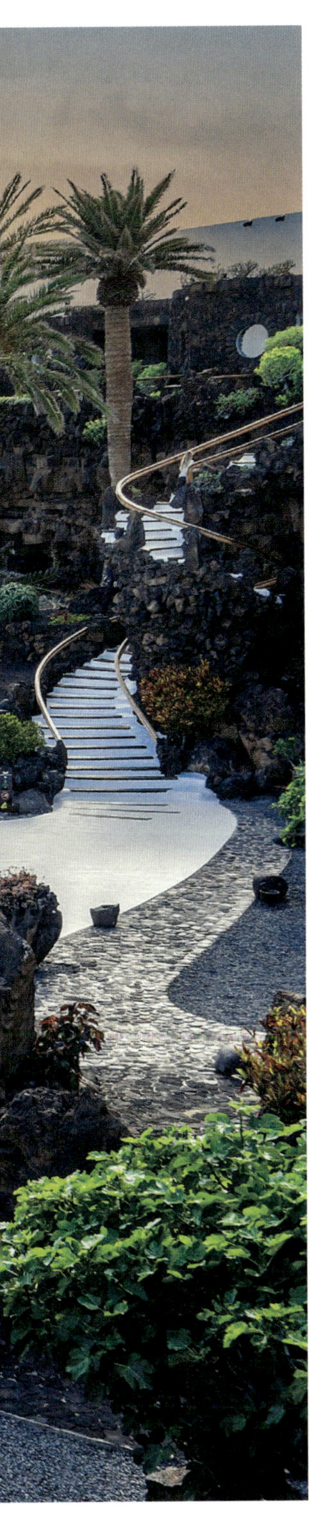

THE MARK OF MAN

~

This island bears the name of a man who probably would have preferred Lanzarote to be known as something else. Lanzerotto Malocello, a navigator from the Republic of Genoa born in Varazze in 1270, arrived here in the 14th century, perhaps looking for a more profitable route or simply because the wind had blown him here by mistake. He found the Majòs, an indigenous population that had preserved rather primitive customs despite earlier colonization by the Phoenicians and then by the Romans. Lanzerotto settled on the island and remained there for 20 years before being forced to flee due to a native uprising. Nonetheless, he left behind a name that would outlive him, making him as eternal as a fossil embedded in lava. Centuries later, another man decided that Lanzarote would be more than just a remote piece of rock in the Atlantic Ocean. César Manrique, a visionary architect and artist born in 1919 in Arrecife, studied, understood and valorized the true wealth of his island, that profound essence he was committed to protecting. He fought to keep the houses white and low, to ensure that buildings and nature blended together and that tourism was not an invasive concrete sprawl but a sustainable idea based on respect. Today, visitors to Lanzarote can enjoy the fruits of Manrique's vision: villages that look like something out of a painting, lava tunnels, viewpoints and volcanic caves transformed into gardens and swimming pools, such as the Jameos del Agua, the Mirador del Río and the Jardin de Cactus. Here, man has learned to fit into the landscape without disturbing it, to establish a dialogue with the rock without sculpting it in his own image.

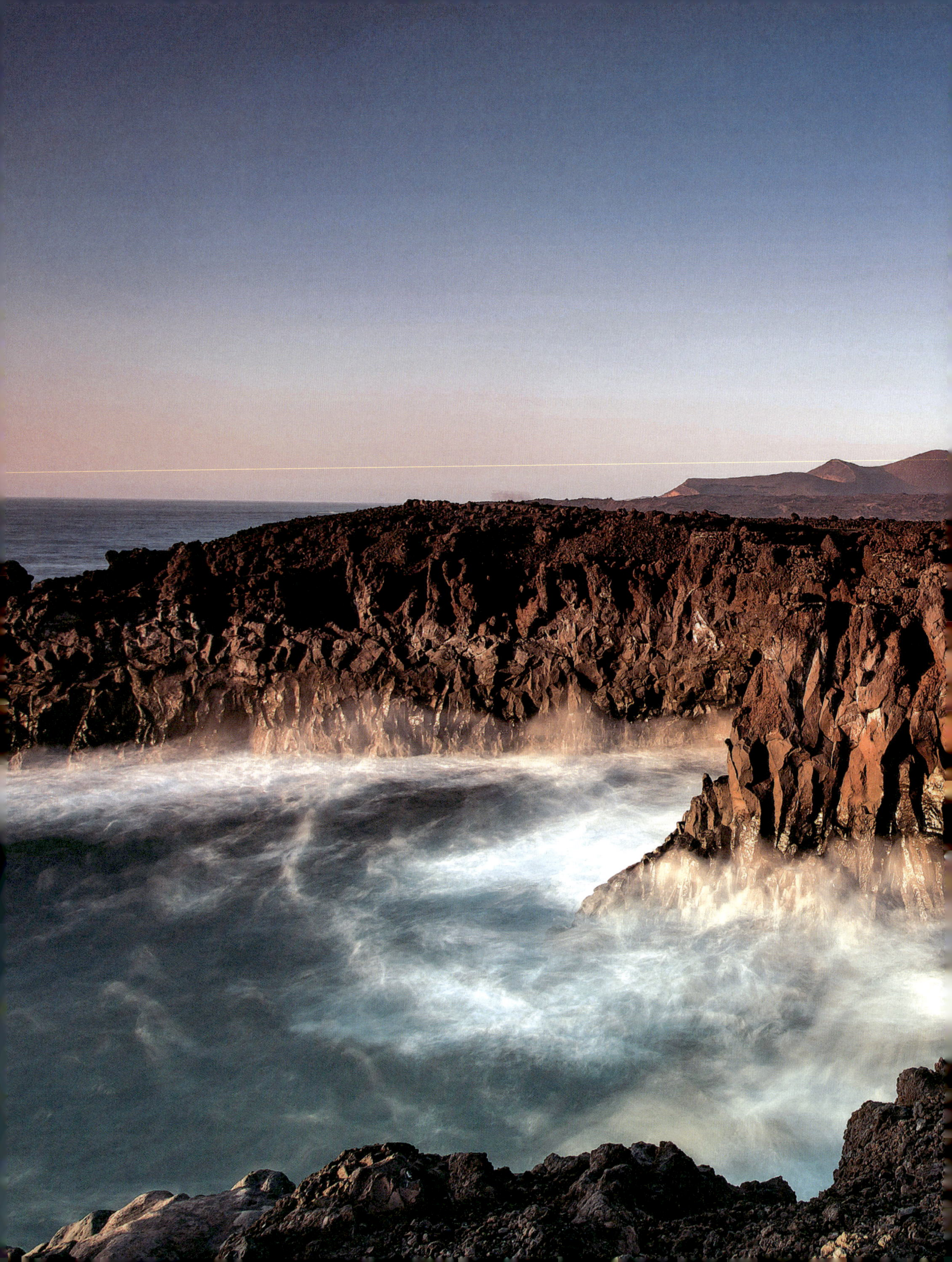

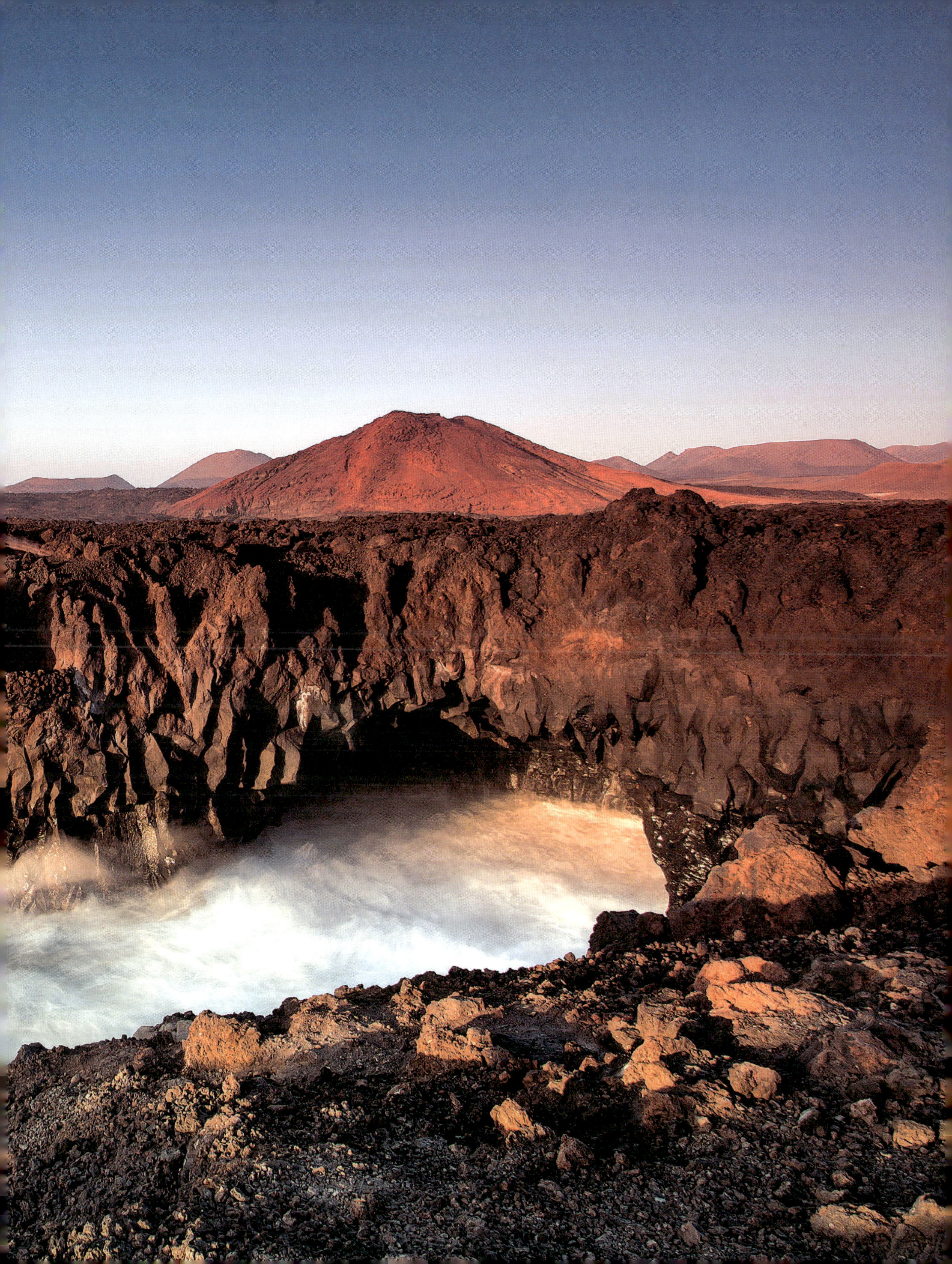

THE DAY THE WORLD ENDED AND BEGAN AGAIN

IT WAS THE 1ST OF SEPTEMBER 1730 WHEN THE BOUNDARY BETWEEN THE LAND AND WHAT LAY BENEATH IT VANISHED. FOR SIX YEARS, THROUGH TO APRIL 1736, THE FIRE THAT HAD BEEN COMPRESSED FOR TOO LONG IN THE BOWELS OF THE EARTH VIOLENTLY ERUPTED, CLAIMING FIELDS, VILLAGES AND HUMAN LIVES. THE LAVA ADVANCED RELENTLESSLY, WIPING OUT VEGETATION AND REWRITING THE LANDSCAPE WITH AN ALPHABET OF BLACK, ROCKY CHARACTERS.

Many of the surviving farmers fled, while others decided to stay, hoping that the fury would eventually subside. And when it did, Lanzarote was no longer the same. It was dead, petrified under its own congealed blood. Those who remained rolled up their sleeves in search of a way to live with the disaster. La Geria was born, an agricultural miracle: fields of volcanic ash transformed into fertile vineyards. The vines, protected from the fury of the wind by semicircular stone walls, sink their roots into the volcanic soil. The nighttime humidity condenses on the dark earth and soaks down to nourish the plants. Since that period, man has adapted and put himself to the test with the typical meticulous skill that characterizes wine producers, developing techniques and traditions that have been perfected and renewed over the centuries. Today, those who traverse Lanzarote walk through these lunar vineyards, drink wine born of an eruption and recognize that this island is a paradox: a land that has rediscovered life in its own death.

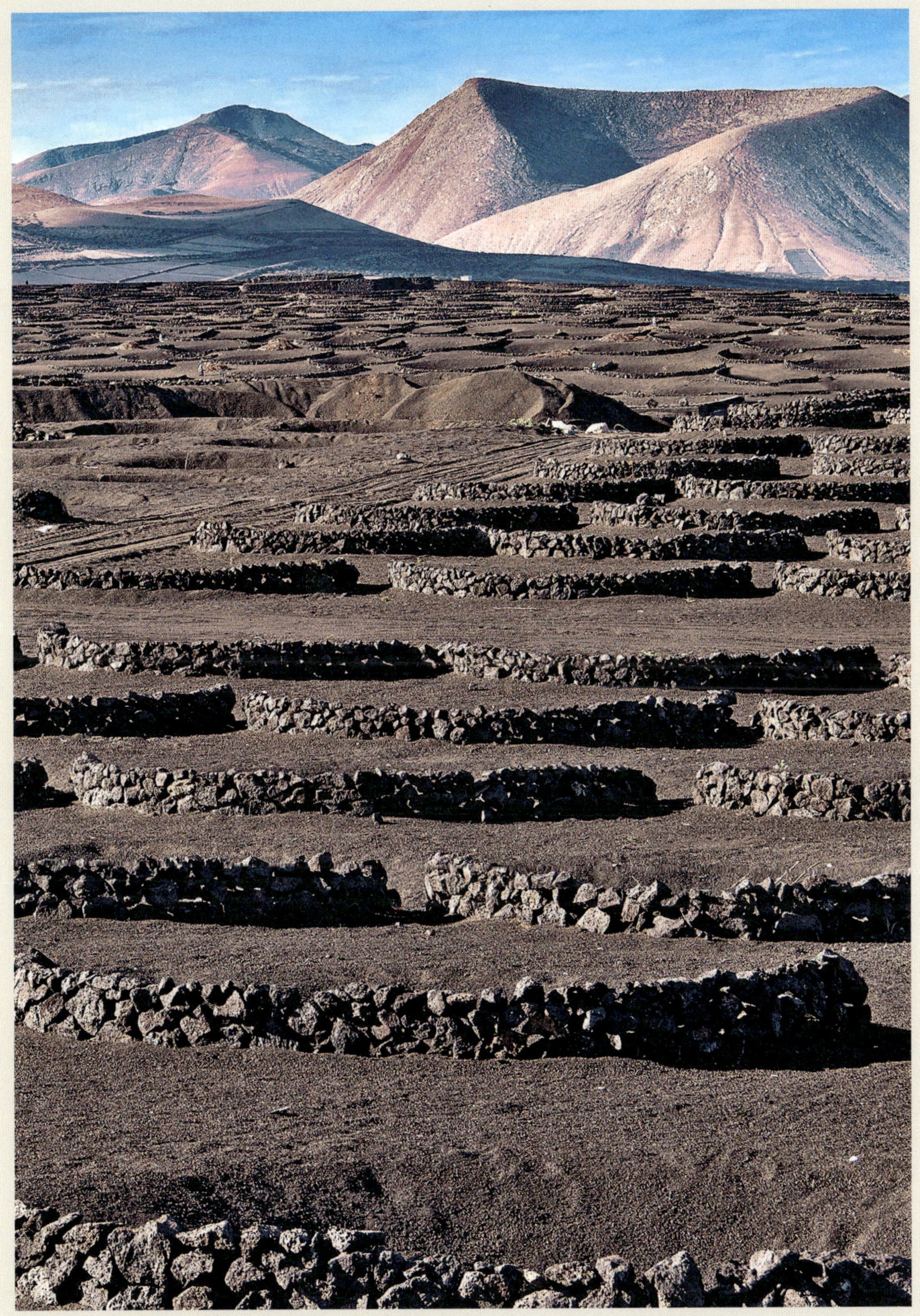

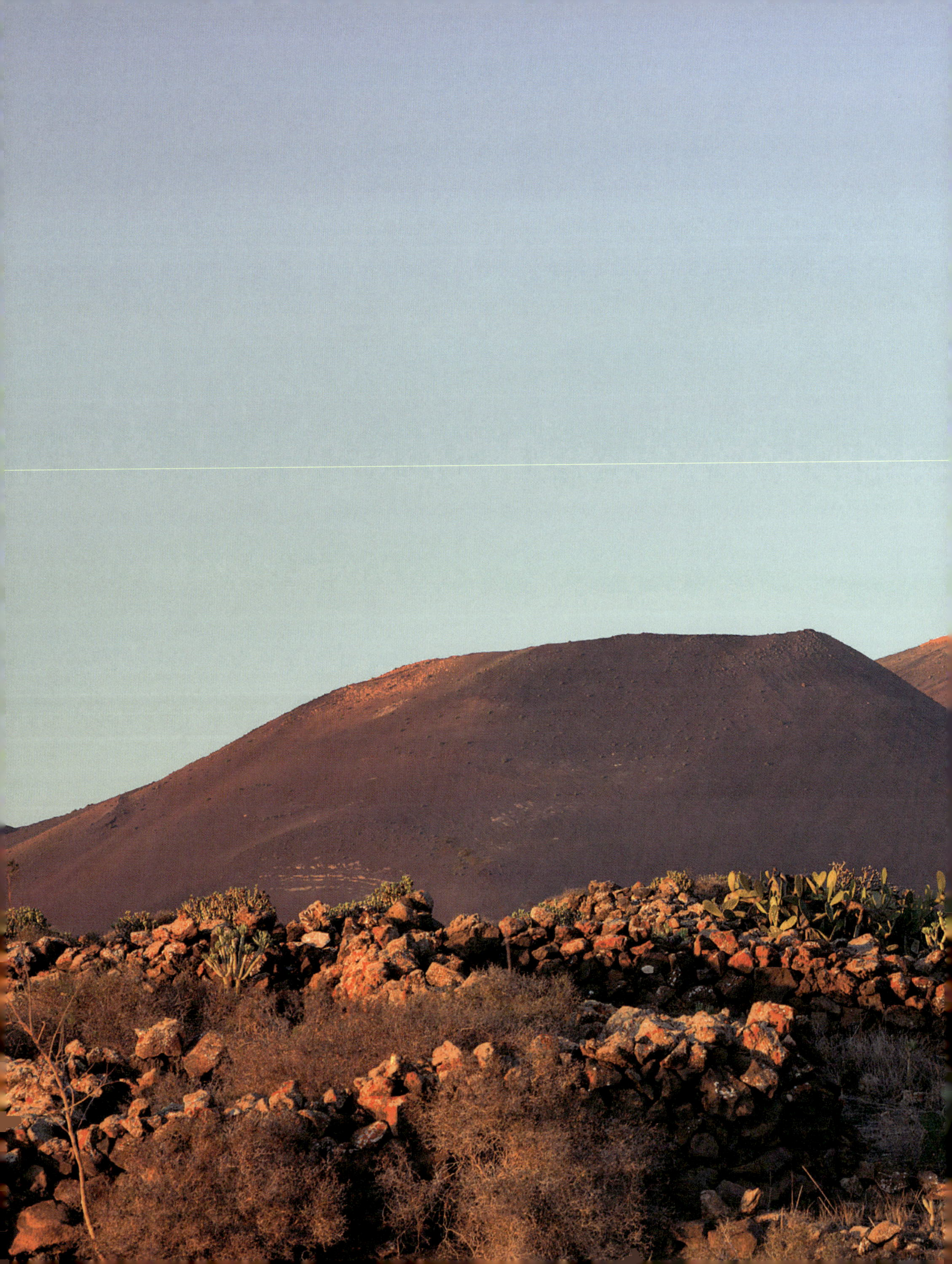

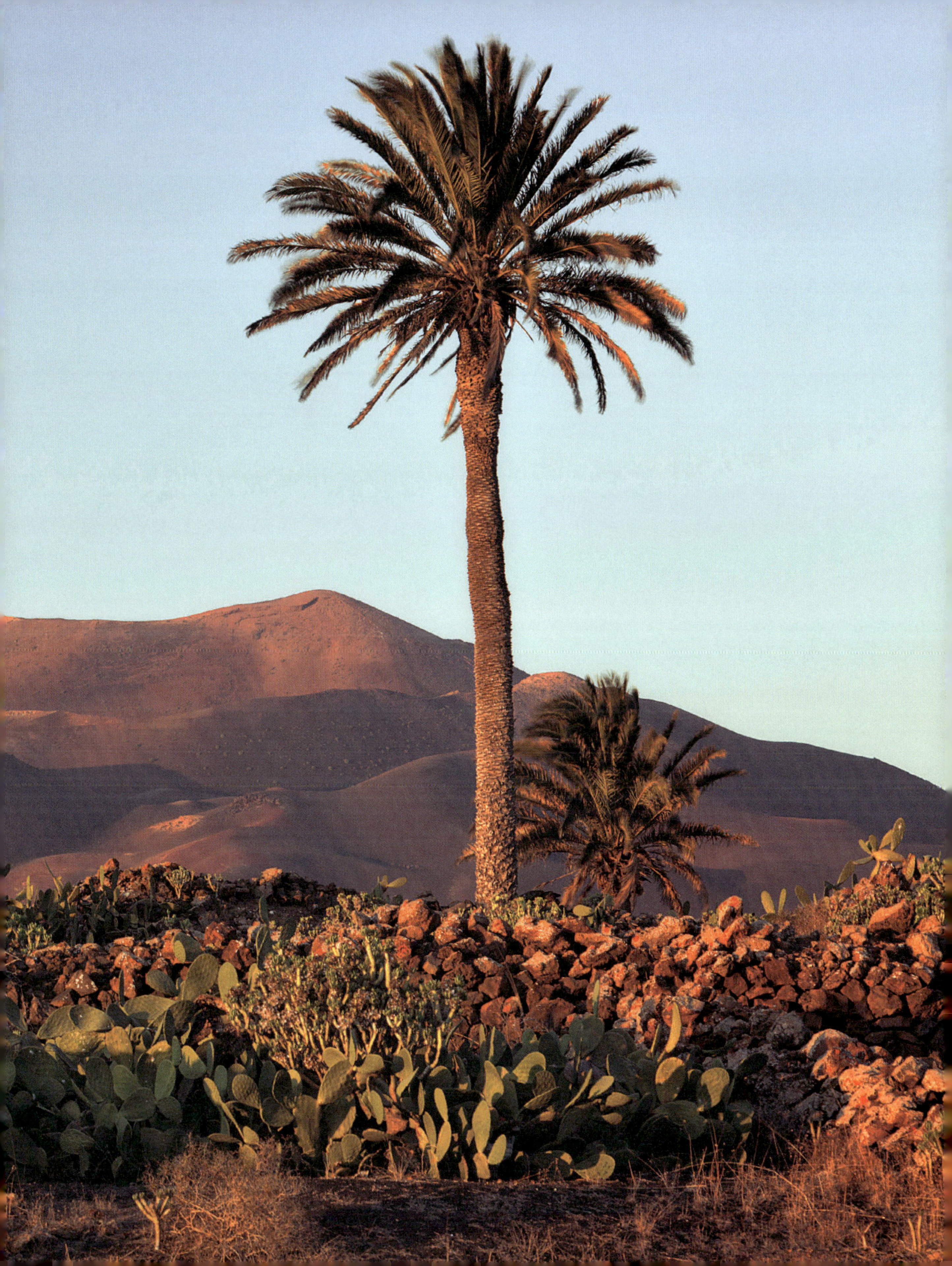

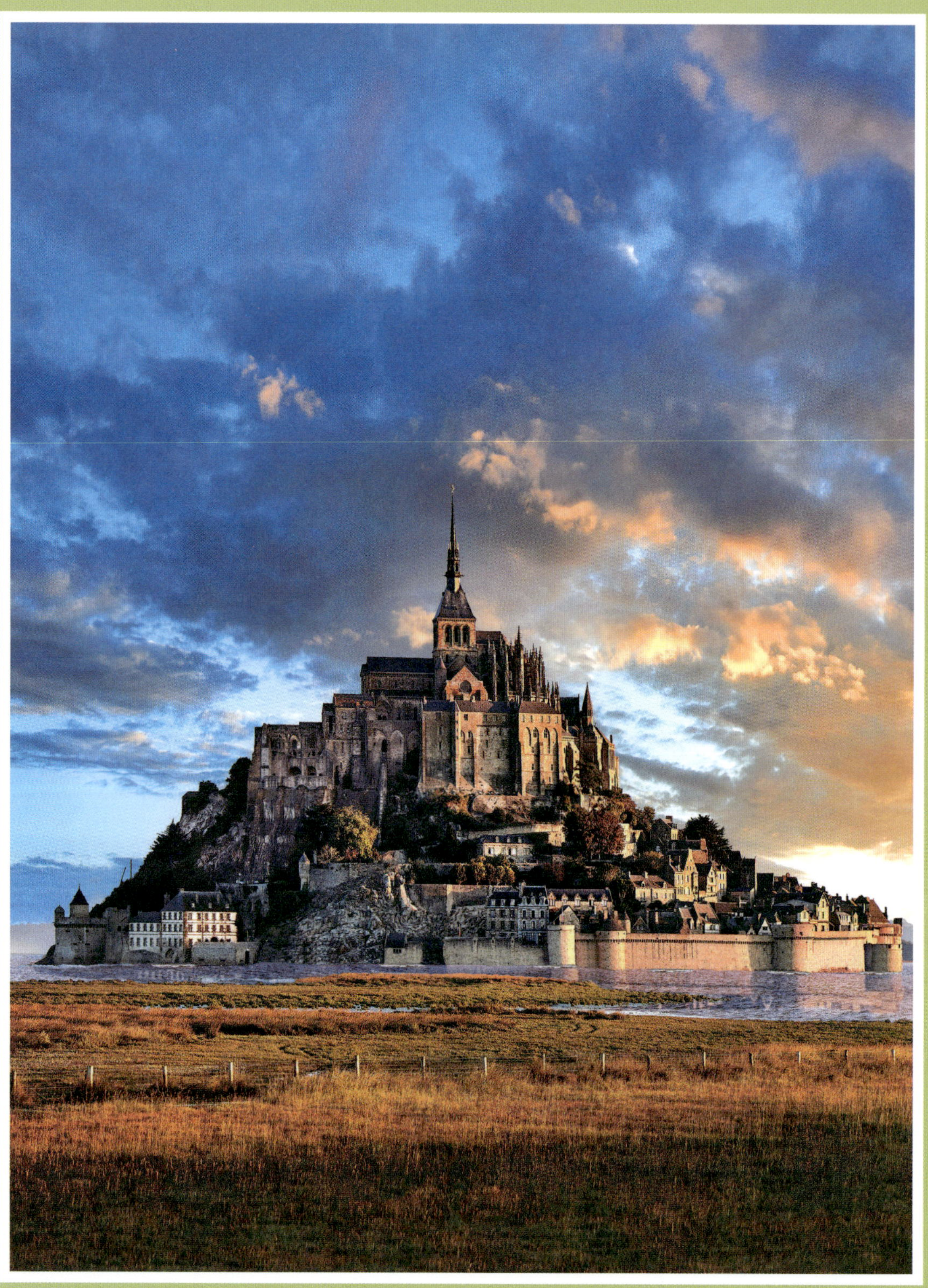

France

MONT SAINT-MICHEL

Geographical coordinates: 48°38'10" N; 1°30'40" W
Waters: Atlantic Ocean
Population: 23 inhabitants
Surface area: 1.53 square miles (3.97 km²)

WHEN IS AN ISLAND NOT AN ISLAND?

They are known as tidal islands and are, by definition, unstable. A strip of sand called a tombolo connects them to the mainland, but this only emerges at low tide. When the water level rises, these strips of land become inaccessible again, making them ideal locations for fortresses, monasteries and castles. These structures combine human ingenuity with the infallible defence offered by the sea. The most famous formation of this type in the world is Mont Saint-Michel, whose profile traced by rocks and the abbey in the center echoes in our unconscious memory like the constellations of our hemisphere or the mountain ridges of familiar places. Located in the bay of the same name, the granite rock islet lies opposite the mouth of the Couesnon river, on whose sediments its deepest layers rest. The river once marked the boundary between Brittany and Normandy and it is thought that a change in its course caused Mont Saint-Michel to shift between the two regions. The tide, which follows variable seasonal and annual cycles, gives rise to a height difference of 45 feet (14 meters). The flat terrain means that these changes occur very quickly, with a wave invading the sandy expanse and endangering anyone in the area. Areas of quicksand are also treacherous even at low tide. Much of the bay was once occupied by the Scissy forest, which was gradually swallowed up by the sea from the 3rd century onward due to land subsidence. According to medieval accounts, a particularly powerful tide finally wiped it out in 709.

THE HUMAN HAND

~

Here, it is unthinkable to separate what nature has provided from what man has created, not simply because of the architectural skyline, but also because of the natural height of 300 feet (92 meters), which becomes 555 feet (170 meters) at the tip of the golden statue of St. Michael surmounting the church. This rock was already sacred to the ancient Celtic tribes who inhabited the Scissy forest before it was swept away by the sea. The sanctuary dedicated to the Gallic sun god Beleno dates back to that period. The first Christian oratory dates back to the 4th century, and legend has it that it was dedicated to the Archangel Michael in 709 at the behest of the Bishop of Avranches after the saint appeared to him three times in a dream and requested it. Twice ignored, Michael decided to speed things up by leaving a hole in the bishop's skull with a touch of his finger. The Benedictine abbey was built around the year 1000 and was subjected to various modifications over the centuries. Following the French Revolution in 1791, Mont Saint-Michel was turned into a prison and remained in use until 1863. A place of study, prayer, art, culture and pilgrimage, and now mass tourism with over three million visitors a year, the mount is always full of life and became a UNESCO World Heritage Site in 1979. The bay surrounding the island is no less important, but it was endangered by the 1880 connecting dam, which blocked the passage of water and debris and threatened to transform the intermittent body of water into salt marshes. To remedy this, a new footbridge designed by Dietmar Feichtinger was built in 2014. This structure allows the sea to flow freely between the piers and consists of two pedestrian walkways and a central lane for shuttle buses.

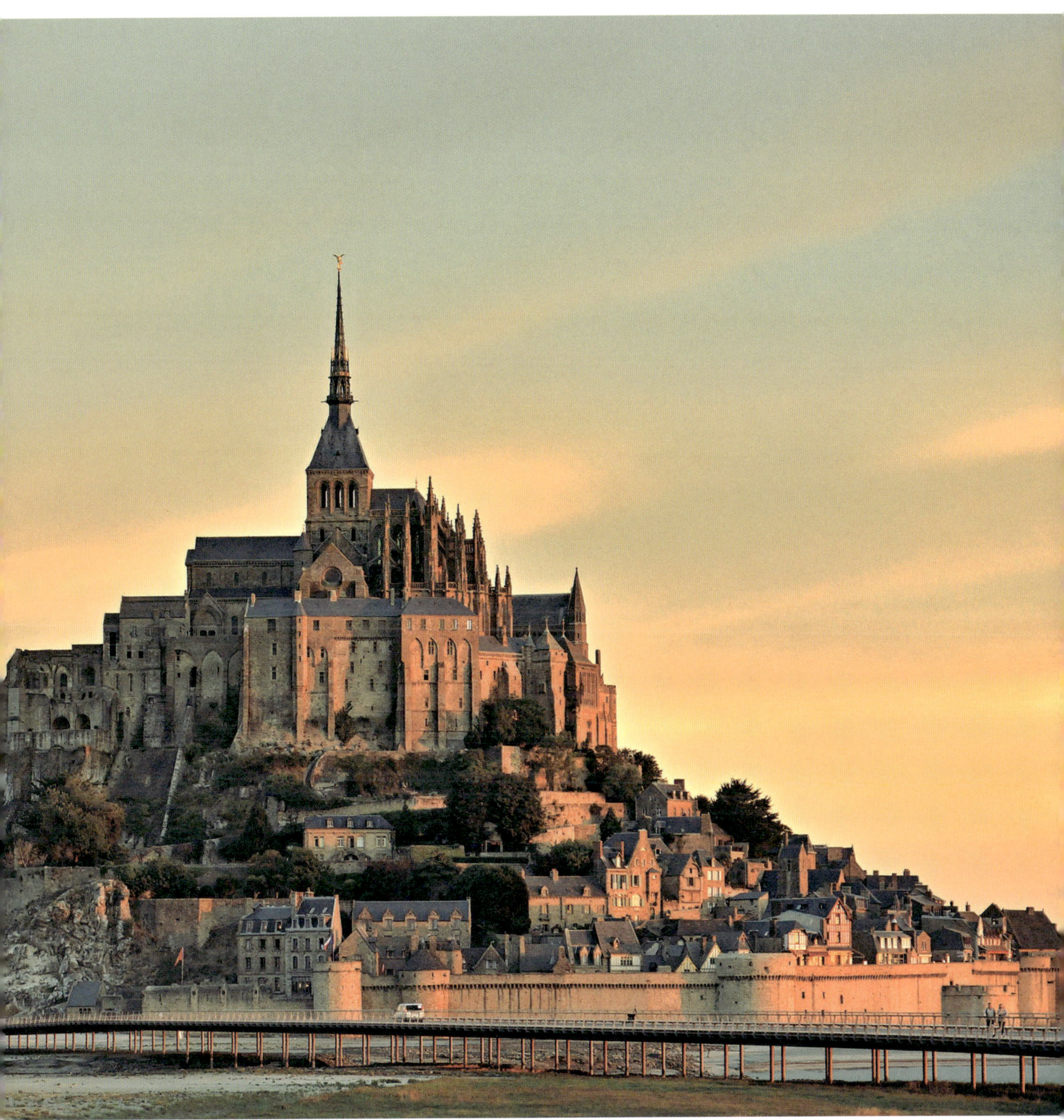

THE FARMER SAINT AND THE POOR DEVIL

∾

MONT SAINT-MICHEL HAS ALWAYS STIMULATED THE IMAGINATION. VICTOR HUGO DESCRIBED IT AS RISING FROM THE SEA LIKE THE PYRAMID OF CHEOPS RISING FROM THE DESERT, WHILE CLAUDE DEBUSSY DREW INSPIRATION FROM THESE SHORES. IN HIS SHORT STORY *LA LÉGENDE DE MONT SAINT-MICHEL (THE LEGEND OF MONT SAINT-MICHEL)*, GUY DE MAUPASSANT DESCRIBES THE ECSTASY OF SEEING THIS MONSTROUS, CHISELLED, ETHEREAL JEWEL FOR THE FIRST TIME.

It is within this atmosphere, somewhere between the frightening and the sublime, that a traveller hears the legend of Saint Michael from a farmer: a man shrewd enough to be a saint. First, he built the church on the island with his own hands and then he surrounded it with quicksand for protection. The devil instead lived in a hut on the coast and led a modest existence; however, he owned huge tracts of fertile land, while the angel starved in his splendid palace. It is he who proposes a deal to Satan. This sui generis devil is naive and hospitable and hardly expects a saint to cheat him. Michael offers to cultivate the land in exchange for half of the harvest and the devil gladly accepts. However, the arrangement turned out to be devious: the carrots, turnips and onions yielded only useless leaves, leaving the saint with the fat, appetizing roots. The devil protested, but Michael raised the stakes: "Next harvest, you keep the underground part and I'll take the above-ground part. Is that okay?" It was. This time, the saint planted wheat, oats, cabbage, peas and artichokes. Satan flew into a rage. Michael let him cool down, then invited him to lunch. "I don't want any misunderstandings between us," he said, offering him food and wine in abundance. The devil overindulged and ended up vomiting in front of everyone, a decidedly unpleasant sight. Seeing his chance, the perfidious Michael pounced on the poor devil, chasing him with a club, beating him and throwing him so high that the unfortunate creature crashed to the ground, leaving permanent marks on the rock and remaining lame forever.

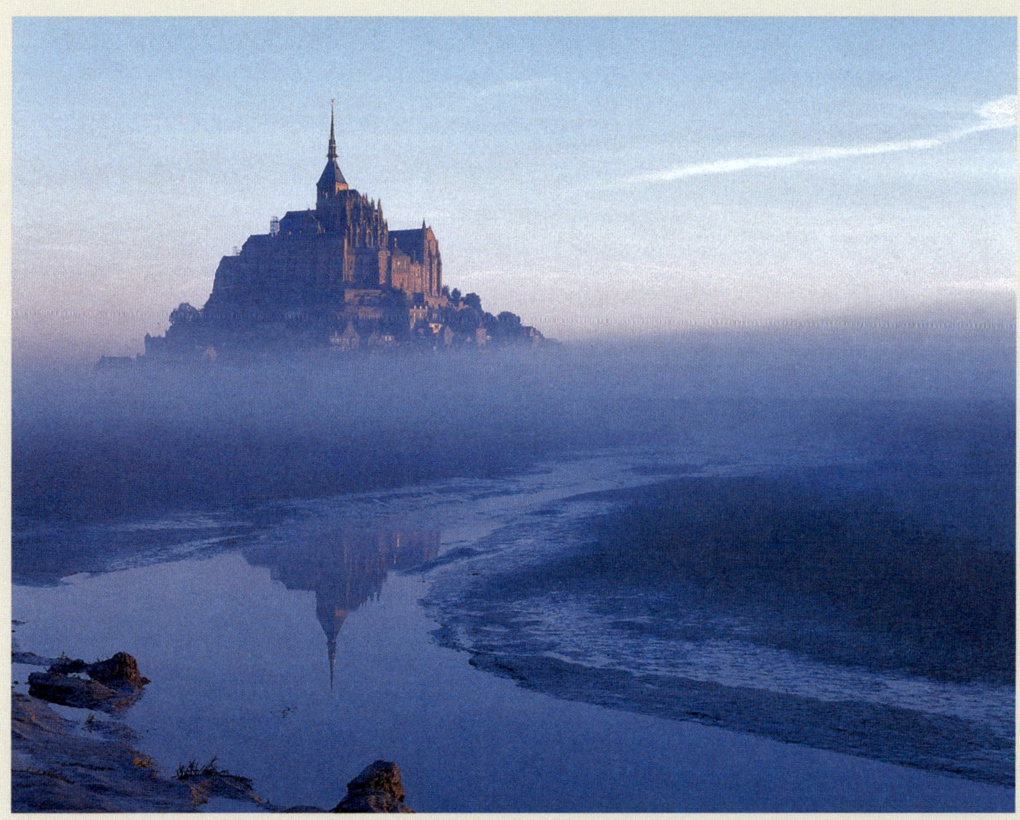

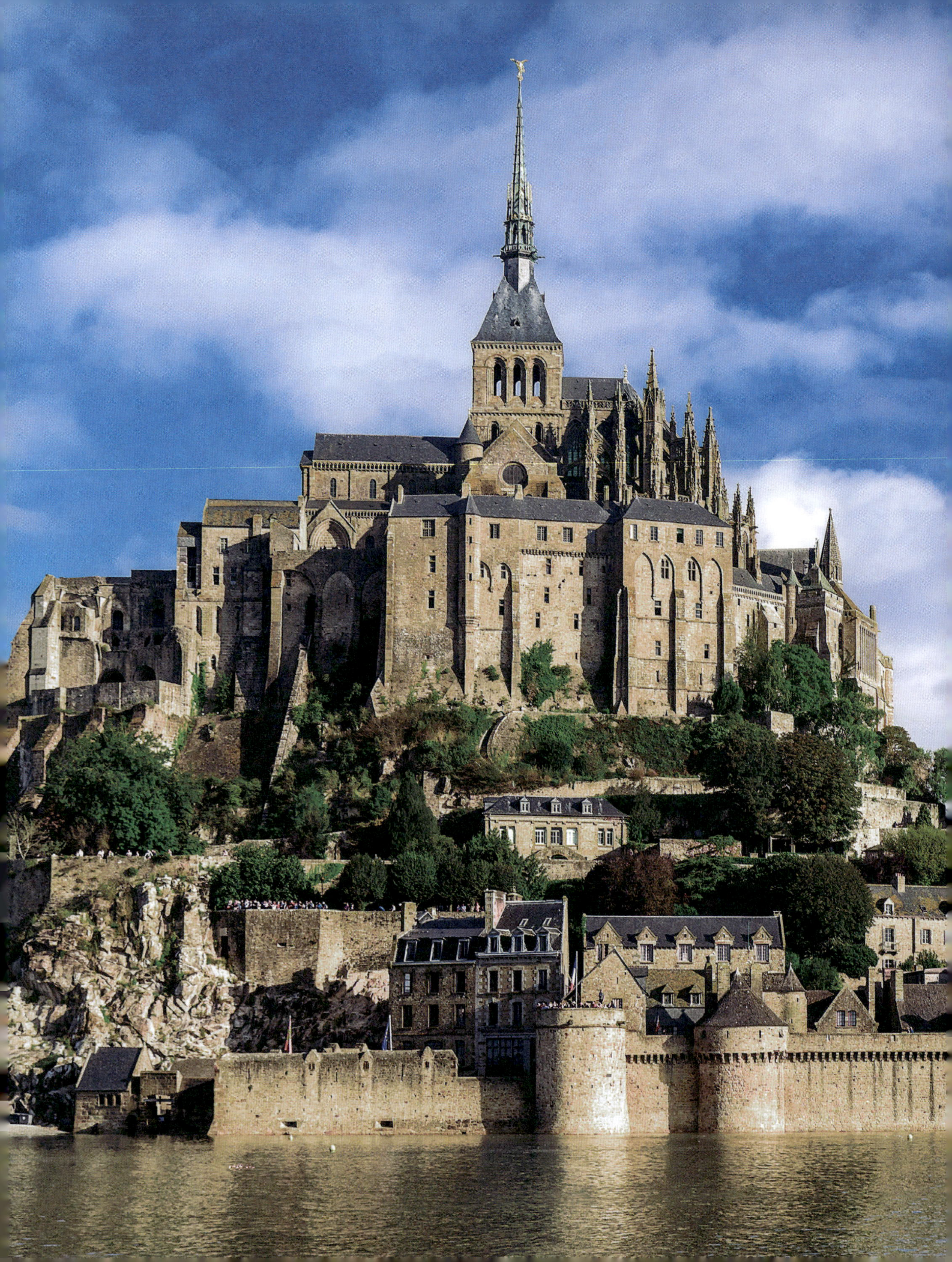

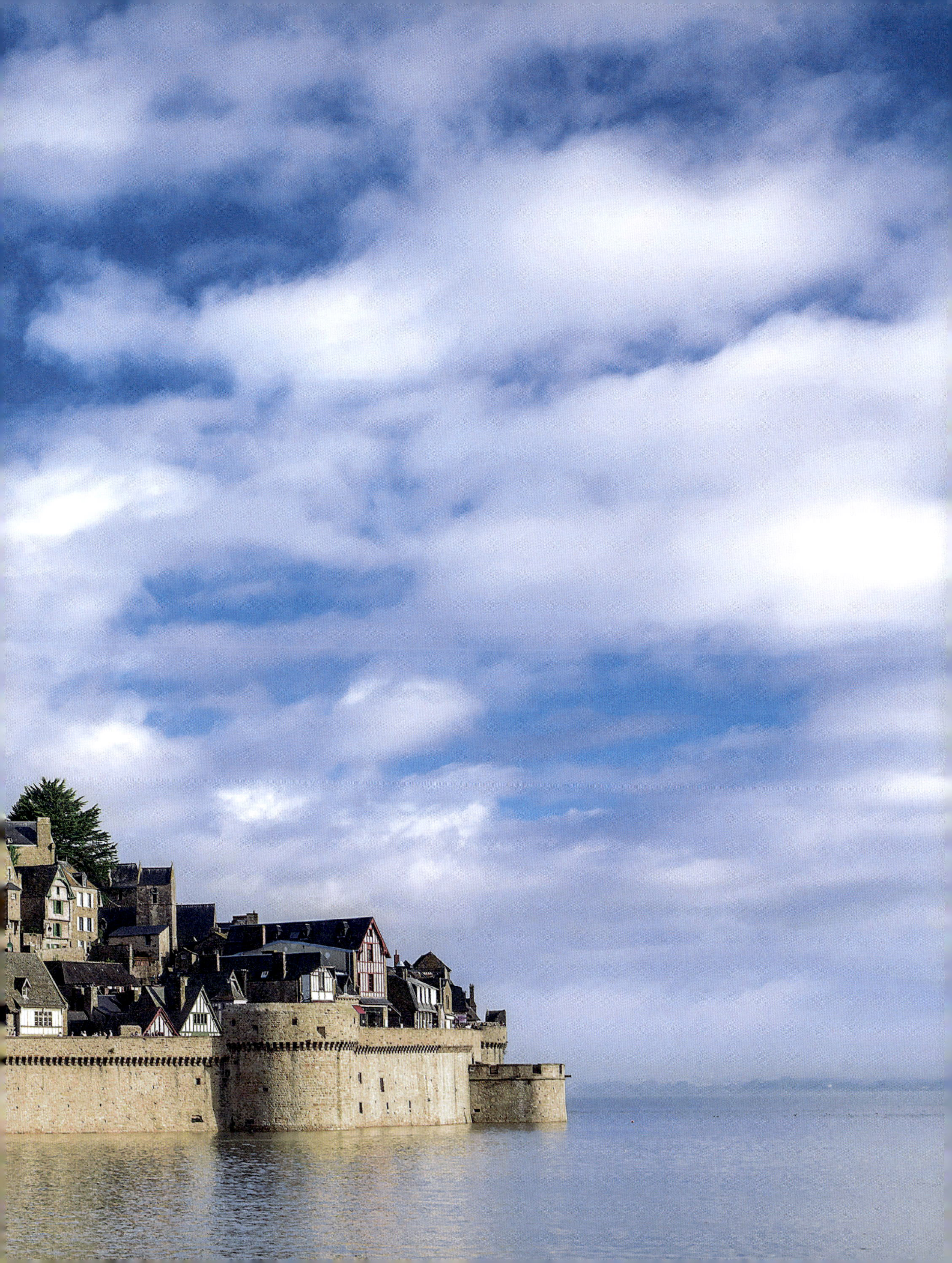

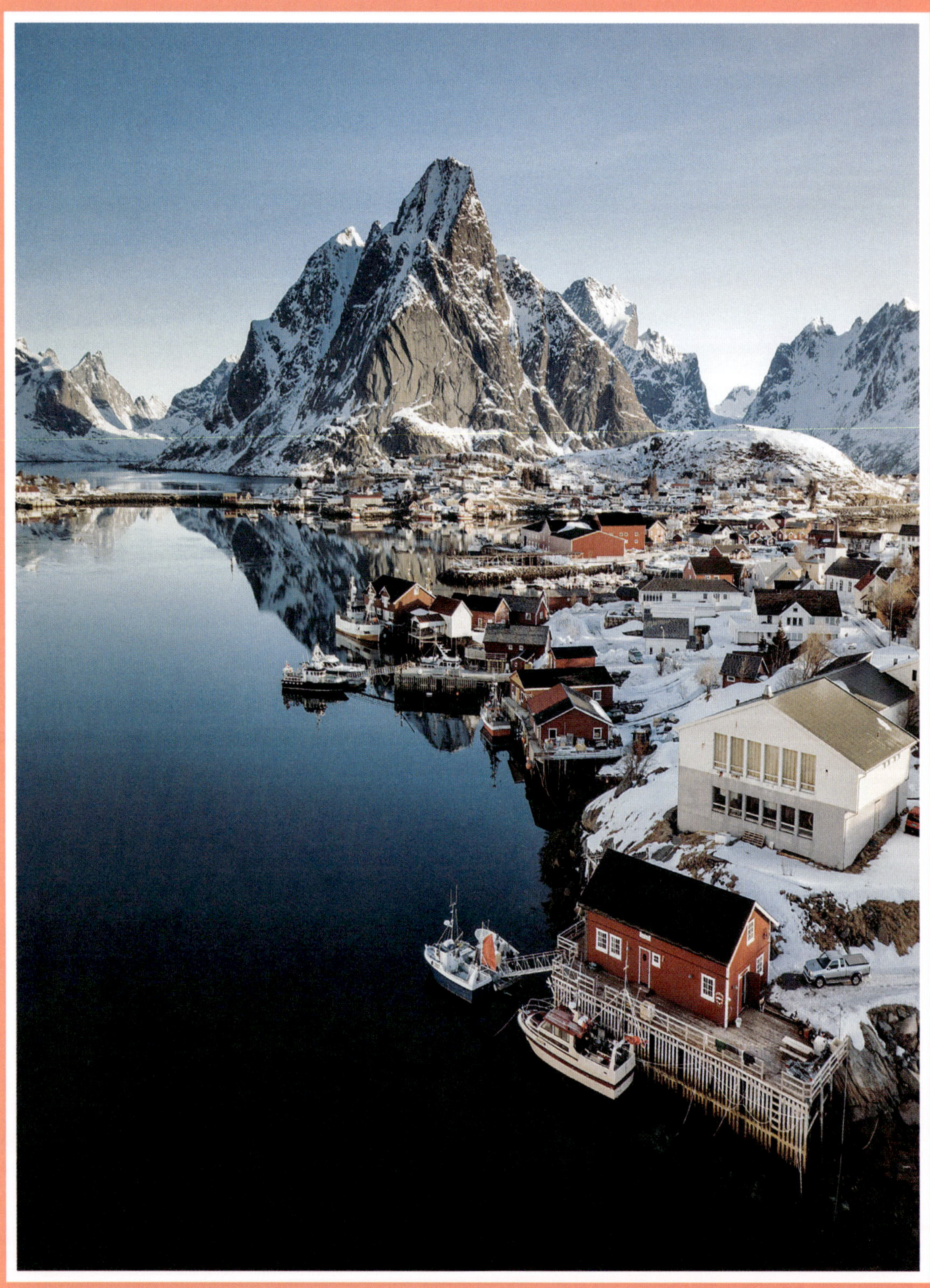

LOFOTEN

Geographical coordinates: 68°20'00" N; 14°40'00" E
Waters: Norwegian Sea
Population: 24,500 inhabitants
Surface area: 473.74 square miles (1,227 km²)
Principal settlement: Svolvær

DAY AND NIGHT

They appear after hours on the ferry or miles of lonely asphalt: jagged, sharp, rising out of the water like an alpine chain that has broken away from the continent to lie in the Norwegian Sea. Sheer cliffs, spires of gneiss and granite rise to the 3,766 feet (1,148 meters) of the Higravtindan, the highest peak. Geologically, the rock strata date back almost three billion years, making them among the oldest in Europe, but their current appearance is the result of retreating glaciers, which have left fjords carved with surgical precision, serrated ridges and valleys like clean cuts in a body of stone. In this archipelago of unpronounceable, long, Viking-like names, crammed with consonants and guttural sounds, the point is not so much to memorize the words—Austvågøy, Gimsøy, Vestvågøy, Flakstadøy, Moskenesøy and Værøy—as to come to terms with the contemplative yearning of this clear, shimmering beauty, almost painful in its melancholic immensity, raw in its distinct contrasts of light and dark. Opposing faces, transfigured between summer and winter, under the caress of a sky capable of remaining light late into the night or of remaining dark even in the middle of the day. Here, in this bizarre contrarian scratch that juts out from the back of Scandinavia, in this sequence of islands like dashes of a broken line that penetrates into the Norwegian Sea for more than 90 miles (145 kilometers) in a climate tempered by the Gulf Stream, respectful and sustainable tourism oscillates between two peaks: that of the midnight sun and that of the hunt for the Northern Lights. In the meantime, the stark, silent mountains are reflected in the sea and together embrace the fishing villages that color the Lofoten islands.

E10

~

The E10, a winding road that hugs the land, that gets under the skin of the landscape through tunnels and connects the islands with bridges, is the clearest symbol of the relationship that has been established between mankind and nature in these parts. Humans have introduced themselves, built and undertaken ambitious projects, yet have not lost that deep respect that borders on reverential awe. The houses may be red, but many roofs are covered with grass, as if to underline this bond. Today, more and more people are arriving, attracted by Arctic scenery that is neither uninhabited nor tamed. A place where every street seems to end in a cliff, where every village is a fragile settlement in which rather than clashing the human presence fits in, like a solidly rooted shelter in the middle of a storm. In the meantime, nature plays its own game: the light—that of the summer months, which is never completely extinguished, but remains suspended in a milky twilight—sculpts the mountains as if they were animated paintings; the Northern Lights in winter instead glow with a magical aura; the beaches of Ramberg, Haukland and Kvalvika confuse you with their Caribbean appearance. On the other hand, tourism aside, living here, among birch trees, shrubs, pastures and fjords as narrow as canyons, is an exercise in adaptation, if not an ongoing confrontation with oneself and one's environment. The first signs of human presence can be traced back to the Stone Age: remnants of fishing activities date back more than 6,000 years and more structured settlement began from the Iron Age onward. In the Middle Ages, Kabelvåg and Borg—on the island of Vestvågøy—became centers of Viking power. On the site of Borg, the imposing residence of the most powerful local chieftain was erected: reconstructed in the Lofotr Vikingmuseum, it brings to life the rituals, festivals and hierarchies of a people who dominated the sea.

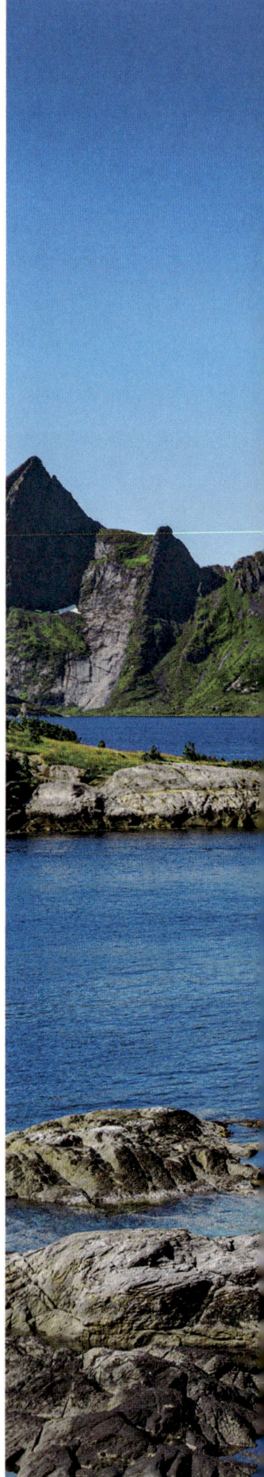

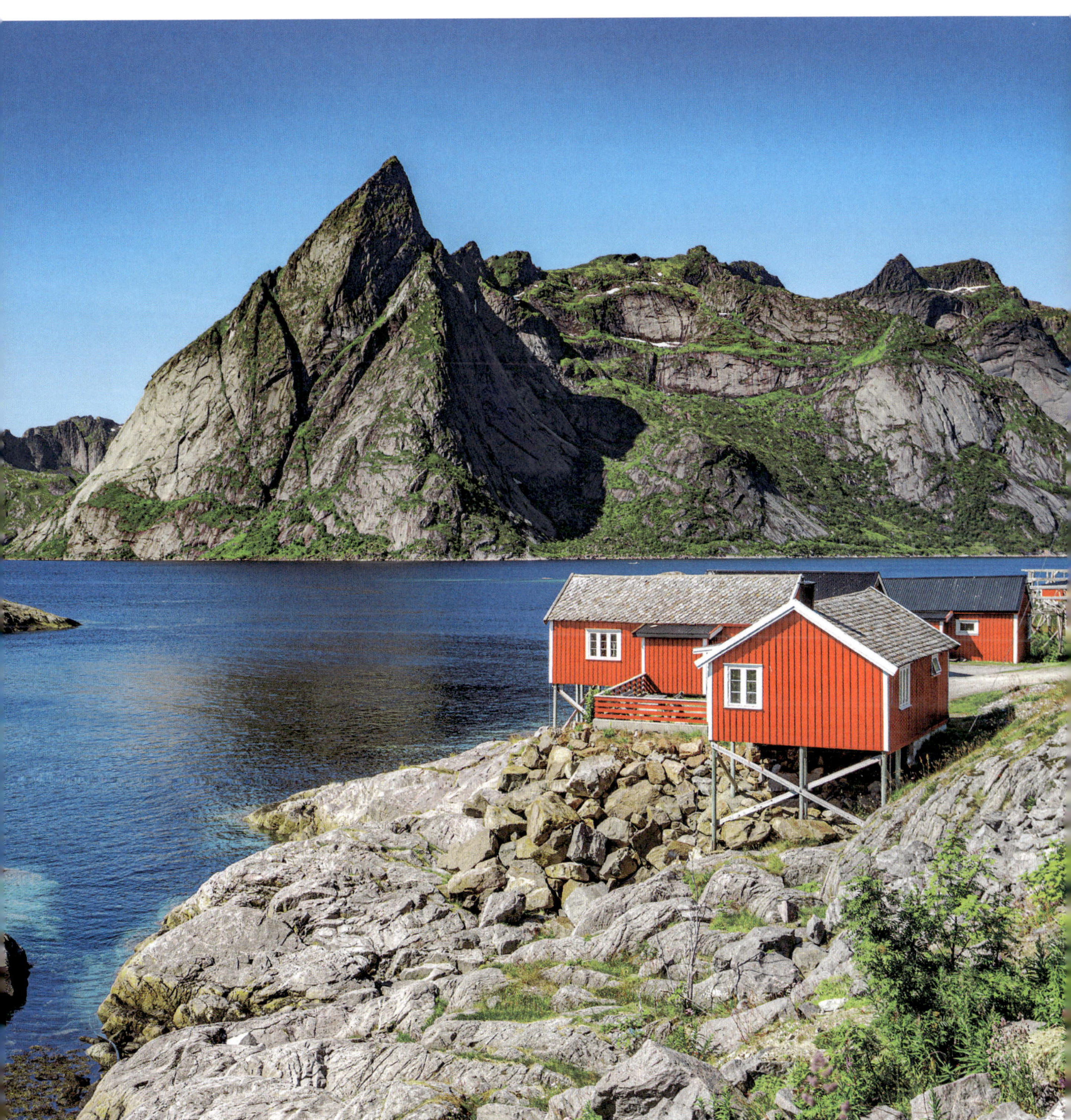

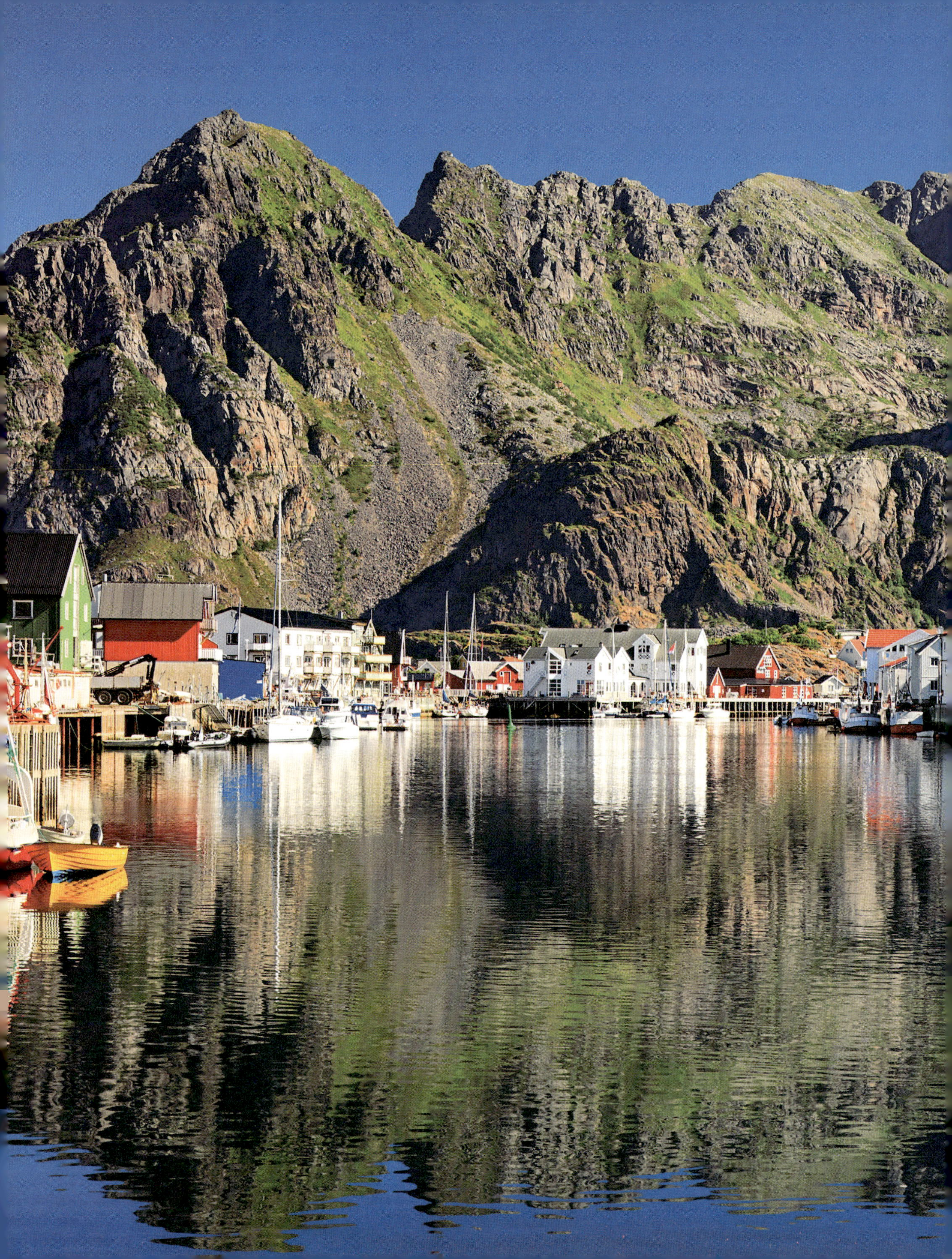

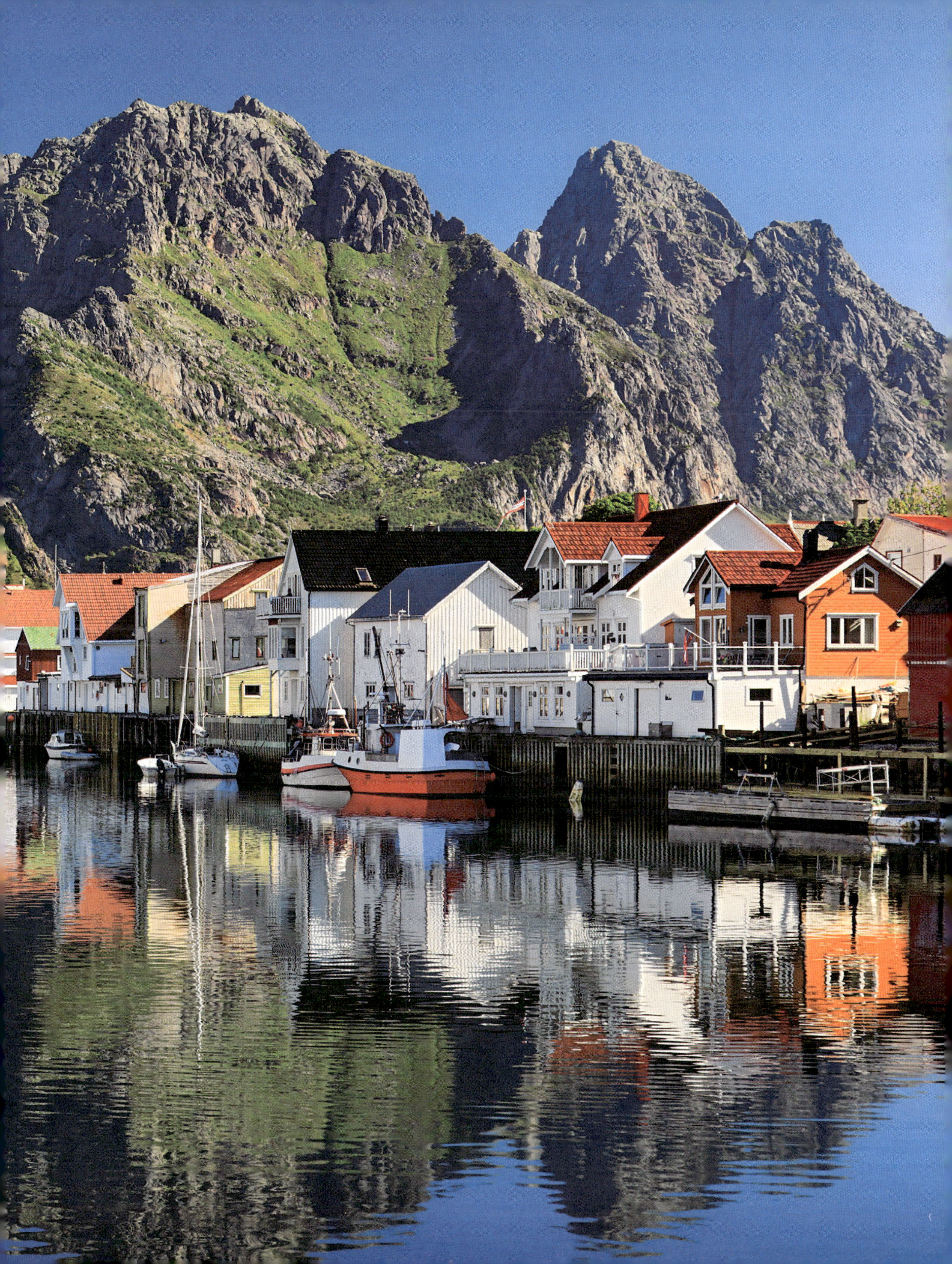

Å FOR END

~

IRONICALLY, THE VILLAGE OF Å—JUST LIKE THE LAST LETTER OF THE NORWEGIAN ALPHABET THAT GIVES IT ITS NAME—IS THE FINAL STOP ON THE E10 ROAD THAT WINDS THROUGH LOFOTEN AND CONTINUES ON FOR A TOTAL OF 528 MILES (850 KM) TO LULEÅ IN SWEDEN.

This minimalist name, pronounced *o* and also meaning *stream*, tells of a small group of red-painted wooden stilt houses, inhabited by a few dozen permanent residents but famous the world over. We are on the island of Moskenesøy, and that blue sign with the name, an inevitable photo opportunity, marks the entrance to one of the best-preserved fishing villages: not a chocolate box tourist trap, but a living, vital place, willing to show its energy to travelers, a fragment of Arctic Norway that still preserves, in full, the past. The old *rorbu*, the fishermen's huts, overlook the water as discreetly as ever. The smell of dried fish mingles with the dampness of the rain. Everything is suspended in a cyclical time of waiting and returning. In the depths of winter, when the storms come thick and fast and the sun barely appears above the horizon, the village prepares to fish for the *skrei*, the Arctic cod that each year ascend the icy currents of the Barents Sea to spawn along the Norwegian coast. The catch is gutted and hung to dry in the wind on large wooden racks. After months of exposure to the cold, salty air, it becomes *tørrfisk*, stockfish: food, commodity, tradition. Å lives around this cycle and narrates it in two small museums: one dedicated to stockfish and one to the village itself, with its houses, its nets, its stories. It is neither folklore nor theater: it is the living memory of a way of inhabiting the world.

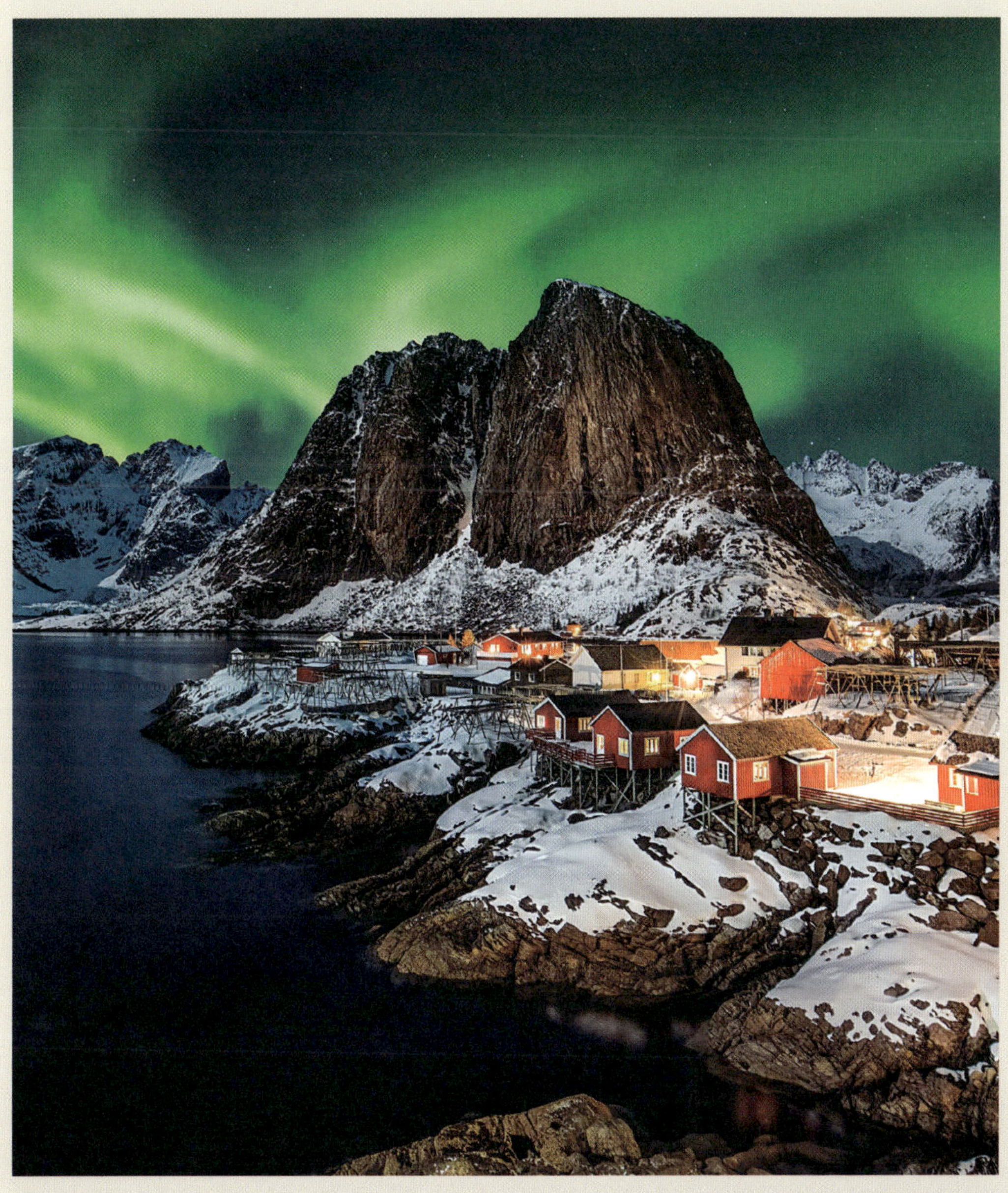

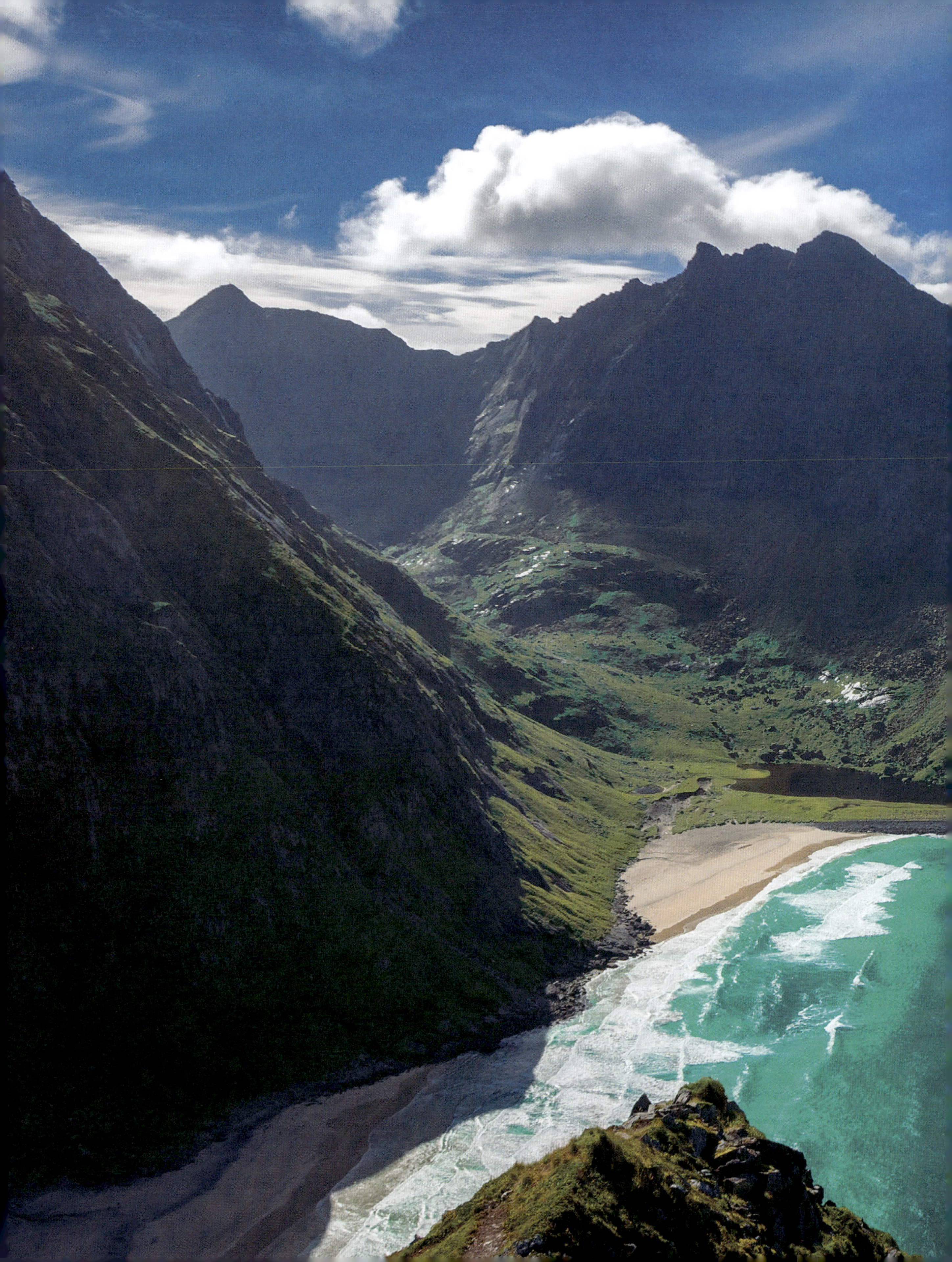

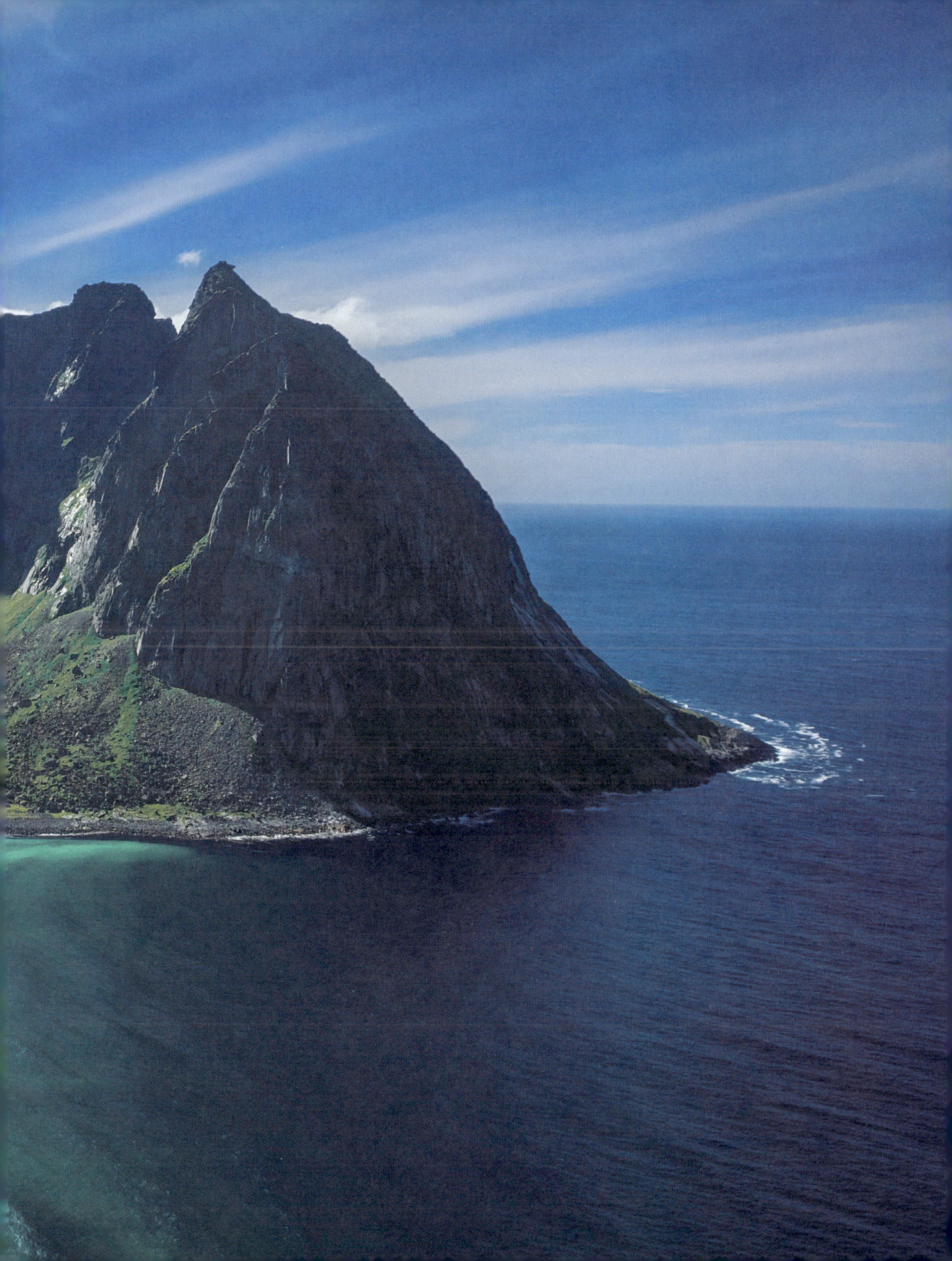

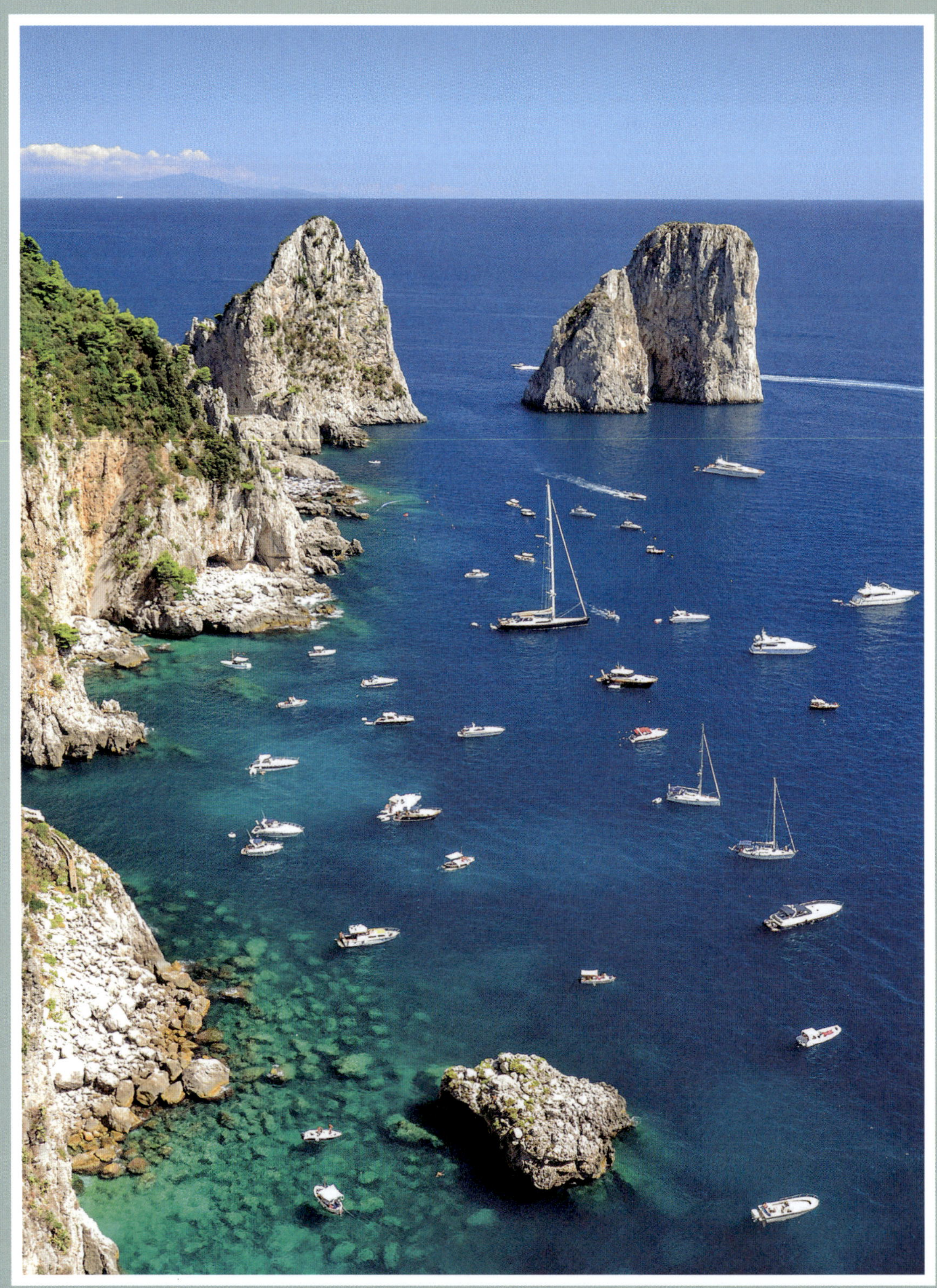

CAPRI

Geographical coordinates: 40°33'03" N; 14°14'33" E
Waters: Tyrrhenian Sea
Population: 13,672 inhabitants
Surface area: 4 square miles (10.4 km²)

THE ISLAND OF THE SIRENS

There is a long history of sediment and stratified fossils leading to the birth of Capri, an icon of Italy throughout the world. Situated on the imaginary extension of the Gulf of Sorrento, it looks out over Naples and the other Neapolitan islands, but is unique, different even in its geology. While Ischia and Procida are of volcanic formation, Capri is of karstic origin. Up until ten thousand years ago—a remote time for us, but negligible for the earth—at the height of the last ice age, that imaginary line was still part of the mainland and Capri represented the tip of the Sorrentine peninsula, as the remains of mammals that lived in the Pleistocene period also confirm. Not only the great movements of the earth, including a slow and progressive subsidence that has taken certain Roman remains below sea level, not only the ancient rocks spewed out by Vesuvius, but also the incessant work of the elements has contributed to the island's current form, so severe, so poetic, so beloved: the wind and the waves have sculpted like tireless artists a landscape destined to steal the eyes and heart of anyone with eyes and a heart. The famous Faraglioni, but also the numerous caves, the steep cliffs alternating with coves, the slopes of the Solaro, Cocuzzo, Cappello and Tiberio hills that dominate the view and the uplands covered with agaves, prickly pears and broom: the whole of Capri is an up and down, a perennial tension of emotions, aspirations and inspirations that transcend time and in a certain sense even space, the same that over the years have bewitched those who have set foot here and breathed this air.

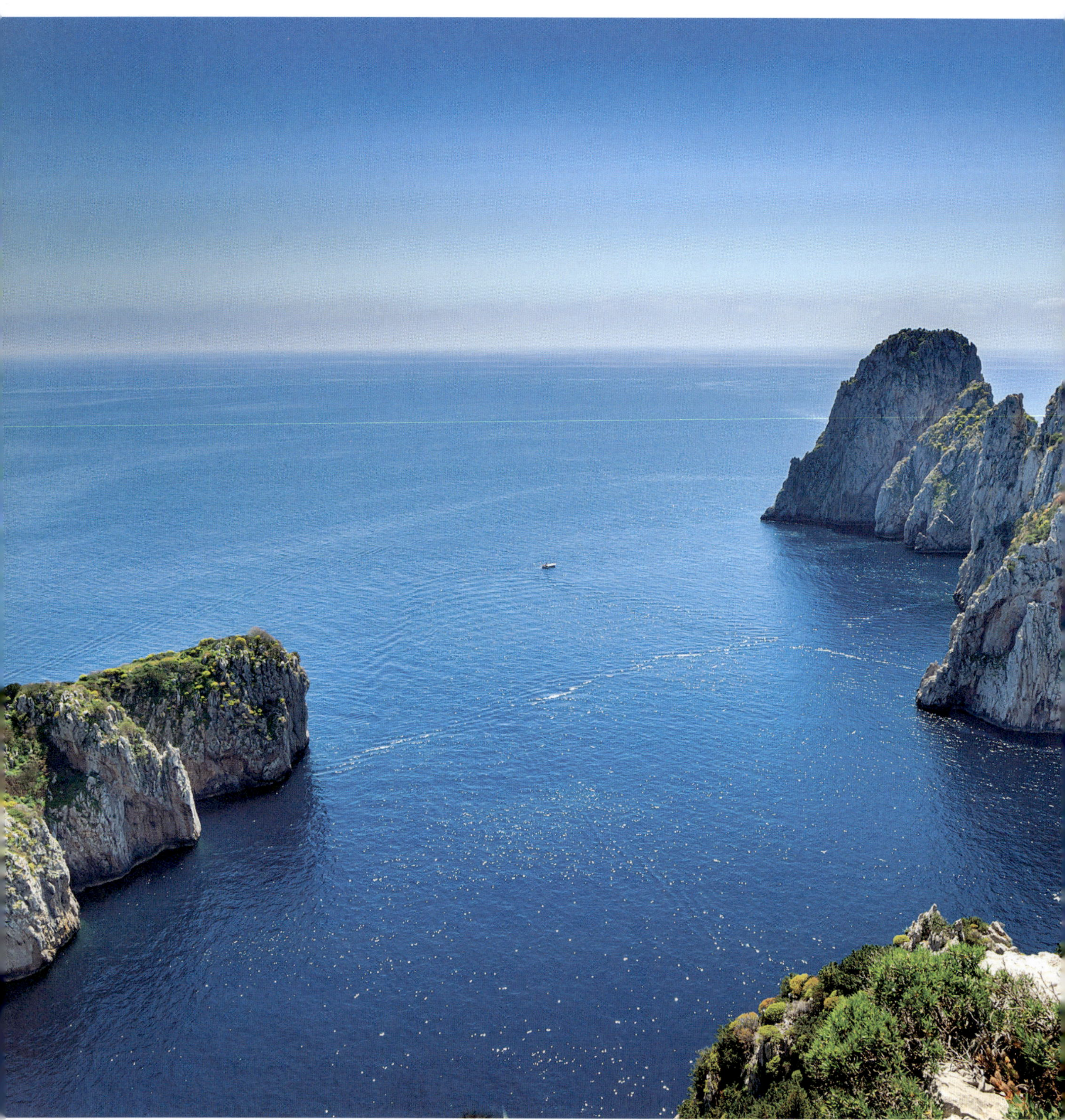

THE VISIBLE WORLD AND THE INVISIBLE WORLD

~

There is no need to see them every day, no need to know them inside out and perhaps, come to think of it, not even any need to have actually seen them at all: the Faraglioni of Capri are part of us, embedded somewhere in our collective memory like an unconscious thought, like a deeply rooted memory we cannot pinpoint but which we can sense perfectly well. They are there, motionless like statues of young daughters of the island captured by a paralysis that rendered their beauty eternal just as they stepped away to plunge into the water and swim. For Homer, they were the boulders thrown at Odysseus by Polyphemus, for Virgil they were the home of the sirens who lured sailors with their song and then killed them, for others they have been guardians or symbols of fertility: indeed, it is difficult to escape the temptation to attribute to them a further meaning, one that goes beyond concrete reality. What is certain is that Stella, the closest to land, the Faraglione di Mezzo, with its famous arch and Scopolo, home to the endemic species of blue lizard, will continue to mesmerize the entire world, as from one hour to the next the light bathes them in different shades, as if they were meant to be admired endlessly. Then there is the submerged world of the Blue Grotto, a minimal opening in the rock that gives access to a cavity of about 195 feet (60 meters) in which the refraction of the sun's rays illuminates the water with an unreal light; the play of reflections touches every surface, transforming the color into a presence capable of upsetting and overturning every impression of what many call "the liquid cathedral." A place already known to the Romans, as evidenced by several submerged statues, it was rediscovered in the 19th century and, since then, many more times, as many as the number of guests who have entered it, willing to be ensnared by its magic.

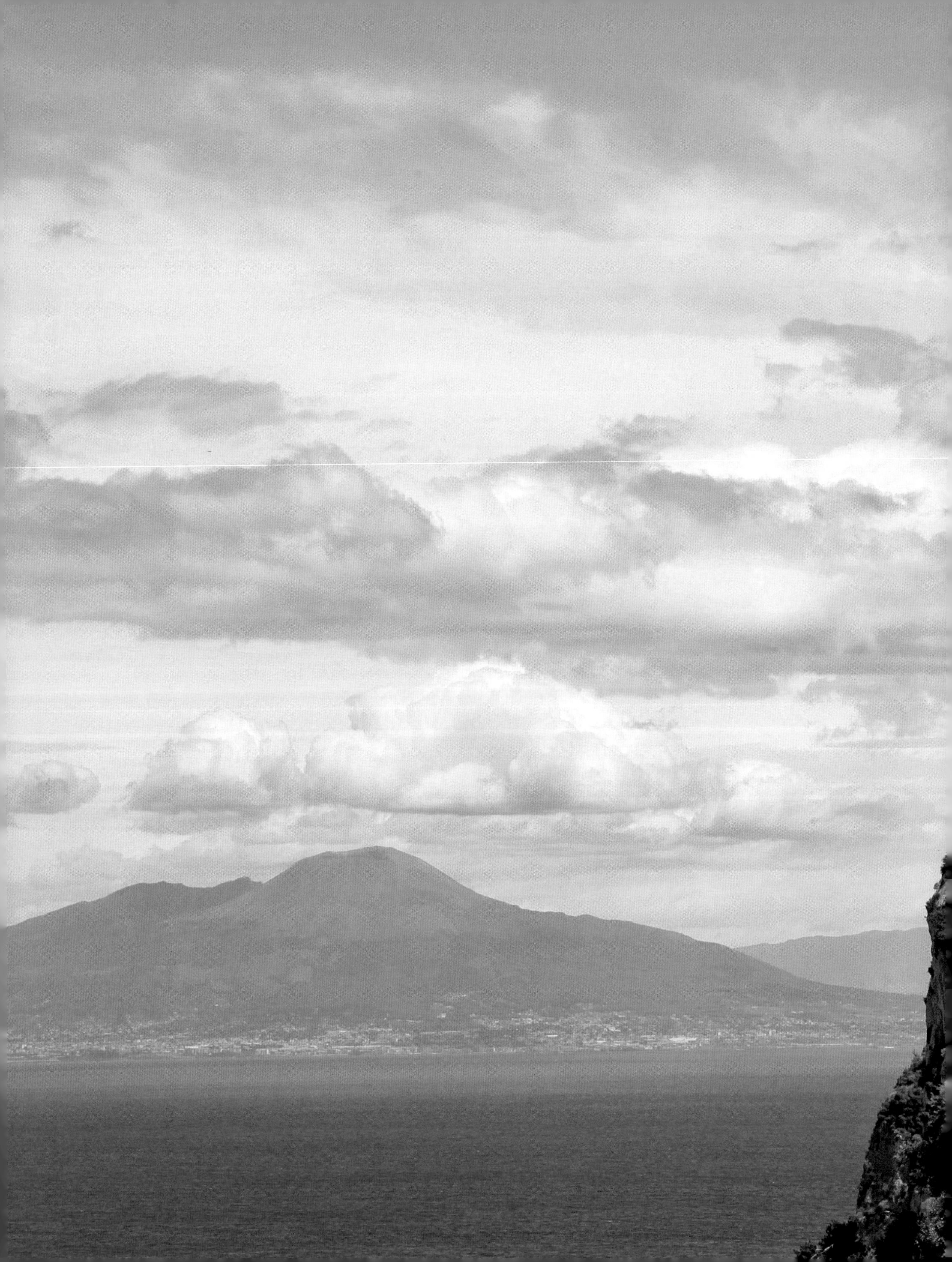

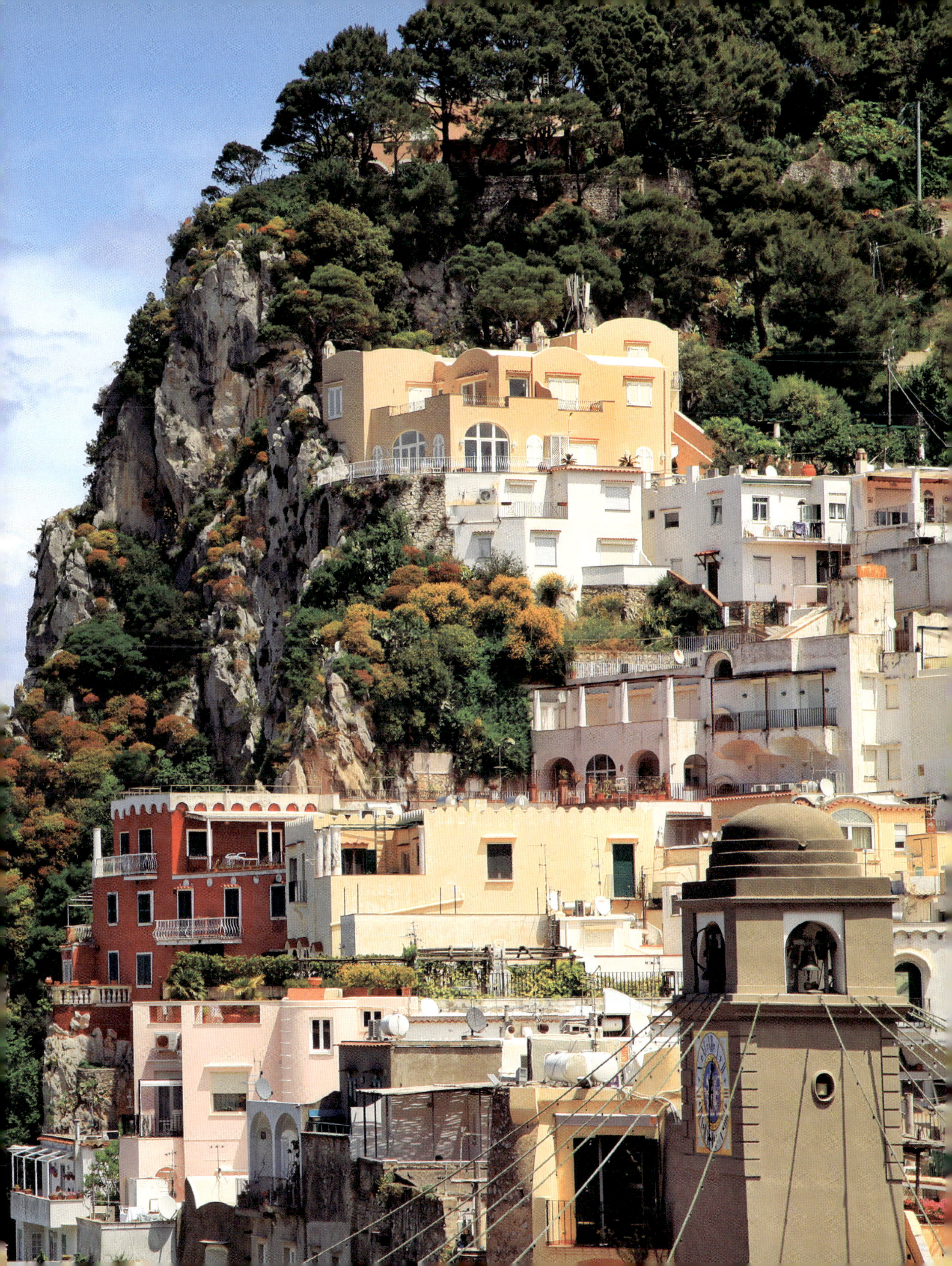

CAPRI FOR US

∾

LIKE ALL JEWELS CONSECRATED TO TOURISM, CAPRI RISKS BEING TRAPPED IN A GLASS SPHERE WITH FAKE SNOW, ONE OF THOSE SOUVENIRS THAT BETRAY THE VERY THING THEY ARE MEANT TO CELEBRATE.

It is impossible to ignore the ungainly throng that floods the famous piazzetta, the barbarian horde that invades the quarters and assaults the grottos and stacks, dotting the sea with boats, nor the presence of a wealthy elite that has made the prices of this sort of living brand unaffordable. This is life, this is fame. However, there is so much more to the place that has inspired writers, painters and directors such as Rainer Maria Rilke, Pablo Neruda, Norman Douglas, Alberto Moravia and Luigi Comencini. Mankind arrived here long before tourism, the Grotta delle Felci holds traces of prehistoric life, the Greeks passed through here, the Romans built sumptuous palaces here as a counterpoint to the wonders of the natural environment. Tiberius settled in the Villa Jovis residence, ruling the empire from afar; the ruins are still there, like a broken bridge between past and present. The island is divided into two towns, Capri and Anacapri, as different as two brothers who have made opposite choices in life can sometimes be and complement each other. The former is the showcase, the stage on which the international myth is staged, the latter is quieter, higher and more hidden, as precious as the views it offers. The same play between the visible and the invisible of the natural elements is repeated in the relationship between Capri and its people: on the one hand the high society, the ready-made and almost brazen offer, on the other the secret footpaths, the old memories and something that is only revealed to those who have the courage and patience to slow down or even stop for a while.

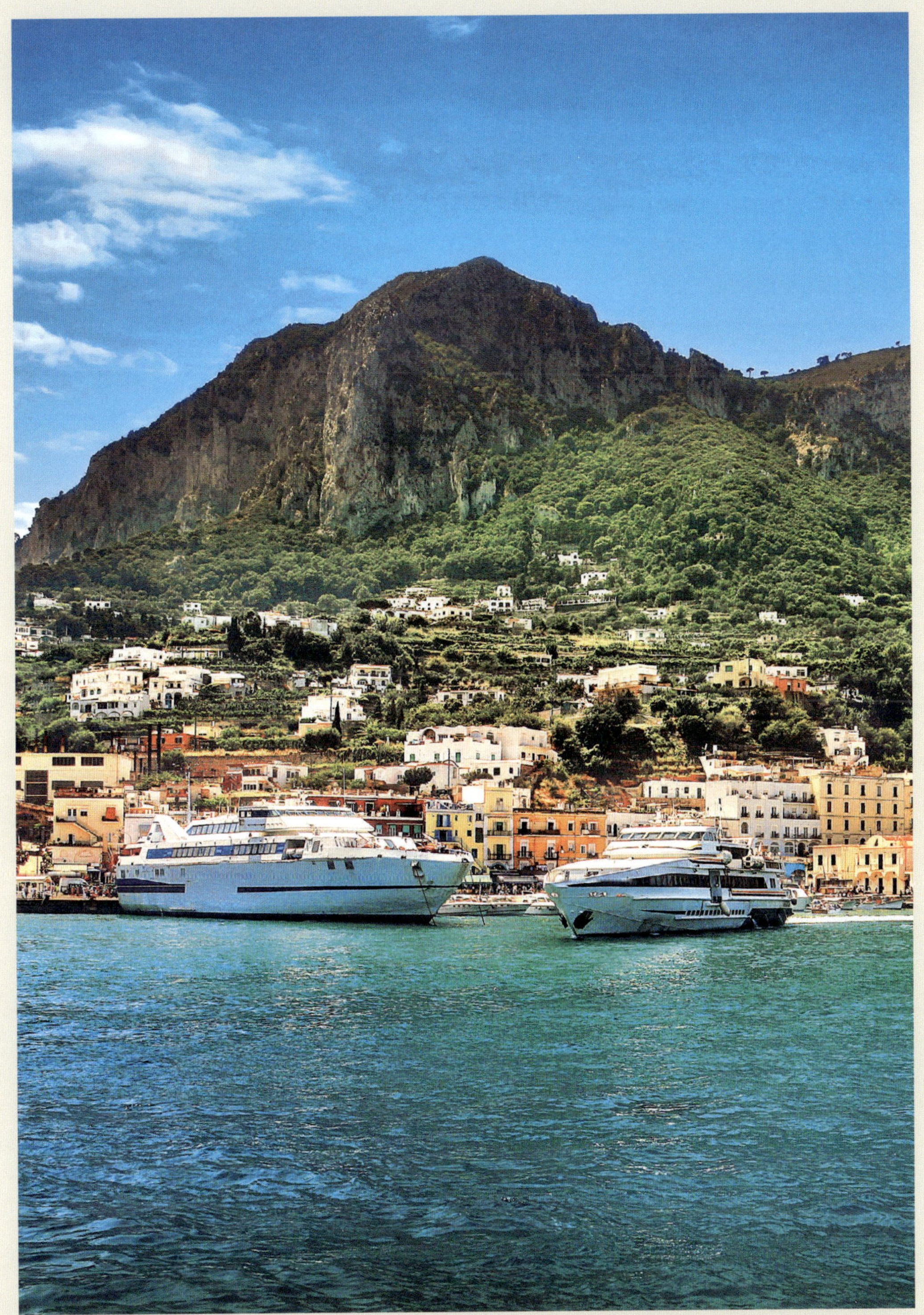

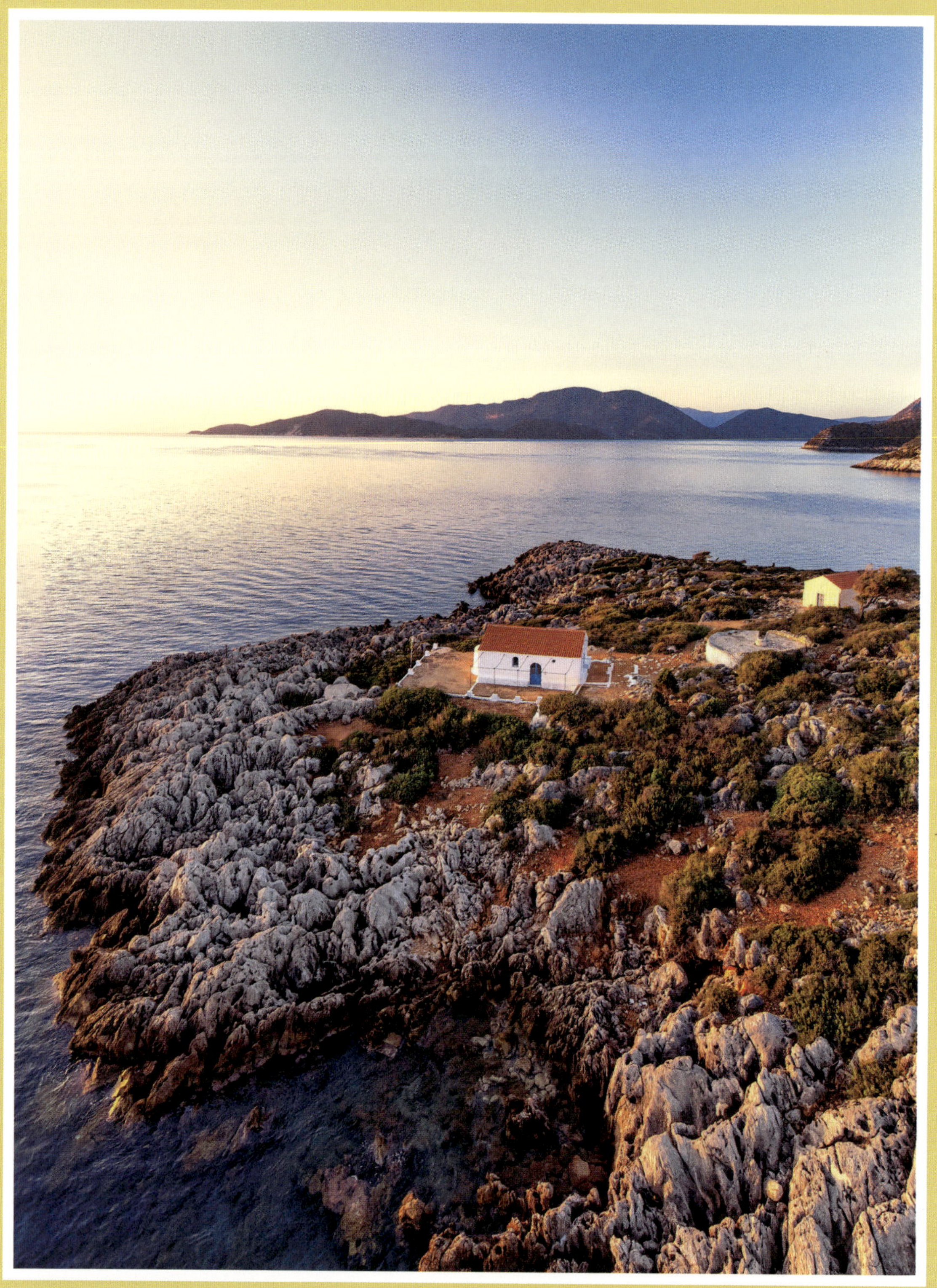

ITHACA

Geographical coordinates: 38°23'59" N; 20°41'21" E
Waters: Ionian Sea
Population: 2,863 inhabitants
Surface area: 45.09 square miles (116.80 km²)
Capital: Vathi

ITHACA, A PLACE TO STRIVE FOR

Ithaca does not show itself, does not reveal itself. Look it up on a map and you realize that it is smaller than you might have expected, set in the waters of the Ionian Sea like a pebble tossed for fun, without much thought. It has none of the theatrical profile of Santorini or the picture-postcard beaches of Mykonos. It is a stark island, stripped down but nonetheless precious, a place that gives itself only to those who have the patience to seek it out. Seen from afar, it resembles the lumpy back of a great marine animal, surfacing between Kefalonia and Lefkada. It has no plains, no easy roads, no shameless, effortlessly admired elegance. Here, the landscape is composed of rock and Mediterranean scrub, olive trees bent by the wind, cypresses like spearheads pointing skyward, cliffs plunging dramatically into the water, like a child who has grown tired of waiting for permission. Rather than long stretches of golden sand, the beaches are small, concealed coves of polished pebbles that disappear when the tide changes mood. The interior is a tangle of hills, dirt tracks and dry stone walls that no one knows who built or why. In certain places, the silence is so dense as to seem like noise. Then there is the sea, which makes its presence felt everywhere, even far from the coast. An Ionian Sea that changes color with the passing hours, from the pale blue of morning to the deep blue of sunset, through to the black of night that erases every nuance. Ithaca, severe and authentic, is not an island that welcomes you a priori, does not flatter, does not promise. If anything, it puts you to the test. And those who pass are unlikely to forget it.

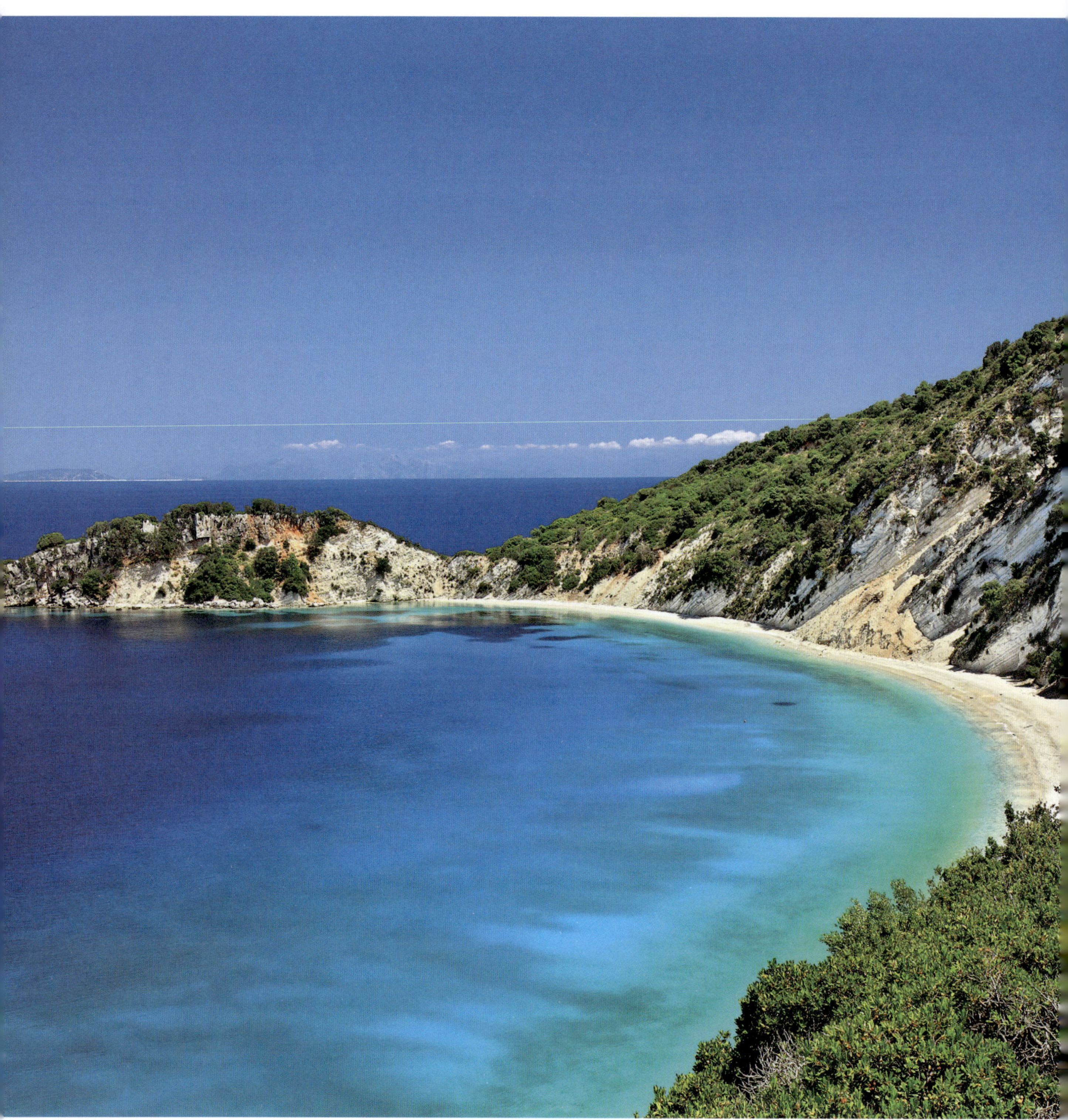

AN ENDLESS JOURNEY

~

Odysseus is both everywhere here and nowhere. Ithaca is his obsession, his destination, the horizon of a journey that does not end even when it ends. Wander around the island today looking for his palace, his olive bed, his bow or Penelope's famous web, any trace, no matter how timid, of his passage, and all you find is speculation. Archaeologists dig, they discuss, they compare fragments of pottery, but the truth is that Ithaca is more an idea than a place, or rather, the place exists as much as the idea, but the bridge connecting them concerns each individual's spiritual quest, without too many concrete footholds, and that's fine. Because Ithaca is not important for what it is, but for what it represents. It is the return, the yearning for home, the point from which one departs and to which one dreams of returning, but truly returning is pure utopia. Odysseus, who 20 years after setting out finds a different island, one undermined by arrogant suitors, knows this. Anyone who travels knows it: the place you leave is never the same when you return. So what remains? A name, a suggestion, the comfort of a place that awaits you even if it is different to how you remember it. Ithaca is a necessary illusion, the mirage that keeps us moving. There is more to Odysseus than his Homeric version, who, despite myriad difficulties, returns home and reclaims his throne; Odysseus is above all the figure Dante meets in the *Divine Comedy*. "Lo maggior corno della fiamma antica" tells a story that does not end in Ithaca at all. Indeed it is precisely this return that reveals that nothing can erase the desire to see the world: neither the sweetness of his son Telemachus, nor the pity that binds him to his father Laertes, nor his love for Penelope who had waited so long for him. And so Odysseus departs once again, without even stopping at the Pillars of Hercules, crossing the Strait of Gibraltar that marked the confines of the known world; here he pronounces the famous speech "Ye were not form'd to live the life of brutes, but virtue to pursue and knowledge high" and leads his companions on their last mad flight that would take them within sight of Mount Purgatory, interrupted by a divine storm that sinks the ship and swallows it into the sea.

THE ISLAND BEYOND THE MYTH

∾

IF YOU TAKE AWAY ODYSSEUS, WHAT IS ITHACA? AN ISLAND THAT LIVES WITHOUT CLAMOR OR COMMOTION. A PLACE THAT HAS NOT SOLD OUT TO MASS TOURISM, THAT HAS NOT TURNED ITS LEGEND INTO A THEME PARK. HERE THERE ARE NO MUSEUMS OR EVENING SHOWS ON HOMERIC SHIPS.

There are villages with white houses and blue shutters, streets that peter out in the middle of nowhere, taverns where time is marked by the glass of ouzo that someone fills for you as soon as you have emptied it, without even needing to ask. Vathi, the capital, is a quiet harbor, a semicircle of Venetian-style houses overlooking the sea, fishing boats swaying slowly, cats waiting for scraps of fish. Higher up, Anogi is a time warp village from another era, with Byzantine churches that no one advertises and an air of stubborn loneliness. Filiatro, Gidaki, Sarakiniko and Kaminia are just some of the beaches where the white pebbles exalt the color of the sea, often difficult to reach by land, protected by a backdrop of olive trees and tamarisk shrubs. Those who come here do so by choice, not by chance. Ithaca, as we have said, does not concede itself easily, but if you stay long enough and learn to follow its slow rhythm and respect its silence, you will feel part of her just as she will be part of you, and then it will be easier to convince yourself that you understand what Ulysses experienced and the reasons why it has been and will continue to be talked about for centuries.

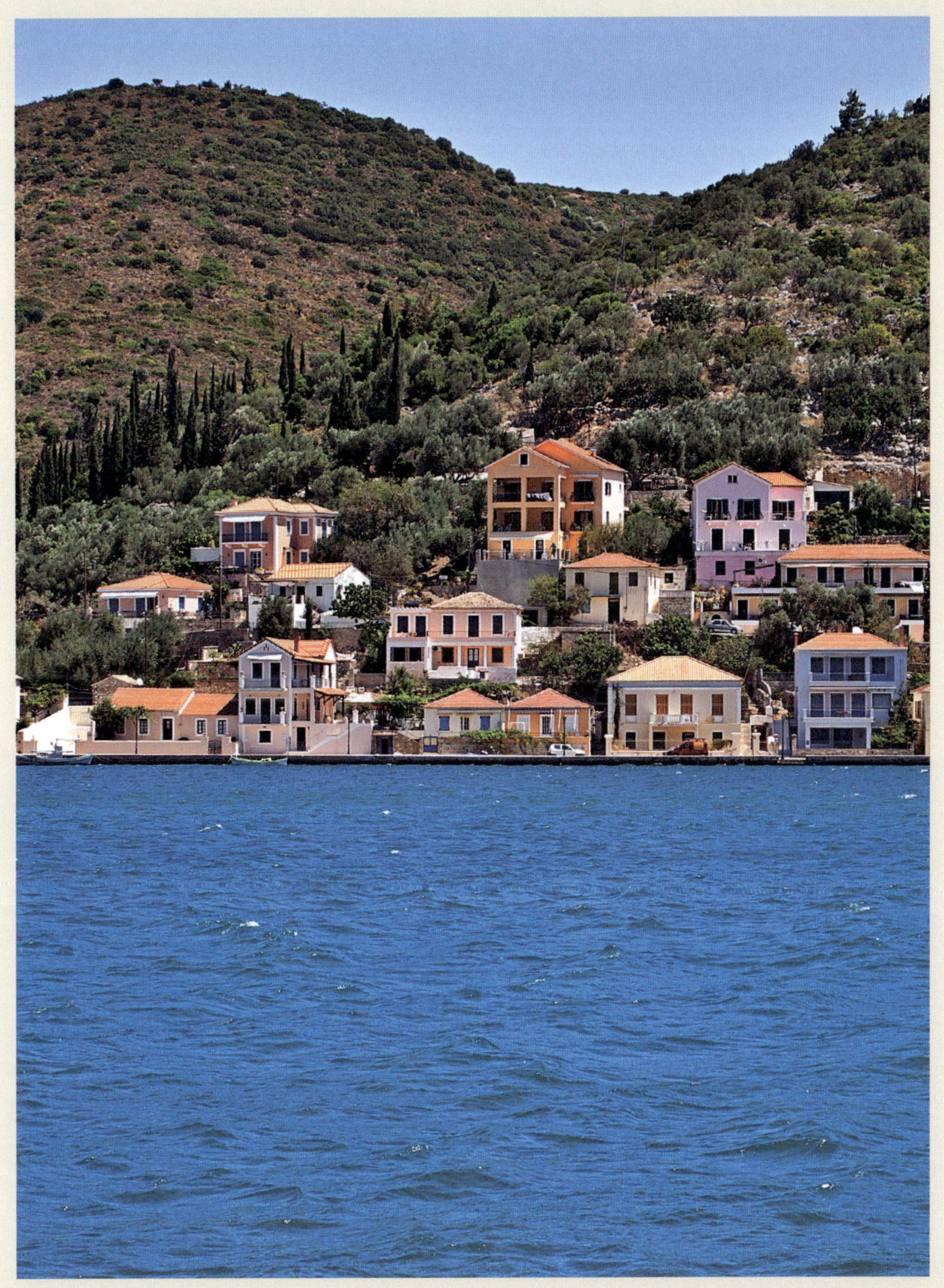

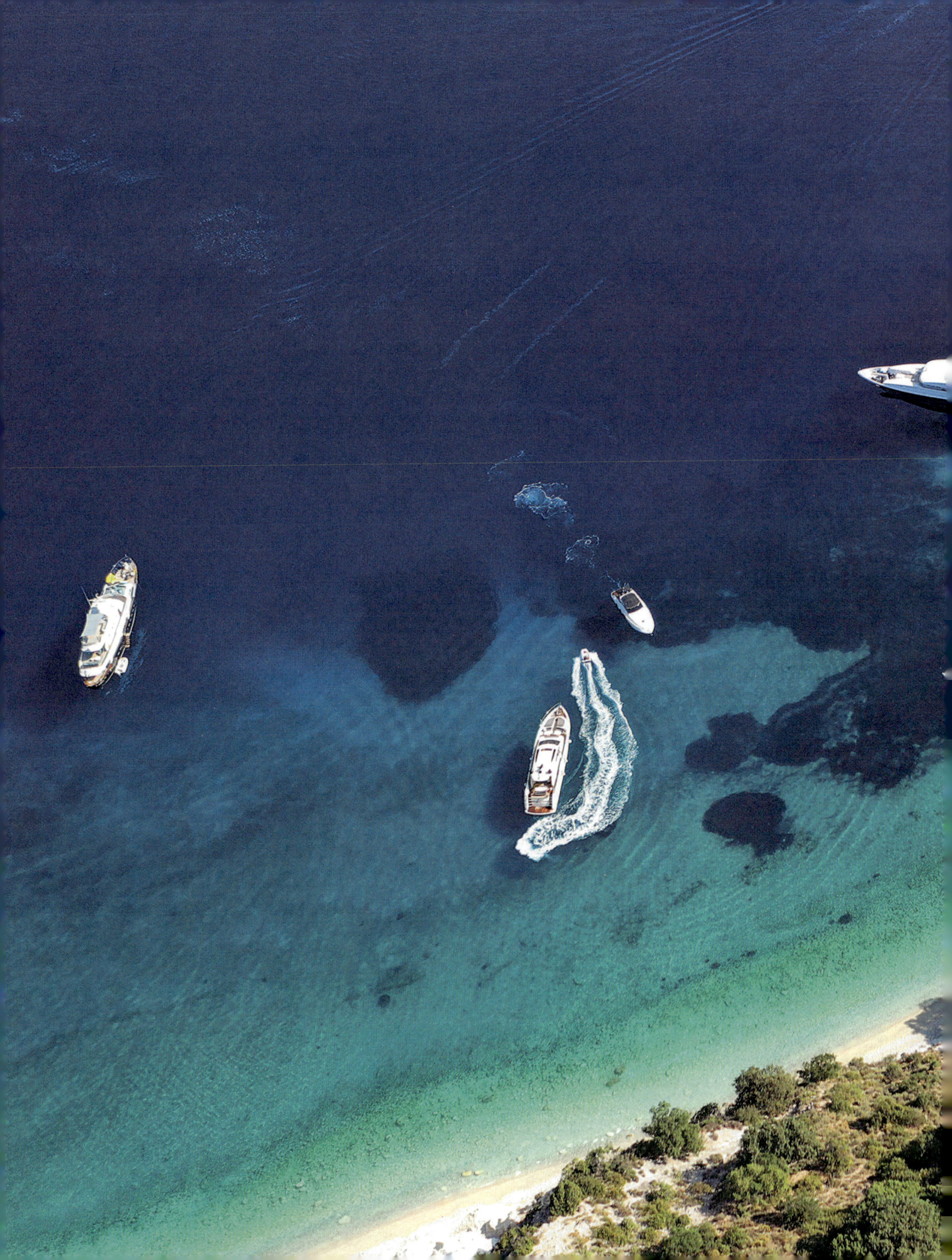

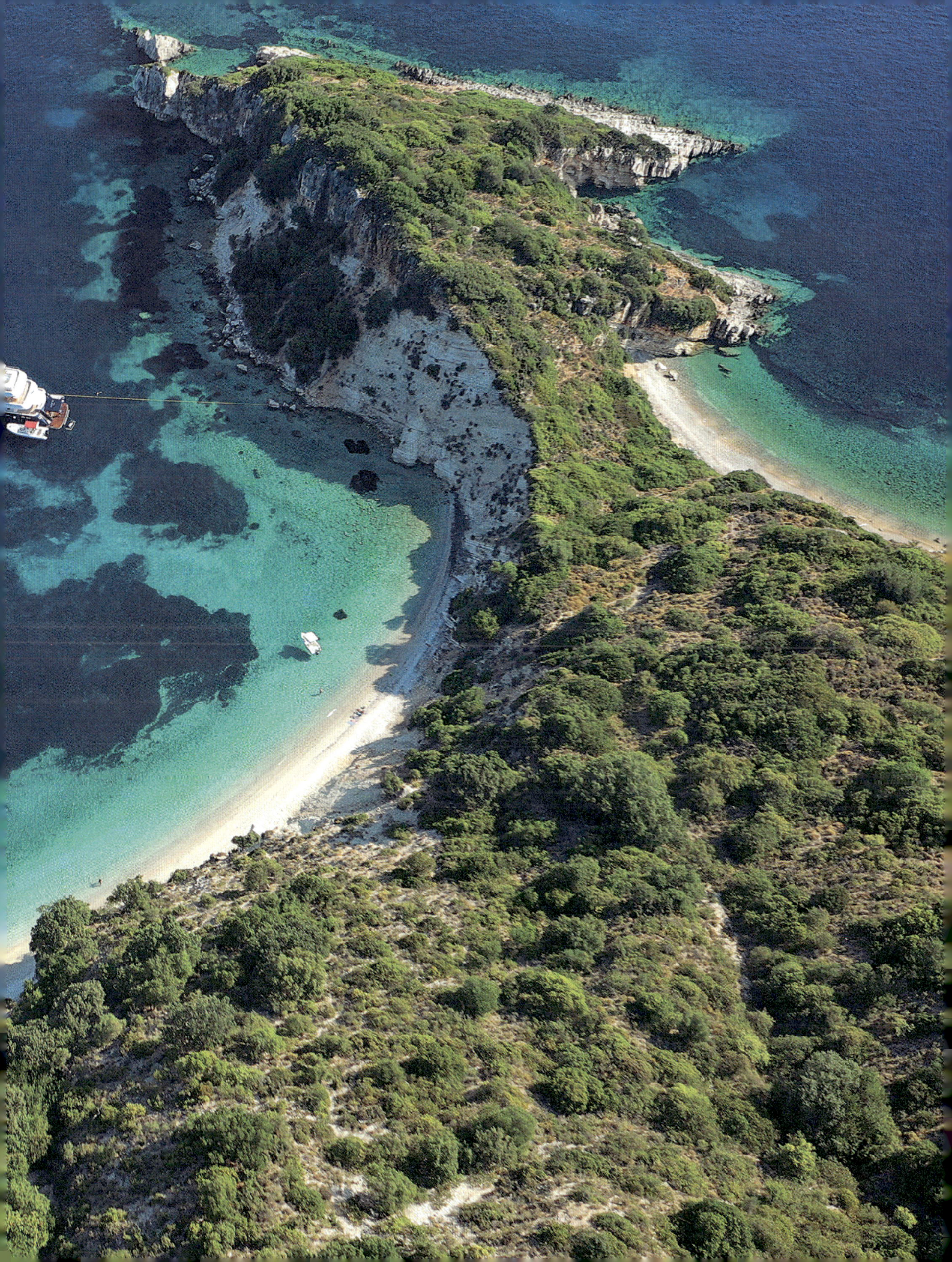

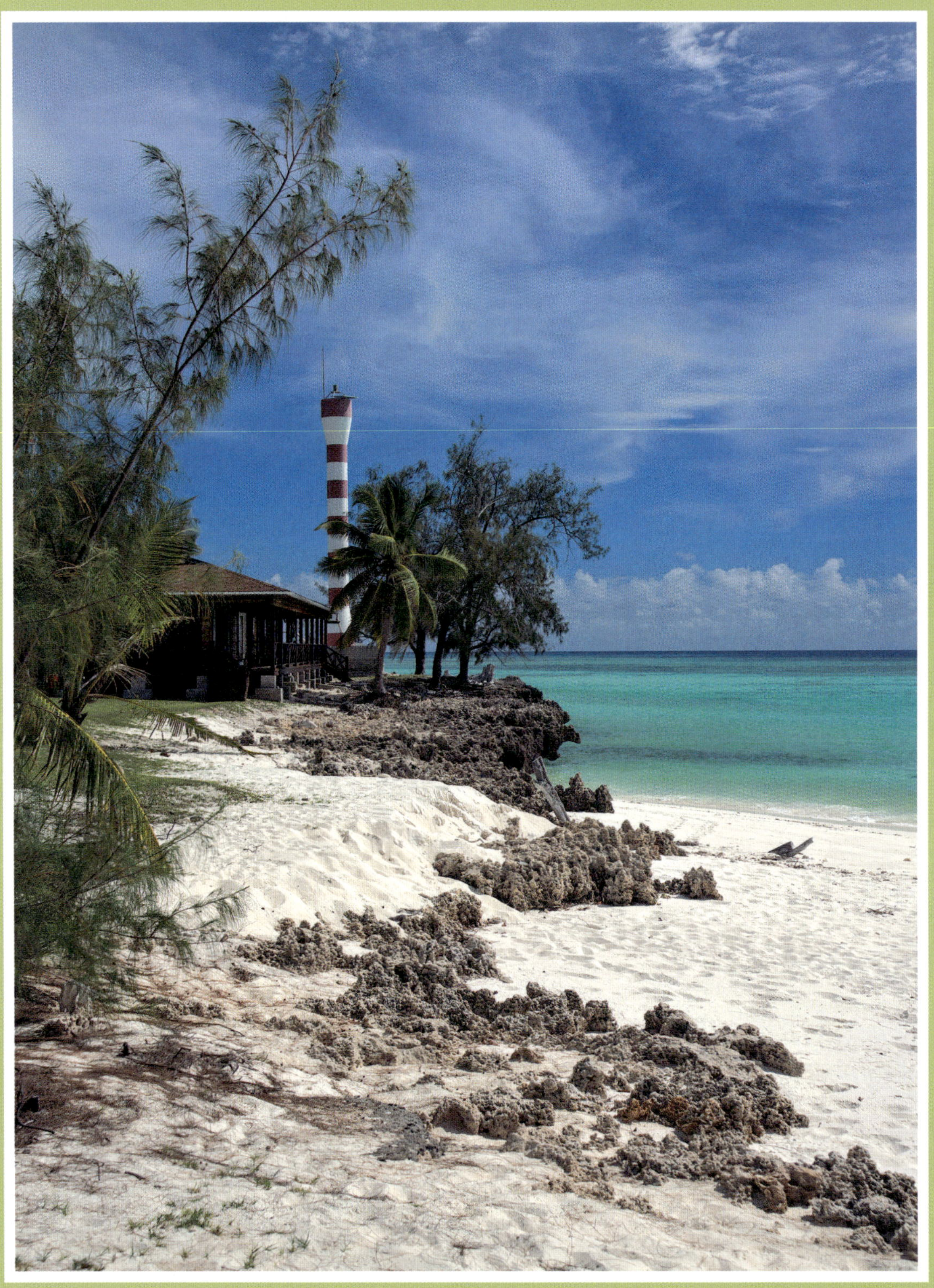

ALDABRA

Geographical coordinates: 9°25'00" S; 46°22'00" E
Waters: Indian Ocean
Population: no permanent inhabitants
Surface area: 59.84 square miles (155 km^2)

A PLACE OF DREAMS

Aldabra is a coral atoll in the Indian Ocean. It is located more than 620 miles (1,000 kilometers) from Mahé, the main island of the Seychelles, around 250 miles (400 kilometers) from Madagascar. Shaped like an immense ring, Aldabra consists of four main islands—Grande Terre, Malabar, Polymnieli and Picard—surrounding a vast inner lagoon connected to the open sea by a network of channels. The entire complex, which also comprises around 40 rocks and islets, sits on an ancient submerged volcano. The landscape is arid and windswept with scarce and seasonal rainfall. There are no rivers or sources of fresh water and the vegetation has adapted to the porous, relatively infertile limestone soil. The tides constantly reshape the atoll's interior, periodically submerging and revealing mudflats, coral reefs and ephemeral lakes. Mangrove swamps alternate with fossil coral formations, white sand and inaccessible stretches of sharp rock, making it almost impossible to move around on foot. Aldabra is remote, exposed to the elements, rough, precarious and wild. Landing here is difficult, and any attempt at permanent settlement is rejected like a foreign body. It is precisely this indomitable and inhospitable nature that makes it a unique place of environmental and scientific interest. Only a handful of scholars and a very restricted number of determined, patient and fortunate visitors have the privilege of setting foot here. Everyone else can only dream of this untouched place from home, leaving it unblemished, imagining it and admiring it through the photos and words of those who have been there.

A NARROW ESCAPE

~

Aldabra nonetheless has a history of contact with humanity and has risked becoming a victim of these landings. Known to the Arabs in the Middle Ages, who named it Al Khadra, the atoll was then visited by the Portuguese in the 16th century and skirted by French and British sailors, traders and slave traders. However, no one settled there permanently. The lack of fresh water and easy moorings along with the logistical difficulties discouraged any attempts at colonization. Aldabra was only used as a makeshift landing place for supplies or to gather natural resources. As early as the 18th century, giant tortoises were captured by the thousands for their meat and oil. In the 20th century, the introduction of invasive species such as goats and cats threatened the local ecosystem. In the 1960s, Aldabra faced its most serious threat when the British Royal Air Force drew up plans for the construction of a two-mile (three-kilometer) runway for a military base. This project was only blocked thanks to opposition from international scientists and environmentalists, including the Royal Society, in one of the first examples of global mobilization to safeguard the environment. Since then, Aldabra has taken a different path. The remains of a 19th-century settlement on Picard Island's coast—including a chapel, a prison, rainwater collection tanks and a few dwellings built to service economic activities such as turtle hunting and soon abandoned farming ventures—were given a new lease of life in 1971 when the Royal Society established a research station on the atoll. Aldabra has been recognized by UNESCO as a World Heritage Site since 1976 and is closed to tourism, except in extremely regulated forms. Around 15 researchers and support staff live in spartan conditions at the scientific base, which is now managed by the Seychelles Islands Foundation (SIF). They are dedicated to monitoring and conserving this unique ecosystem, with occasional external connections and scarce supplies.

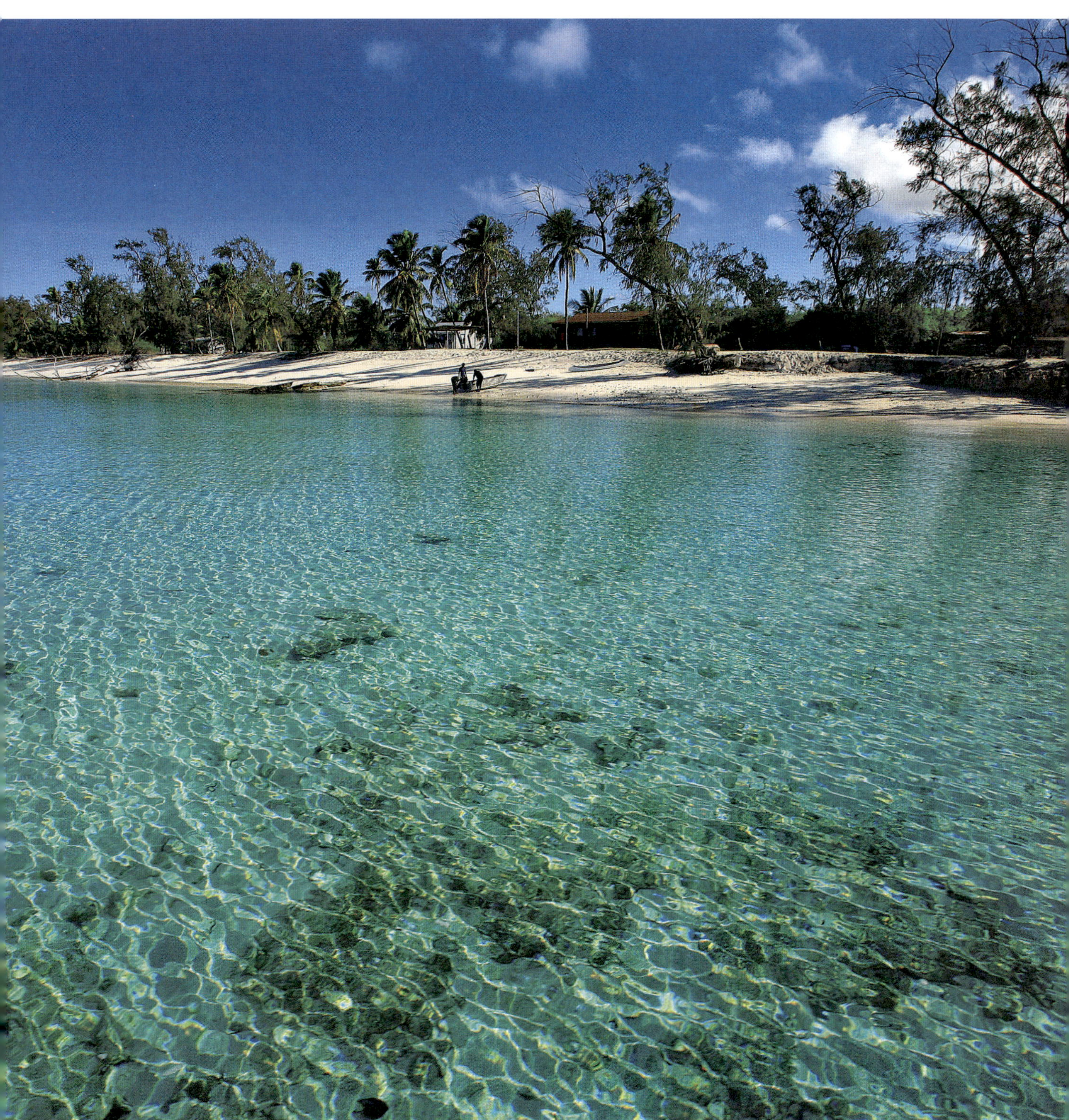

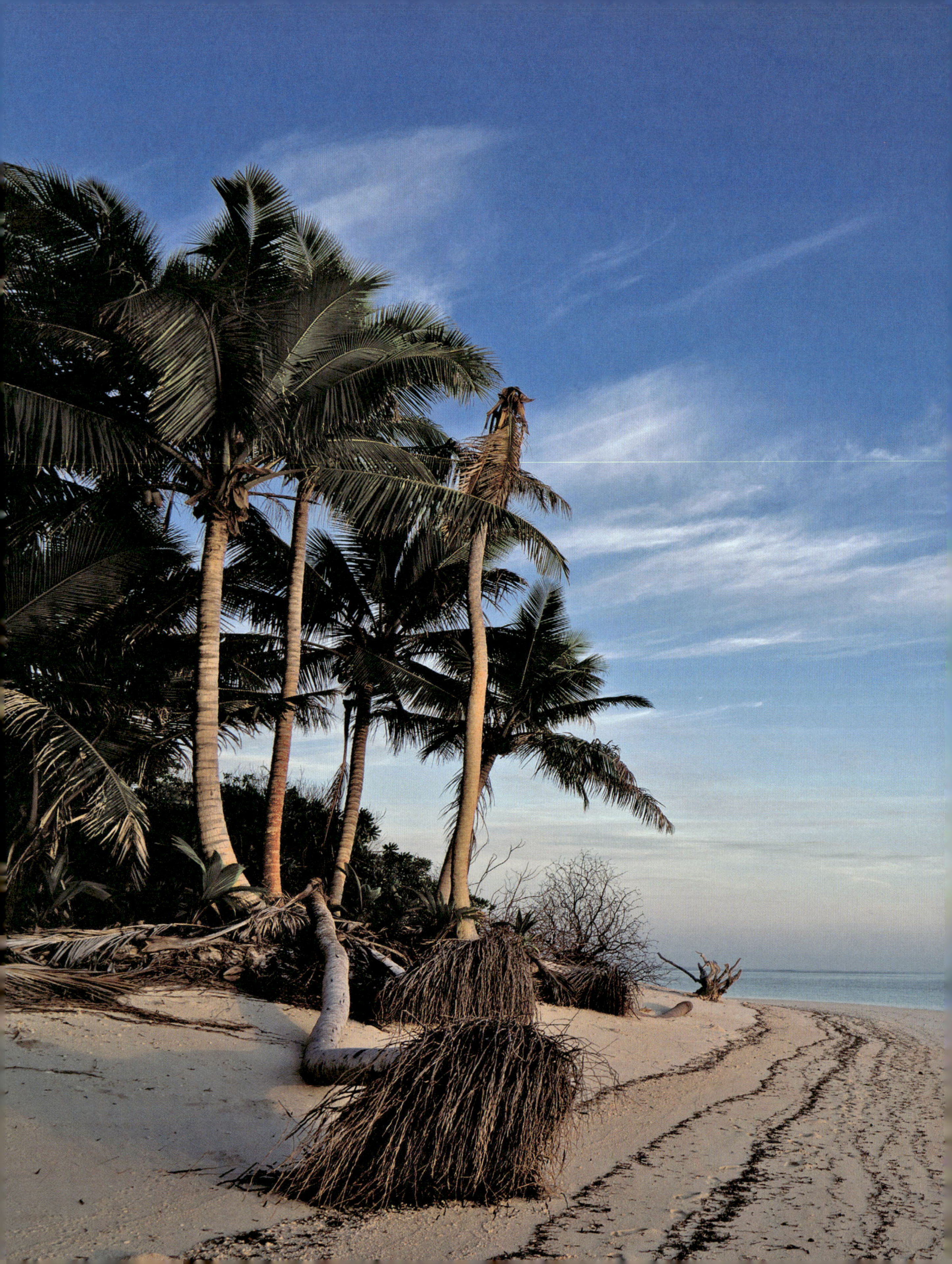

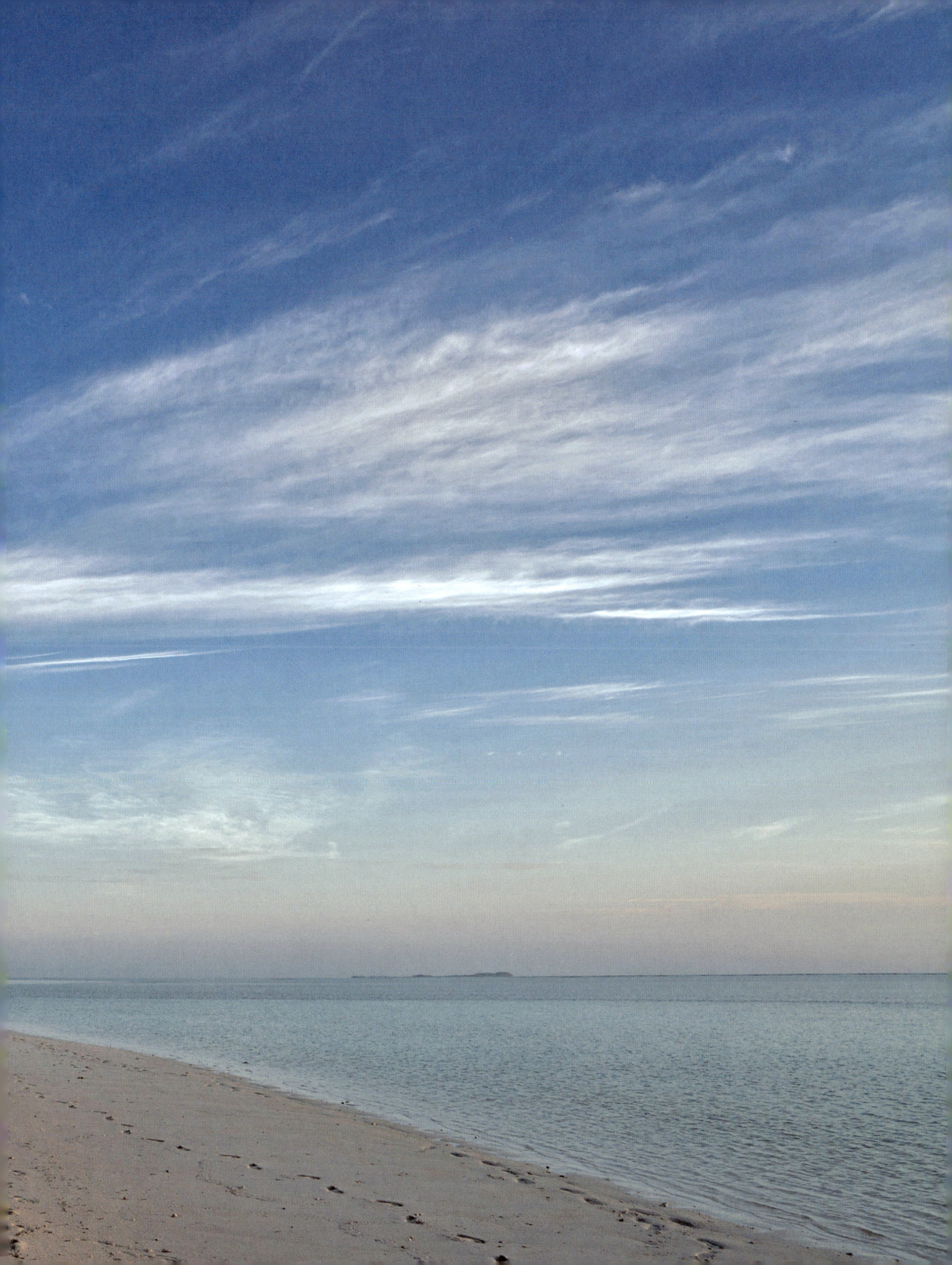

THE TURTLE ARMY

NATURE HERE HAS FOLLOWED ITS OWN PATH, WITHOUT COERCION OR MANIPULATION. OVER 400 PLANT SPECIES HAVE ADAPTED TO THE POOR LOCAL SOIL. THESE INCLUDE ENDEMIC SPECIES THAT ARE UNIQUE TO THIS PART OF THE WORLD.

There is an absolute synergy between the plants and animals: the plants provide shelter and refuge for the animals, who in turn help to disperse seeds and regenerate the flora. Immense colonies of birds dominate the skies—frigatebirds, gannets, herons and terns—and nest along the coast and among the mangroves. Lemon sharks, stingrays, moray eels and sea turtles swim in the water, and Aldabra's beaches offer turtles an ideal place to lay their eggs. However, the most iconic creature is the Aldabra giant tortoise, the sole survivor of an ancient group of tortoises that once inhabited the islands of the Indian Ocean. Today, there are around 100,000 of these tortoises, making it the largest wild population on the planet. The tortoise has become such an integral part of the landscape that it influences the distribution of vegetation: it moves slowly among the rocks, rests in the shade of trees and bushes, and digs with its feet to search for food, creating paths on the ground as it goes. Despite being at risk of extinction for centuries, the tortoise has managed to survive here thanks to the inaccessibility of this habitat. It is a sad ecological paradox: the more inhospitable a place is to humans, the more likely it is to harbor biodiversity. However, we must remain vigilant, as tourism projects such as the one planned by a Qatari fund on the nearby island of Assumption could threaten the delicate balance of Aldabra, which currently resists, defended by its army of placid tortoises.

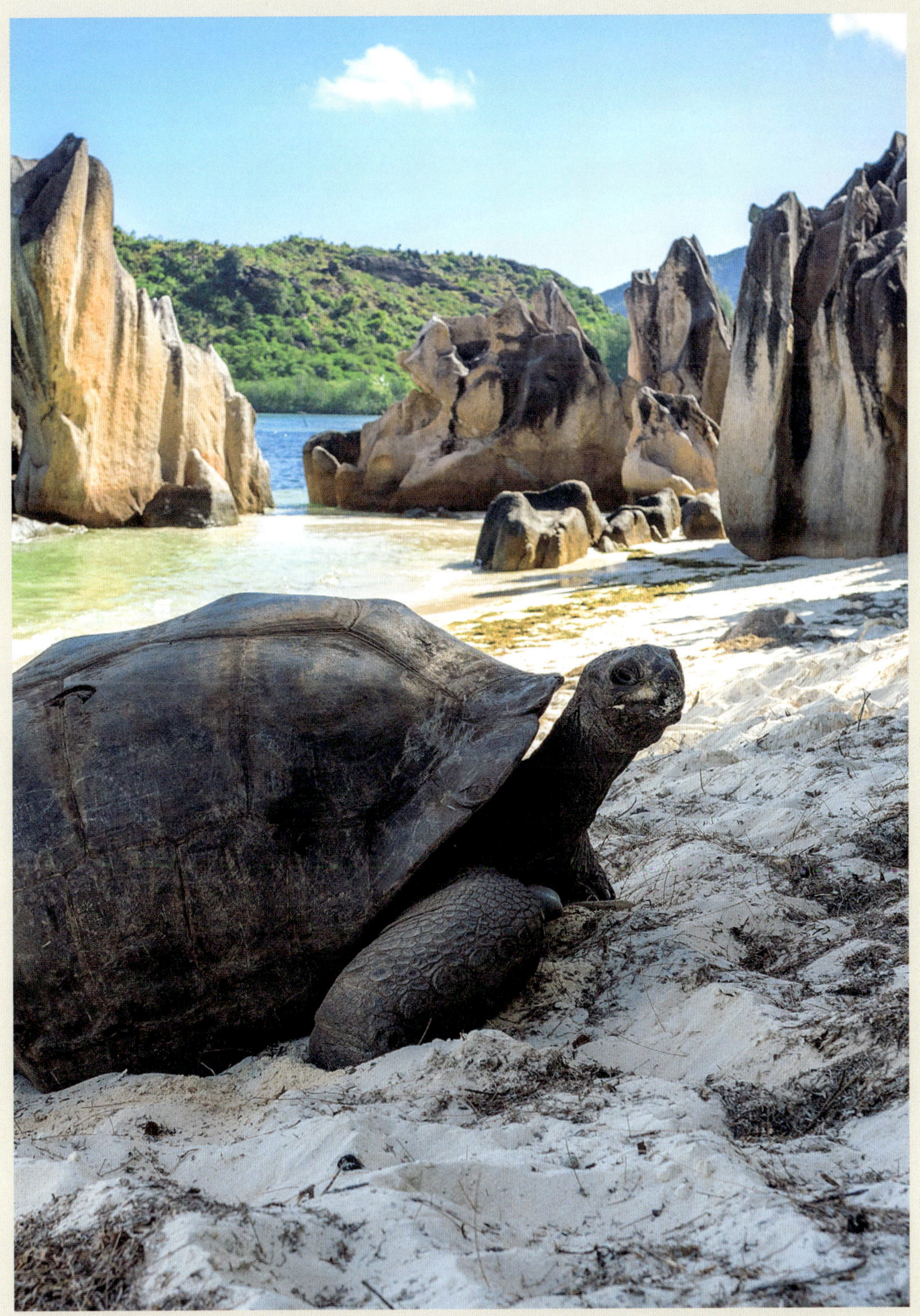

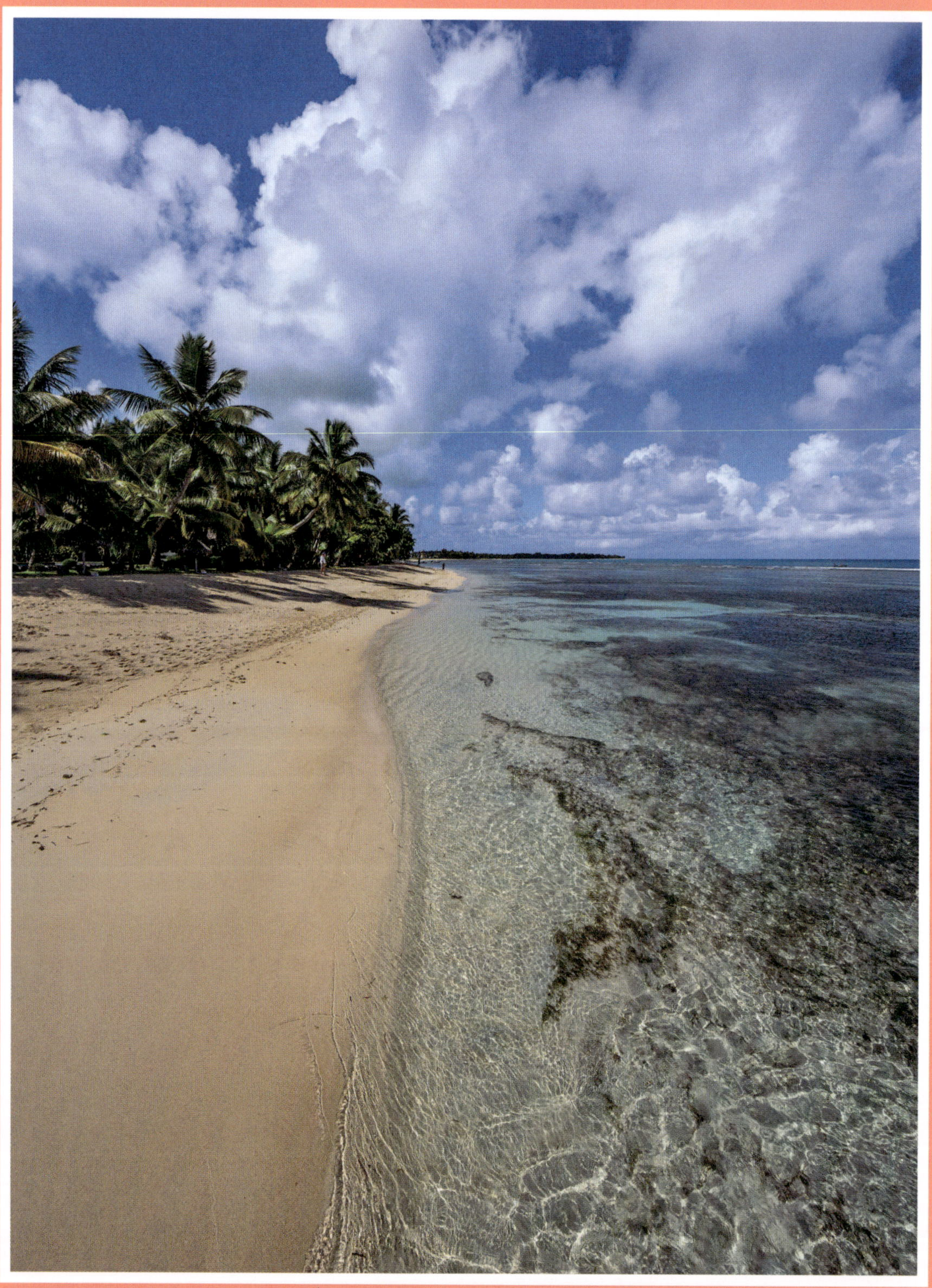

SAINTE-MARIE (OR NOSY BORAHA)

Geographical coordinates: 16°54'0" S; 49°54'0" E
Waters: Indian Ocean
Population: 26,547 inhabitants
Surface area: 85.71 square miles (222 km^2)

THE QUEEN OF MADAGASCAR

This long, thin strip of land, a granitic island around 37 miles (60 kilometers) in length and 3 miles (5 kilometers) wide, offers a stark contrast between the colors of the sea, the white sand and the bright green of the inland trees. Just 5 miles (8 kilometers) from the east coast of Madagascar, the island of Nosy Boraha was sighted by Portuguese navigators on the 15th of August, 1503, Assumption Day, a detail that prompted the explorers to name it after the Virgin Mary. In fact, according to local legends, the discoverer of the island was a humble fisherman named Boraha, who was dragged and tossed around by a whale while on his pirogue, only to be rescued by a dolphin that helped him closer to the shore; according to other versions, the man was some kind of explorer, and rather than tossing him around, the whale actually rescued him from a shipwreck and deposited him safe and sound on the island. Perhaps it was precisely the island's seclusion and its wealth of subsistence resources, a remote yet welcoming place, that made it an ideal landing stage for vessels plying the Indian Ocean trade routes. Still today, its waters conserve the remains of ships sunk in the 18th century, stranded on its rich and colorful seabed. In addition to the wonders of the coral reefs, this place is also home to a pristine tropical forest, populated by lemurs and precious plants such as the orchid *Eulophiella roempleriana*, endemic to the area, which clings to the leaf axils of trees for nourishment. Waterfalls, caves and the natural pools sacred to the locals also complete the landscape.

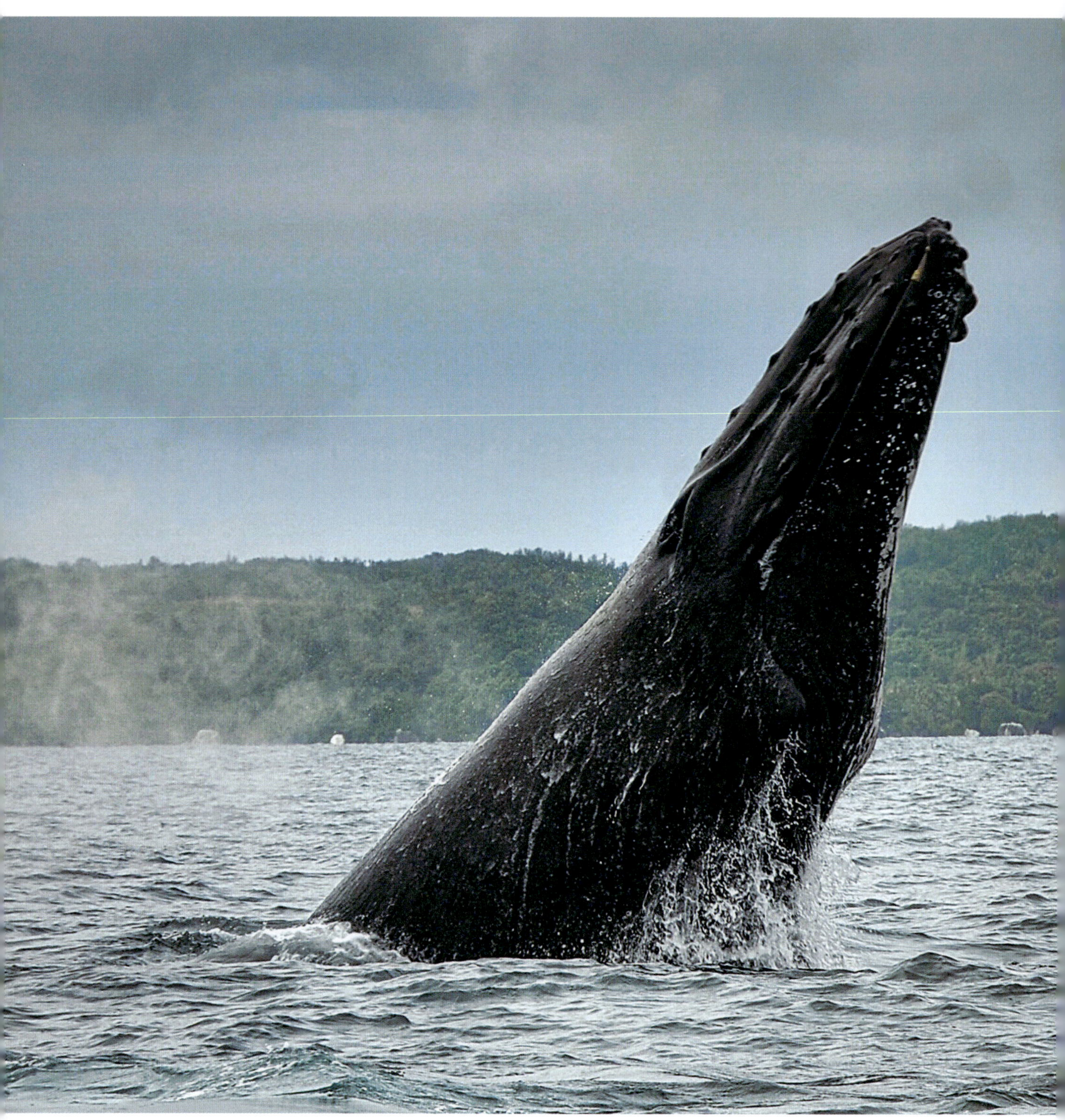

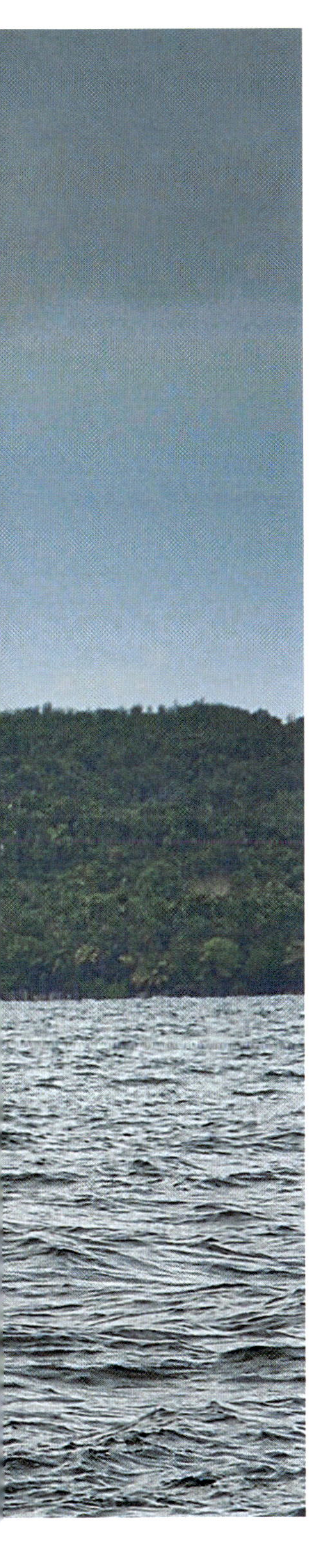

THE DANCE OF THE HUMPBACK WHALES

~

Ranging in length from 50 to 65 feet (15 to 20 meters) and weighing up to 40 tons, humpback whales are much smaller at birth, 10 to 13 feet (3 to 4 meters) long and 1.5 tons in weight. They can ingest up to 4,450 pounds (2,000 kilograms) of plankton per day, but feed mainly in cold waters near the poles. They trap fish in a kind of net created with air bubbles and then swallow them by rushing to the surface. When they move to tropical waters to reproduce, they use their accumulated fat reserve. Despite their size, they are capable of leaping clear of the water and perform a variety of manoeuvres; they are sociable and curious animals, even toward humans; they sometimes sing. Humpback whales, which live to between 50 and 80 years old, are among the most extraordinary creatures we can observe, and fortunately their numbers are increasing. They can swim at around 15 miles per hour (25 kilometers per hour) and they travel great distances, completing immensely long migrations between the poles and the equator, grinding out thousands of miles. The channel between Nosy Boraha and Madagascar is an ideal area for the mating and reproduction of these majestic cetaceans, so between July and September there is an intensive coming and going of humpback whales, a remarkable spectacle destined to leave a mark on your soul.

IN THE PIRATES' LAIR

THE STORIES SURROUNDING SAINTE-MARIE HAVE AN APPEAL CLOSELY LINKED TO THE IMAGINATION OF CHILDREN. GIVEN ITS STRATEGIC LOCATION ALONG THE EAST INDIES TRADE ROUTE, IT PROVIDED AN IDEAL REFUGE FOR MARAUDING SEAFARERS DEDICATED TO WAYLAYING THE VESSELS PLYING THOSE WATERS. OVER THE CENTURIES IT BECAME A TRUE ISLAND OF PIRATES WHO LIVED HERE PERMANENTLY AND CONCEALED THEIR SHIPS IN THE NUMEROUS INLETS AFTER THEIR RAIDS.

Today, it is still possible to visit what remains of the pirates' cemetery, which now has only about thirty graves: apparently many were desecrated by seekers of imaginary treasures, who in all probability were left empty handed. According to several unconfirmed theories, Sainte-Marie was also the site of the famous anarchist colony Libertalia—which, however, many place elsewhere, if it is not purely imaginary—an enclave of marauders described by Captain Charles Johnson in his *A General History of the Pyrates* in 1724. In the name of God and freedom, this handful of revolutionaries had declared war on civil society, founded on prevarication and oppression. Hence the *freemen* plundered ships and rescued the slaves carried on them, inviting them to join their community based on sharing and direct democracy. While the fate of this legendary experience also seems to be linked to bloody conflicts with the Malagasy populations, in reality it seems that on the island the pirates integrated with the locals, giving rise to a new mixed-blood ethnic group called the Zana-Malata. Among those said to have lived on Sainte-Marie, the names of Robert Culliford, Thomas Tew and William Kidd resonate. The latter, according to some, is buried in the island's cemetery—upright, standing, to atone for his earthly sins, of which there was no lack—while it is historically known that his death sentence was pronounced in London, followed by a long display of the body hanging as a warning to those who would emulate him. Captain Kidd, in fact, had begun his career as a privateer in the pay of the crown tasked with attacking French ships, but then turned to the craziest and most nefarious raids, obviously also at the expense of the East India Company.

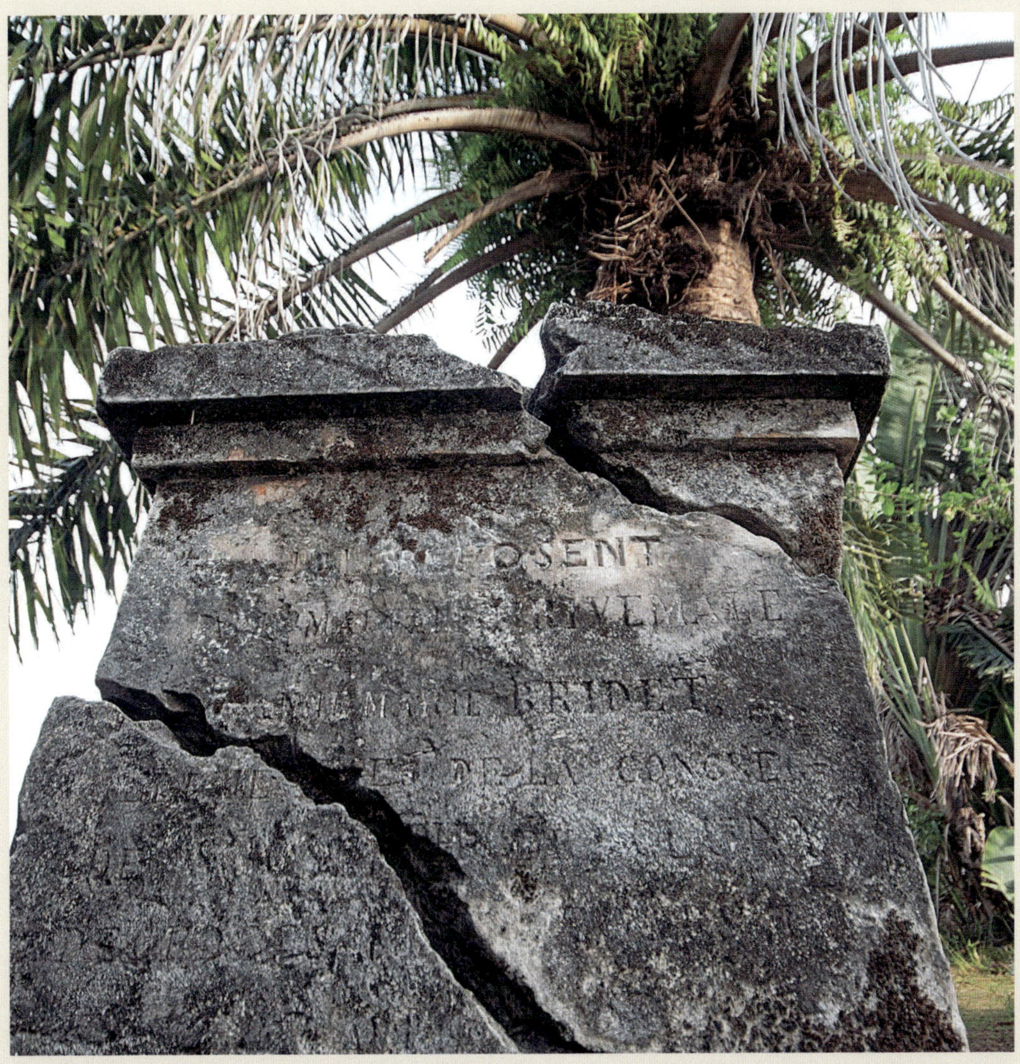

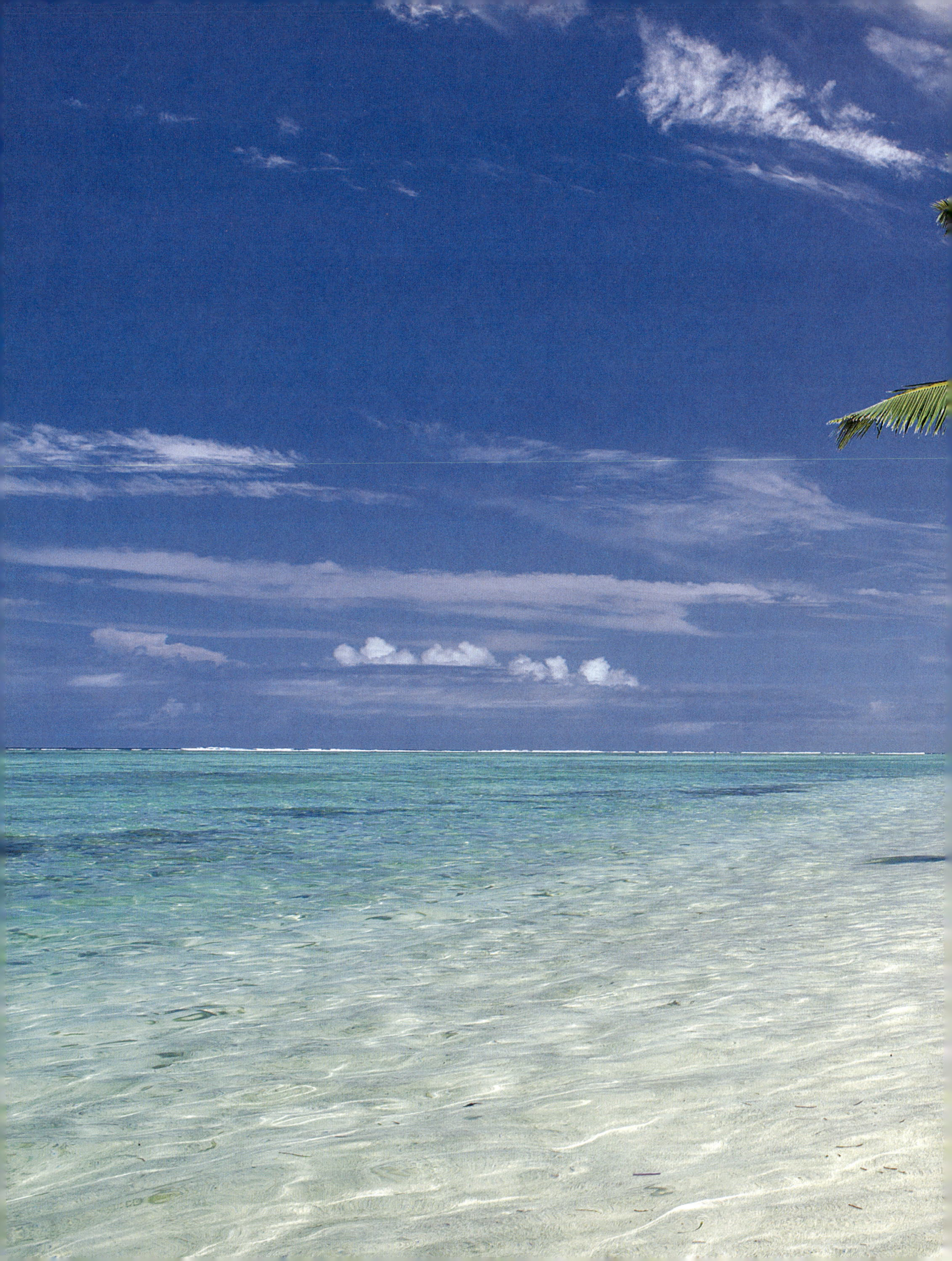

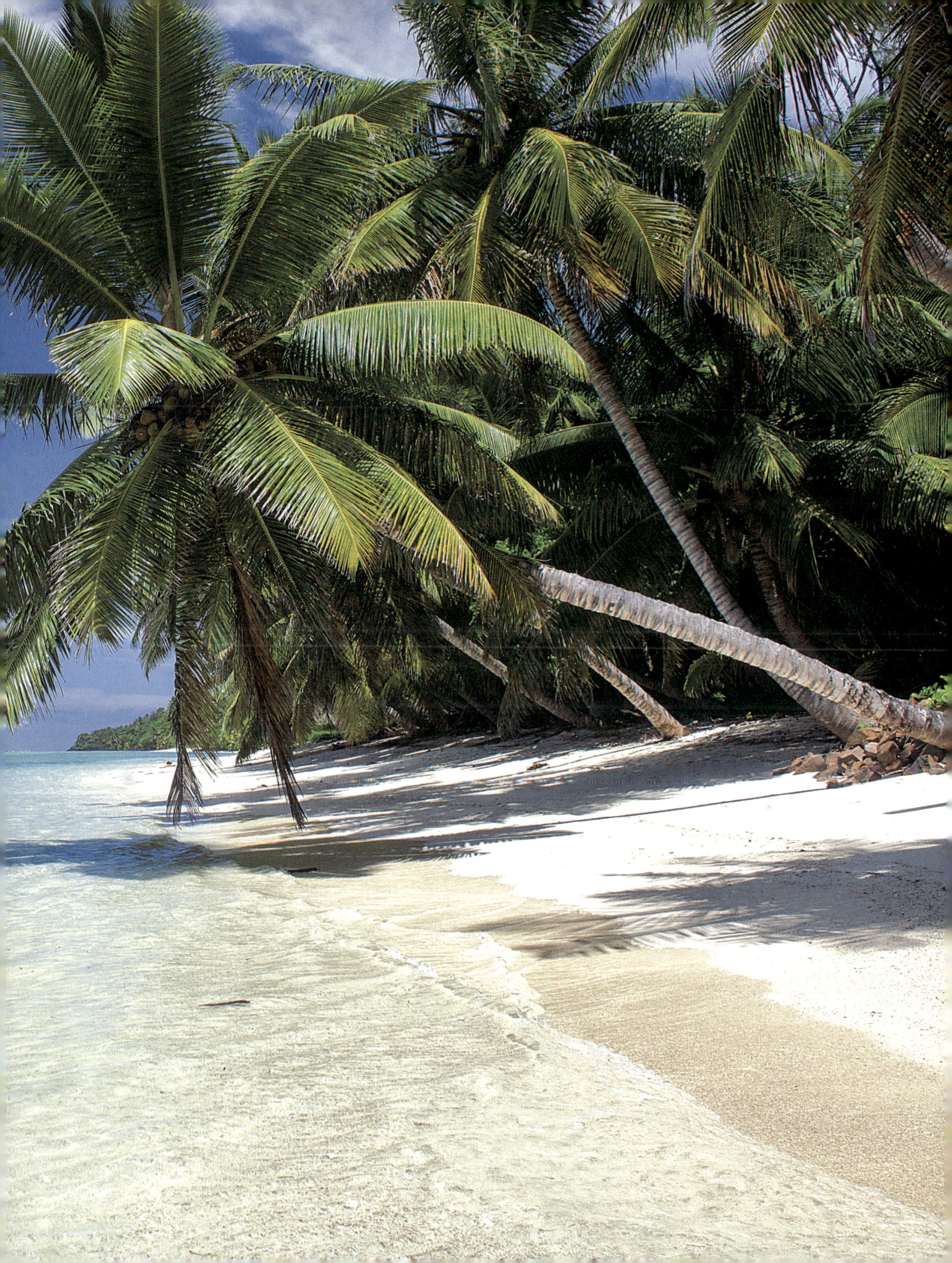

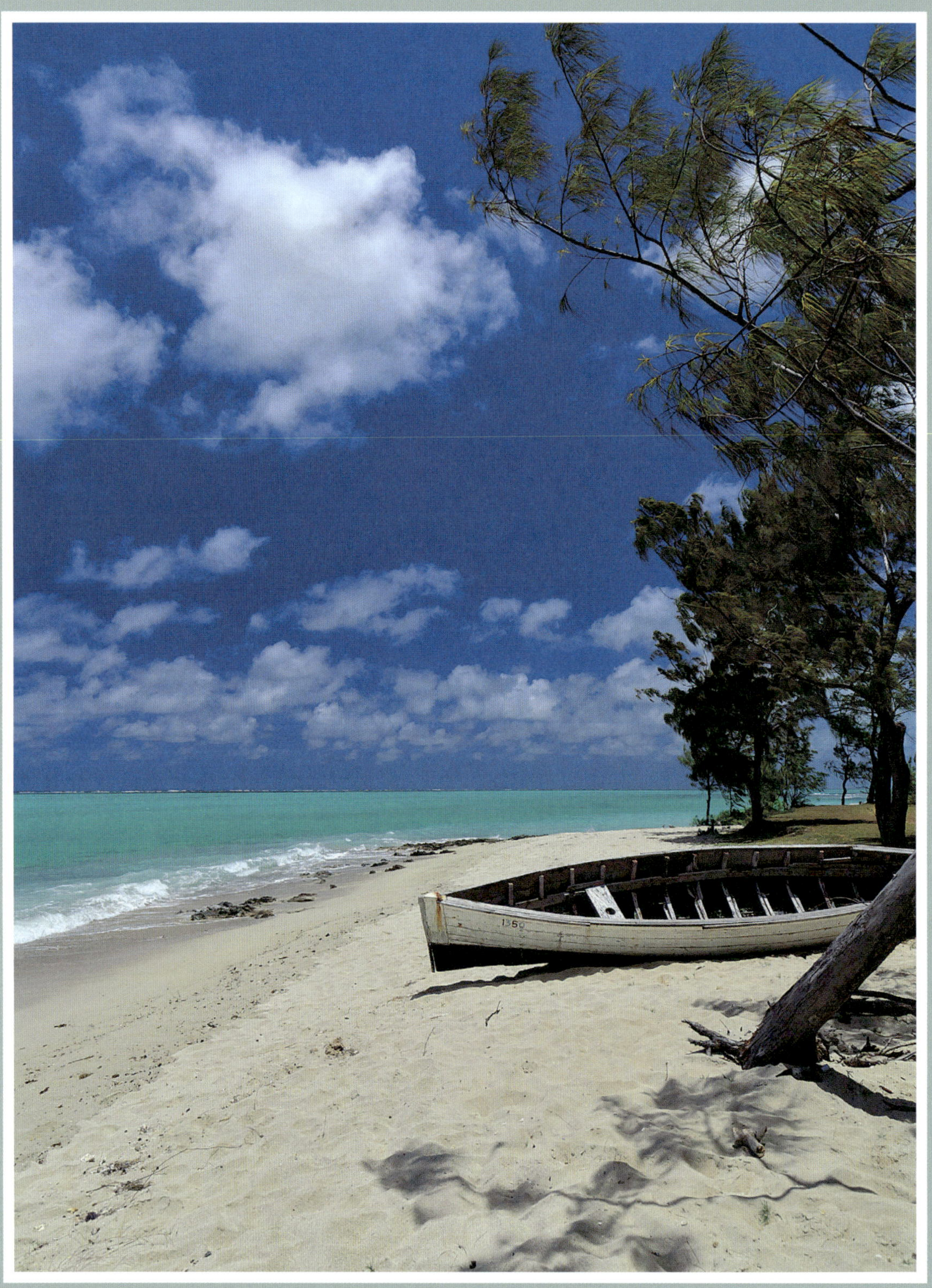

Mascarene Islands, Mauritius

RODRIGUES

Geographical coordinates: 19°43'00" S; 63°25'00" E
Waters: Indian Ocean
Population: 44,427 inhabitants
Surface area: 41.69 square miles (108 km²)
Capital: Port Mathurin

PRESENT AT A REMOTE DISTANCE

It lies there in the midst of the blue, a remote dot in the Indian Ocean we might vaguely liken to Madagascar, but only to note how far away it is from everything else. This is a place that shows us just how big our little planet is and just how insignificant and tiny we are. However, the concepts of center and periphery become blurred and overlap, because this is a microcosm in its own right: we are on Rodrigues, the easternmost and most remote of the Mascarene Islands, located over 370 miles (600 kilometers) from Mauritius, to which it belongs politically but from which it is distinguished by its geography, atmosphere and lifestyle. Of volcanic origin, the island is relatively young—one or two million years old—and has an undulating, never harsh landscape. The highest point, Mont Limon, reaches an altitude of 1,275 feet (389 meters), but rather than dominate the landscape, it accompanies the gaze along green ridges and flat cultivated areas. Around the island lies one of the largest lagoons in the Indian Ocean, protected by a continuous coral reef. The inland area alternates between pastures, family plantations and wooded areas undergoing regeneration. The soil, of poor quality but workable, has favored a simple rural lifestyle based on subsistence farming and the raising of livestock. The climate is tropical. The hot, humid summer from December to April is punctuated by typhoons, while a drier and windier season exists during the rest of the year. The overall effect is discreet, harmonious and sober: Rodrigues is small and self-sufficient; life goes on a stone's throw from the sea and far from everything else.

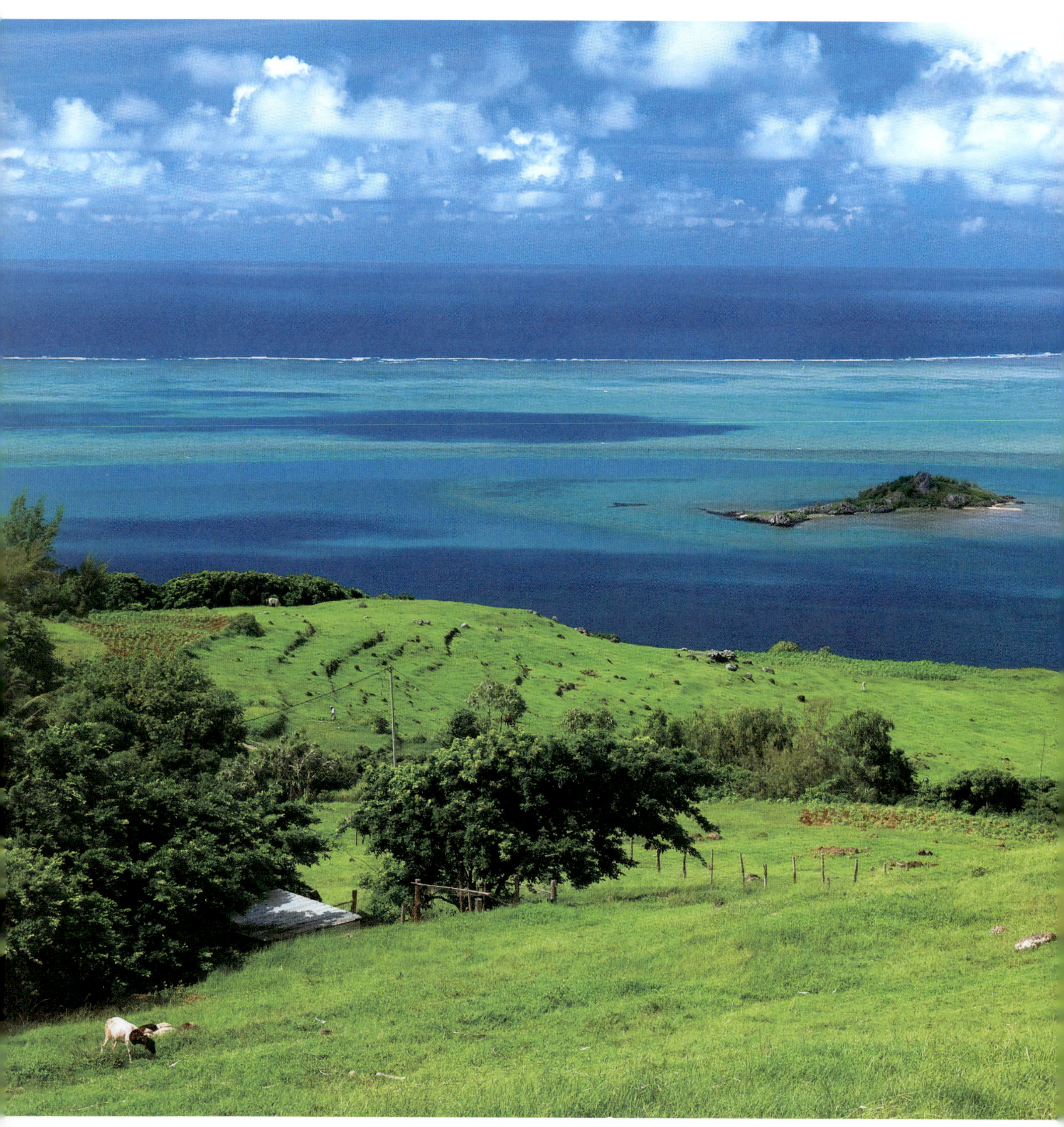

A PERIPHERAL HISTORY

~

Rodrigues takes its name from the Portuguese explorer Diogo Rodrigues, who sighted it in 1528. During the course of the following century, it was used sporadically by the Dutch as a staging post. In 1691, the Huguenot François Leguat and seven other men were left on the island for a couple of years to try to establish an agricultural colony, but without success. The experiment ended with a dramatic return to Europe, but the descriptions Leguat subsequently wrote are considered to be of great naturalistic value. The island remained uninhabited until the 18th century, when the French began to colonize it with small but strategic settlements. Like elsewhere, the introduction of slavery transformed the place into a hub for the mustering and exploitation of African and Malagasy labor, some of which was used to cultivate coconuts, corn and manioc. After Mauritius passed into British hands in 1810, Rodrigues also flew a different flag. Slavery was abolished, but the descendants of slaves continued to form the basis of the local population, which is now predominantly Creole, with Indian, European and Chinese minorities. Its marginal location and its lack of major resources have preserved Rodrigues from over-development. For centuries, it remained a rural, agricultural backwater. It was only in 2002 that it gained a degree of political independence with the creation of the Rodrigues Regional Assembly, which administers the island with limited legislative powers. Today, life revolves around a mixed economy of subsistence farming, fishing, small-scale livestock farming, honey production and handicrafts. Tourism, which is limited in numbers, focuses on visitors who appreciate nature and a slow pace of life. Port Mathurin, the capital, is little more than a village. The impression is of a place that has succeeded in establishing balance, preserving a strong local identity and a rare sense of limits.

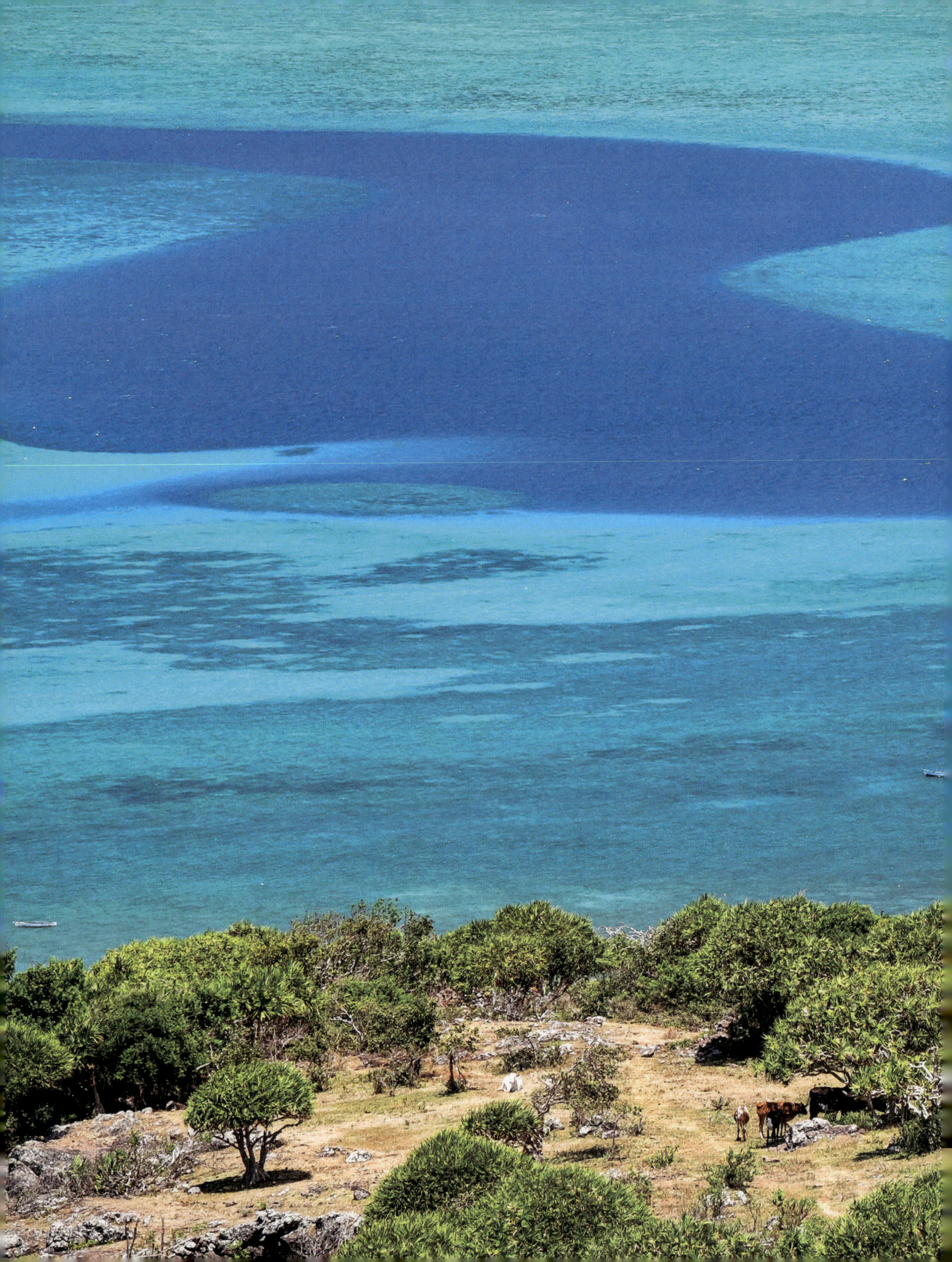

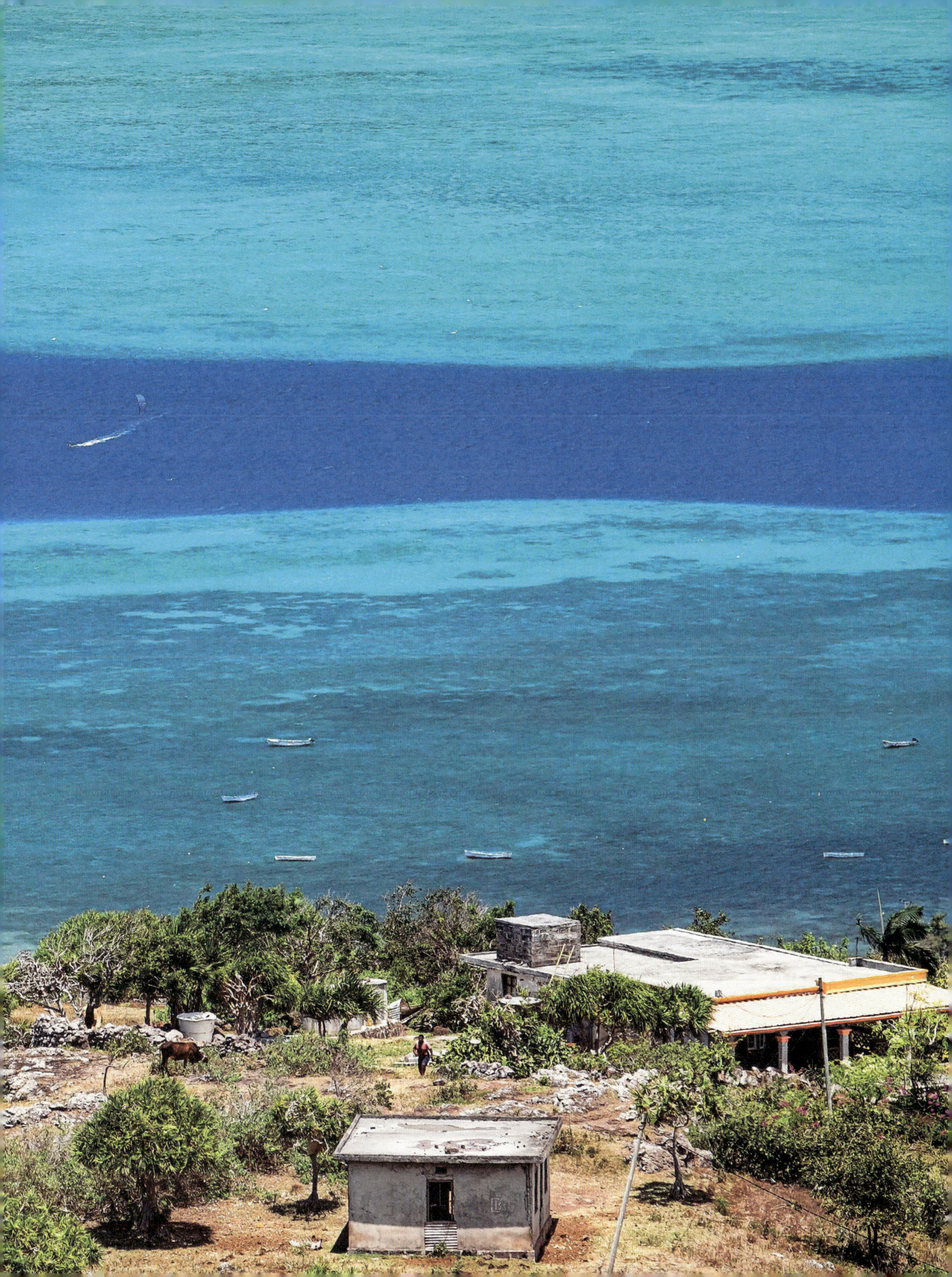

THE RETURN OF THE TORTOISES

WHEN THE FIRST EUROPEANS SET FOOT ON RODRIGUES, THEY FOUND A RICHLY BIODIVERSE ISLAND. TWO SPECIES OF GIANT TORTOISES GRAZED IN HERDS AMONG THE CLEARINGS, WITH A POPULATION OF OVER 300,000.

According to Leguat's description, you could walk more than a hundred steps on their shells without ever setting foot on the ground. Yet in less than two centuries they were exterminated: because they were docile and easy to catch, because they provided a large amount of meat and were often loaded alive onto ships, where they survived for months without food before being slaughtered, because their fat was useful both in cooking and for lamps, because they laid huge, protein-rich eggs and, finally, because of the beauty of their shells. By the late 18th century, they were extinct, along with numerous other endemic species such as the famous Rodrigues solitaire, a flightless bird closely related to the dodo. Today, the island is trying to recover some of what has been lost. Since 2007, the François Leguat Reserve has been active in the southwestern part of the island: more than 50 acres (20 hectares) of land where two species of giant tortoises (those of Aldabra and Madagascar) have been reintroduced and live semi-wild in a reconstructed ecosystem. There are currently more than 5,000 examples. Similarly, attempts are being made to protect some surviving species, such as the Rodrigues flying fox, and work is underway to restore the original flora: the Grande Montagne Nature Reserve, on the opposite side of the island, is an example of environmental recovery, with over 150,000 native plants having been replanted. Below the surface of the sea, the coral reef survives with a reasonable degree of autonomy: here you can find endemic damselfish, rare crustaceans and seabeds that, although affected by bleaching, do show great resilience. In the absence of predators and without excessive tourism, wildlife is finding space to thrive. On Rodrigues, turtles are no longer prey: they are a living, breathing, slow moving legacy of the past.

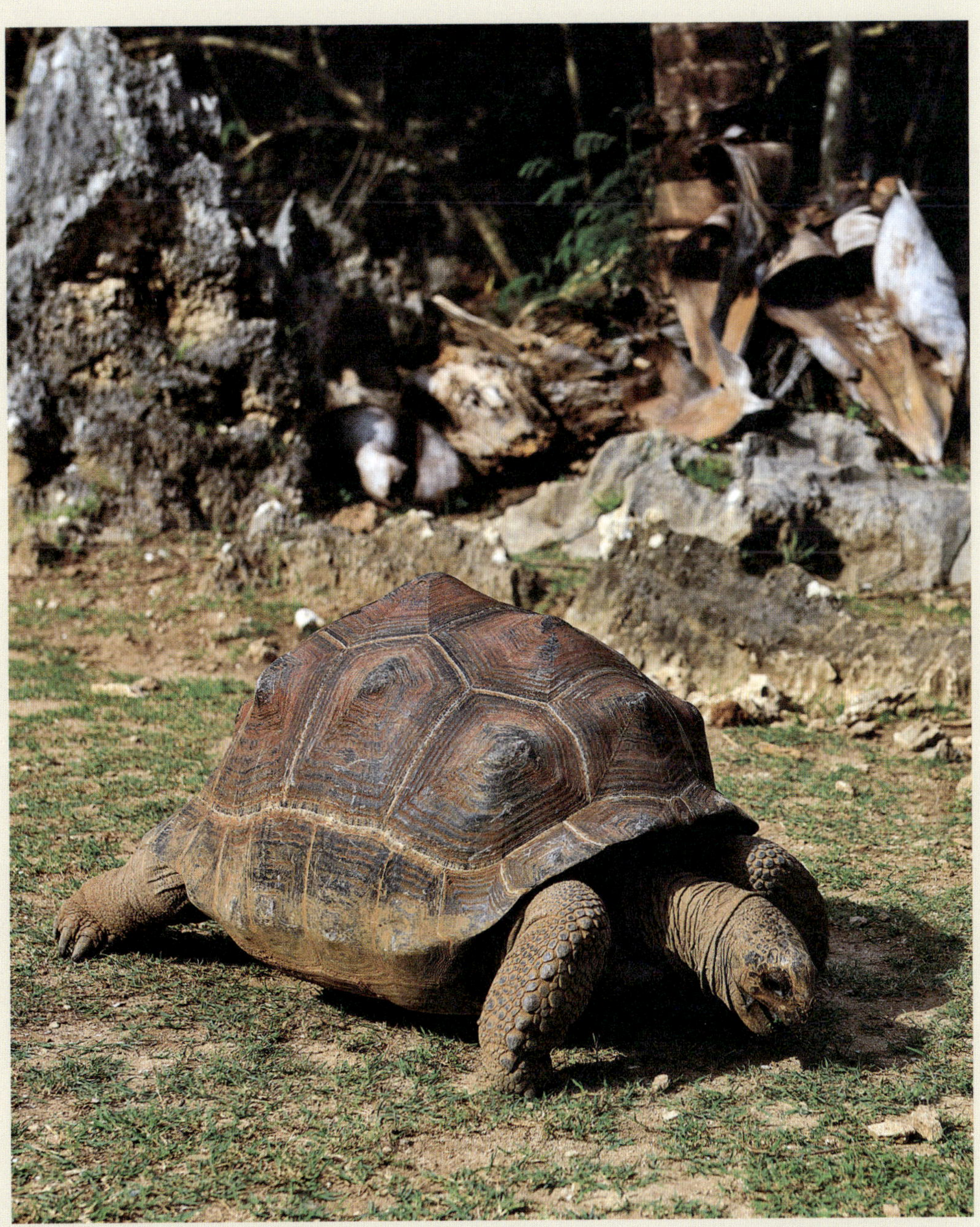

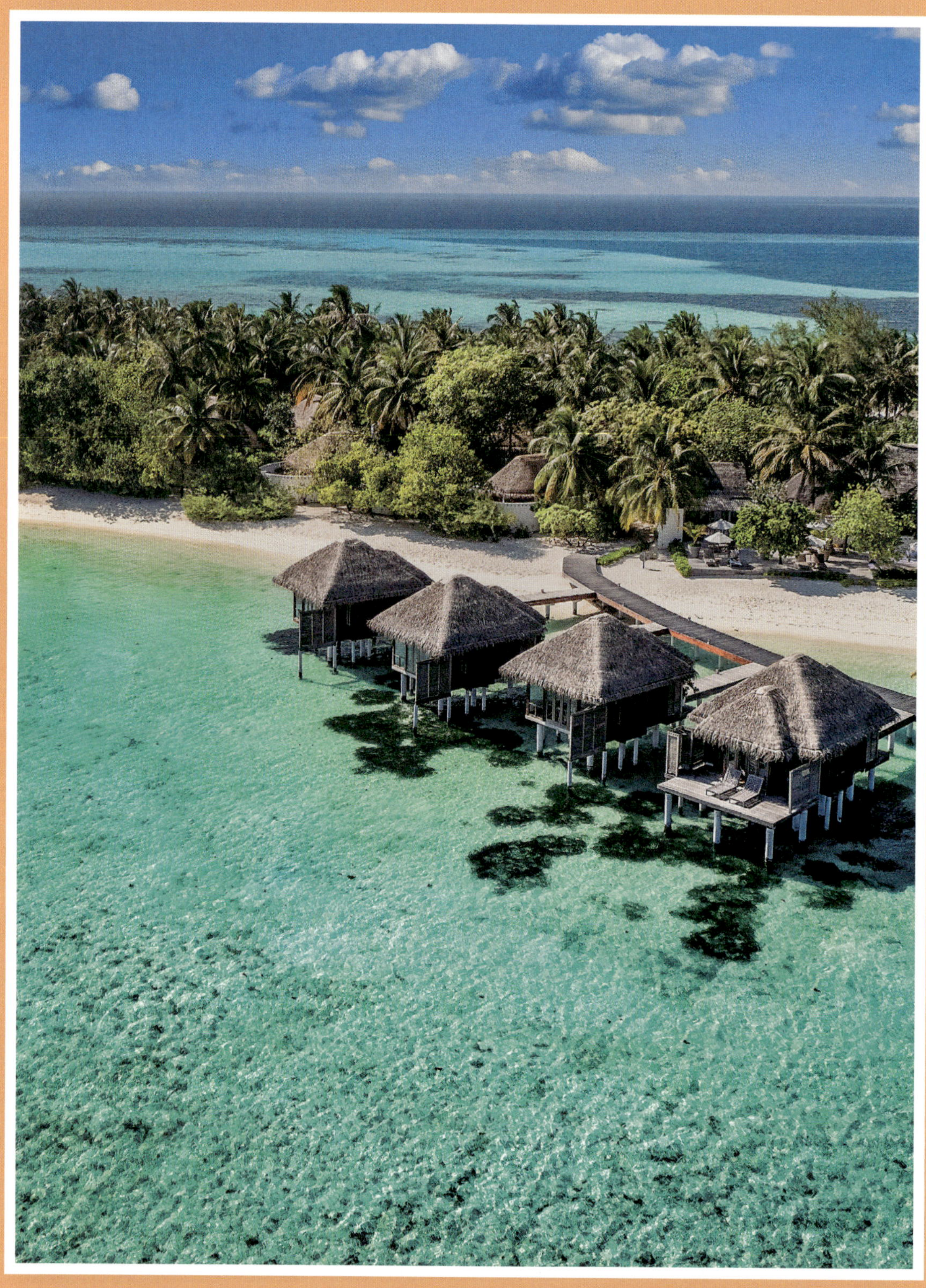

The Republic of Maldives

THE MALDIVES

Geographical coordinates: 4°10'48" N; 73°30'36" E
Waters: Laccadive Sea, Indian Ocean
Population: 529,414 inhabitants
Surface area: 114.98 square miles (297.80 km²)
Capital: Malé

THE PERFECT ILLUSION

If you look down at these islands from above, they look like random marks on a map; only with a great effort of imagination can we trace them back to a constellation emerging from the blue of the Indian Ocean. The Maldives barely rise above the water and might very well not exist. Rather than a real place, they are more a precarious geometric pattern of coral sand drawn amidst the waves. Over a thousand microscopic, fragile islands scattered along an invisible axis southwest of Sri Lanka, so flat that they resemble a geological miracle destined to disappear: the Maldives have no mountains, rivers or mainland in the strict sense of the word. There are 26 atolls, coral rings enclosing transparent lagoons, submerged reefs protecting tongues of white sand and vegetation reduced to the bare essentials. Palm trees, mangroves, a few shrubs resisting the salt air. The rest is water and wind, currents that move like invisible fingers, redrawing the line between land and sea every day. Living here is to make a pact with the ocean, which decides who can stay and who cannot. The atolls have no deep roots: all it takes is a storm or a higher wave for a beach to disappear, a house to sink. Yet for centuries, man has inhabited these precarious fragments of the world, building villages, even cities, on islands that might be mistaken for a cartographic error and navigating the currents with the confidence of those who know the sea better than the land. A bird's eye view of Malé reveals the Maldivian paradox: buildings up to twelve stories high crammed together with no apparent logic, and a population density far higher than that of New York. Every inch is covered with asphalt, concrete, thrumming motors, lives piled on top of each other.

PARADISE FOR HIRE

~

For the rest of the world, the Maldives are a pre-packaged dream. A glossy catalogue of fluorescent waters, bungalows perched on stilts, cocktails sipped at sunset with your feet lapped by the sea. Paradise reduced to an experience to be purchased: you arrive on an island, plunge into the sea amidst a surreal silence and forget that elsewhere there is a planet moving on without you. Here, time crumbles, the present dilates and everything is constructed to be perfect. However, the Maldives are not just a luxury five-star resort, they are also the miracle of existence reduced to the essential. There is no need for roads, the horizon is always in sight, the most familiar noise is that of the wind in the palm leaves. Everything is reduced to simple gestures and vivid images: freshly caught fish roasted over a fire, the silhouette of a boat slipping across the water, the rhythmic sound of the waves breaking on the coral reef. The true protagonist is of course the sea. A parallel universe can be found just a few inches below the surface: corals like submerged cathedrals, shoals of fish moving like splinters of colored light, sharks lazily swimming with the air of those who have nothing to fear. Diving here is to enter a world where man is nothing more than a guest. However, even in paradise there are invisible confines. The Maldives are a divided archipelago: on the one hand the island-resorts, with their promise of solitude and perfection, on the other, the islands inhabited by the locals, where life goes on shielded from the eyes of the tourists. Two parallel realities, separated by a distance that is more than merely geographic.

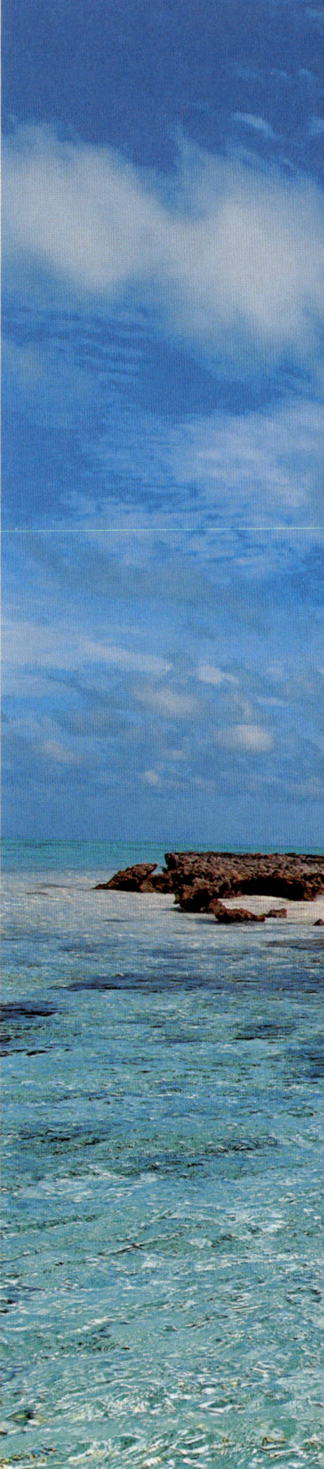

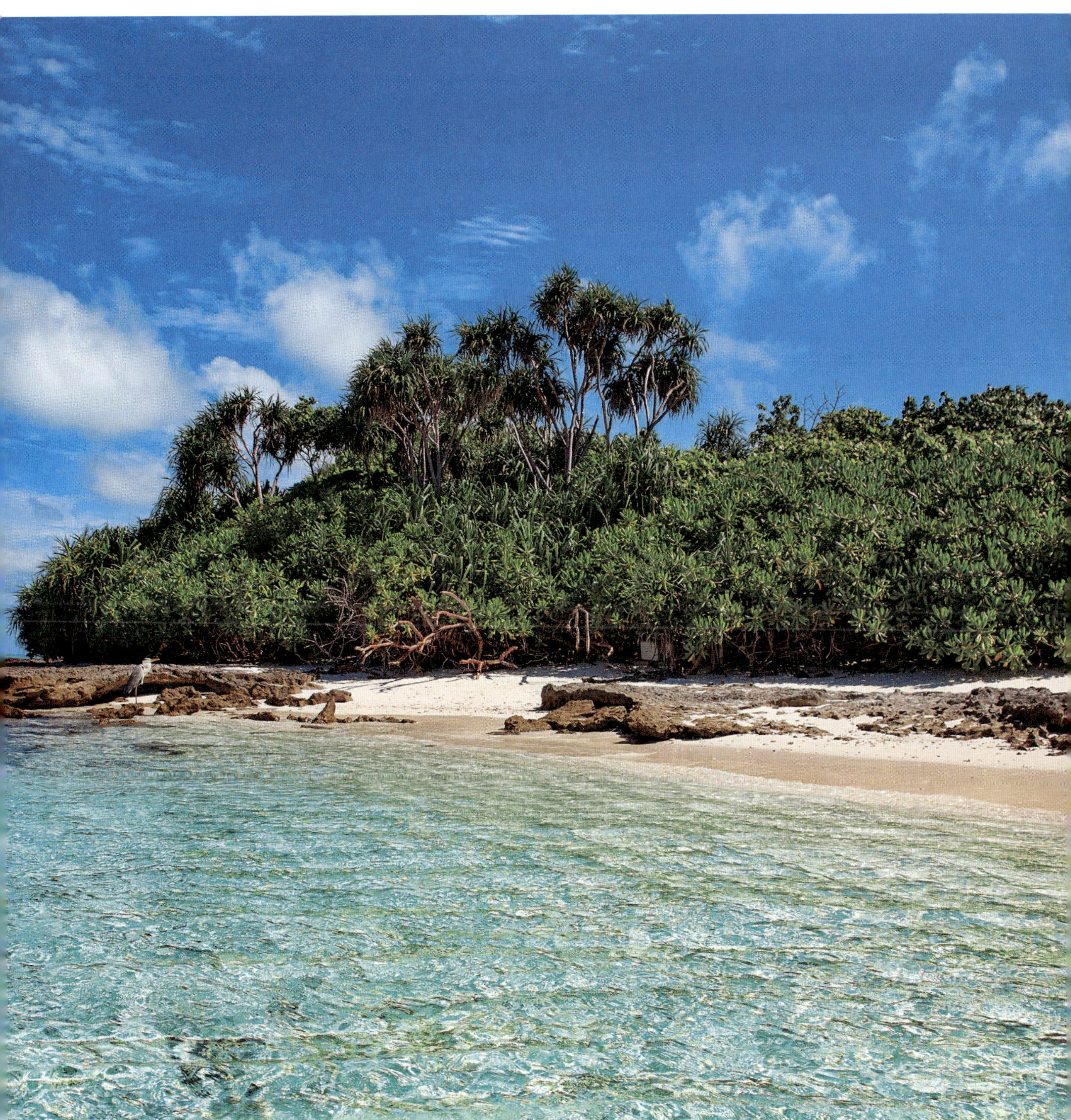

A SINKING WORLD

THERE IS MORE TO THE MALDIVES THAN A DREAM-LIKE SETTING. THERE IS ALSO AN ARCHIPELAGO CONTROLLED BY A POWER THAT SMILES AT VISITORS BUT KEEPS ITS INHABITANTS IN A VICE-LIKE GRIP. THE LUXURY VILLAS AND THE OPEN-AIR SPAS CONCEAL A REGIME THAT FOR DECADES HAS SUFFOCATED DISSENT, CONTROLLED THE PRESS AND INCARCERATED POLITICAL OPPONENTS.

For almost 30 years, the Maldives have been governed by Maumoon Abdul Gayoom, a president who has constructed a throne of silence and repression. There are just a few dozen islands that the tourists see, but the archipelago contains more than a thousand. Many have been used as floating jails, in which political prisoners were exiled and forgotten. Change only came in 2008 with the first democratic elections, but the transition has been fragile, marked by coups, arbitrary arrests and suspect and contested election results. Religious freedom is also a mirage: even the constitution says that all citizens shall be of the Muslim faith and the public practice of other religions is prohibited. There is then a very real threat looming over the Maldives, their blessing and their curse: the sea. This is the country with the lowest average altitude in the world, with a highest point of just 16 feet (5 meters). With climate change and rising sea levels, many islands risk disappearing within a few decades. Paradise is sinking, inch by inch. While the government is constructing artificial islands to save the saveable, the coral reef, the living heart of the Maldives, is dying. The whitening of the corals, pollution and mass tourism are putting at risk the very ecosystem that has made life on these atolls possible for centuries. The Maldives are a perfect illusion, a precarious Eden, relying on a crumbling equilibrium. A place of dazzling beauty, but one with a concealed price, payment of which is continually postponed. The tourists continue to dream on the turquoise waters and the immaculate beaches, but with the ocean rising slowly but inexorably, the day of reckoning is approaching.

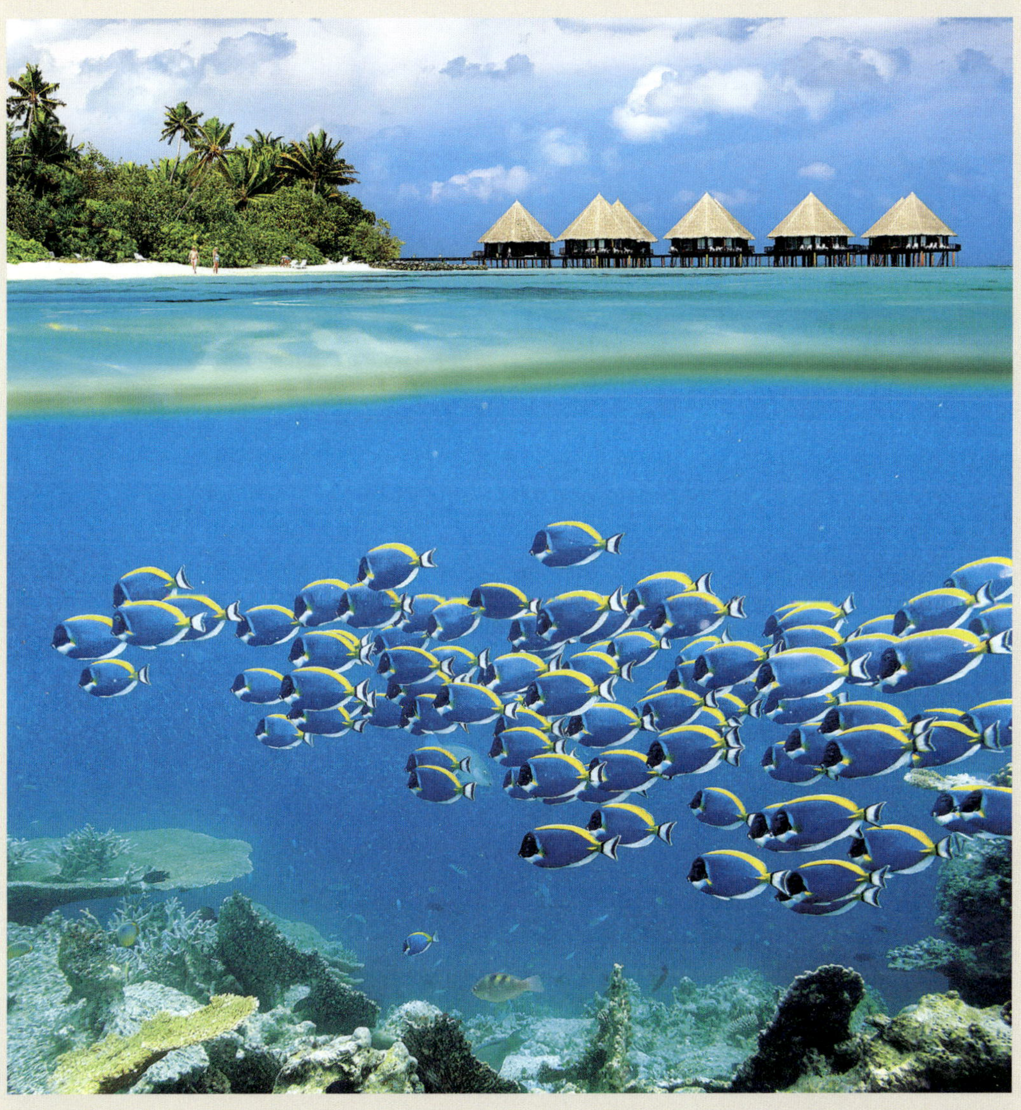

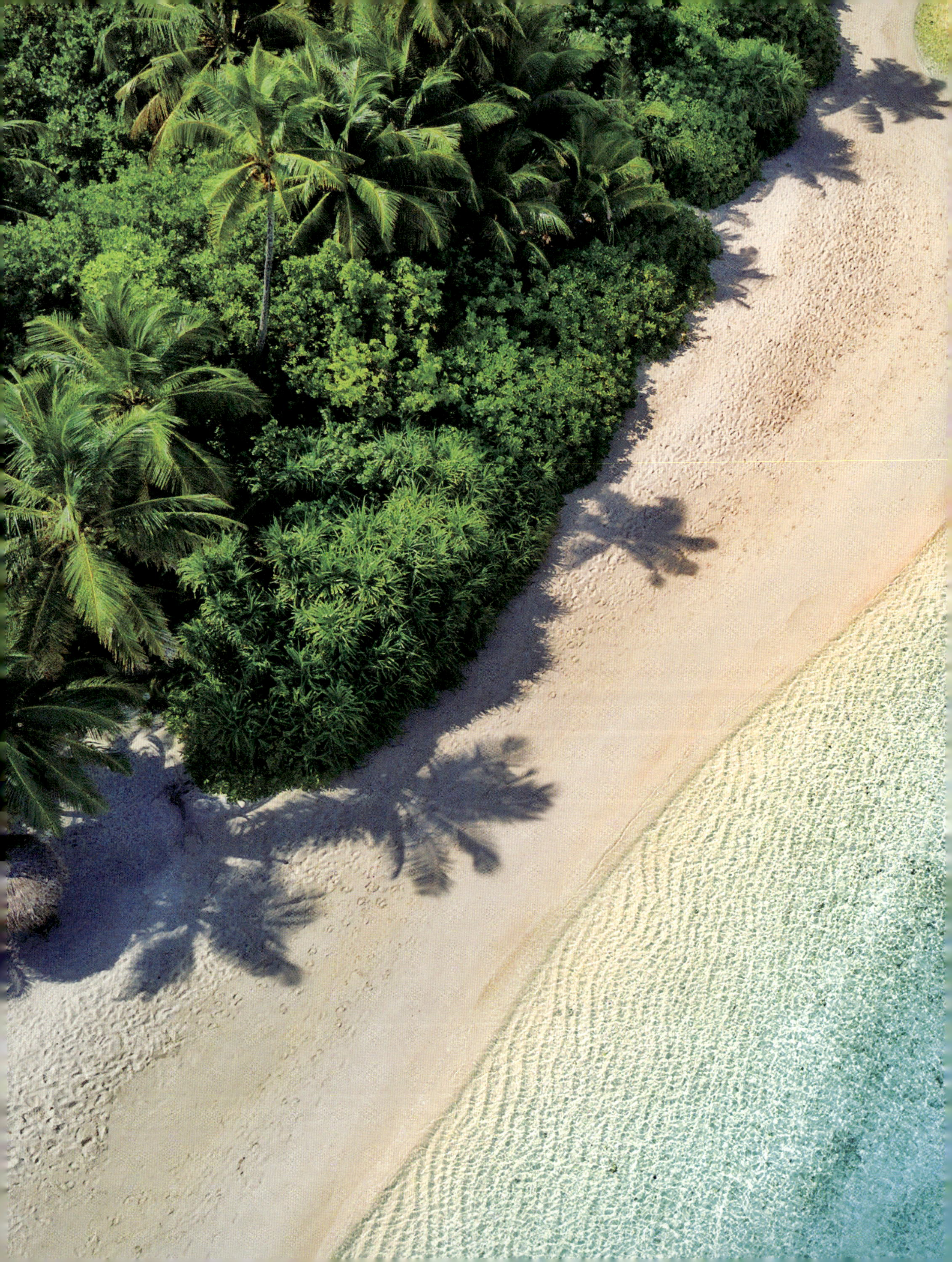

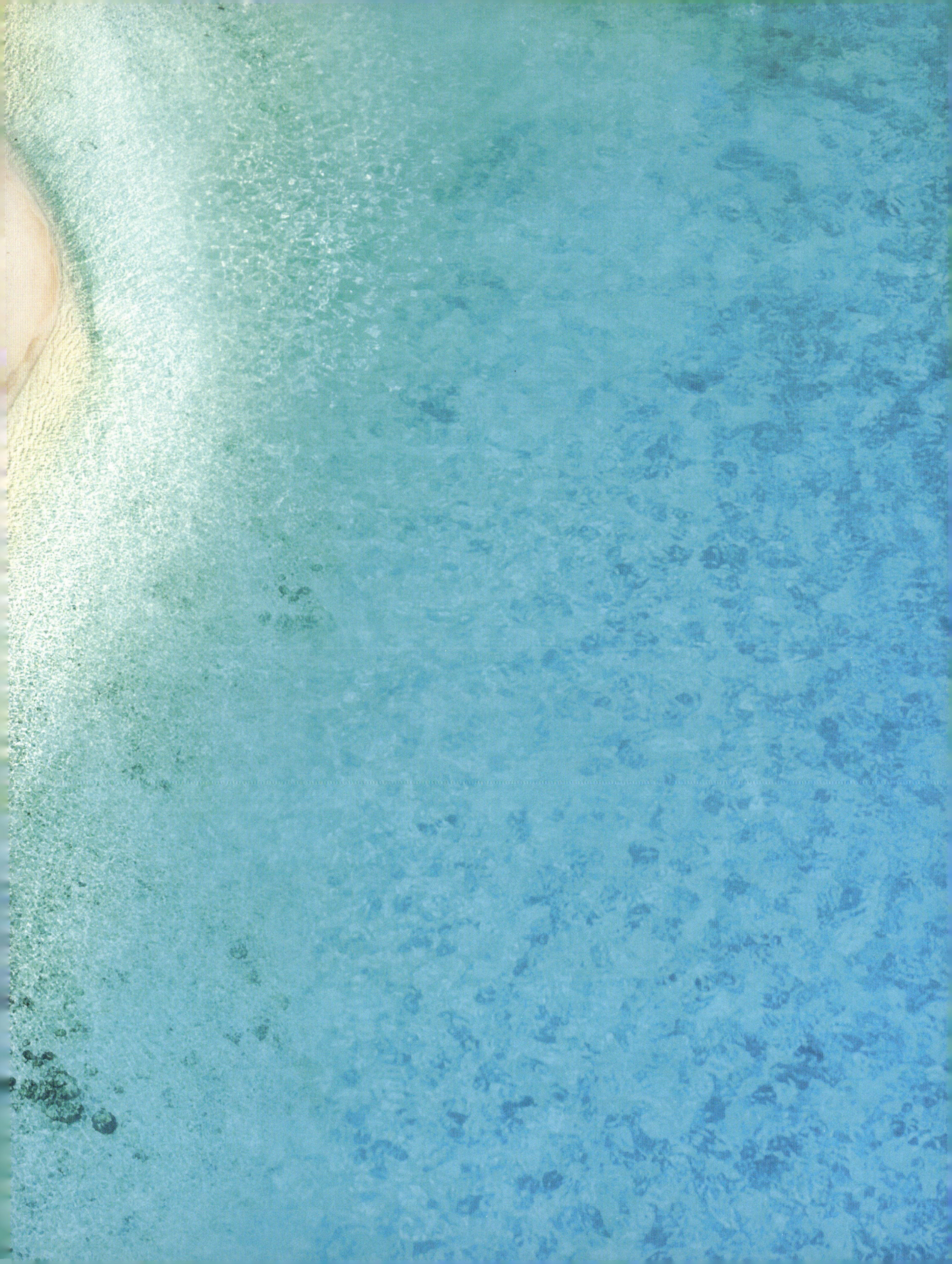

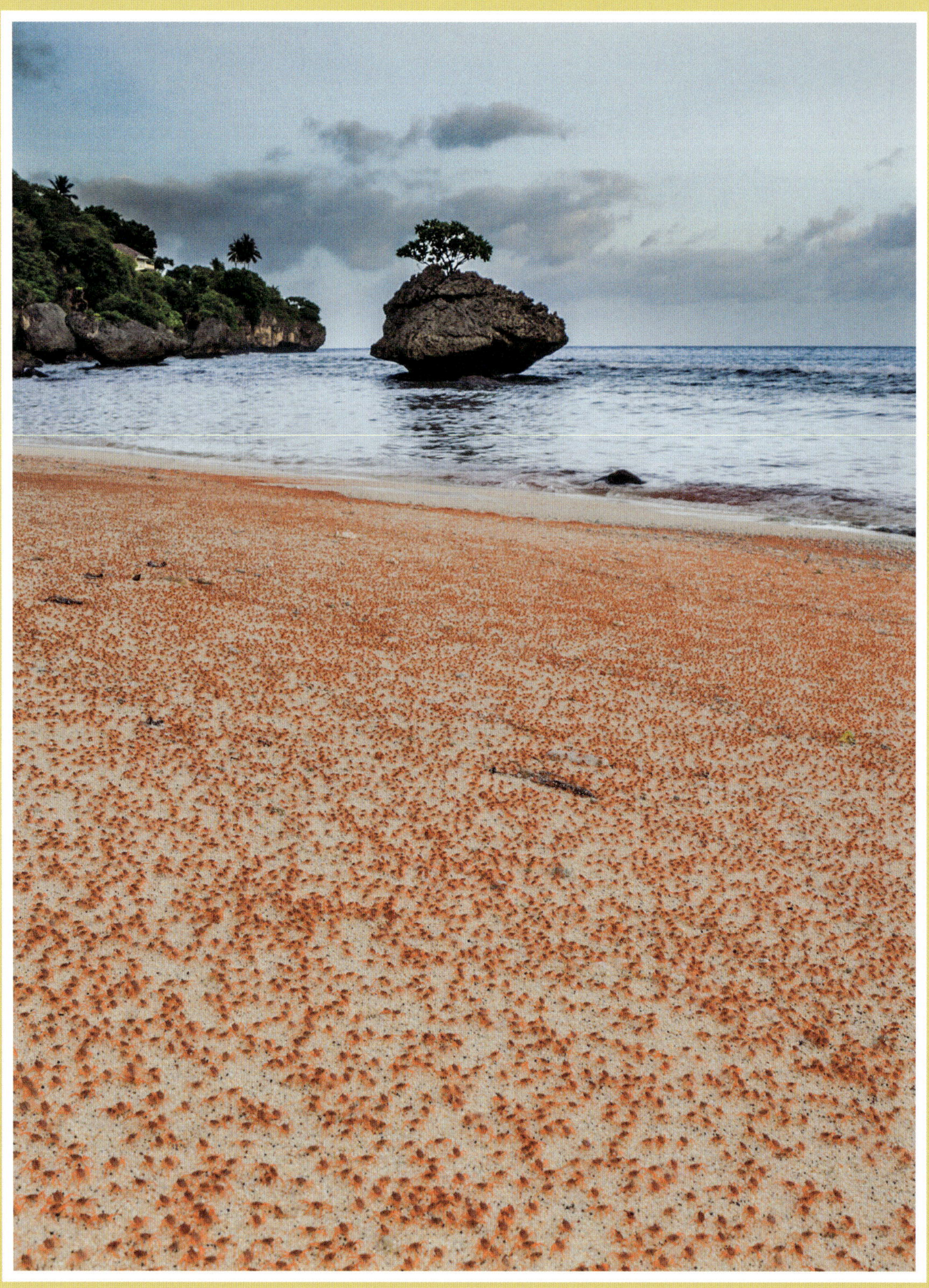

CHRISTMAS ISLAND

Geographical coordinates: 10°29'24" S; 105°37'39" E
Waters: Indian Ocean
Population: 1,692 inhabitants
Surface area: 52 square miles (134.70 km^2)
Capital: Flying Fish Cove

A WILD RED CARPET

Nature reigns supreme here; plants and animals are in the driving seat and man's respect for the environment is unquestionable. Perhaps this is because here, more than anywhere else, a basic principle is evident: human beings belong to their habitat. Thus it is that on this island, for once, human beings—more accustomed to cutting down trees to make way for roads and buildings—are working hard to facilitate the natural cycles. The ritual that has become a symbol of Christmas Island is staged between October and December, at the beginning of the rainy season. Fifty million red crabs, *Gecarcoidea natalis,* leave their inland shelters and head to the beaches. It is a journey of weeks through forests, over cliffs, around buildings and across paved roads: the island is blotched red, as if covered by a moving carpet. Having reached the coast, the males dig holes in the sand where mating will take place and, after fertilization, they retreat to the center of the island. The females brood the eggs, which they lay at the time of the spring tide—the moment in the lunar cycle when the difference between high and low tide is greatest—and only then do they leave. It takes about four weeks for the eggs to hatch into tiny .2-inch (5-millimeter) crabs. At that point, the youngsters are ready to set out on their long march inland, where they will remain hidden for three years before being able to reproduce, following in the footsteps of their parents. Local residents and authorities contribute to the spectacle of this seasonal migration by closing the roads affected by the passage of the crabs and building bridges and tunnels to facilitate their passage.

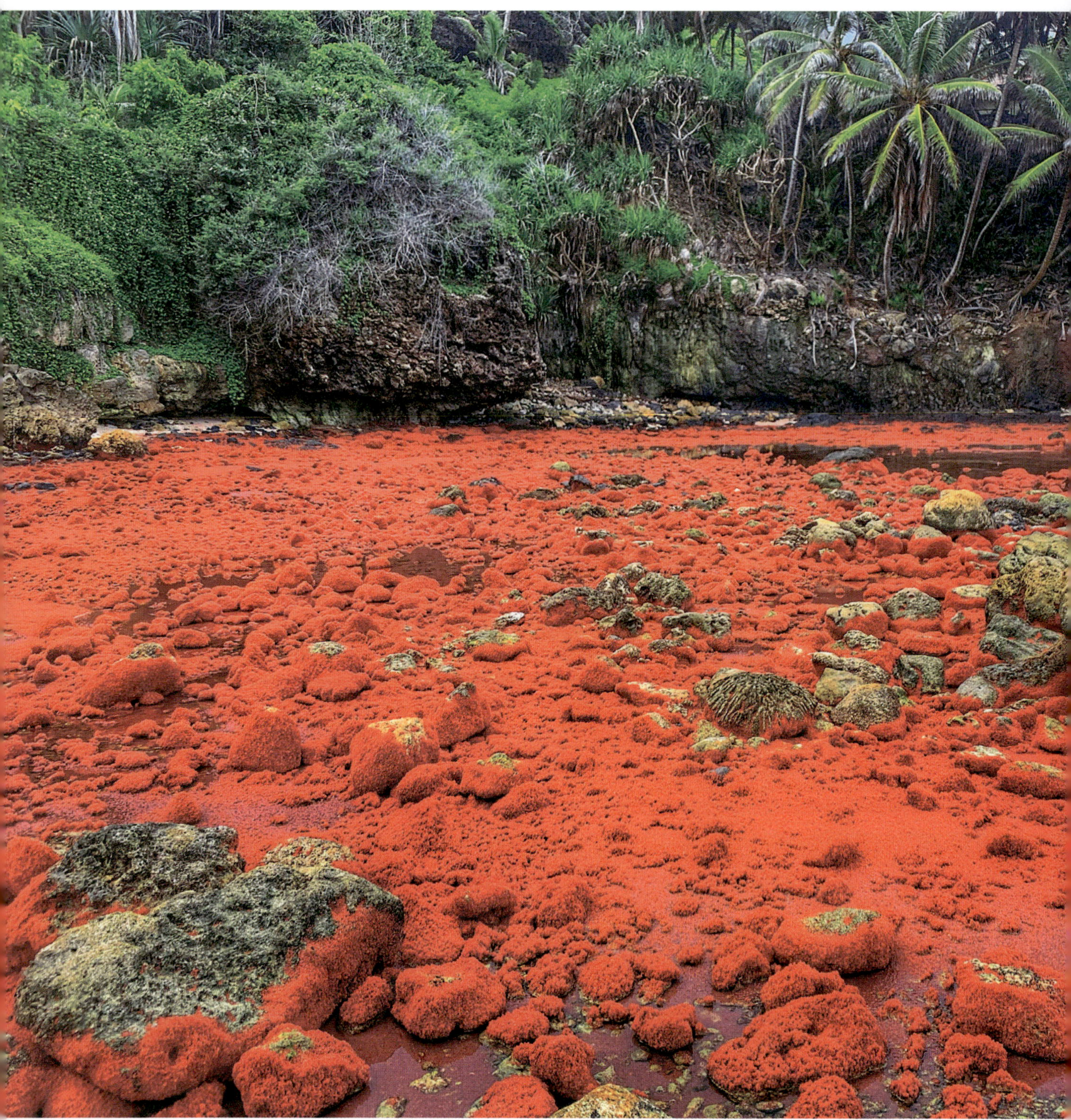

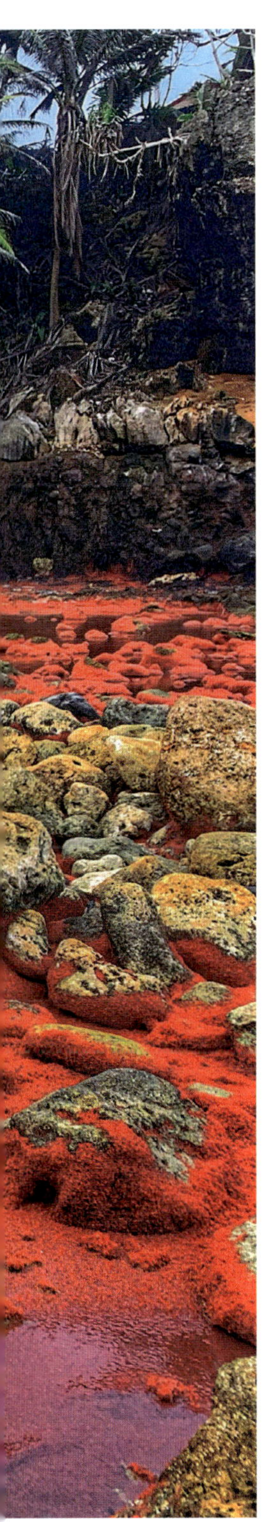

A FRONTIER ISLAND

~

In political terms, this island belongs to Australia, but geographically it is close to Indonesia. Spotted by the British in 1615, it was given its current name in 1643 by Captain William Mynors, who actually sailed past it on Christmas Day. The first landings took place in the late 17th century, but it was not until the end of the 19th century that more systematic explorations began, when the island was annexed by Great Britain and exploited firstly for its timber and then for the extraction of phosphate, an industry that attracted around a thousand Chinese and Malaysian workers, supervised by a handful of Europeans. On the 14th of March 1942, in the middle of the Second World War, the Japanese Imperial General Headquarters gave the order launching Operation X for the occupation of Christmas Island. All that Captain L.W.T. Williams had to oppose the Japanese fleet was an old cannon, four British NCOs, an officer and 27 Indian soldiers. The latter then mutinied, killed Williams and surrendered to the Japanese. At the end of the war, the island returned to British hands without the spilling of further blood, under the sovereignty of Singapore, through to 1958 when it was sold to Australia for 20 million dollars. Since the late 1980s, Christmas Island has been at the center of repeated migratory waves. The Australian government's reluctance to accept refugees has frequently given rise to controversial situations. In 2001, the Norwegian ship *MV Tampa* was refused permission to dock and disembark 433 asylum seekers, while in 2010 a wreck off Flying Fish Cove resulted in 50 refugees drowning. Bitter arguments have also arisen around the detention center for immigrants, a structure with 800 beds, built in 2006, closed in 2018 and reopened in 2019.

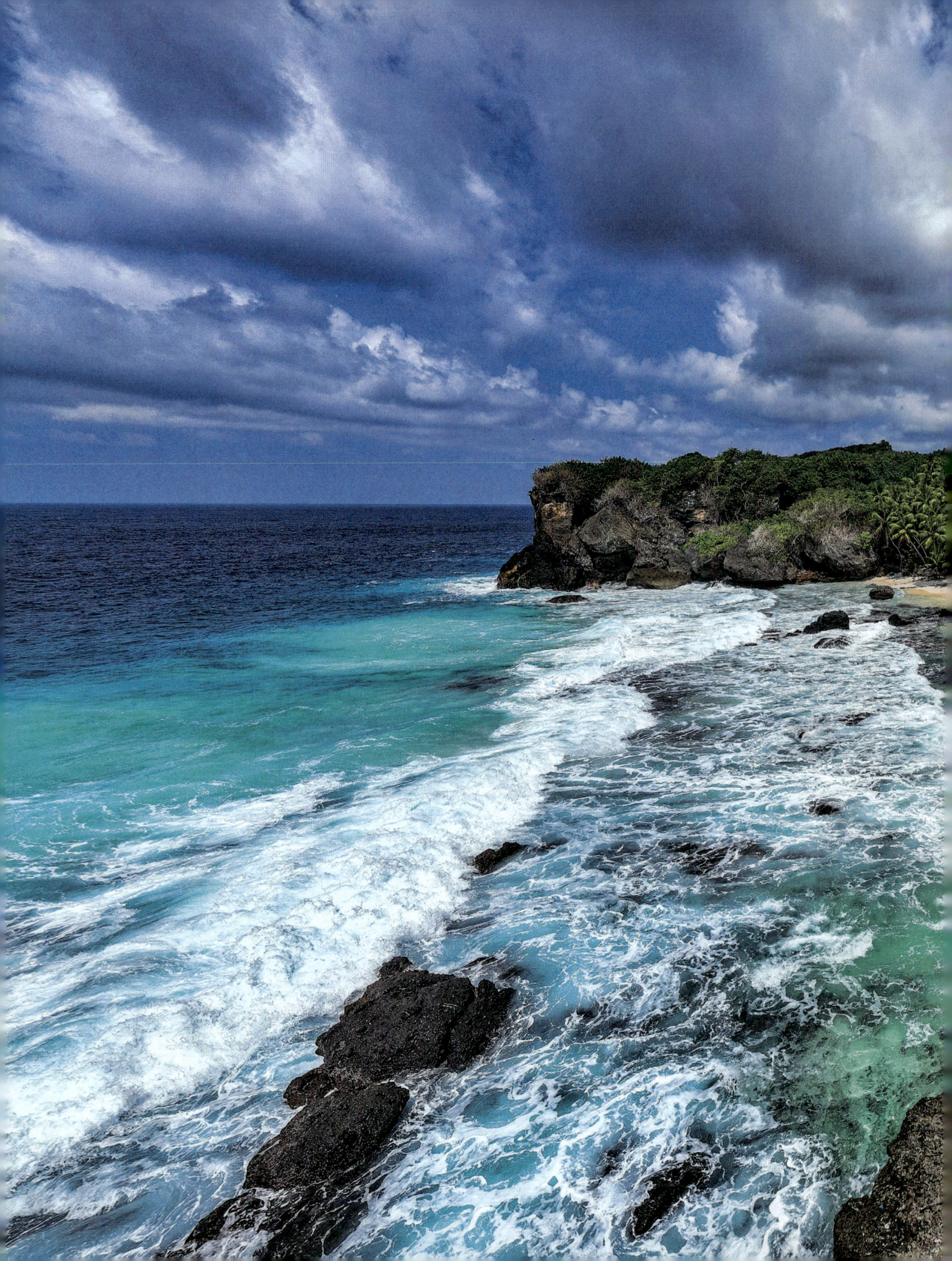

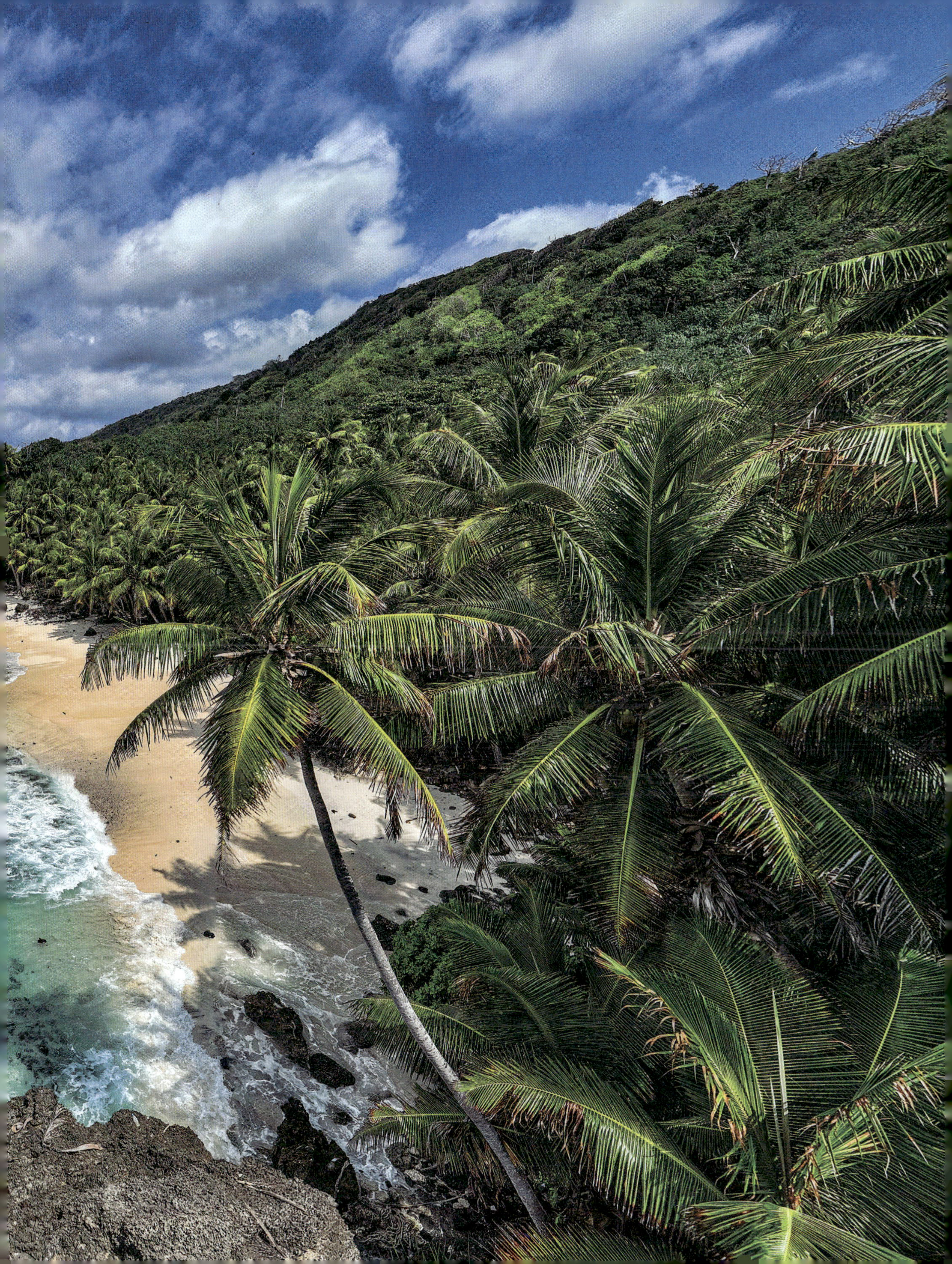

FLYING FOXES AND CRAZY ANTS

~

MORE THAN HALF OF THE ISLAND IS A PROTECTED NATURAL PARK. THE ISLAND IS THE SUMMIT OF AN UNDERSEA MOUNTAIN THAT RISES OVER 13,000 FEET (4,000 METERS) FROM THE OCEAN DEPTHS BUT PEAKS AT JUST 980 FEET (300 METERS) ABOVE SEA LEVEL.

Of volcanic origin, it nonetheless has a surface area that is largely composed of coralline deposits. The karst terrain is made up of sheer cliffs, caves and anchialine pools. The conditions of these remote places, never frequented by humans until 150 years ago and prevalently covered by tropical rainforests, has favored the evolution and conservation of endemic species, lending the site a scientific interest comparable to that of the Galápagos islands. The flora is a synergic system: tall trees protect the undergrowth of ferns, orchids and climbing plants, with the blessing of copious rainfall. A number of mammals are now extinct, others are endangered, including the black-eared flying fox, a species of fundamental importance for pollination and the dispersal of seeds. There is also an enviable ornithological variety, with endemic nesting sea birds and endangered migratory species. Here, too, however, human impact and the arrival of non-native creatures has put the environment at risk. An emblematic case is that of *Anoplolepis gracilipes*, eloquently known as the yellow crazy ant, listed among the world's worst invasive species. Introduced accidently in 1915, the ant has spread in various super colonies responsible for chain reaction damage. The ant feeds on the sugars produced by aphids and cochineal insects and in exchange defends them from potential predators, favoring their proliferation. The damage to the flora affects the fauna that lives in it and even the famous red crabs are threatened by the spread of this insect. Attempts have been made to counter this phenomenon by aerial spraying with fipronil, but it is not easy to intervene in what is an already compromised situation without further disturbing it.

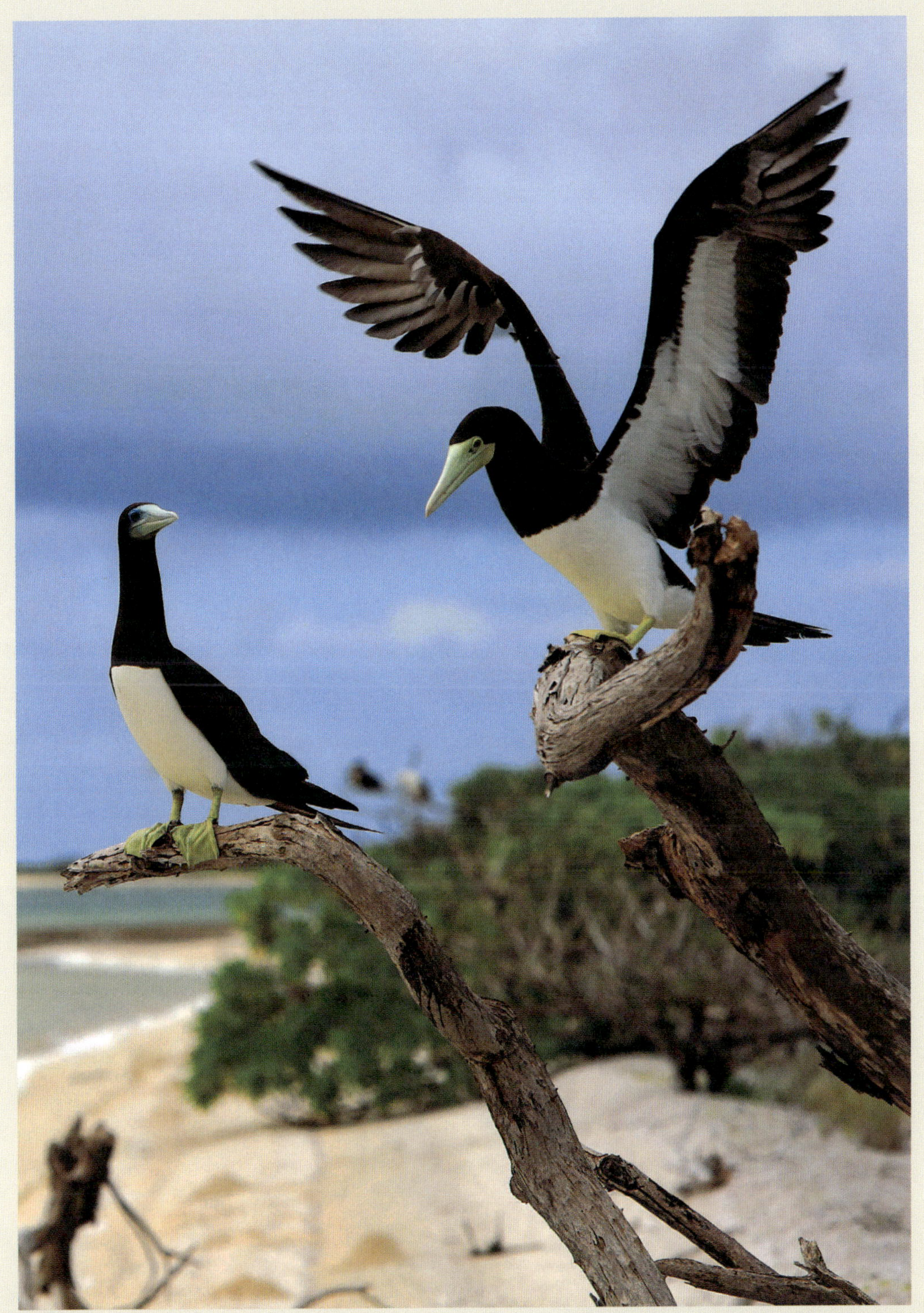

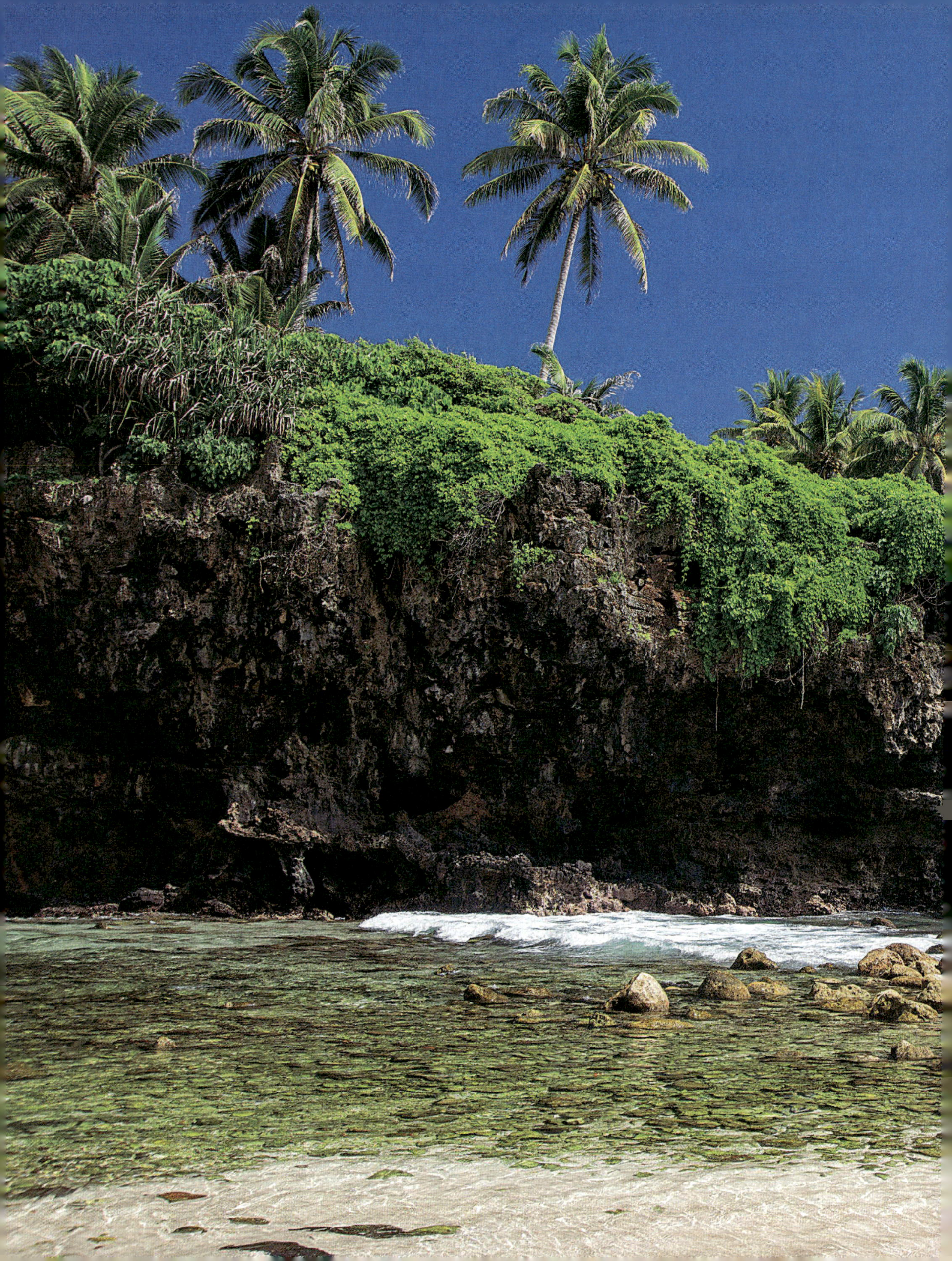

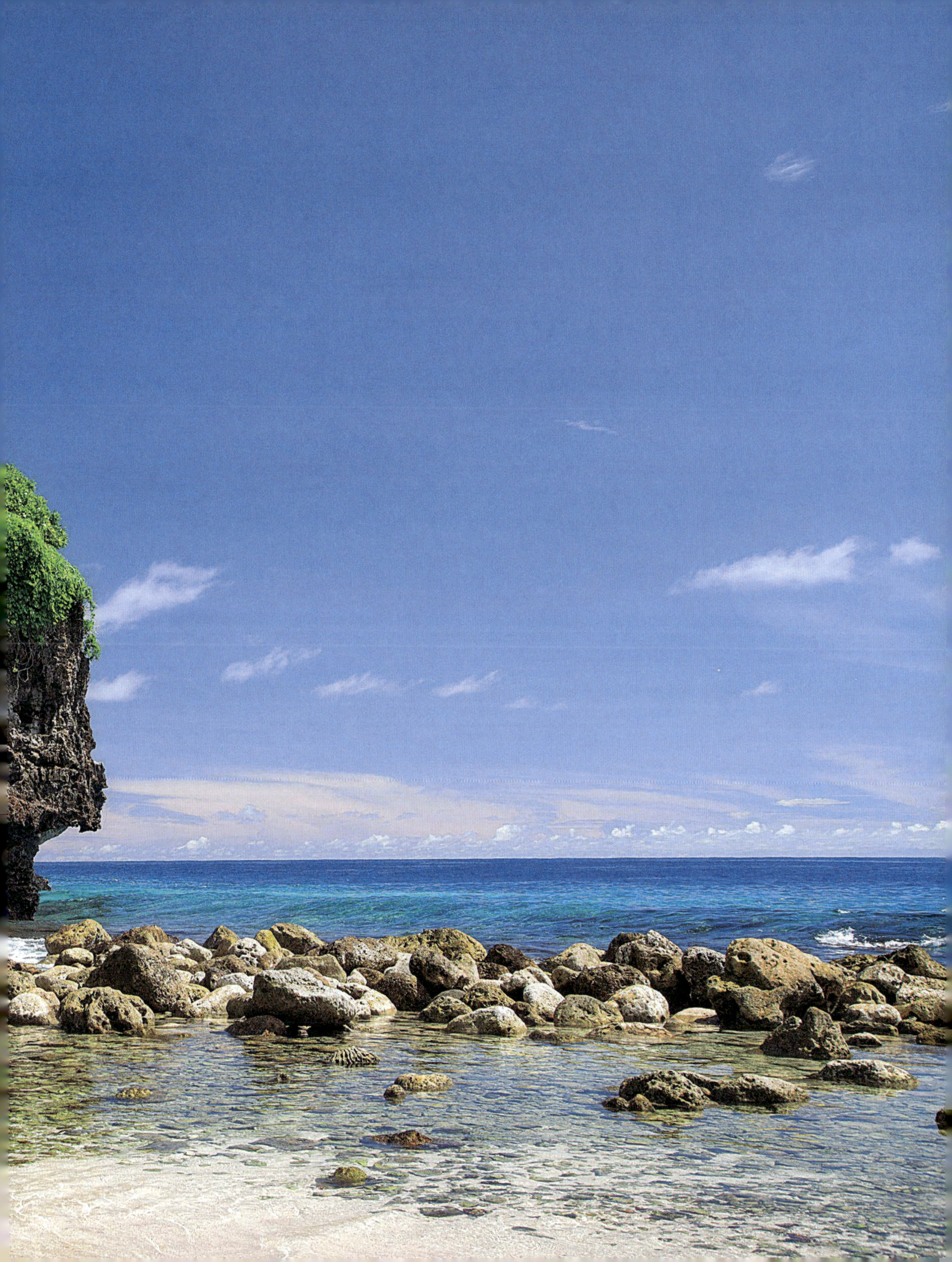

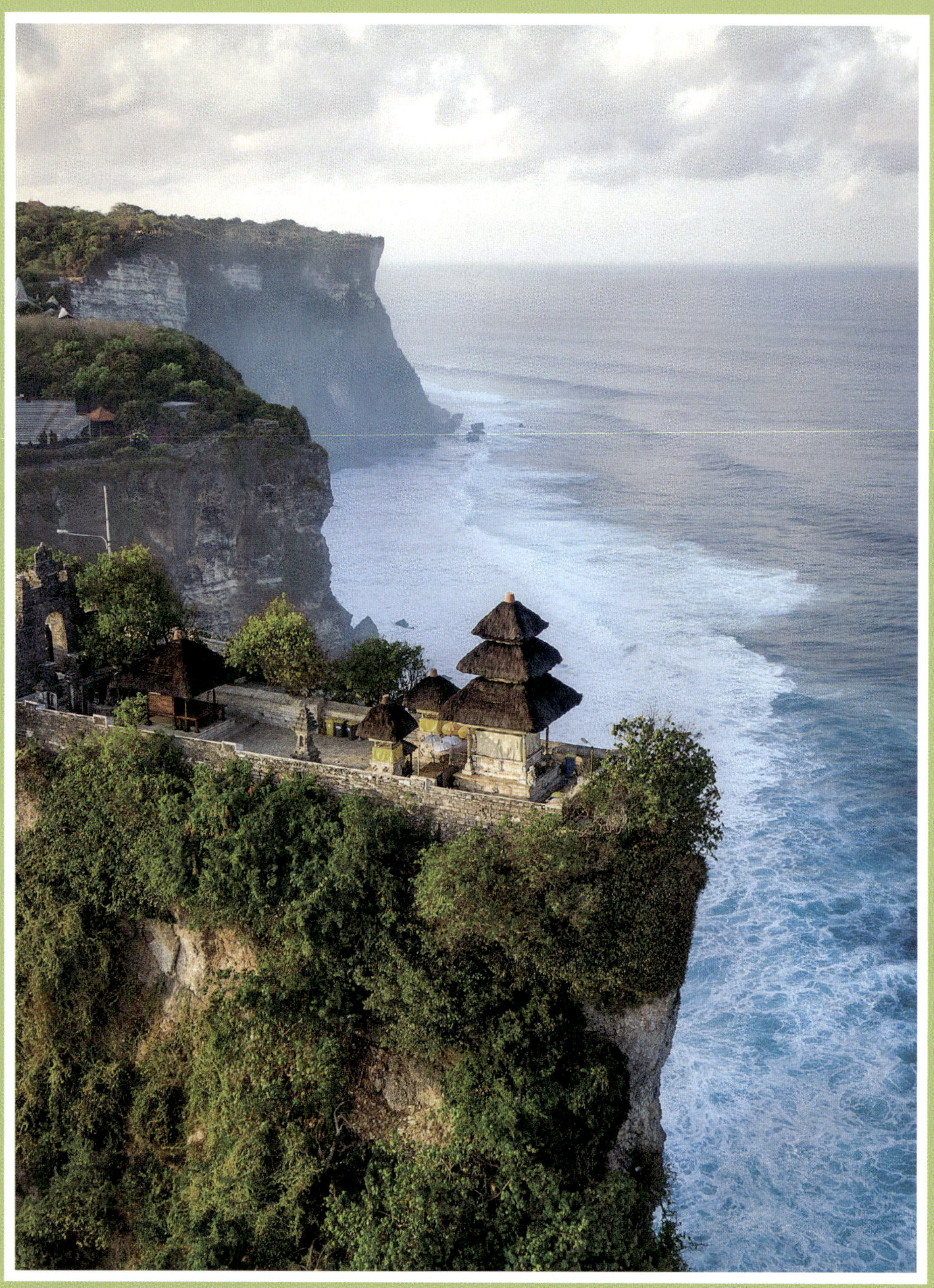

BALI

Geographical coordinates: 8°20'6" S; 115°5'17" E
Waters: Bali Sea, Indian Ocean
Population: 4,404,300 inhabitants
Surface area: 2,158.31 square miles (5,590 km²)
Capital: Denpasar

A BREATH SUSPENDED IN MIDAIR

Rather than just an island, Bali is a ripple in space and time, a precarious balance between natural wilderness and human presence, between chaos and harmony. On the map, it resembles a floating seed in the middle of Indonesia, separated from Java by the Bali Strait and overlooking an expanse of water that stretches toward Australia. However, geography is but a detail. What defines Bali is its breath: moist, fertile, saturated with scents that oscillate between the sweetness of frangipani and the odor of incense and burnt sacred offerings. A breath that rises from the terraced crops, flies over the temples, slides along the beaches and dissolves in the waves. The heart of the island is green: a mosaic of tropical forests and rice paddies shaped by man with the patience of those who understand the rhythm of the earth. In the center rises Mount Agung, the sacred volcano looming like a sleeping god. Over time, it has awoken many times, with all the fury of an offended deity: the last eruption was in 1963, when lava engulfed houses and paddy fields, leaving behind ashes and despair. However, Bali has always been able to rise again, for here destruction is never an end, merely a transformation. Today, in fact, beneath the volcano's shadow lie silent villages, temples hidden among the lianas, waterfalls cascading through gorges. Then there is the coast, with its dual soul: to the south, the power of the ocean that attracts surfers and dreamers; to the north, a quieter sea, where fishing boats move slowly and the sand has the dark tones of ancient magma. Bali is everything and the opposite of everything, suspended between water and sky, prayer and storm.

A THOUSAND SPIRITS ON ONE ISLAND

~

Bali changes depending on who is looking at it. For some it is a surfing mecca, with the sea crashing on the beaches of Kuta and Uluwatu, where the water is an arena of constant challenge and time is measured by the wait between one wave and the next. For others it is a spiritual refuge, a place where the sacred is combined with the everyday: in the temples overlooking the rocks, in the ceremonies transforming the streets into processions of colors and sounds, in the serene gazes of the monks who seem to guard forgotten secrets. The interior is yet another world. Here, nature sets the pace, the terraced paddy fields of Tegallalang and Jatiluwih spread like green scales over the hills, irrigated by a system almost as old as the island itself. Ubud, the cultural capital of Bali, pulses with creativity and mysticism with its handicraft markets, sculptor's workshops and cafes concealed among the palm trees. Here it seems possible to escape the concept of time; even the waiting in restaurants, sometimes of a length that would become frustrating elsewhere, here takes on the value of a spiritual trial. Then there is the more shrouded face of Bali, the one that few visitors get to see: the black sand beaches of Amed, the fishing villages on the east coast, the placid lakes nestling between the mountains. Each corner has a different spirit, an echo of the past that coexists with the present. Bali is never the same because those who pass through it transform it with their gaze.

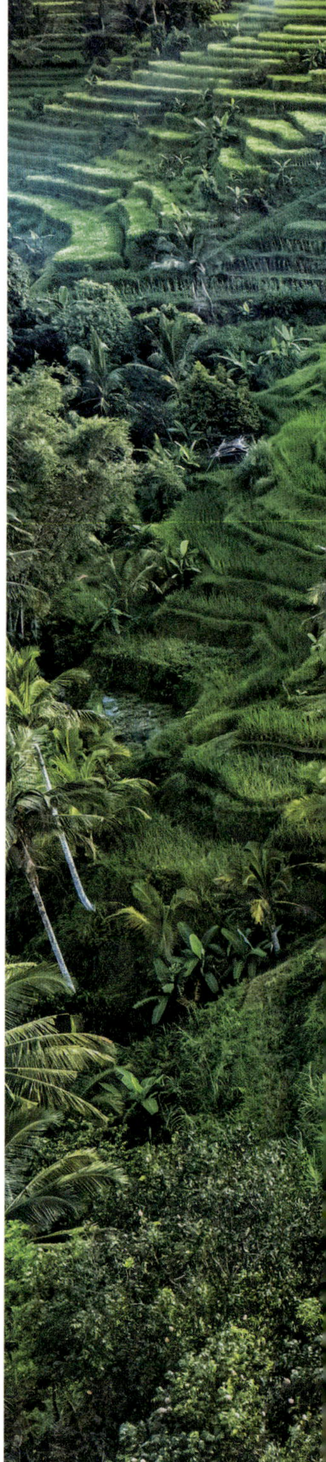

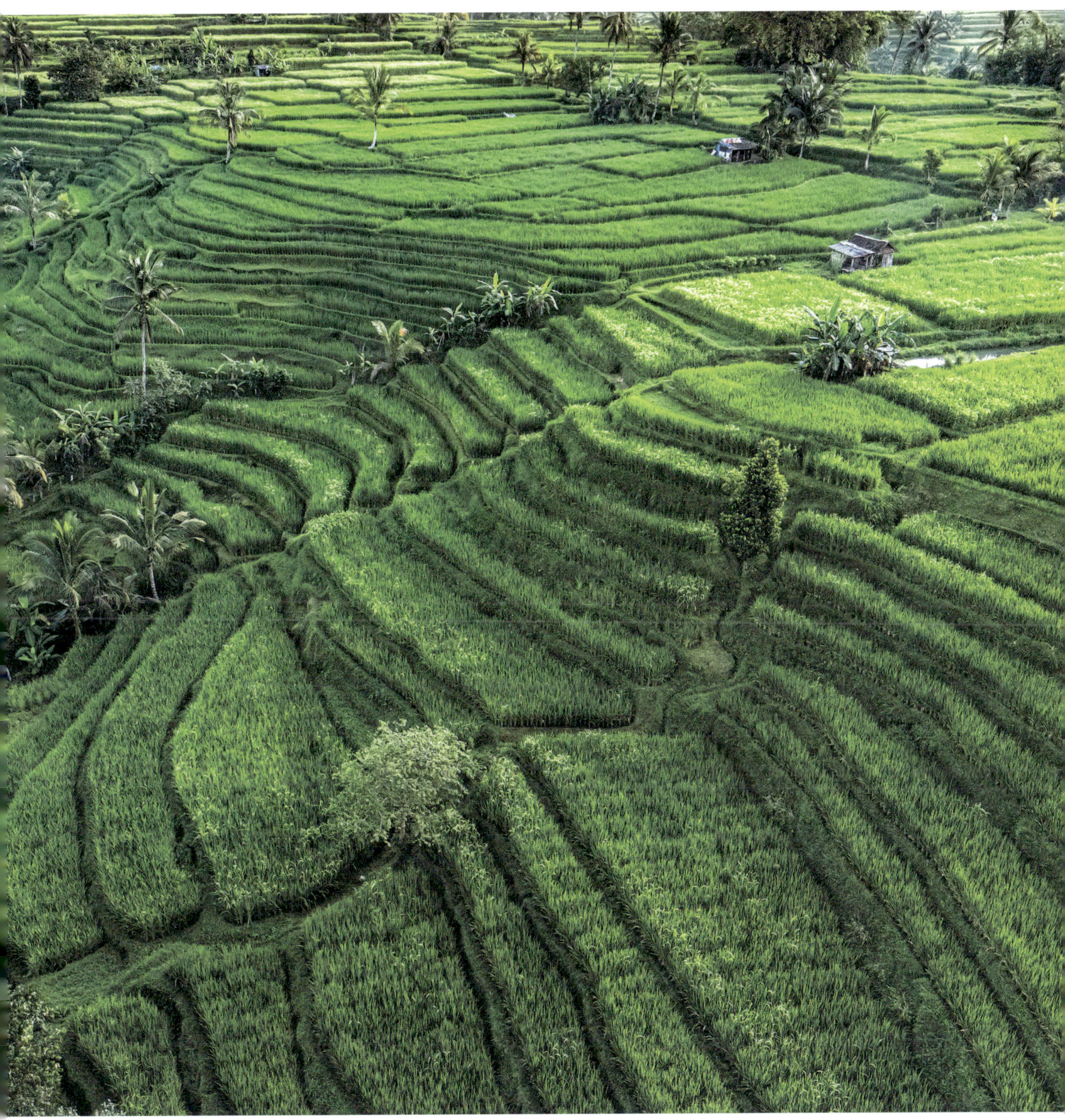

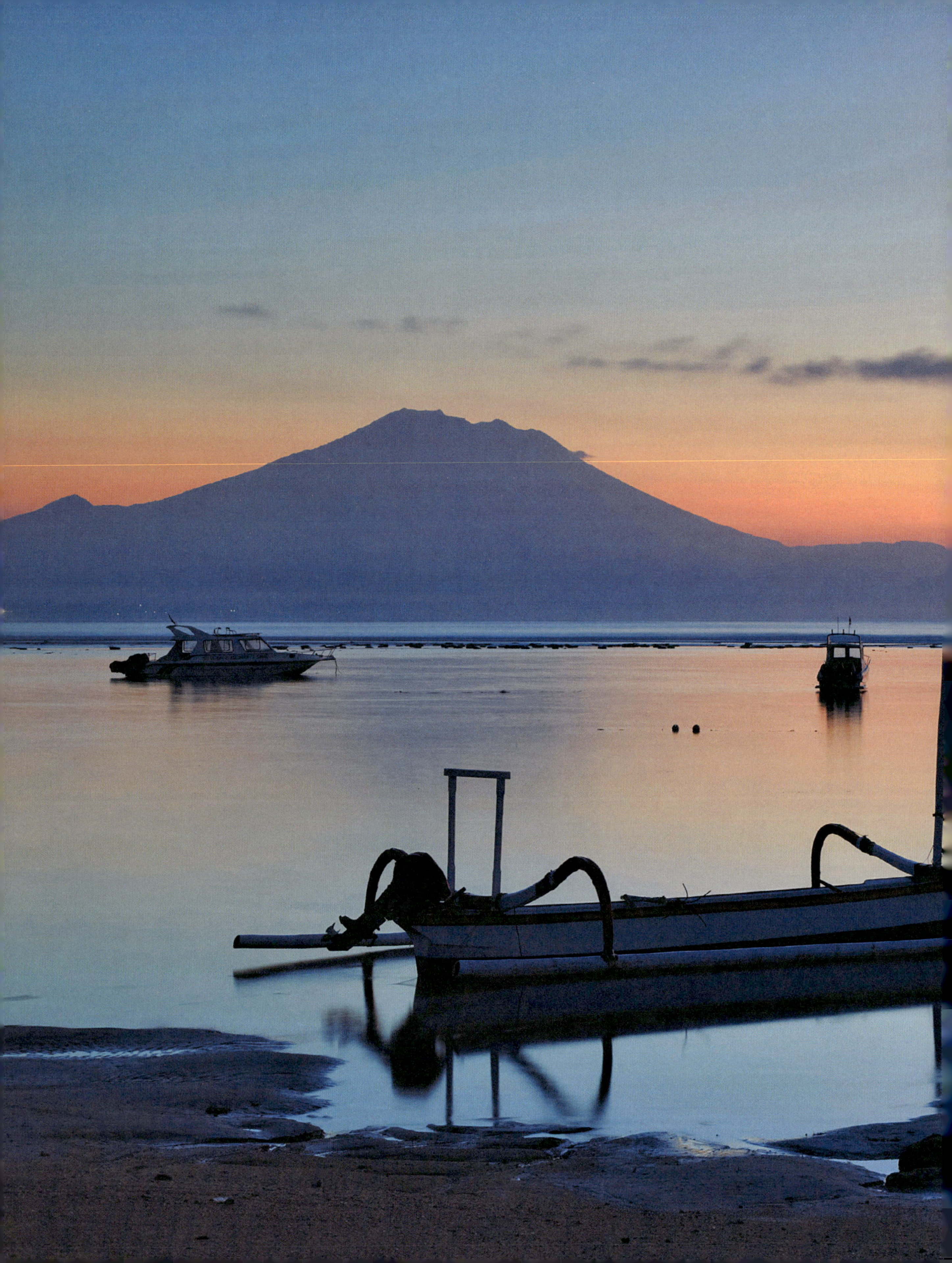

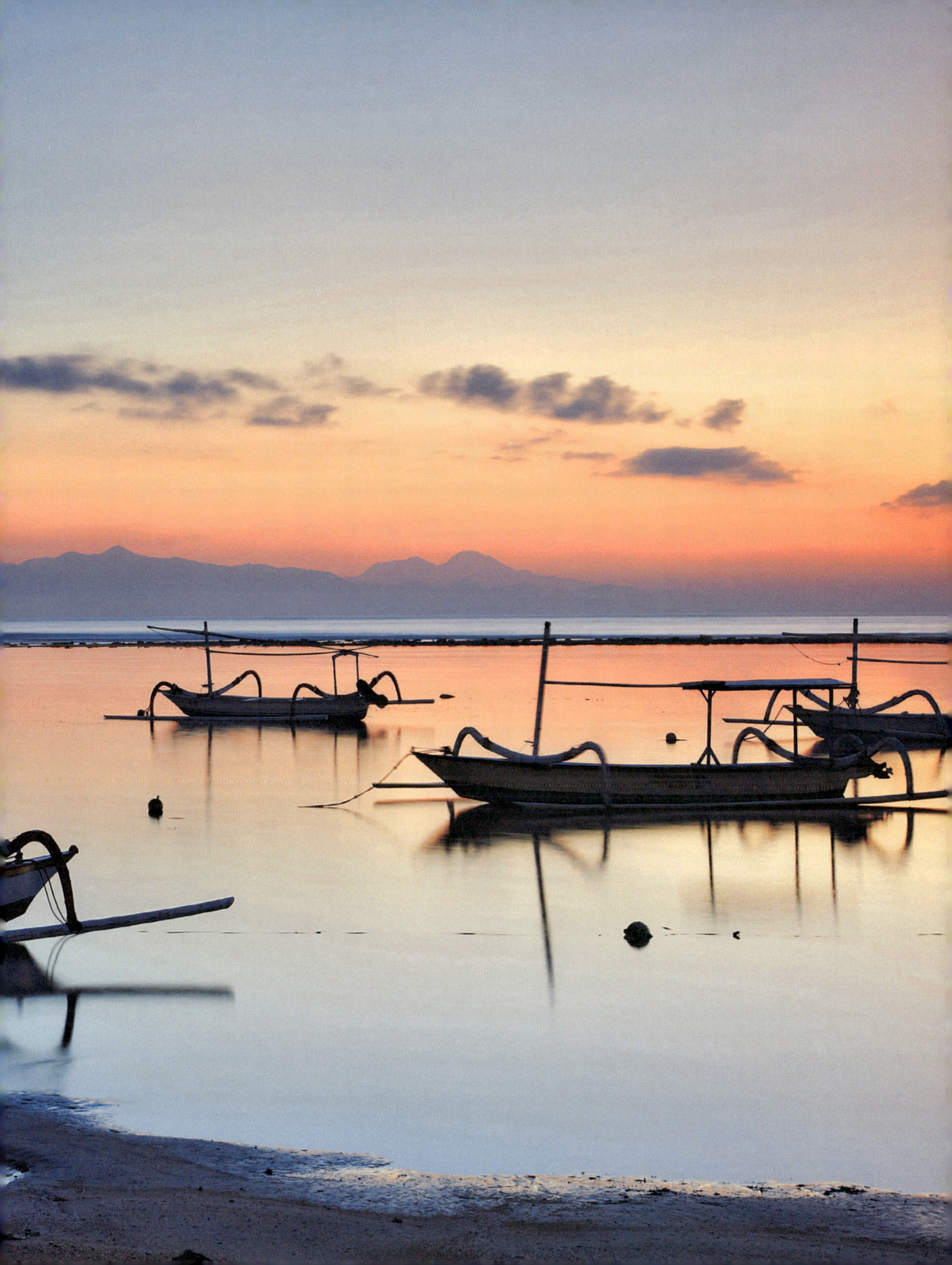

THE WOUNDS BENEATH THE INCENSE

BEHIND THE PICTURE-POSTCARD IMAGE, BALI BEARS THE SCARS OF A TURBULENT HISTORY, MARKED BY ERUPTIONS, CONQUESTS AND THE SPILLING OF BLOOD. INDEED, IT WAS NOT ONLY VOLCANOES THAT LEFT WOUNDS. DUTCH COLONIALISM CRUSHED THE ISLAND FOR OVER A CENTURY, STIFLING REBELLIONS IN BLOOD.

In 1906 and again in 1908, the Balinese rulers, rather than bowing down, chose *puputan*, mass suicide: the men of the court, along with women and children, in ceremonial dress, advanced toward the guns armed only with daggers, in a final gesture of dignity. Certain sources suggest that many of the dignitaries killed each other under the gaze of the Dutchmen, while according to other accounts the latter opened fire on the group: the only certainty is the merciless looting that followed. Fifty years later, between 1965 and 1966, the island was the scene of one of the darkest massacres in Indonesian and world history: in the wave of anti-communist violence unleashed by General Suharto, thousands of Balinese were killed, thrown into rivers or buried in mass graves. The purges directed against the militants of the Indonesian Communist Party—often defenceless or even unsuspecting—were encouraged by the United States, which feared the influence of this movement and its increasingly close relations with China and the USSR. Throughout Indonesia, the number of victims remains uncertain but appalling: an estimated 500,000 to 3 million dead. This is a genocide that has never resonated in the West; it has never been recounted or even clarified, due in part to Suharto's thirty-year dictatorship following those events. A silence that still weighs like a millstone today. And then there is terrorism. In 2002, the Kuta bombs—of Islamist origin—ripped through the island, bringing death to the heart of its nightlife. Bali, a land of harmony and beauty, once again experienced the blind brutality of destruction: this time the 202 victims were mostly foreigners or locals working in the tourism industry. Today, Bali continues to dance between light and shadow, between beauty and memory. It has seen death, and every day it reinvents itself like an offering left on the steps of a temple in the morning: fragrant and precious, but destined to fade and be reborn, over and over again.

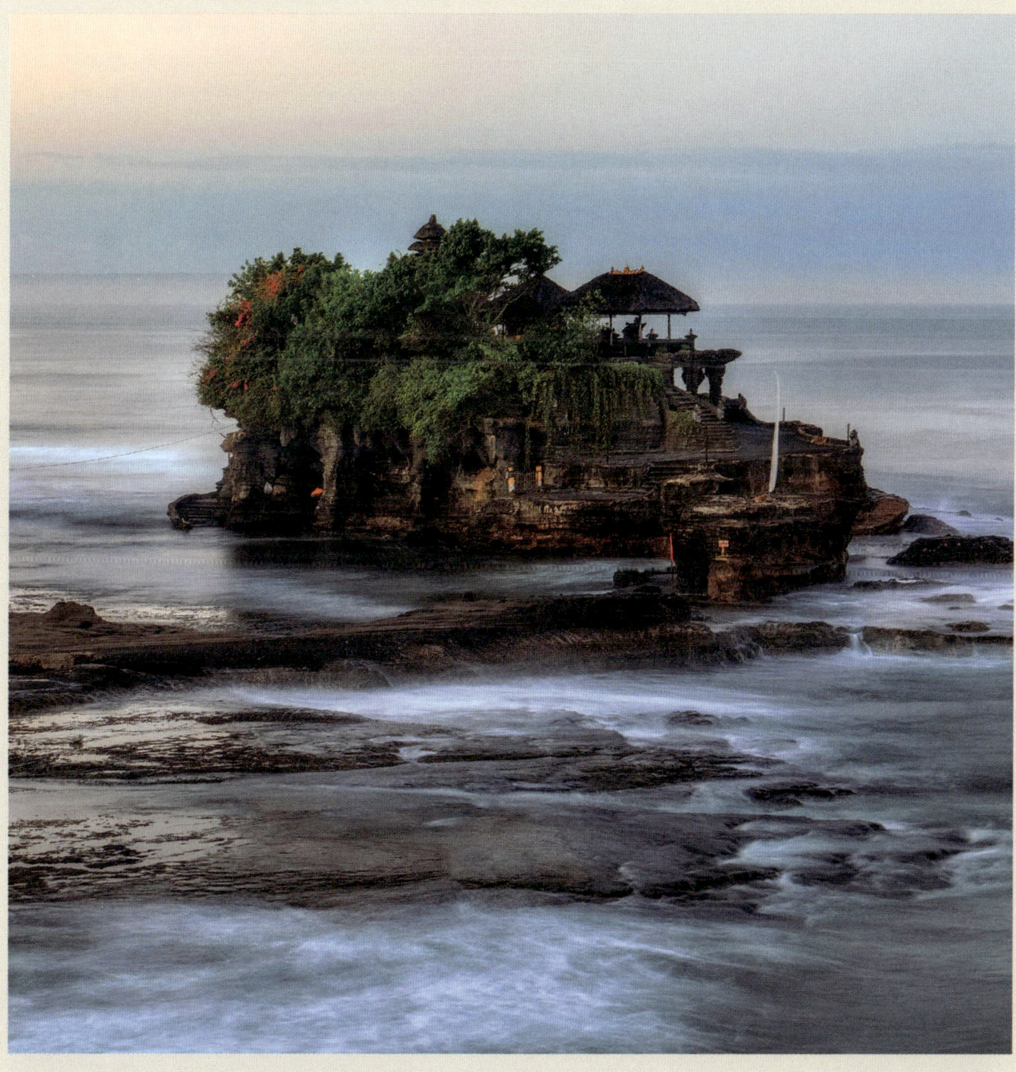

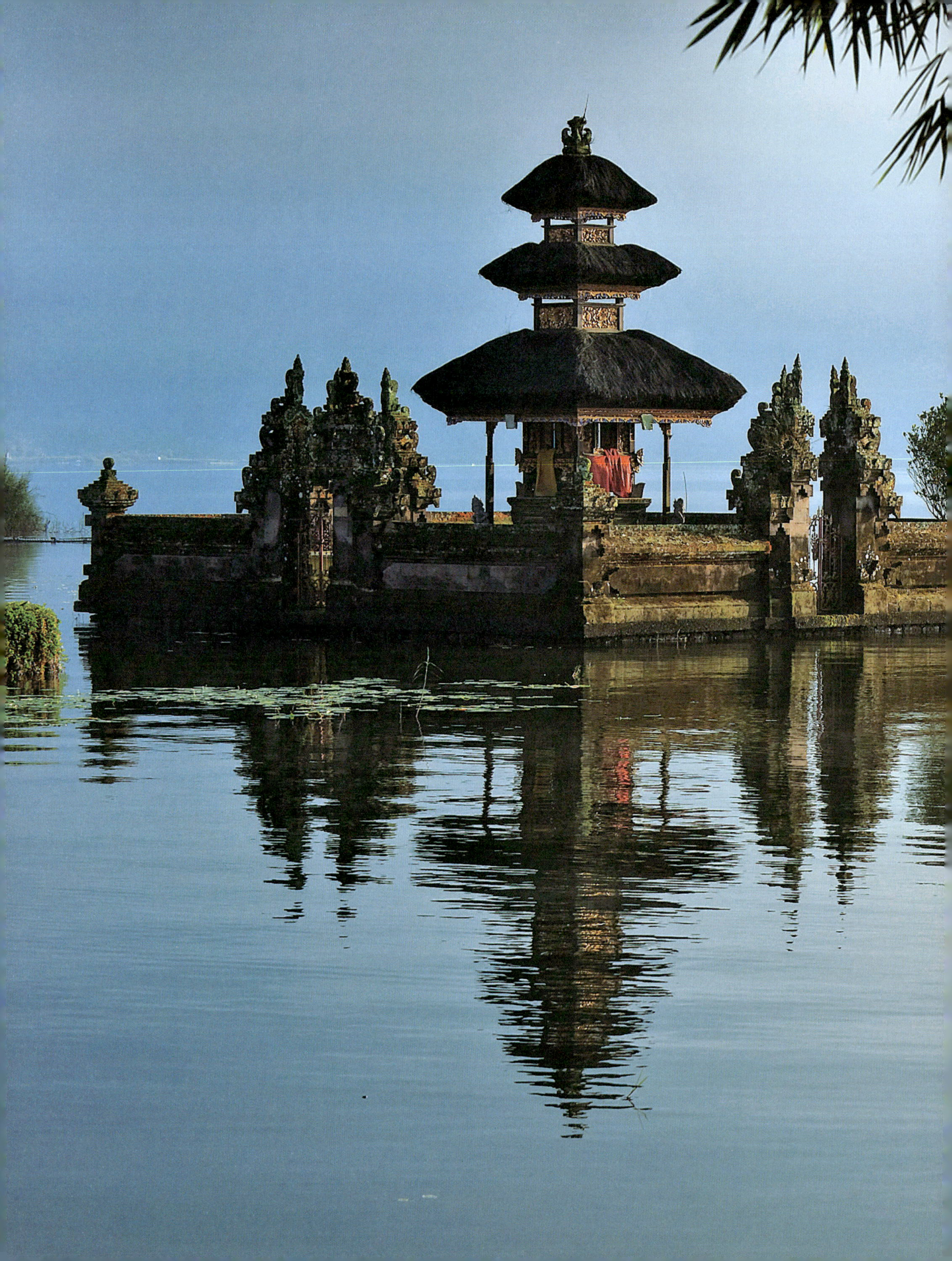

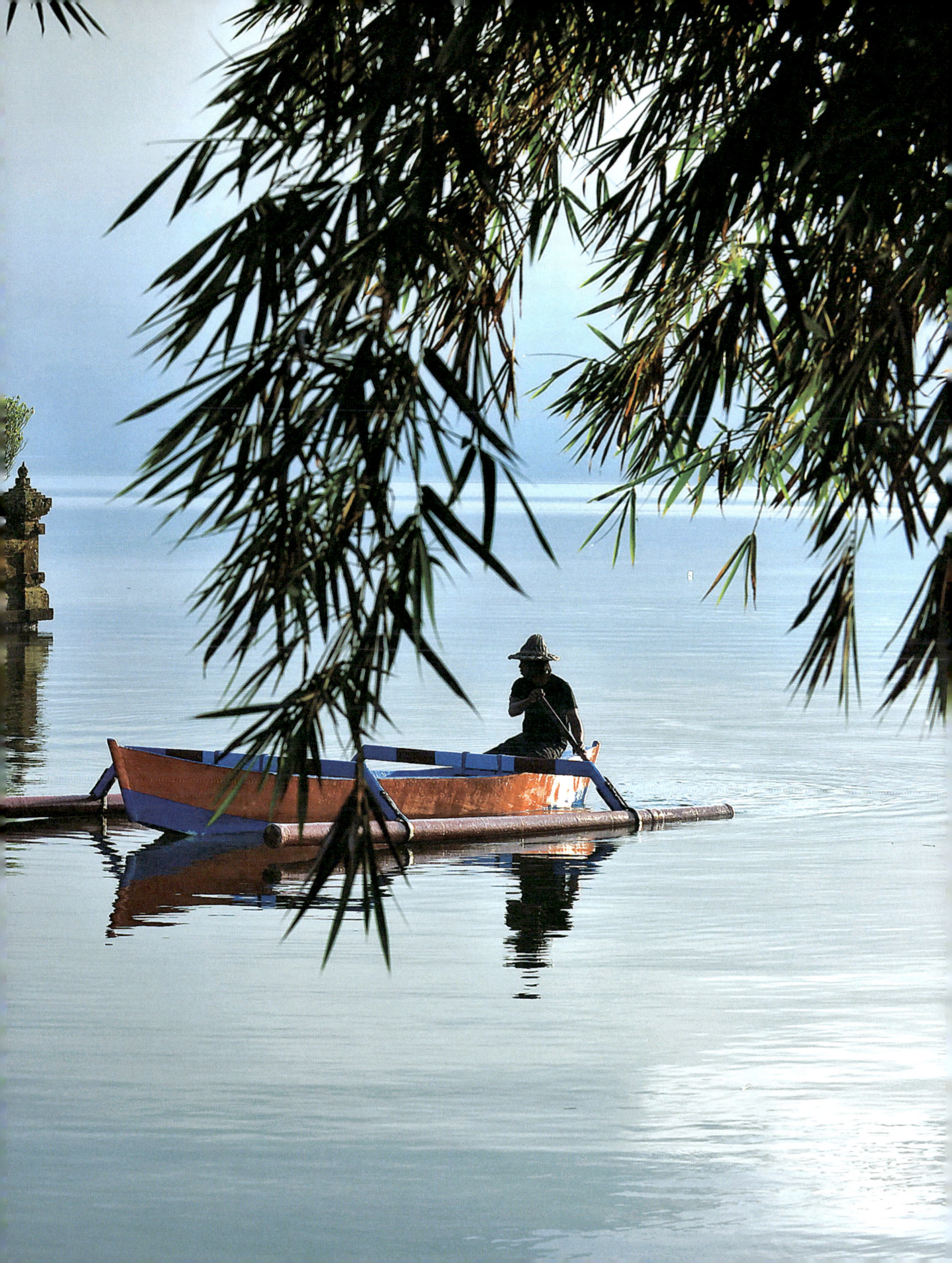

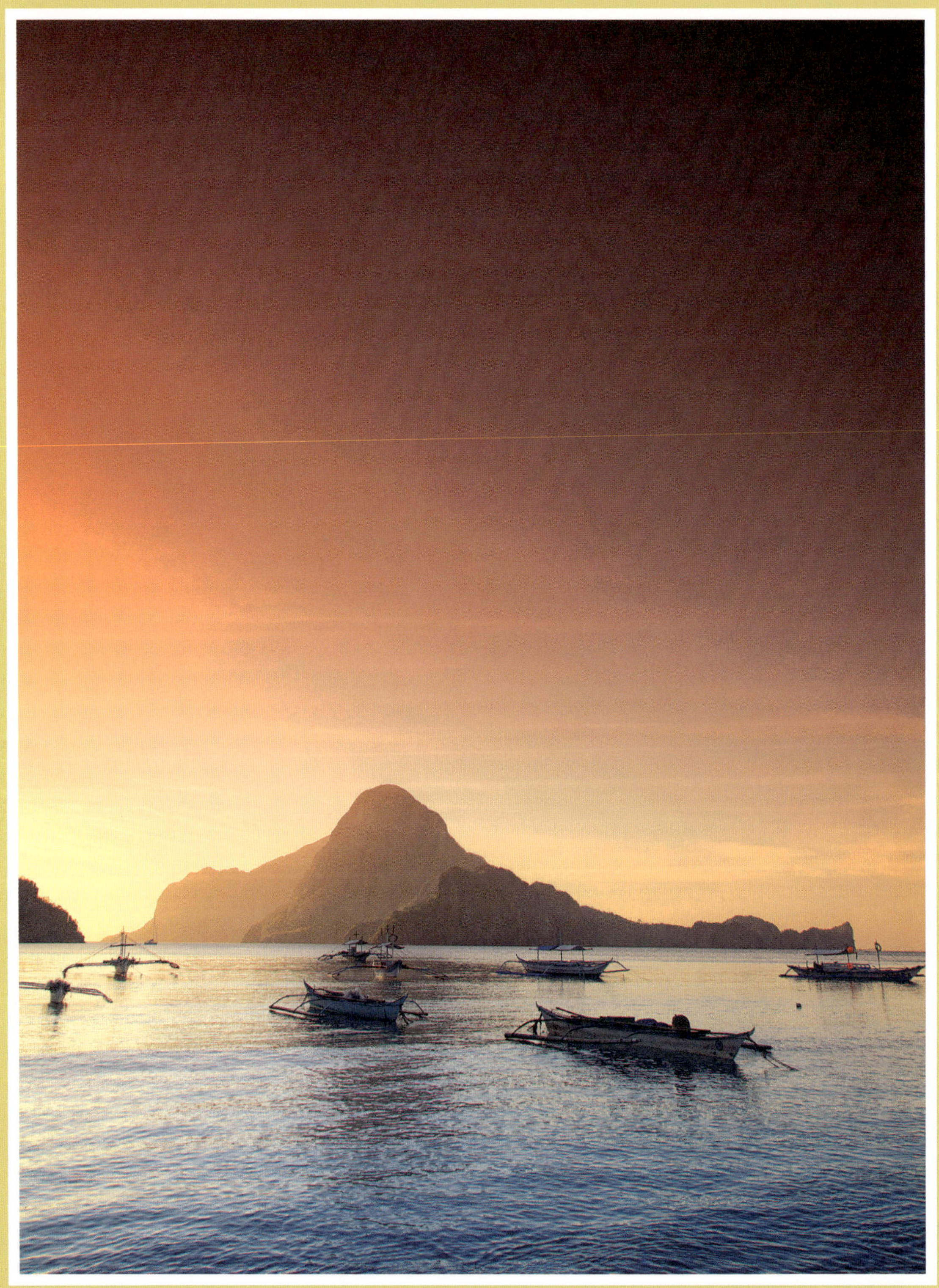

PALAWAN

Geographical coordinates: 9°44'21" N; 118°44'07" E
Waters: South China Sea, Sulu Sea
Population: 939,594 inhabitants
Surface area: 5,751.37 square miles (14,896 km²)
Capital: Puerto Princesa

A JUNGLE SPINE AND THE SEA

In the tropical chaos of the Philippines, a group of more than 7,000 islands scattered between the South China Sea and the Sulu Sea, Palawan is the exception that never passes unnoticed. The main island, which lends its name to the entire archipelago, long and sharp, is an emerald blade sculpted by the wind and the water to the point where it resembles a shattered bridge between Borneo and Luzon. Its 265 miles (425 kilometers) in length and maximum width of 25 (40 kilometers) are more of a journey than a point of arrival: a sequence of mountainous reliefs covered with primordial forests, sharp cliffs that emerge like teeth from the liquid skin of the sea, secret and silent lagoons where time seems to have forgotten to flow. Rather than an island, Palawan is a world apart. Here the jungle is so dense that light struggles to filter through the leaves, the rivers run invisible below ground like veins nourishing life without showing themselves and the beaches are never those you expect: a strip of white sand between two rocky outcrops, a bay where the water is so transparent to make it impossible to distinguish the confine between sea and sky. To the north, the small Bacuit archipelago, with its karstic formations jutting from the water, is the tropical version of a mystic vision. To the south, the nature is wilder, less domesticated, as if it seeks to ward off mankind and maintain its mystery intact. In the middle, the indigenous Tagbanua and Batak tribes continue to live according to ancient rhythms, speaking languages that evoke a distant and remote past, a suspended time forgotten by the rest of the world.

MAGELLAN AND THE GHOSTS OF THE SEA

~

In 1521, when Ferdinand Magellan dropped anchor in the waters of the Philippines, Palawan observed him from a distance, silent and immobile. The Portuguese navigator, convinced he had found a route to the Indies, had instead entered a labyrinth of islands and hidden dangers, where neither the sea nor the land are ever what they appear. Palawan was not the first port of call for that historic expedition, which had left Sanlúcar de Barrameda in Spain on the 20th of September 1519, nor would it be the last. However, while the Philippines marked the end of Magellan's life, mortally wounded on a Mactan beach by a poisoned arrow shot by the chieftain Lapu-Lapu, Palawan became one of the refuges of the surviving fleet, a respite from the slaughter of that battle between indigenous peoples and the Europeans. It is said that here the exhausted sailors found drinking water and food, exchanged gifts with the local inhabitants and perhaps, for a moment, during those finally calm nights lit by the glow of the moon, felt they were safe, reawakening within them that courage that was to push them to complete their voyage. There are legends that speak of a lost treasure, of gold coins buried under the sand of some forgotten beach, where the palm trees dip to touch the water and where time seems to have stopped. There are the mysteries there the sea has never thought to reveal: wrecks of galleons submerged among the corals, faded maps, secrets buried beneath centuries of silence. Palawan, with its broken, mutating geography, is the perfect place for what has been lost and never found.

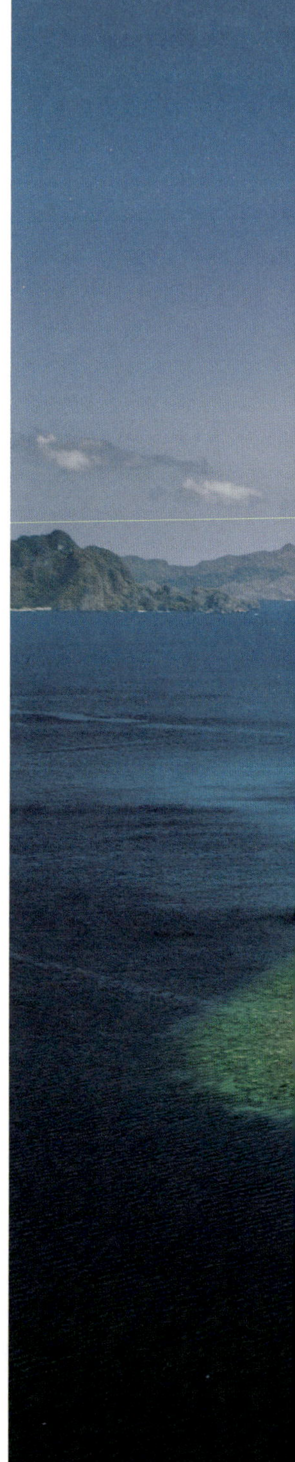

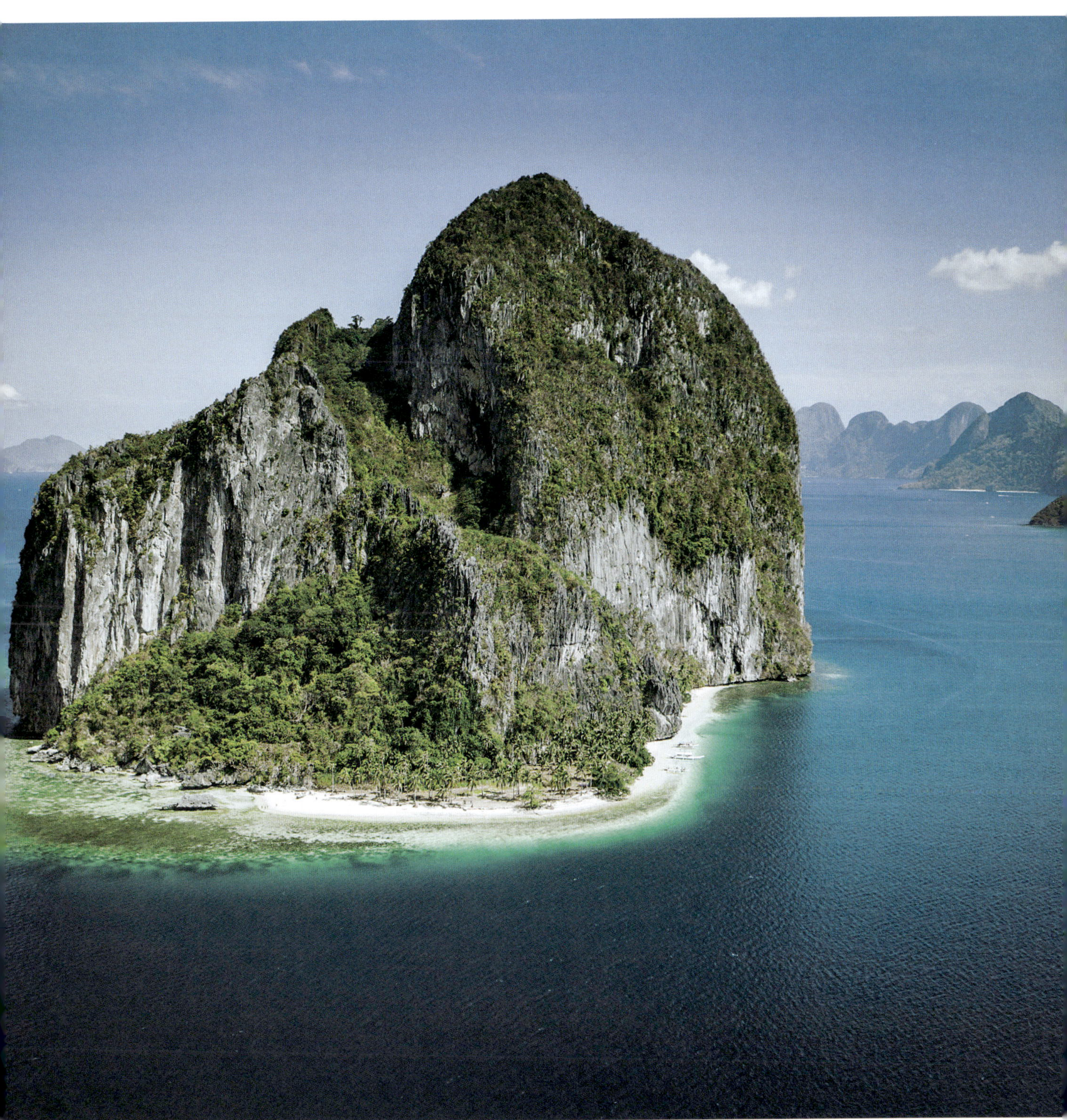

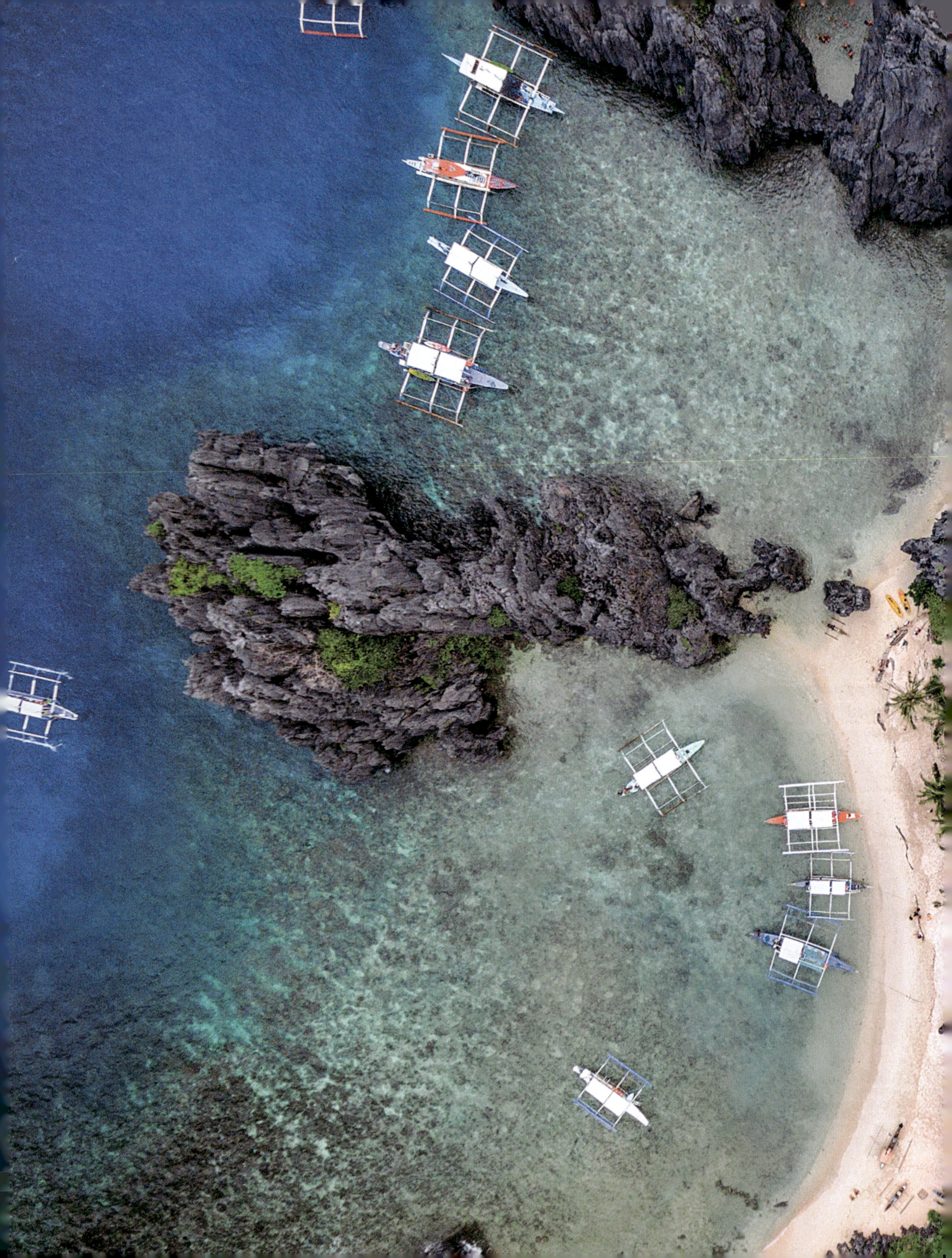

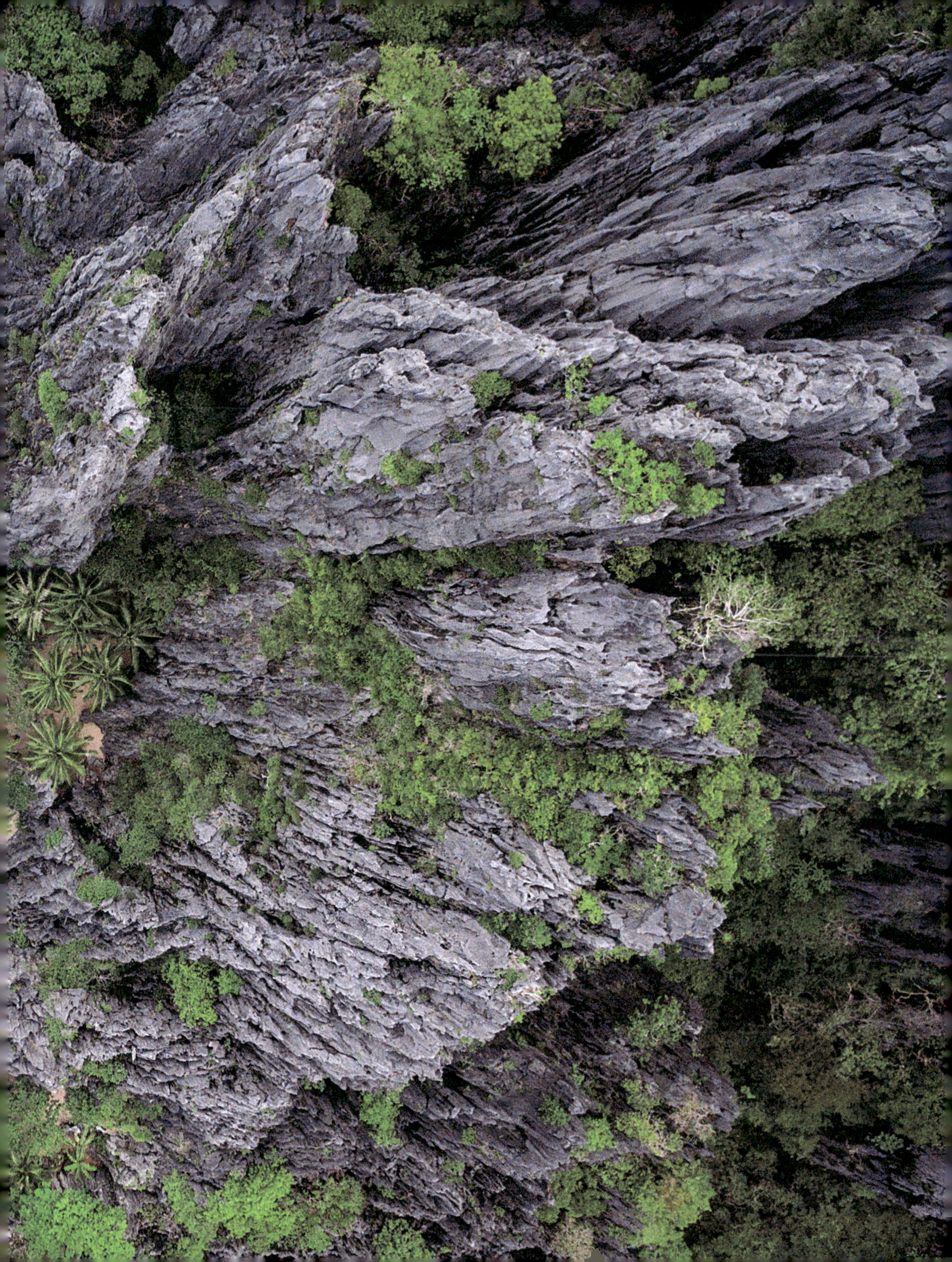

TWO WONDERS BELOW THE OCEAN SURFACE

IF THE EARTH HAD A LAST WISH, IT WOULD PROBABLY ASK TO BE BURIED IN THE DEPTHS OF TUBBATAHA.

This natural park, a submerged cathedral in the heart of the Sulu Sea, is an explosion of life that words can neither contain nor describe: coral outcrops that extend for miles, hammerhead sharks that emerge ghost-like from the depths, turtles that swim with the slow grace of those that know they have all the time in the world, fish that move in hypnotic swarms, like fragments of colored glass drawn by the ocean's very breath. Tubbataha is untouchable, protected by strict laws and its own isolated nature. Few can visit it, only for a short time and only in certain periods of the year. It is the kind of place that reminds you how small and transient you are, while the currents shift the sand and the fish swim as if they do not see you. It is reached after 10 hours sailing, when the coast is but a blurred memory and the all-encompassing blue becomes absolute. Then there is the subterranean river of Puerto Princesa, another anomaly that nature has casually left here. A river that insinuates itself into a mountain, flowing for miles beneath stalactites and caverns illuminated only by the trembling light of torches. The silence is total, broken only by the dripping of the water and the flapping of the bats' wings. It is one of those places where you only ever feel you are a guest, never a master. This is Palawan: a frontier between the visible and the invisible, between what we know and what we continue to search for. Here nature still dictates its rules, with a strong, mysterious voice. An island that has never been tamed, perhaps for the best.

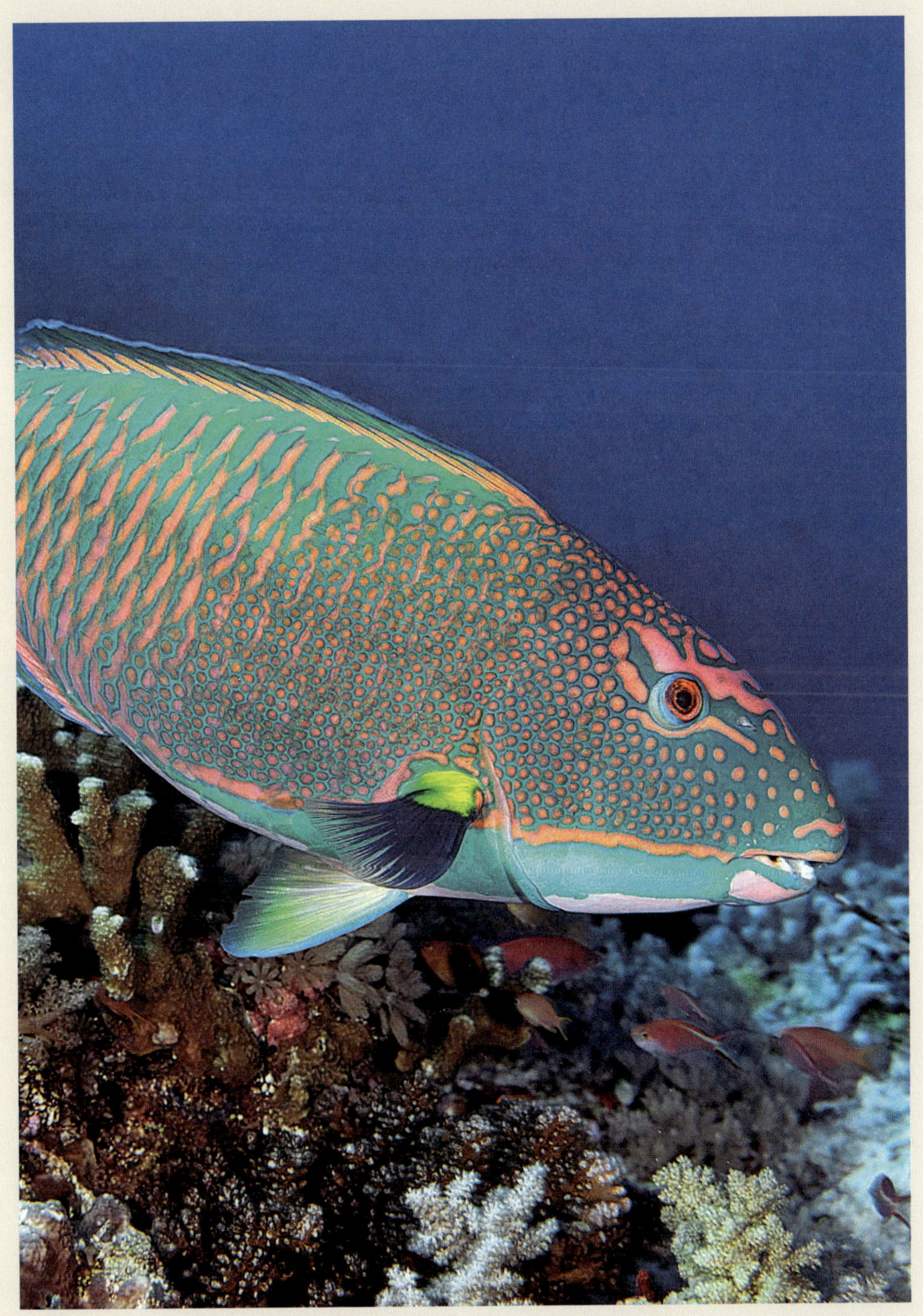

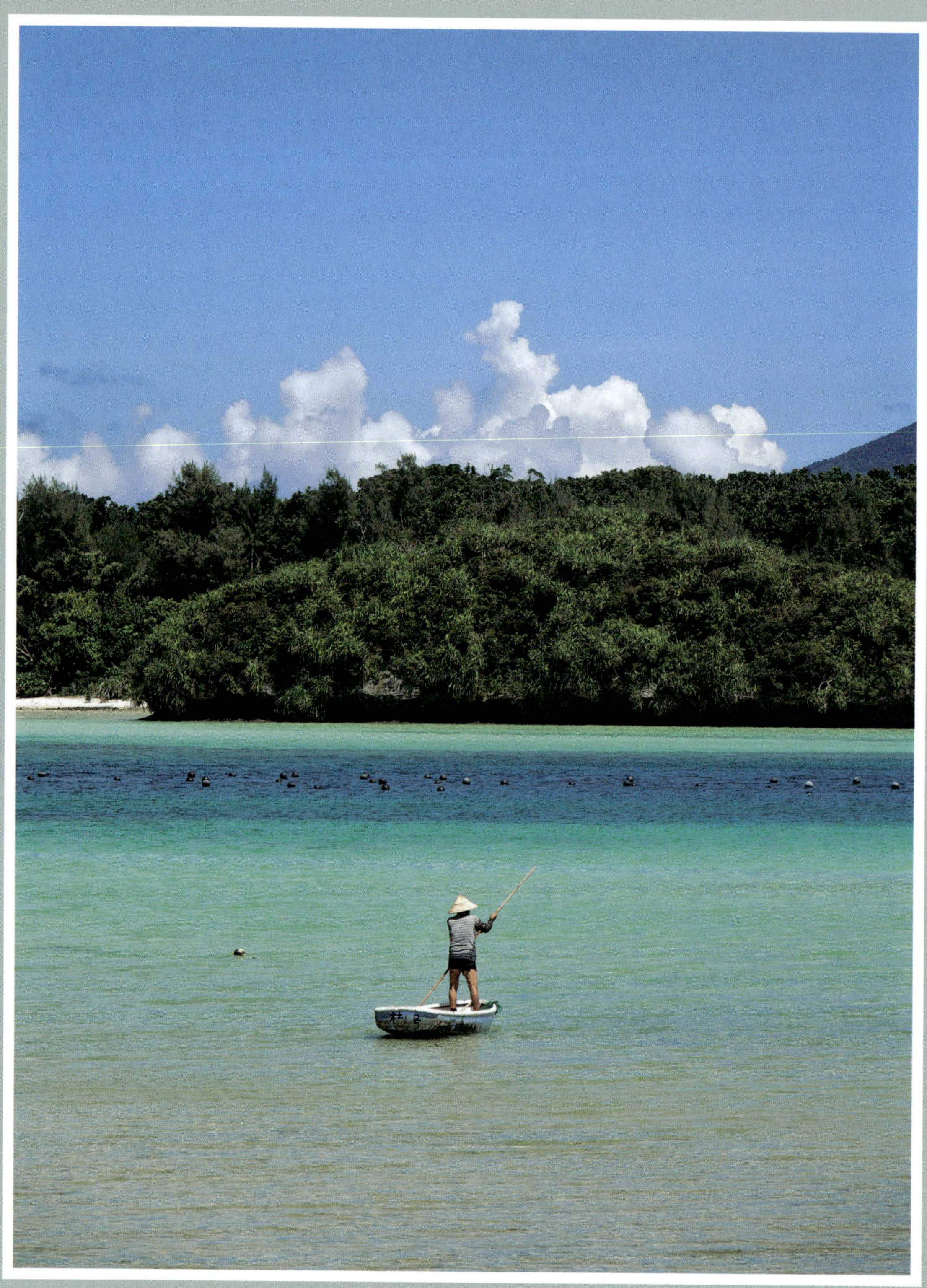

Ryūkyū, Japan

OKINAWA

Geographical coordinates: 26°28'46" N; 127°55'40" E
Waters: Philippine Sea, East China Sea
Population: 1,466,870 inhabitants
Surface area: 466.02 square miles (1,207 km^2)
Capital: Naha

THE HAWAII OF THE RISING SUN

The Okinawa archipelago, more than 160 islands of which only 50 are inhabited, is the heart of the Ryūkyū, a fragmented island chain stretching over 620 miles (1,000 kilometers) between Kyūshū and Taiwan. Politically it belongs to Japan, but geographically, biologically and culturally it is actually a crossroads between East Asia and the Pacific. The main islands—Ishigaki, Miyako, Iriomote and Okinawa—are of volcanic and coral origin: gentle reliefs shaped by centuries of rain, alternating with low-lying formations with beaches of incredibly fine sand. While the southern islands of the archipelago, in particular Miyako and Yaeyama, are lower and flatter, punctuated by coral reefs emerging from crystal-clear lagoons and pristine beaches, Okinawa, about 60 miles (100 kilometers) long and never more than 18 (30 kilometers) wide, is a varied territory: jagged coastlines, limestone plateaus and an interior covered with dense subtropical vegetation. To the north lies the region of Yanbaru, home to one of Japan's last virgin forests, with endemic species such as the Okinawan woodpecker. The climate is hot and humid for much of the year, with long summers and mild winters, but also sudden and violent typhoons. Everything oscillates between delicacy and resistance: the land, the sea, life itself that clings tenaciously to this hidden, kaleidoscopic archipelago. Natural beauty is only one element in its magic circle: it is a world full of precious insights that speak softly to the deepest parts of the human soul. Harmony between opposites, here, is an ideal within reach, courted gracefully in a refined and courageous cultural and spiritual quest, involving both the individual and the community.

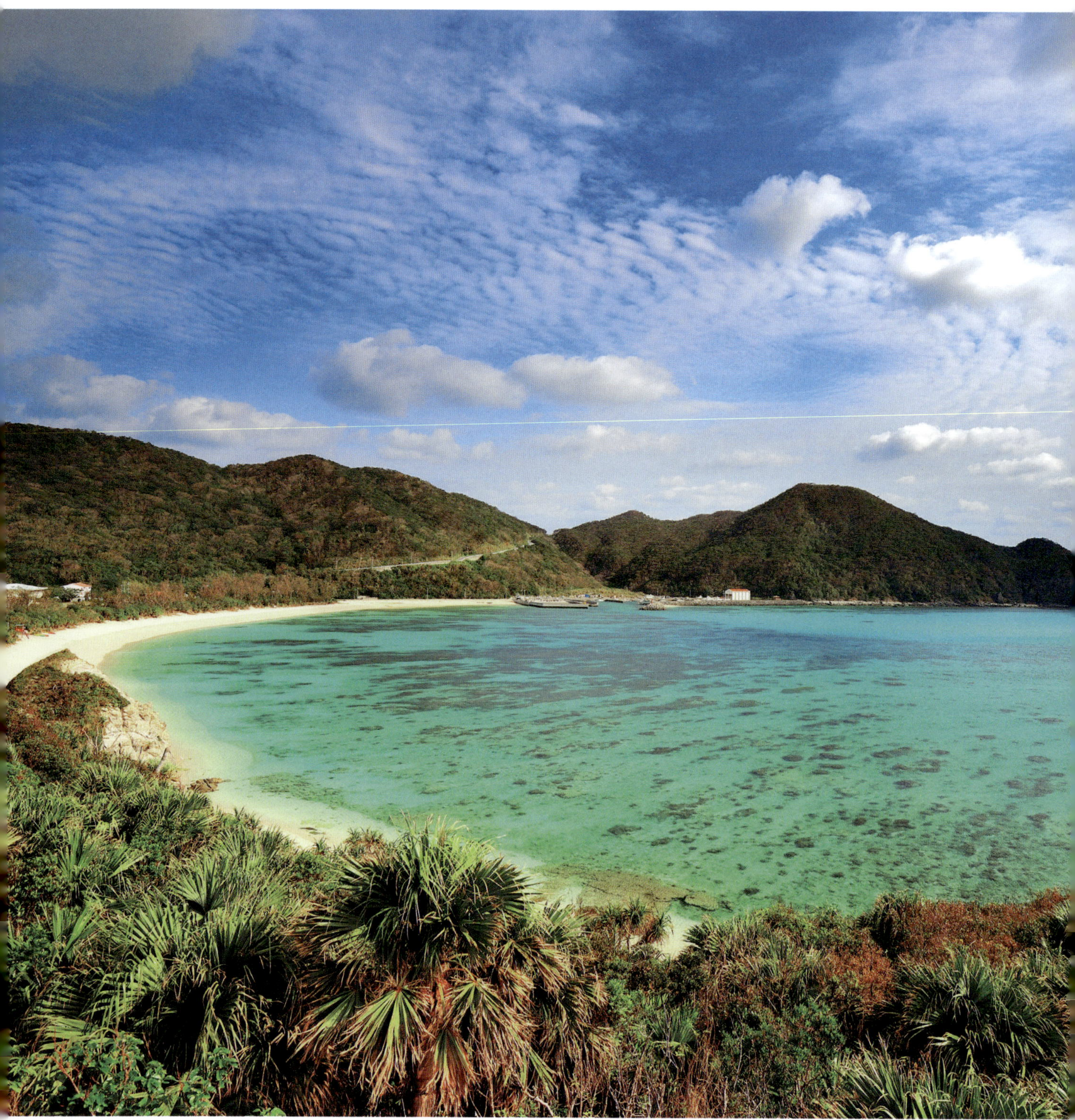

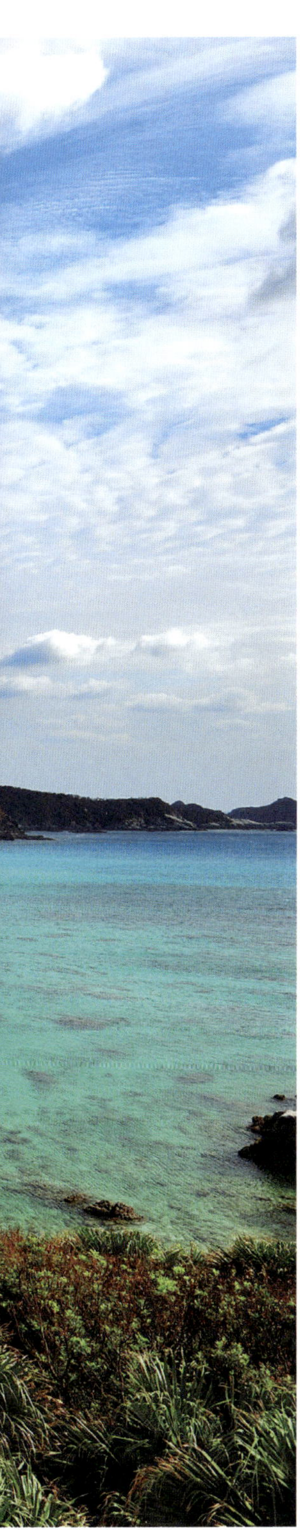

LAND OF IMMORTALS

~

On the island of Okinawa, humanity achieves a degree of physical and spiritual well-being such as to arouse not only wonder among its visitors but also the interest of the scientific community. It is in fact the area of the world where people live longest and the incidence of serious illness, especially those associated with aging, is lowest. There is a remarkably high number of centenarians and like expectancy is more than 13 years higher than the global average—85 against 72. A key role is played by diet, prevalently vegetarian and locally produced, enriched with foods blessed with antioxidant and anti-inflammatory properties such as purple yams, vegetables such as goya—related to the cucumber and zucchini—fruits such as shikuwasa and varieties of alga such as kombu and mozuku. *Hara haci bu* is the name of the custom of stopping eating just before you are satiated, nourishing yourself slowly given that that the brain takes a few minutes to register that the stomach is full. Slowness here is a value, part of an approach to respecting oneself, others and the environment. Another key concept of this network of the spirit is *ikigai*, that is to say, the reason why we wake up in the morning: the idea that every person, at whatever age, has an aim and a responsibility to make a decisive contribution to their well-being. Another pillar of this style of life are the *moai* (which have nothing in common with the Easter Island statues): groups of people who share passions and interests and who are ready to support one another in times of need. Each individual may belong to multiple moai, and this form of amical solidarity lasts a lifetime.

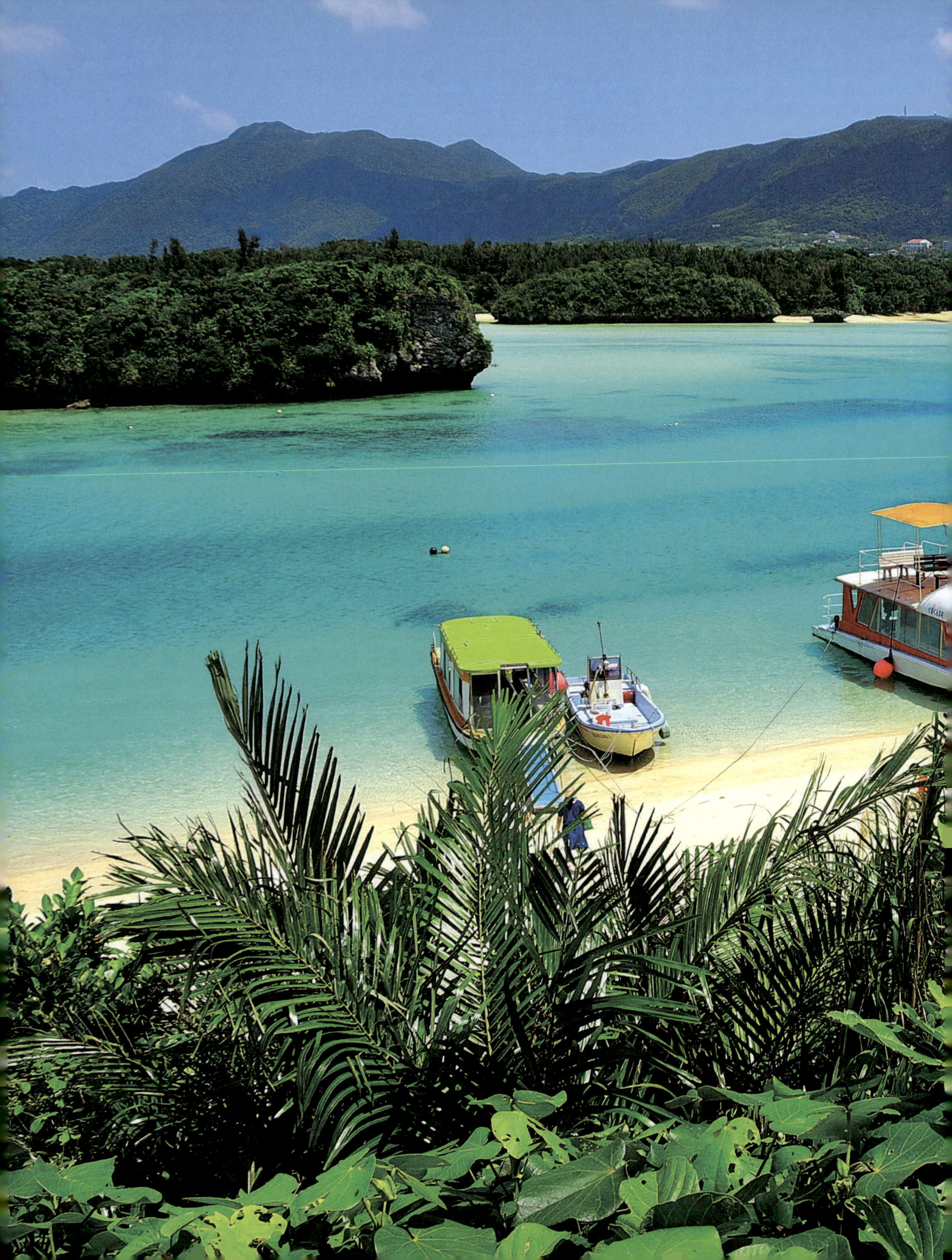

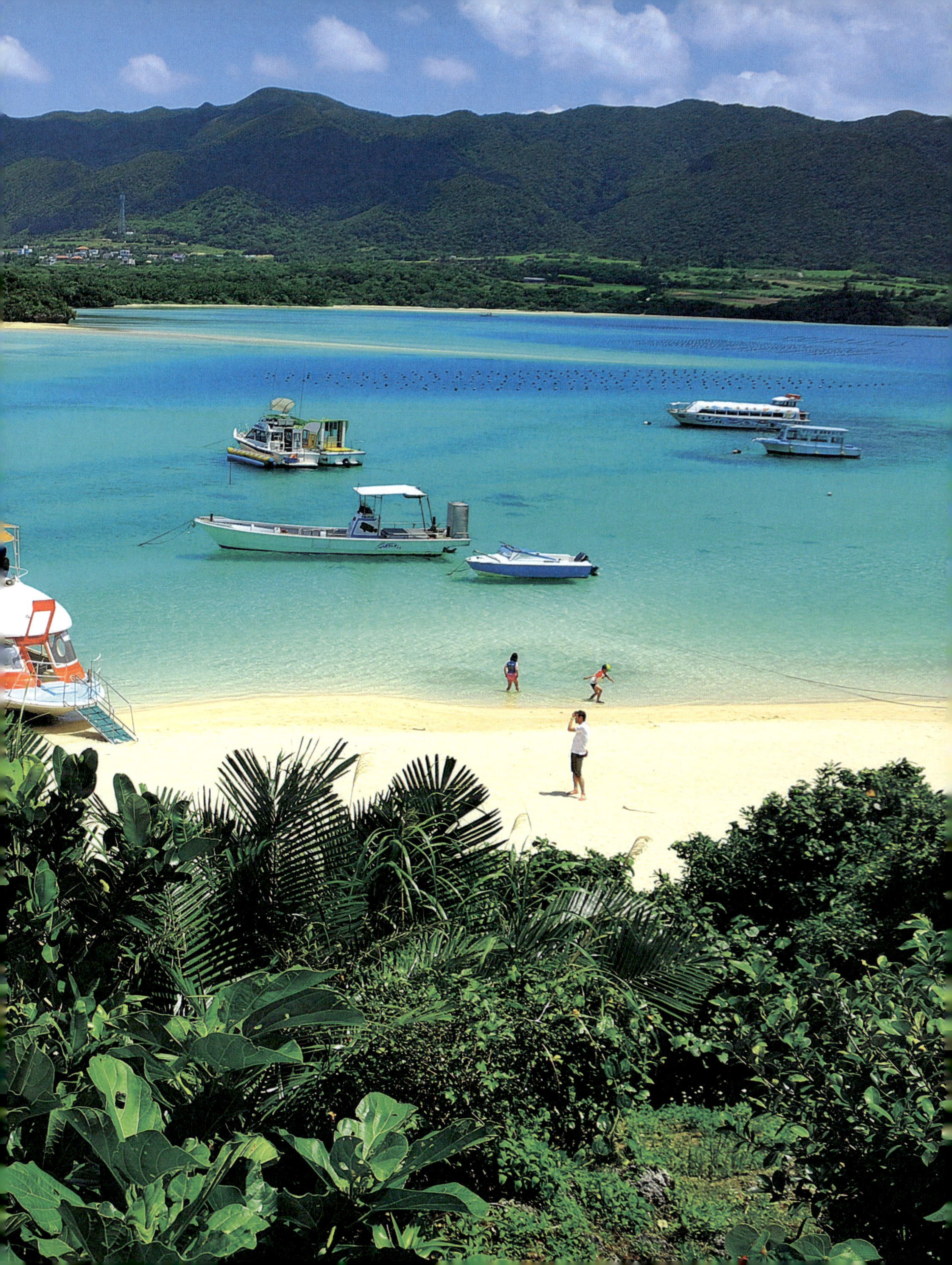

KAMIKAZE

∾

THERE IS NOT ONLY RESPECT AND WISDOM TO THE CHARACTER OF THIS ARCHIPELAGO WRESTED FROM CHINESE DOMINION IN 1879, BUT ALSO TRAUMA AND LACERATION, WITH EXPERIENCES SUCH AS THE SECOND WORLD WAR REVEALING THE MOST CHALLENGING ASPECTS.

The American forces' invasion of Okinawa—Operation Iceberg, preceded by intensive bombardment—began on the 1st of April, 1945, but the resistance of the local population was more tenacious than expected. The first reprisal saw more than 350 kamikaze flights. The ground offensive was slow and painful, with symbolic victims for the Americans, including the reporter Ernie Pyle and General Simon Bolivar Buckner Jr. The advance was encouraged by the admirals, but came up against the difficulties caused by the nature of the terrain and the determination of the locals, who took no prisoners and refused to surrender, imposing continual deadly clashes. The fighting lasted three months and was concentrated along the Shuri line, where the Japanese had dug in, exploiting the numerous natural caves. The struggle involved the local people, with families being supplied with hand grenades to be used in the case of the enemy's approach. On the 22nd of June, with the situation by then compromised, Commanding General Ushijima and Chief of Staff Chō Isamu chose an honorable ritual suicide—*seppuku*, involving decapitation by an adjutant—

leaving just Colonel Hiromichi Yahara alive to report on the event. It is estimated that the American forces lost 12,000 men, while the Japanese victims numbered 150,000, approximately a quarter of the island's population. The island remained under American control through to 1972, but the presence of American bases is still today a source of tension. It should come as no surprise that a martial art such as karate, which combines power, balance and control in the search for a combative spirit that does not stray into aggression, was developed in these parts. It is a long story that began after the unification of the three kingdoms that made up the island in the 15th century, when all arms were locked away in the Shuri castle and their use was prohibited, in favor of an effective defensive technique requiring no weapons.

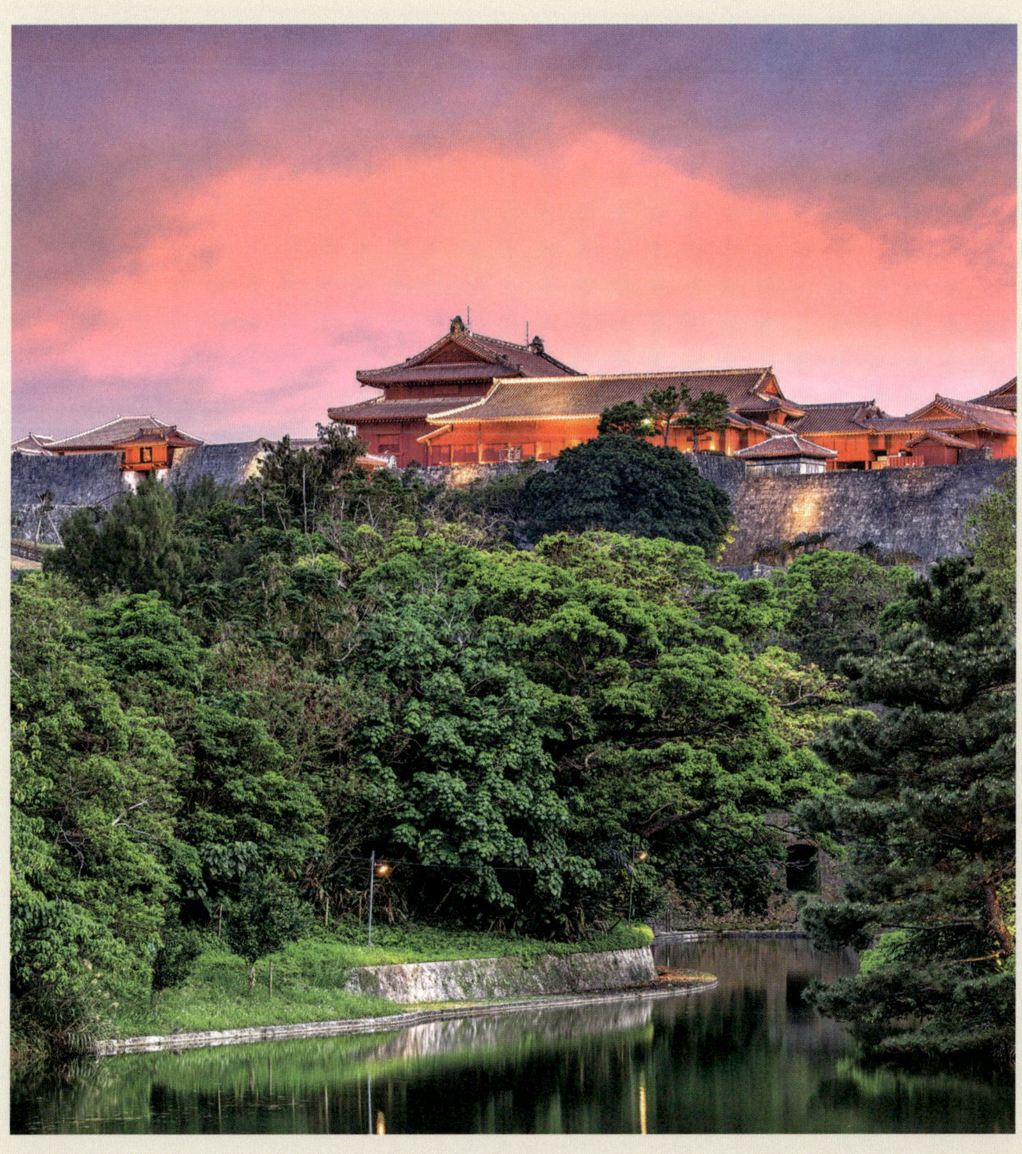

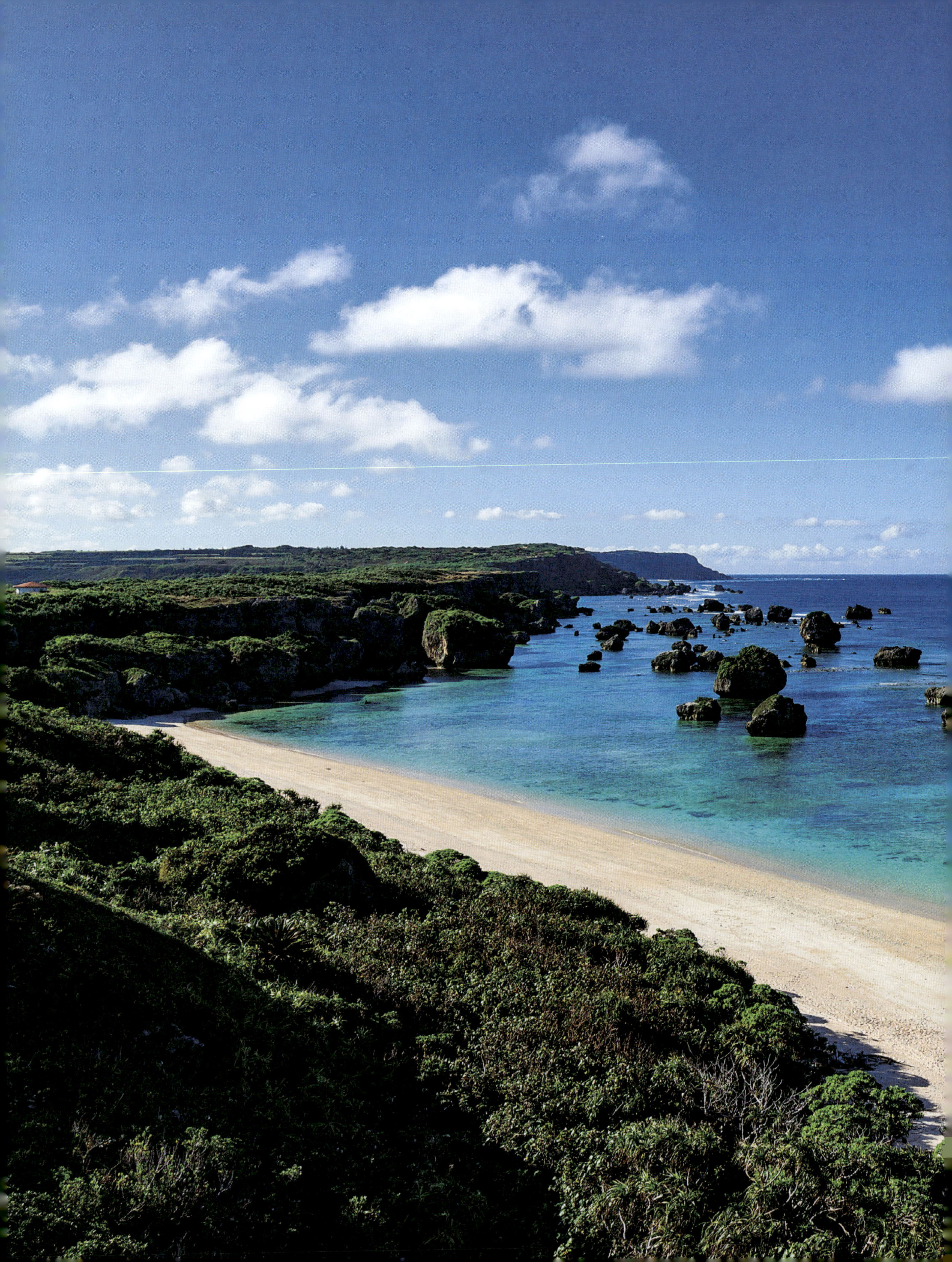

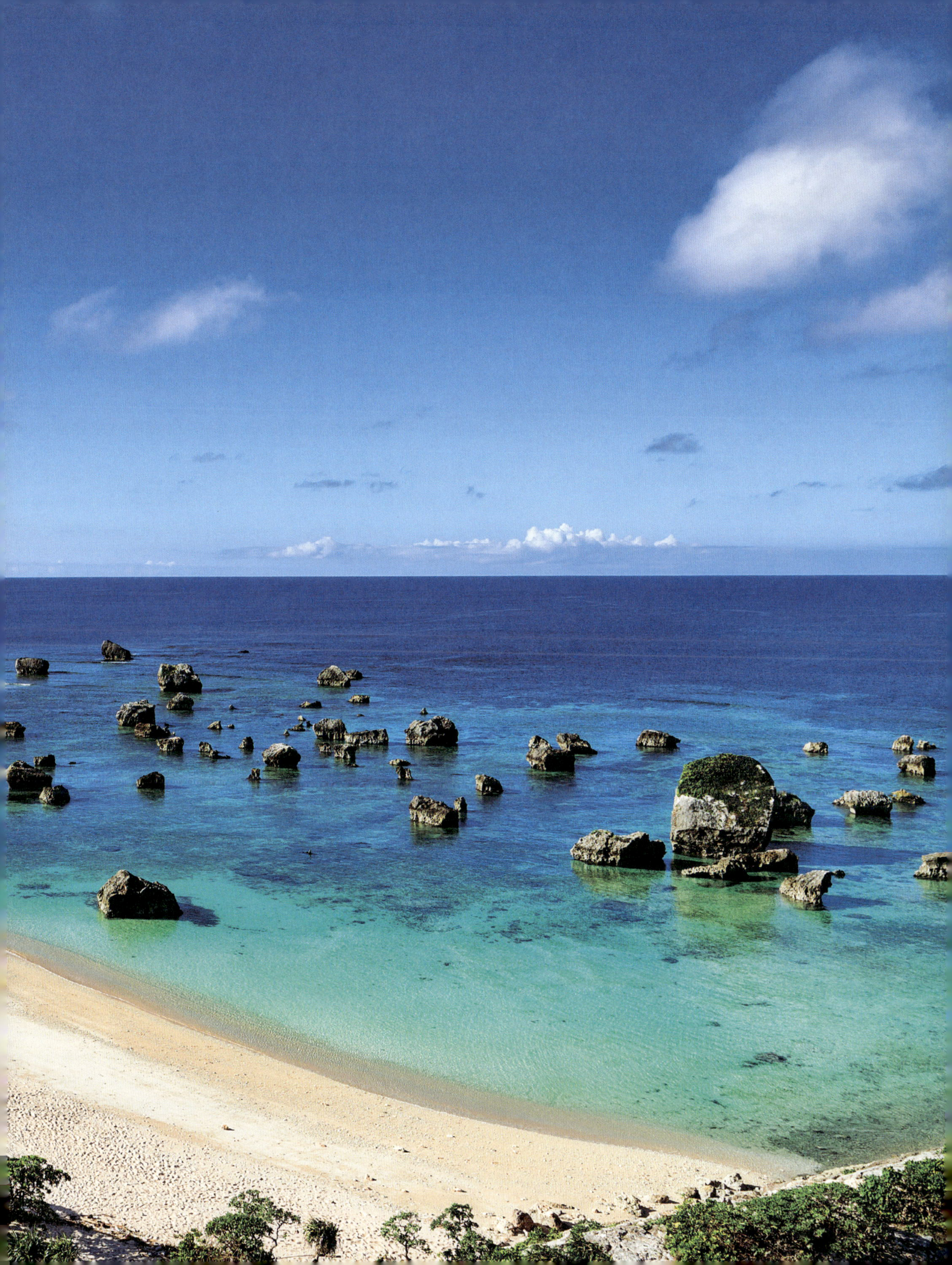

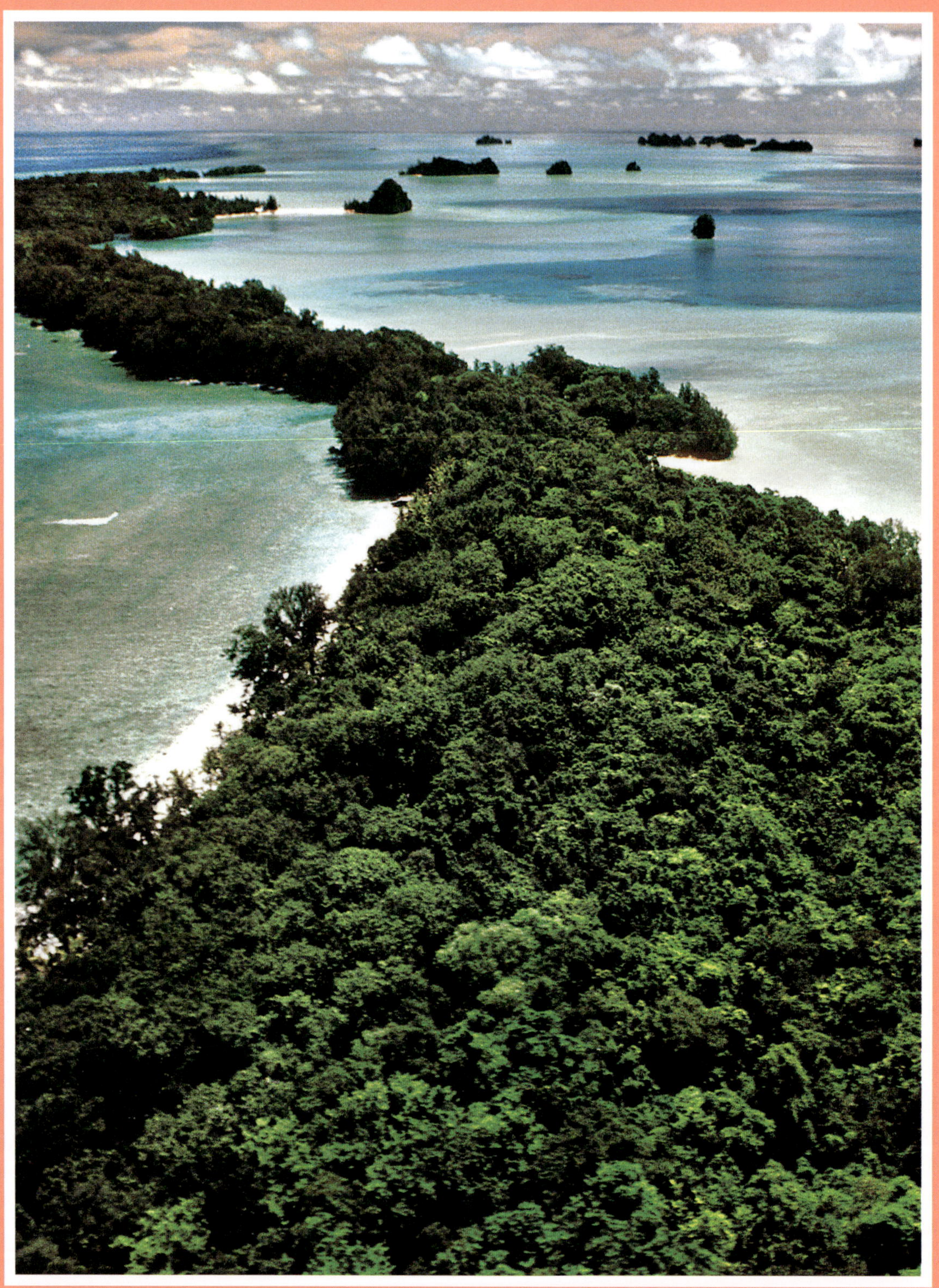

Rock Islands, Palau

EIL MALK (OR MECHERCHAR)

Geographical coordinates: 7°9'15" N; 134°21'45" E
Waters: Philippine Sea
Population: no permanent inhabitants
Surface area: 7.33 square miles (19 km²)

THE MOVING LAKE

It has a body that is incorporeal, ethereal, transparent and elegant; it hypnotizes you, seduces you as it dances, embracing the current. However, touch it and the illusion collapses: the jellyfish unleashes its stinging potential, as unexpected and fierce as an electric shock. Yet this deadly caress is not aggression but merely defence, survival. On Eil Malk, things are rather different: it is here that Jellyfish Lake is to be found, home to a permanent population of golden jellyfish. In this basin of brackish water, separated from the ocean but connected by underground channels, a unique evolutionary event has taken place. The jellyfish, isolated for thousands of years in the absence of predators or perils, have lost their ability to sting. But there is more, an extraordinary phenomenon deriving from the close symbiosis with the single-celled algae that live in their tissues, nourishing the jellyfish in exchange for protection and movement. Every day, millions of specimens make a horizontal migration, slowly moving from one shore to the other following the sun. It is a constant, synchronized, silent movement, a living wave that crosses the lake to maximize exposure to light. At night, the journey is reversed. The jellyfish move in a compact mass, enveloped in a viscous transparency. This primordial procession, governed by simple biological laws, has been repeating itself for thousands of years. The lake is 98 feet (30 metes) deep, but life is concentrated in the first 33 (10 meters). Below that level, the water becomes anoxic, devoid of oxygen and saturated with hydrogen sulphide, preventing the growth of any other organism. It is this vertical separation, together with geographical isolation, that has preserved the lake's balance.

SLIGHT TRACES

~

Eil Malk today appears to be intact with no human traces. The vegetation has engulfed the remains, erosion has obliterated the straight lines, but between the 13th and the 15th centuries the island hosted small coastal settlements devoted to fishing and harvesting the resources of the lagoon: shellfish, fish, turtles and crustaceans. Seasonal groups perhaps, or perhaps permanent inhabitants, in any case few in number. They settled in the low-lying areas and close to sources of fresh water, or in proximity to sheltered bays, ideal for launching canoes. There are no known organized villages nor permanent structures: no roads, stone walls or complex agricultural systems. Just a few signs, but sufficient to indicate a human presence that nonetheless was interrupted around the 15th century for no clear reason. From then on, the island remained uninhabited for centuries, even after the arrival of the Europeans, ignored by colonial interests and never exploited, not even by Japan, which in the first half of the 20th century controlled the Palau archipelago. Today, Eil Malk is part of a protected area, subject to strict environmental restrictions. The traces of the past remain uncertain, camouflaged and difficult to differentiate from the vegetation that has engulfed them. In the past, snorkeling was permitted in the lake—strictly without fins, sun creams or oxygen tanks—but from 2017, access has been restricted to protect a fragile ecosystem threatened by environmental changes. The increase in temperature and the variations in salinity drastically reduced the jellyfish population between 1998 and 2016, although the numbers have revived in recent years. Jellyfish Lake is a time warp; it does not resemble any other ecosystem on Earth. It is a world apart, suspended between biology and geography, between sun and salt.

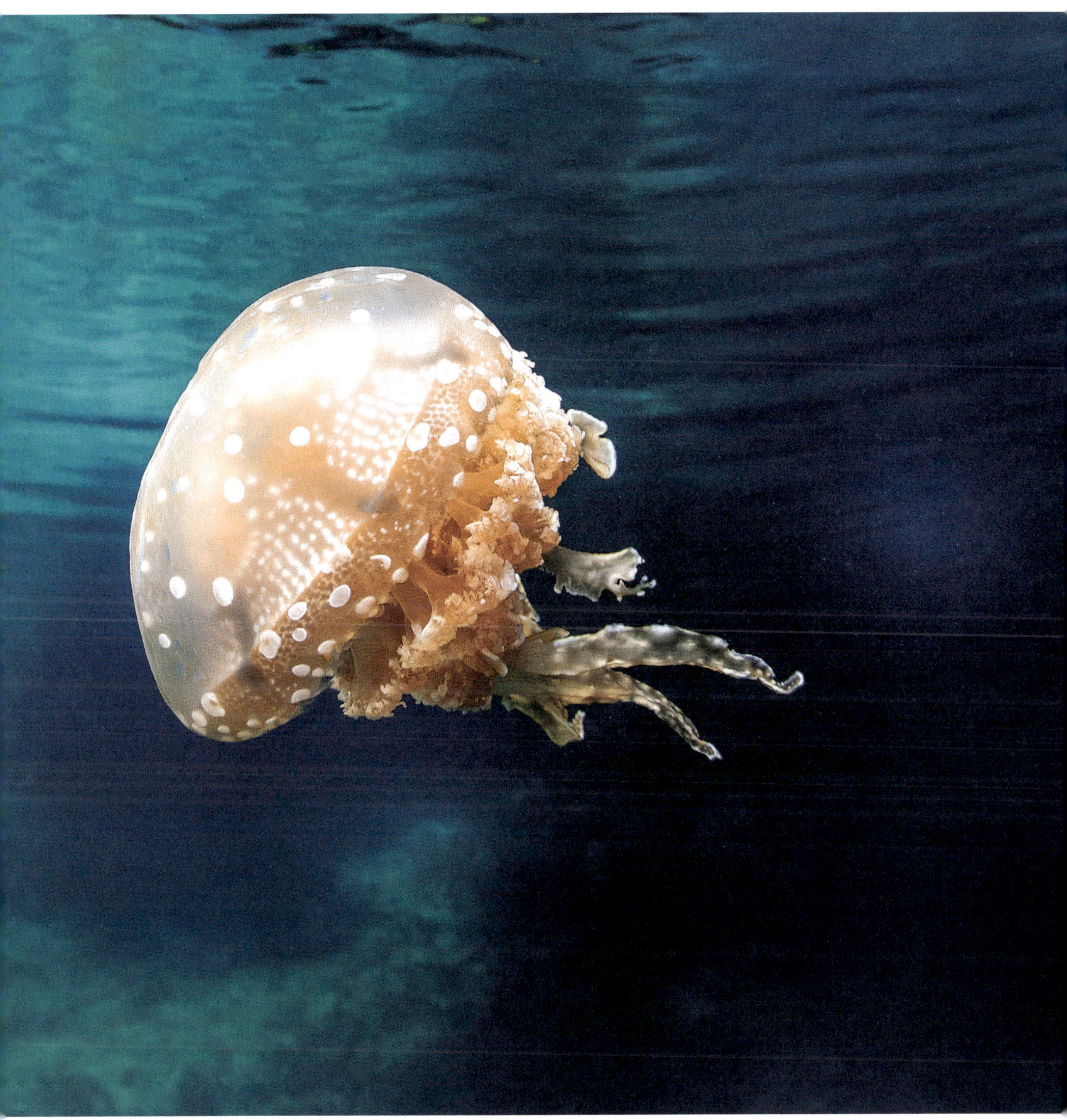

PALAU ARCHIPELAGO

PALAU IS AN ARCHIPELAGO OF MORE THAN 300 ISLANDS, FANNING OUT BETWEEN THE PHILIPPINES AND MICRONESIA. IT HAS A SMALL SURFACE AREA (178 SQ MILES/460 SQ KM) AND JUST NINE ARE INHABITED, BUT THE SEA AREA UNDER ITS JURISDICTION IS VAST. A SOVEREIGN STATE FROM 1994, WITH THE CAPITAL NGERULMUD ON THE ISLAND OF BABELDAOB, THE MAJORITY OF THE INHABITANTS, LESS THAN 20,000, LIVE ON KOROR AND THE NEIGHBORING ISLANDS.

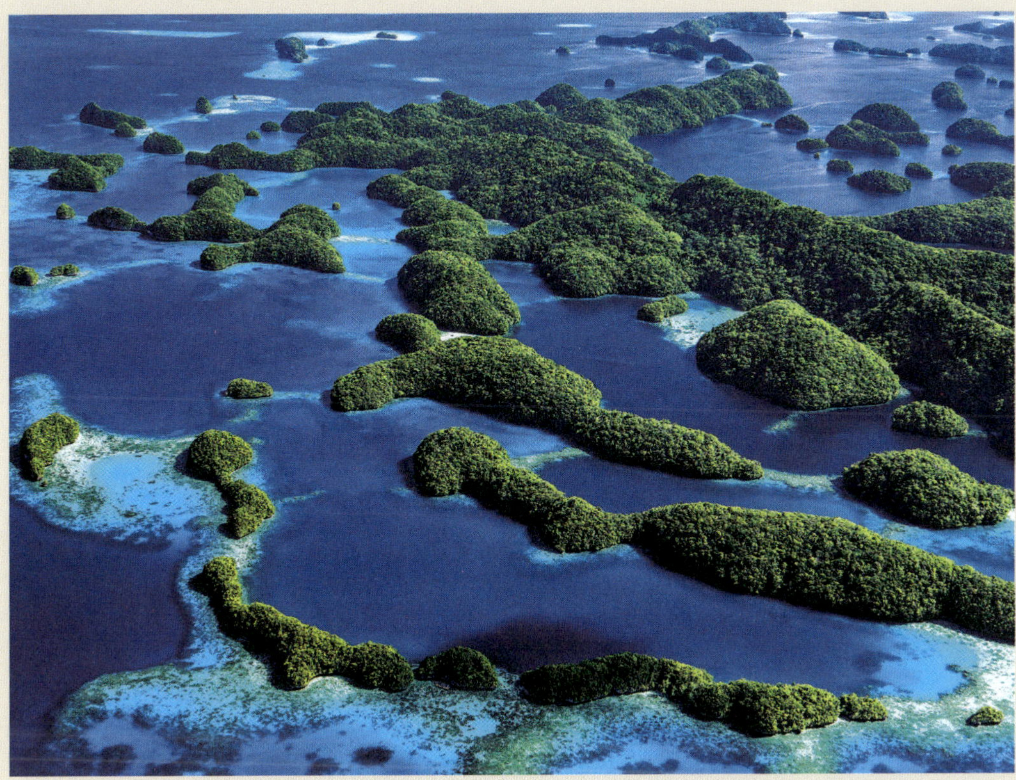

Geologically, the archipelago is a mosaic: older volcanic islands, such as Babeldaob and Koror, alternate with the rock islands—which number more than 300—of which Eil Malk is a part. It is of coral origins, calcareous structures modeled by erosion and covered with vegetation, uninhabited and inaccessible. It has been a UNESCO World Heritage Site since 2012. The sea here is full of surprises: grey sharks, rays, dugongs, sea turtles, thousands of species of fish and coral coexist in a complex network of reefs, channels and lagoons. Since 2015, almost 80% of the territorial waters has been declared a marine sanctuary, one of the most extensive protected areas on the planet. Commercial fishing and the industrial exploitation of the seabed have been banned, in favor of environmental safeguarding and sustainable tourism. From the cultural point of view, too, Palau is a rich and stratified land. The inhabitants speak Palauan and English, follow a traditional matrilineal social system and preserve a living oral heritage composed of myths and genealogies. Palm trees, shells and channels are still parts of everyday life, along with modern schools, a strong American influence and a growing ecological awareness. Palau was the first country to ask tourists to sign a pledge on arrival to respect the local environment: an ethical passport, more symbolic than binding, but in line with the approach of an island aware of its own vulnerability. Eil Malk is the most emblematic island, but the entire archipelago is an open workshop, in which ancient equilibria and modern pressure intertwine, where time is both slow and pressing.

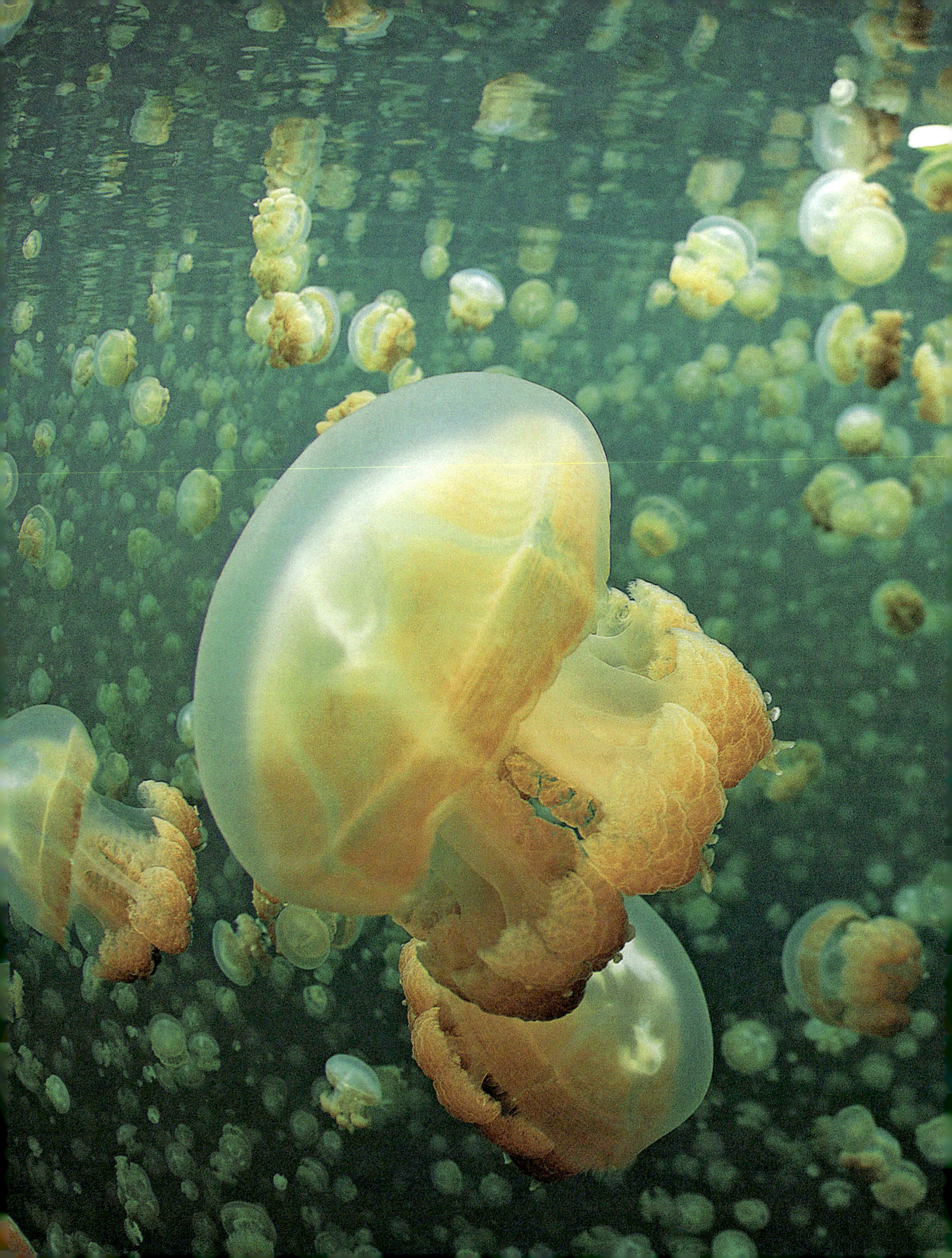

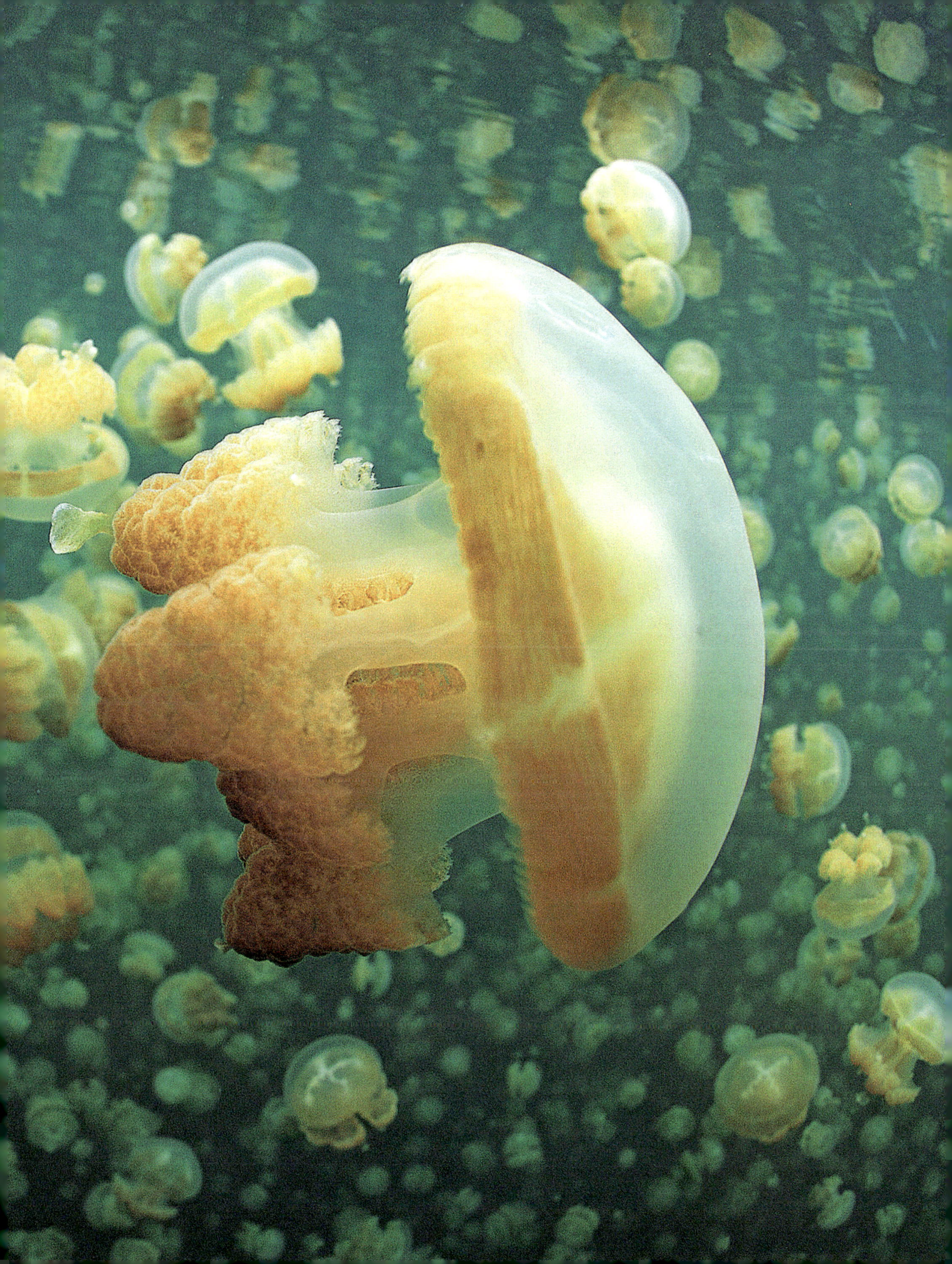

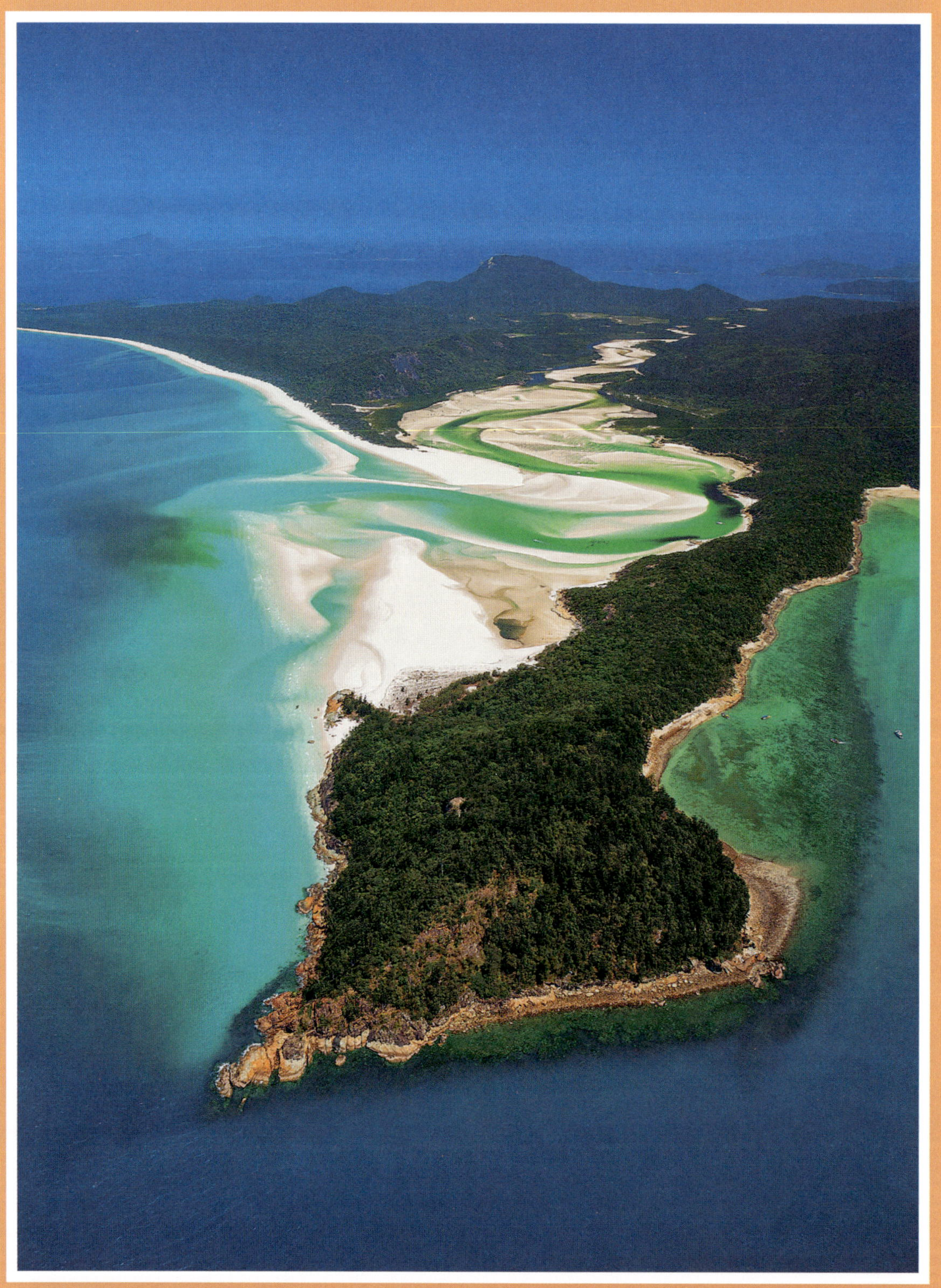

Australia

WHITSUNDAY

Geographical coordinates: 20°18'00" S; 148°56'00" E
Waters: Coral Sea
Population: no permanent inhabitants
Surface area: 42.08 square miles (109 km²)

THE PENTACOST THAT WASN'T

The view from above is enough to make you dizzy. This is due to the streaks of color that combine in a hypnotic vortex, where the deep, shifting tones of the sea merge with the blinding, imperious white of the silica sand beach. The sensation of falling into the spiral is an almost irresistible urge: it is right there we want to fall, where river and sea are indistinguishable and the green seems to protect and guard something precious. We find ourselves at the Hill Inlet viewpoint, which offers a dizzying glimpse of the half-mile-long (one kilometer) Whitehaven Beach on Whitsunday Island, the largest of a group of 74 islands, itself part of a more extensive archipelago in northeastern Australia, the Cumberland Islands. The silica of which this fine, white sand is composed does not retain the heat of the sun. Rather than originating from the erosion of the island's rocks, it was transported here by a play of currents that painstakingly created this spectacle. The island, along with its neighbors, is what remains of mountain ranges that were once connected to Australia. As the seas rose, the valleys flooded, leaving only the granite peaks visible. These were subsequently shaped by atmospheric agents and covered by vegetation. The dense tropical forest gives a semblance of uniformity to a varied landscape of undulating ridges, plateaus, hills and narrow valleys. The place owes its name to an error by James Cook, who passed through here on the 4th of June, 1770, convinced that it was Whitsunday, although he had actually crossed the International Date Line and slipped one day ahead into a common 18th-century Monday.

NGARO

~

Captain Cook's passage is just one of many that have marked the history of man in this territory. There is evidence of the presence of the Ngaro people here for at least 9,000 years and not in an occasional form: they lived, fished and moved between one island and the next following recurring routes, now known as the Ngaro Sea Trail, which can be traveled by tourists. These aborigines, excellent navigators and bark canoe builders, exploited marine and terrestrial resources with skill and precision. They collected shells, used stone traps to catch fish and had a thorough knowledge of what the vegetation had to offer, both for food and for healing purposes. There were no stone dwellings but long-term camps, and there were quarries exploited for the manufacture of tools, found even hundreds of miles away. It was after the mid-19th century that this symbiotic idyll was brutally shattered by the arrival of settlers, determined to exploit timber and introduce animal husbandry. In those years, abuse and violence became systematic, and every small act of rebellion by the natives was followed by broad reprisals, to the extent that within a few decades the native civilization could be considered culturally extinct due to massacres, forced conversions and exiles. Today, no one lives permanently on Whitsunday Island, although descendants of the local peoples living on neighboring islands such as Hamilton are collaborating with the authorities of the Australian state of Queensland to rediscover and valorize the traces of the past through informed and responsible tourism. Nearly all areas of the archipelago are protected by a national park established as early as the 1930s. Naturally, the safeguarding of the environmental heritage has proceeded in parallel with awareness of the need to mend colonial wounds: distant in time but still alive as testimony and warning.

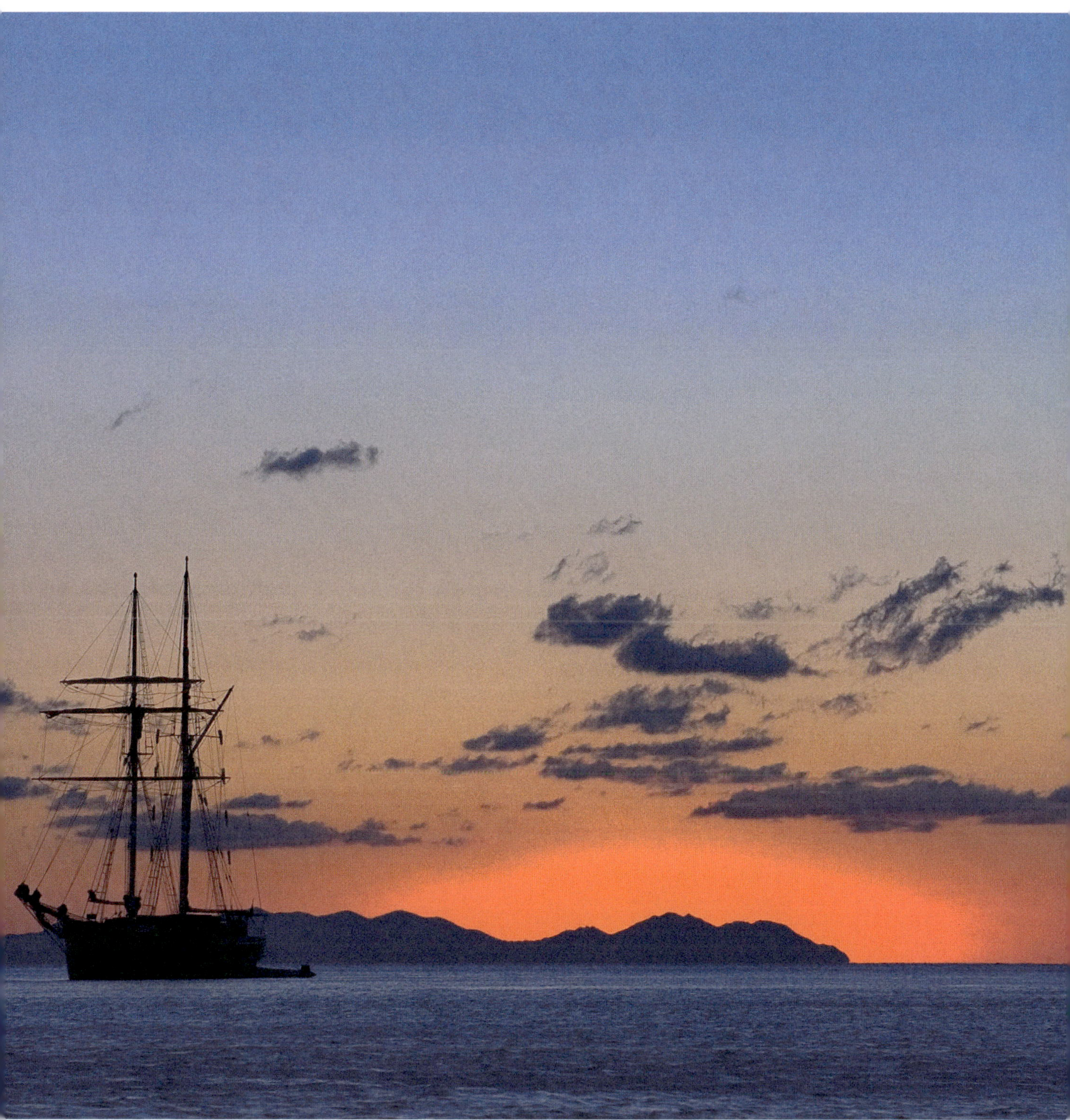

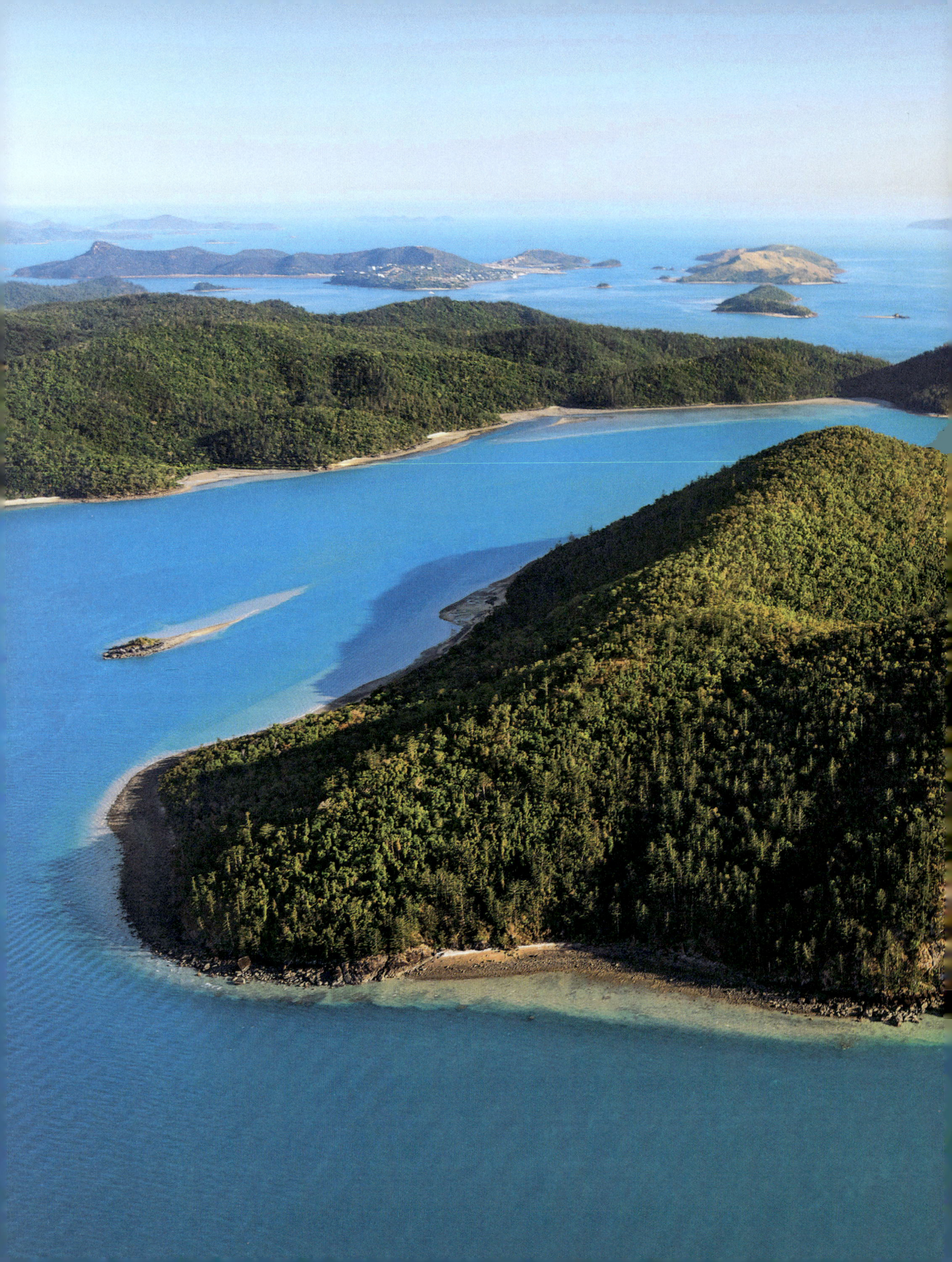

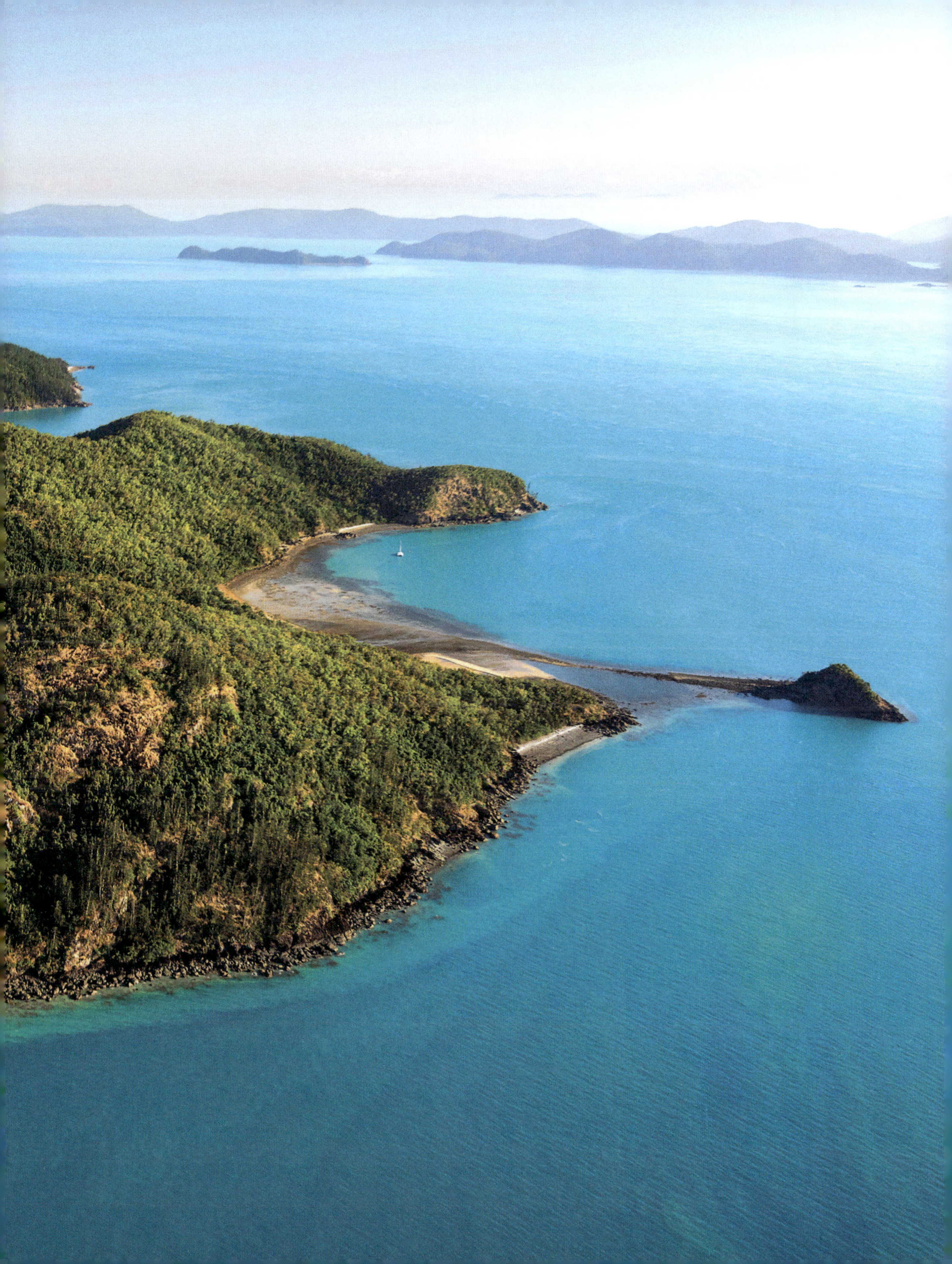

CORAL LIFE

IN THE WHITSUNDAYS, THERE IS MUCH TO PROTECT. THE CHUNNIGAM ARAUCARIA, OF WHICH THERE ARE A THOUSAND SPECIMENS, IS A CONIFER TYPICAL OF TROPICAL COASTAL FORESTS, A VERY ANCIENT SPECIES THAT COEXISTED WITH THE DINOSAURS AND THAT HERE ALTERNATES WITH MANGROVES AND ACACIAS, TOGETHER WITH A RICH UNDERGROWTH.

In terms of terrestrial fauna, you might encounter—although it would perhaps be better to avoid them—the goanna, or lace monitor lizard, a reptile that can exceed 6.5 feet (2 meters) in length, carnivorous and opportunistic, which feeds on small animals, eggs and carcasses, or the rock wallabies, small marsupials similar to kangaroos, threatened by habitat change and competition with other species. There is no shortage of birds, such as gannets, frigates, pelicans and sea eagles, but it is under the surface of the water that wonders are hidden: humpback whales passing through between May and September, sea turtles nesting from November to March and the sensational dugongs, which feed on the posidonia meadows. The corals of the Great Barrier Reef, which are crucial for balance and marine biodiversity, are worthy of special mention. This area is affected by the bleaching phenomenon caused by stress factors such as excessively high temperatures, pollution, ocean acidification and excessive exposure to sunlight. These conditions lead to the expulsion of zooxanthellae, microscopic algae that live in symbiosis with corals and provide them with the energy they need, as well as the bright, vivid color that everyone admires. When this virtuous circle is interrupted, the coral goes pale, stops receiving nutrients and eventually dies. This damage can be reduced by responsible behavior and improved global conditions, but as is often the case, it is much easier to destroy than to construct.

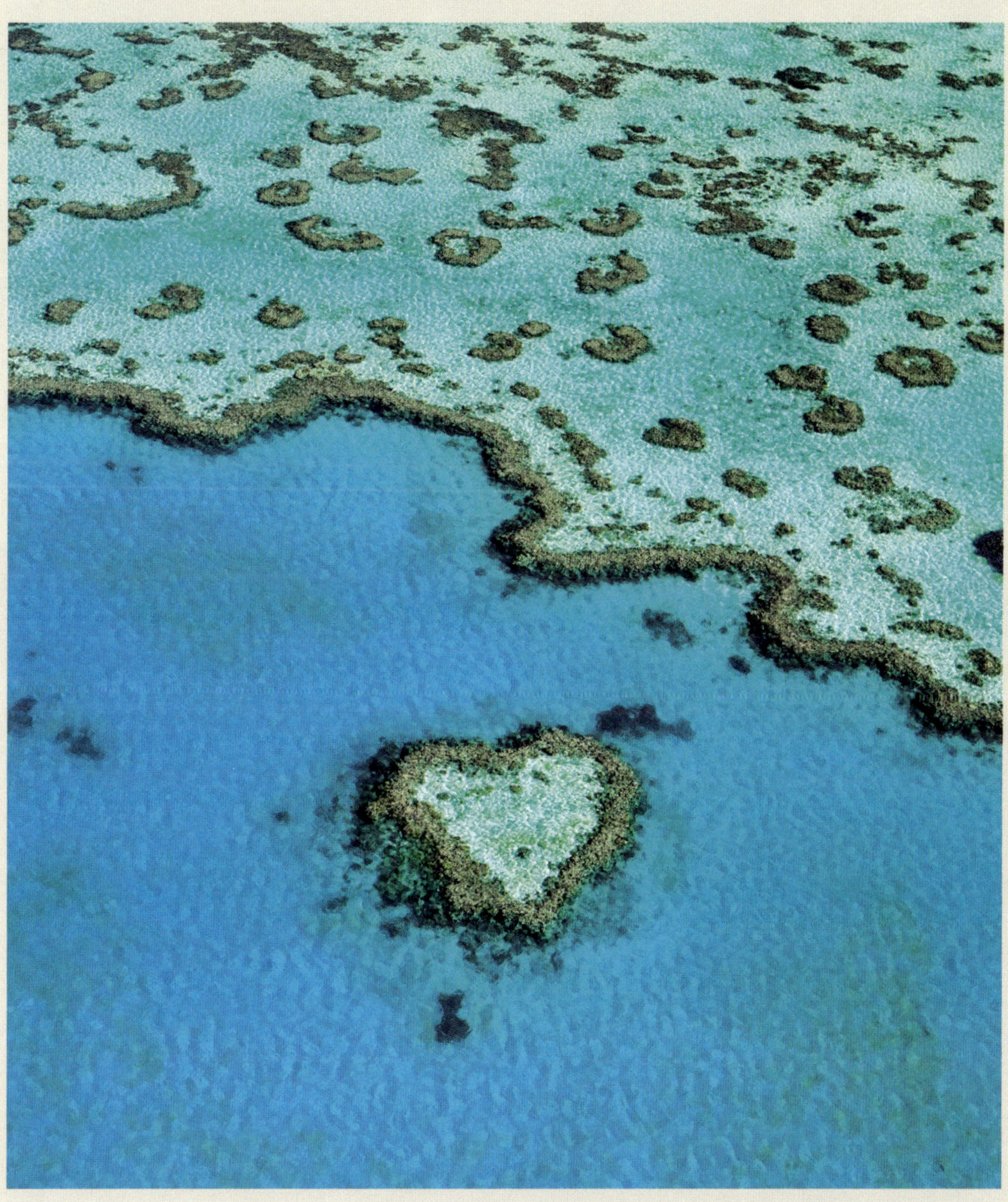

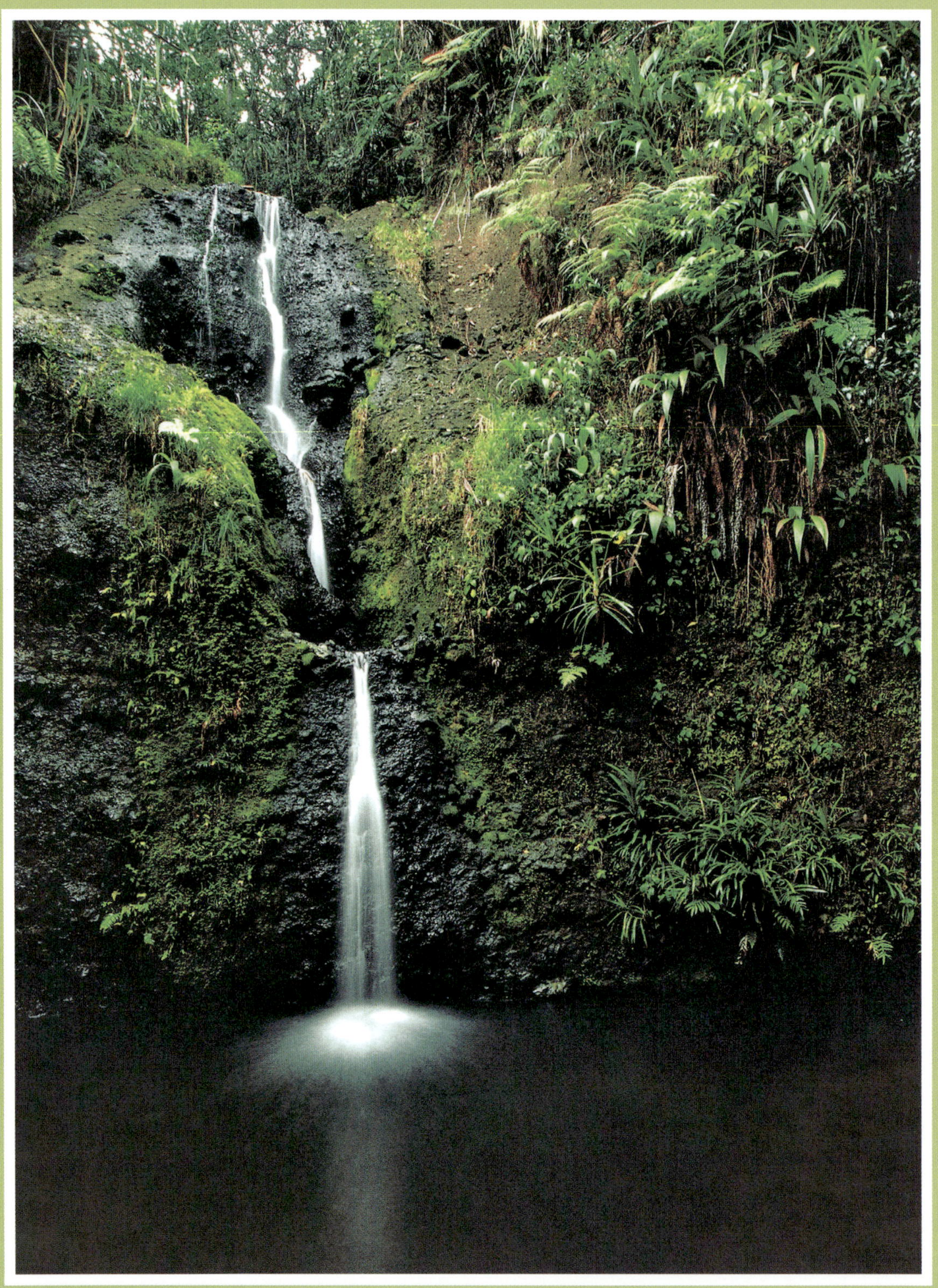

VITI LEVU

Geographical coordinates: 17°48'00" S; 178°00'00" E
Waters: South Pacific Ocean
Population: 740,000 inhabitants
Surface area: 4,066.04 square miles (10,531 km²)
Capital: Suva

A CENTER OF GRAVITY

Viti Levu, the largest island of Fiji, has a vaguely oval shape, traversed by a range of sharp peaks that highlight its changeability. The island is a weave of extinct volcanoes, ancient crests, alluvial plains and red earth striped with green. Water is everywhere: it descends the valleys in gushing cascades, excavates dark ravines, soaks the roots of the forest and extends in broad, slow rivers like the Sigatoka, which rises on Mount Tomanivi and runs for 75 miles (120 kilometers) from east to west with the patience of inevitability. The southernmost part of the island catches the most sun and is the driest and most domesticated. Fields planted with sugarcane alternate with pastures, tropical grasslands and villages scattered along dusty roads. Here are to be found Nadi and Suva, the two main towns and the access points for those arriving on the island. As you climb toward the central area—where Mount Tomanivi reaches 4,345 feet (1,324 meters) above sea level—Viti Levu reveals its true indomitable nature. Dense forests of mahogany, breadfruit trees and arboreal ferns cover the highlands, which in the damper months hide beneath blankets of thick fog. The slopes descend toward deep valleys, inhabited by remote communities for which time passes leaving little trace. The contrast between the coast and the interior is sharp, as it is between Viti Levu and the smaller islands that surround it: Ovalau, the Yasawas and the Mamanucas, which seem to float on the ocean, almost as if to compensate for the weight and gravity of the mother island. It is in fact Viti Levu that keeps the system in balance, like a miniature continent in the middle of the Pacific.

A PRECARIOUS LAND

~

Viti Levu has been inhabited for at least 3,000 years. The first to land here were Austronesian sailors, followed by the Melanesians. Subtle traces of that era remain: ceramics from the Lapita culture, traditional agricultural techniques, languages combined and transformed. However, the true revolution came in the 19th century, when Fiji and Viti Levu found themselves on the route of the European powers. In 1874, after decades of British pressure and internal conflicts, the island became a colony of the empire and the most excruciating period of its history began. The British exploited the fertility of the soil to establish intensive sugarcane plantations. Labor was required and between 1879 and 1916, more than 60,000 contracted workers arrived from the Indies. The so-called Girmitiya lived in terribly harsh conditions, segregated and deprived of human rights. When the period of recruitment ended, many remained, giving rise to a mixed community that today constitutes a third of the population. Since then, Fiji has had two strong and frequently conflicting identities: the indigenous, bound to the land and tribal hierarchy, and the Indian, urban, commerical and more secular. Independence was achieved in 1970, but democracy has wavered: between 1987 and 2006, there were a sequence of coups d'état, suspensions of the constitution and military governments. Certain regimes promoted the supremacy of the natives, others for more inclusive citizenship. The elections in 2014, the first after years of authoritarianism, ushered in a period of partial normalization, but the debate remained heated. Viti Levu embodies this complexity. Suva, the capital, is the face of the melting pot of indigenous peoples—the iTauke—Indians, Chinese and Europeans who compose a lively mosaic, while the inland villages still follow ancient rhythms and customs. This is a geologically young island, but one marked by strata, wounds and experiments.

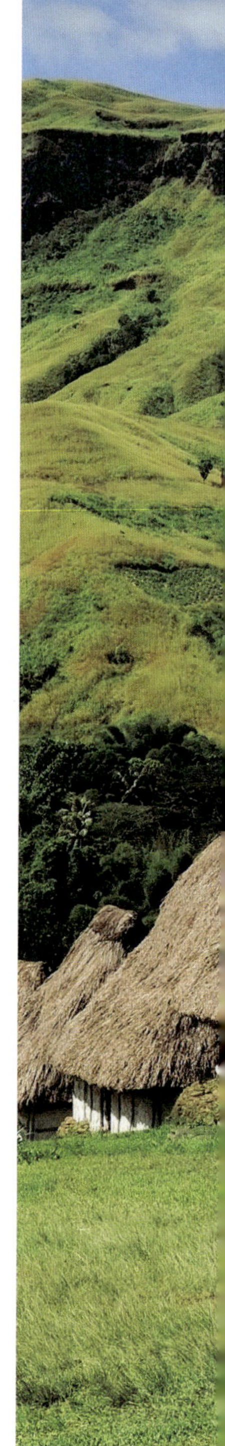

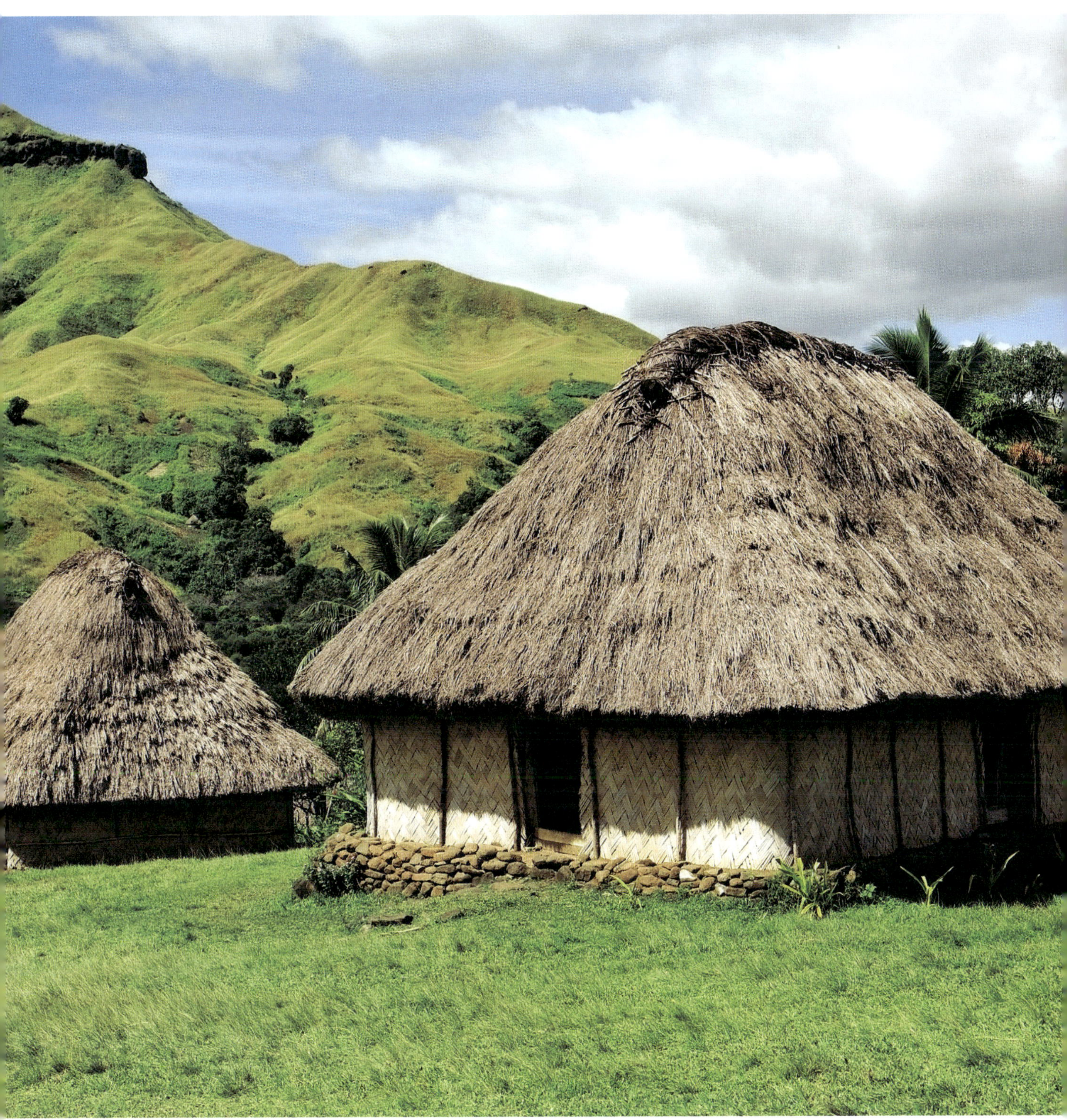

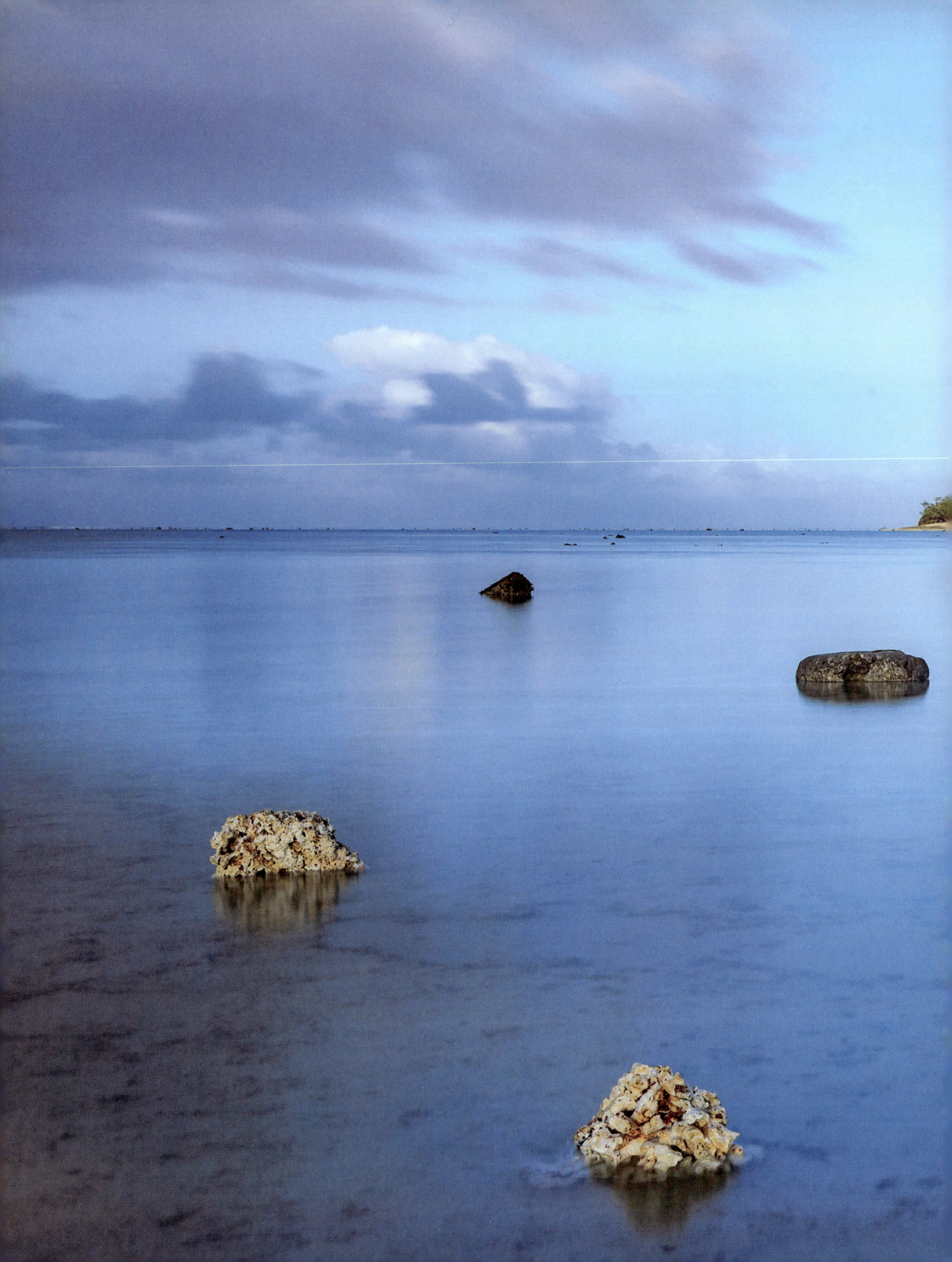

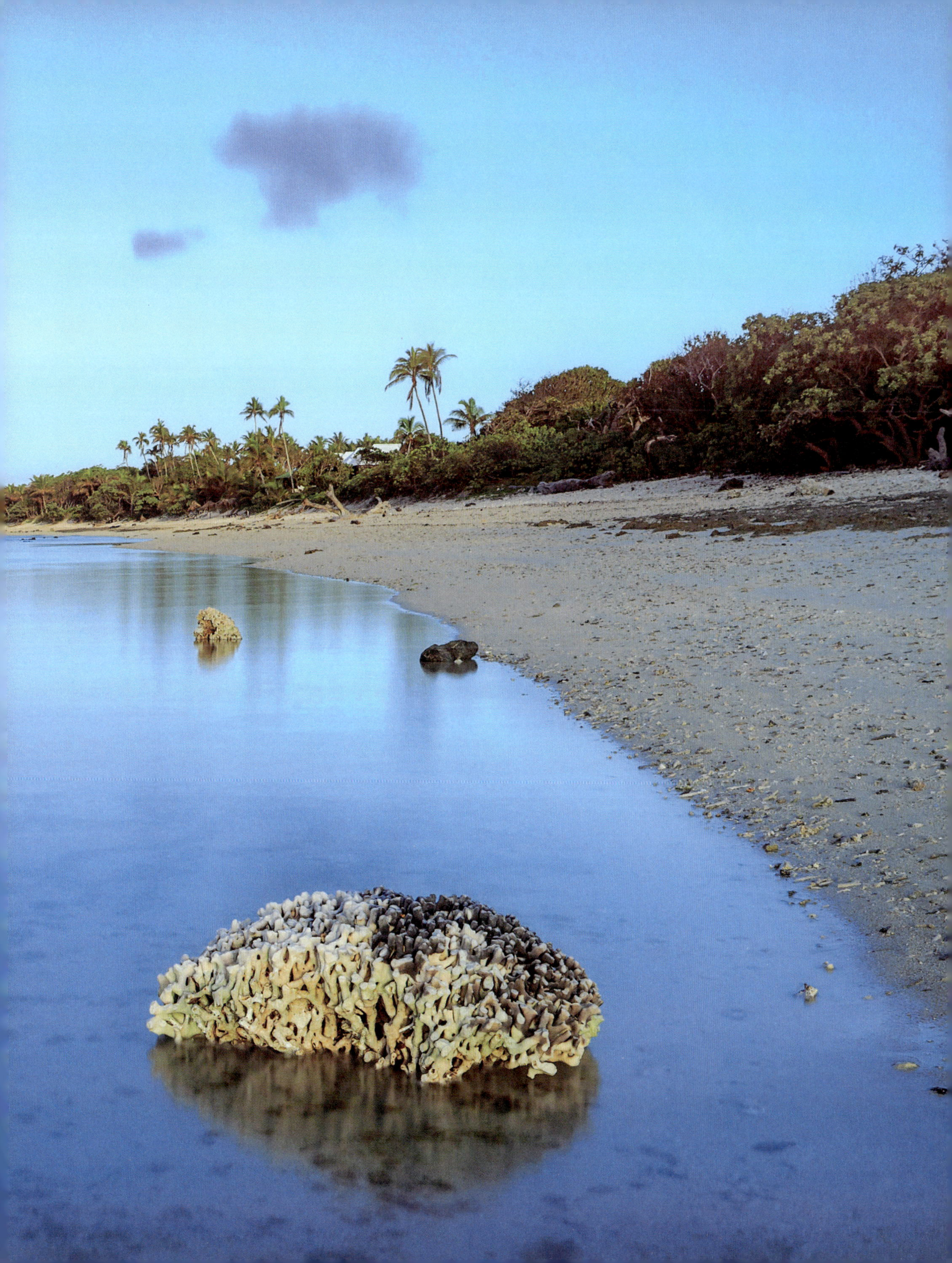

WILD, PRIMARY, MYSTICAL

~

ENORMOUS TREES SINK THEIR ROOTS INTO SOIL SMELLING OF ANCIENT ASH AND PERPETUAL HUMIDITY. THEIR CANOPY CLOSES OVER THE PATHS, FILTERING A GREEN, AQUATIC WATER THAT RENDERS EVERYTHING EVEN MORE STILL AND PROFOUND. HERE, NATURE IS NOT JUST A LANDSCAPE; IT IS A LIVING, CLOSED, AUTONOMOUS AND UNFATHOMABLE SYSTEM.

The area boasts extraordinary biodiversity: endemic birds such as the Fiji goshawk and the masked shining parrot with its acid-green feathers live in the highlands, as does the rare silktail, a small black sparrow with glossy wings. Migratory eels and armored crayfish swim in the streams and rivers, and fruit bats nest in caves, emerging at sunset like a dark cloud. The emerald-green Fiji crested iguana with blue stripes is one of the symbols of the archipelago and is considered sacred in many local legends. Still today, some clans worship it as a totem and guiding spirit. Beyond the forest lie fertile plains, plantations and palm groves. Then there are the coasts: the Coral Coast in the south with its shallow lagoons and pristine coral reefs, and the more rugged eastern coast battered by rain. The landscape's primordial nature is evident everywhere: despite being touched by man, the island continues to follow a different, pre-human rhythm. It is said that the central mountains were created by a god who occasionally turns in his sleep, causing the earth to tremble. In some valleys, stories are handed down about ancestral spirits associated with rocks, plants and water courses. Anyone who cuts down a sacred tree or disturbs a river without first offering a prayer will suffer the consequences. Some fishermen tell of a deep-sea creature similar to a huge, dark manta ray that only appears offshore during certain phases of the moon. It is no coincidence that many film productions looking for an unspoilt location arrive in Fiji, often on Viti Levu, as seen in *Blue Lagoon*, the second chapter of the film saga *Anaconda* and *Survivor*. In short, this island has not been tamed; it remains a place where you can lose yourself in tropical rain that seems to come not only from the sky, but also from below, from the very center of the world.

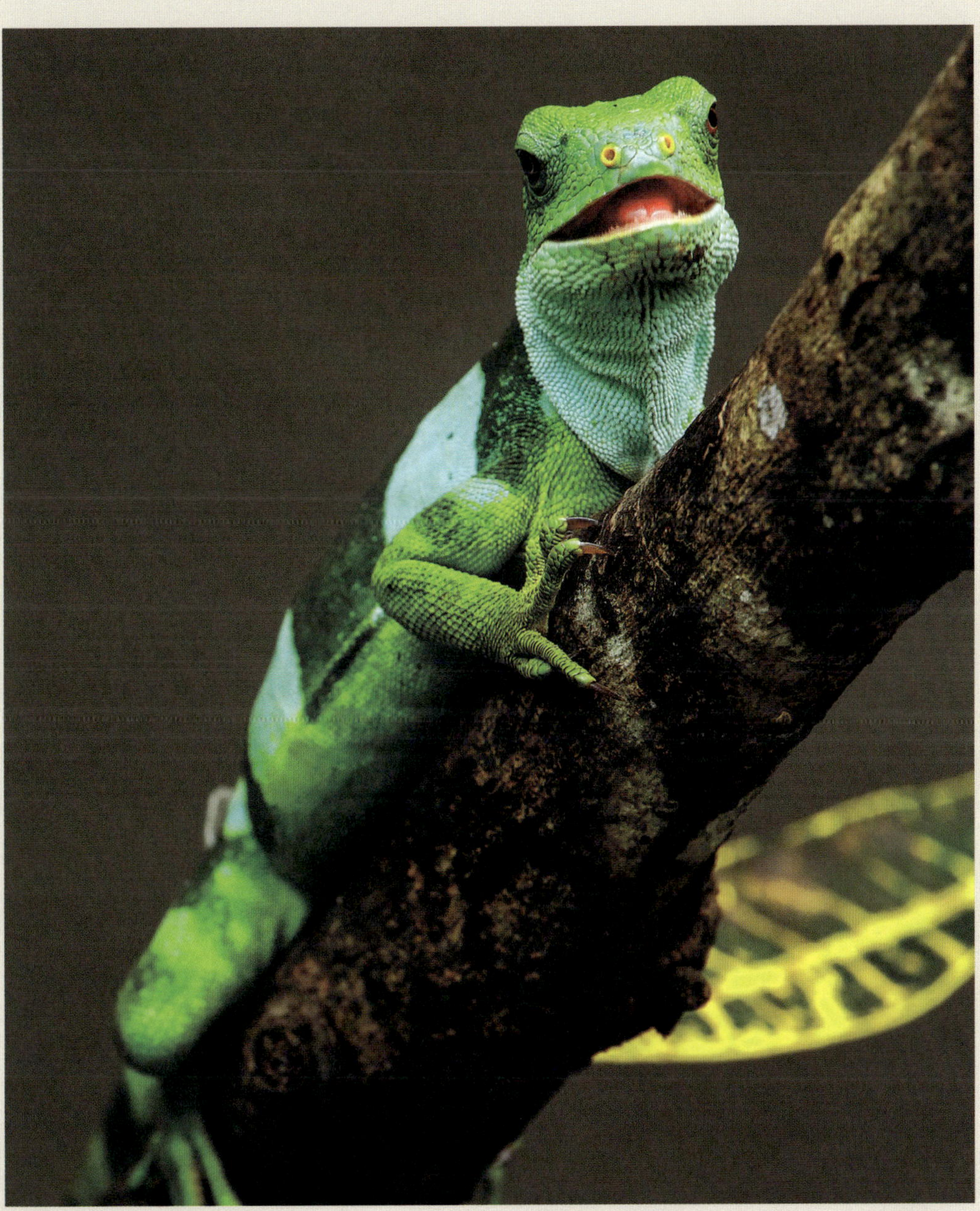

PHOTO CREDITS

p. 9 javarman/Shutterstock
p. 10 Andia/Universal Images Group/Getty Images
p. 12 Maridav/Shutterstock
p. 15 LuisMorenoFineArtPhotos/Shutterstock
p. 16 Billy McDonald/Shutterstock
p. 19 Maridav/Shutterstock
p. 20 Alexander Demyanenko/Shutterstock
p. 22 Naeemphotographer2/Shutterstock
p. 25 ITPhoto/Alamy
p. 26 Holger Leue/Lonely Planet RF/ Getty Images
p. 29 Joe Kras/Alamy
p. 30 Maridav/Alamy
p. 32 Sergio TB/Shutterstock
p. 35 FCG/Shutterstock
p. 36 Karol Kozlowski Premium RM Collection/Alamy
p. 39 abriendomundo/Shutterstock
p. 40 Andia/Universal Images Group/Getty Images
p. 42 Jesse Kraft/Alamy
p. 45 C.MALE/Alamy
p. 47 VW Pics/Universal Images Group/Getty Images
p. 48 Maridav/Shutterstock
p. 50 Arizona By Michael M/Shutterstock
p. 53 Dylan Garcia Photography/Alamy
p. 54 Szilard Toth/Shutterstock
p. 57 KristinRita/Shutterstock
p. 58 JKcreative/Alamy
p. 61 Hemis/Alamy
p. 63 John Mitchell/Alamy
p. 64 Paolo Costa/Shutterstock
p. 66 Michele Falzone/Alamy
p. 69 Travel Pix/Alamy
p. 70 Pulsar Imagens/Alamy
p. 73 Diane Stoney/Alamy
p. 74 Luciano Albano/Shutterstock
p. 76 Westend61 GmbH/Alamy
p. 79 HomoCosmicos/Alamy
p. 81 Richard Wadey/Alamy
p. 82 Matjaz Corel/Alamy
p. 84 irisaimages/Shutterstock
p. 86 Sopotnicki/Shutterstock
p. 88 Image Professionals GmbH/Alamy
p. 91 Graham Mulrooney/Alamy
p. 92 robertharding/Alamy
p. 94 funkyfood London - Paul Williams/Alamy
p. 97 Michal Stipek/Alamy
p. 99 Tristan Deschamps/Alamy
p. 100 Artem Evdokimov/Alamy
p. 102 franckreporter/E+/Getty Images
p. 105 Nanisimova/Shutterstock
p. 106 rusm/E+/Getty Images
p. 109 Hamase parsa/Shutterstock
p. 110 Stefano Zaccaria/Shutterstock
p. 112 Darios/Shutterstock
p. 114 Boris-B/Shutterstock
p. 116 Vlad Ghiea/Alamy
p. 119 Valery Bareta/Alamy
p. 120 Giovanni Rinaldi/Shutterstock
p. 122 Heracles Kritikos/Shutterstock
p. 125 PANAGIOTIS KARAPANAGIOTIS/Alamy
p. 126 Aerial-motion/Shutterstock
p. 128 Cindy Hopkins/ Alamy
p. 131 AfriPics.com/Alamy
p. 132 Janos Rautonen/Alamy
p. 135 Jan Bures/Shutterstock
p. 136 Michael Lutz/Alamy
p. 138 BIXQUERT Loriane/Shutterstock
p. 141 Matjaz Corel/Alamy
p. 142 Charles-Henry THOQUENNE/Shutterstock
p. 144 sebastien bonaime/Alamy
p. 146 guichaoua/Alamy

p. 148 Hemis/Alamy
p. 151 imageBROKER.com GmbH & Co. KG/Alamy
p. 152 icemanphotos/Shutterstock
p. 155 Anna Komissarenko/Alamy
p. 157 Jan Wlodarczyk/Alamy
p. 158 Jag_cz/Shutterstock
p. 160 WaterFrame/Alamy
p. 162 Carl Nelson/Shutterstock
p. 164 robertharding/Alamy
p. 167 Natalia Harper/Alamy
p. 168 Big State Images/Alamy
p. 170 R.M. Nunes/Alamy
p. 173 monticello/Shutterstock
p. 174 robertharding/Alamy
p. 177 Joana Kruse/Alamy
p. 178 Hemis/Alamy
p. 180 Michele Falzone/Alamy
p. 183 Igor Tichonow/Shutterstock
p. 184 .M. Nunes/Shutterstock
p. 187 SeaTops/Alamy
p. 188 BERENGERE CAVALIER/Alamy
p. 190 Sean Pavone/Alamy
p. 192 shikema/Shutterstock
p. 195 Sean Pavone/Shutterstock
p. 196 dreamsky/Shutterstock
p. 198 Olivier Blaise/Moment Open/Getty Images
p. 201 Reinhard Dirscherl/Corbis/Getty Images
p. 203 Suzuki Kaku/Alamy
p. 204 Helmut Corneli/Alamy
p. 206 Shane Pedersen/Alamy
p. 209 Michele Falzone/Alamy
p. 210 Ingo Oeland/Alamy
p. 213 Travelscape Images/Alamy
p. 214 DEA/F. BARBAGALLO/De Agostini/Getty Images
p. 217 Peter J. Hatcher/Alamy
p. 218 Kim Petersen/Alamy
p. 221 Don Mammoser/Alamy

Cover: SasinT Gallery/Getty Images

NICOLA BALOSSI RESTELLI

~

Nicola Balossi Restelli is an author and ghostwriter born in Milan, where he lives with his family An aficionado of stories, nature, travel, and sports. He also works for various publishers, and for White Star he has published *Beautiful Peaks*.